The New Behaviorism

Behaviorism was the dominant movement in American psychology in the first half of the twentieth century, culminating in the radical movement of B. F. Skinner—the most influential psychologist since Freud. This book begins with a brief history of behaviorism and goes on to explain and criticize radical behaviorism, its philosophy and its applications to social issues. The mission of the book is to help steer experimental psychology away from its current undisciplined indulgence in "mental life" toward the core of science, which is an economical description of nature. The author argues that parsimony, the elementary philosophical distinction between private and public events, even biology, evolution and animal psychology—all are ignored by much contemporary cognitive psychology. The failings of a theoretical radical behaviorism as well as a philosophically defective cognitive psychology point to the need for a new theoretical behaviorism, which can deal with problems such as "consciousness" that have been either ignored, evaded or muddled by existing approaches.

This second edition, which will be published nearly fifteen years after the first edition, surveys what, if any, changes have occurred within behaviorism and whether it has maintained its influence on experimental cognitive psychology or other fields.

Since publication of the first edition, John Staddon has published extensively in journals and magazines, offering insightful commentary on everyday events, usually exposing how our preconceptions are often illogical and inaccurate, yet have become deeply entrenched in our collective conscience. In 2012, he published a successful trade book called *The Malign Hand of the Markets*, which exposed the insidious forces affecting our financial markets. John has used his developed writing skills to make the second edition of *The New Behaviorism* richer and more accessible, with illuminating and engaging examples to illustrate his points.

The book will appeal to scientists in fields that are influenced by or eschew behaviorism, graduate students and advanced undergraduates interested in the psychology of learning, curious about the history and philosophy of the behavioral approach and wanting a glimpse of current developments in the behaviorist tradition.

John Staddon is James B. Duke Professor of Psychology and Emeritus Professor of Biology and Neurobiology, at Duke University, and an honorary visiting professor at the University of York, United Kingdom. He is a fellow of the American Association for the Advancement of Science and the Society of Experimental Psychologists, and has a Docteur, Honoris Causa, from the Université Charles de Gaulle, Lille 3, France. His research is on the evolution and mechanisms of learning in humans and animals, and the history and philosophy of psychology, economics and biology. He is past editor of *Behavioural Processes* and *Behavior & Philosophy,* and is the author of more than 200 research papers and five books. He writes and lectures on a wide range of important public policy issues.

The New Behaviorism

Second Edition

John Staddon

Ψ Psychology Press
Taylor & Francis Group

NEW YORK AND LONDON

Second edition published 2014
by Psychology Press
711 Third Avenue, New York, NY 10017

and by Psychology Press
27 Church Road, Hove, East Sussex BN3 2FA

*Psychology Press is an imprint of the Taylor & Francis Group,
an informa business*

© 2014 Taylor & Francis

First edition published by Psychology Press 2001

Library of Congress Cataloging-in-Publication Data

The New Behaviorism: Second Edition / John Staddon.
    pages cm
    BJ1533.R42H825 2014
    179—dc23
    2013016485

ISBN: 978-1-84872-687-1 (hbk)
ISBN: 978-1-84872-688-8 (pbk)
ISBN: 978-1-315-79817-2 (ebk)

Typeset in Times
by Apex CoVantage, LLC

SUSTAINABLE
FORESTRY
INITIATIVE

Certified Sourcing
www.sfiprogram.org
SFI-00555
The SFI label applies to the text stock.

Printed and bound in the United States of America by
Walsworth Publishing Company, Marceline, MO.

Contents

Preface

This edition is almost completely rewritten and about twice as long as the first. I cover two new social issues and also devote more space to the philosophy of cognitivism and the science behind theoretical behaviorism. B. F. Skinner figures less prominently in this edition than the previous, but his work is a theme that still runs through many chapters because his influence has been so great and his writings raise so many provocative issues that are identified with behaviorism. But, as readers of the first edition detected, my position is far from Skinnerian.

Many reviewers thought well of the first edition but, naturally, I want to attend to those who did not. Some felt I was too hard on Skinner. One even accused me of an *ad hominem* attack. Several thought that I did not present a favorable enough view of behaviorism and that my own position was little short of . . . *cognitive.* One otherwise sympathetic critic thought the book "conservative"—not a term that will endear it to most psychologists.

The critics are right to this extent. The book was not and is not an advertisement for radical behaviorism. It is, first, a short history of a fascinating movement in psychology. Second, it is an analysis of what I think went wrong with behaviorism as time went on. Third, it is a proposal for a theoretical behaviorism. I describe the philosophy behind theoretical behaviorism as well as some more or less detailed applications of the approach to laboratory phenomena, ranging from choice behavior in animals to human perception. I believe that theoretical behaviorism can provide a unified framework for a science of behavior that is now fragmented. And finally, I suggest how it can provide insights into broader practical issues such as law and punishment, the health-care system and teaching.

Behaviorism began with a healthy skepticism about introspection. Conscious thought tells us very little about the springs of action. Behaviorism of all types is right about that. It is right to emphasize action over information and representation, which is the theme, even the preoccupation, of cognitive psychology. On the other hand, not all cognitive psychology is philosophically or experimentally flawed. It should not be ignored. Behaviorism is right also to emphasize biology and evolution, which is driven not by thought but by action. And radical behaviorism, as advanced by Skinner and his students, was wonderfully right in developing new experimental methods for studying the behavior of individual organisms in real time. The discovery of reinforcement schedules was a great advance and opened up a huge new field to be explored.

But behaviorism also lost its way in several respects. Methodological behaviorism, Skinner's term—neo-behaviorism was their own term—went along with the standard methods of psychology: between-group comparisons rather than the study of individuals, and settling for statistical significance as a measure of scientific success. I have little to say about it. I do discuss the serious flaws of null-hypothesis statistical testing in Chapter 9.

Although radical behaviorism accepts evolutionary continuity between man and animals, it has consistently neglected the *nature* part of the nature–nurture dyad. It also imposed ridiculous strictures on theoretical development, to the point that *behaviorist theory* became an oxymoron. Radical behaviorism also became increasingly isolated from the rest of psychology through a self-consciously idiosyncratic vocabulary and a naïve epistemology (theory of knowledge) that caused many philosophers to dismiss the whole field. Skinner bears much responsibility for that and for the limits he placed on theory.

And finally, Skinner's pronouncements on society and its reform led him to extrapolate an infant laboratory science to social realms far beyond its reach. My response to this is not so much "conservative" as just cautious. Human society is immensely complex. Political decisions involve values as much as techniques. Much has been written on the organization of society. Not all of it is worthless. Almost none was addressed by Skinner. To "design a culture" as one might design a lawnmower is to confuse "culture" with contraption, and place oneself far above humanity in general as a sort of all-wise, all-knowing philosopher king. We would all like to find a philosopher king, but they are in short supply. Skinner was not one.

The book is in four parts. The first part (Chapters 1 and 2) is a brief history of behaviorism. The second part (Chapters 3–12) is the longest. It discusses the experimental methods and theory associated with Skinnerian behaviorism and the single-subject method (Chapters 3 and 4), Skinner's views on theory, the parallel between learning and evolution and the theoretical relations between behavioral psychology and "rational-choice" economics (Chapters 5–8). In Chapter 4, I have a longish discussion of choice behavior and matching, a laboratory phenomenon that has played an important part in the development of behaviorist theory. This section ends with a discussion of the new consensus on a Darwinian, selection/variation approach to learning, the limitations of Skinner's utopian ideas and finally Skinner's idiosyncratic view of mental life (Chapter 9–12). Two chapters deal with Skinner's still-influential proposal to "design a culture." The popularity of behavioral economics, exemplified by books like *Nudge,*[1] the policies of New York's longtime mayor Michael Bloomberg and the United Kingdom's David Cameron about things like smoking and obesity, and the continuing efforts, especially in Europe and the United Kingdom, to diminish the role of punishment in the legal system, all reflect the influence of Skinner's ideas. Skinner, like many "scientific imperialists" today, believed that science provides the ends as well as the means for enlightened social policy. So it's okay to use science to trick the citizenry as long as it gets them to do the right thing. I examine all this in Chapters 10 and 11.

The third part expands the discussion of theoretical behaviorism that I began earlier in connection with choice and timing. I describe what it is, how it deals with some new learning phenomena and with phenomena of consciousness, in humans and in animals (Chapters 13–16). Part IV is a beginning attempt to analyze three major areas of society—the legal system, health care and teaching—from a behavioristic viewpoint.

John Staddon
Durham, North Carolina, June, 2013

Note

1. Thaler, R. H., & Sunstein, C. R. (2008). *Nudge: Improving decisions about health, wealth, and happiness* (New Haven, CT: Yale University Press). See also www.nytimes.com/2010/05/16/magazine/16Sunstein-t.html?pagewanted=all.

Acknowledgments

Many people were kind enough to comment on chapters and on talks I have given on some of the topics of the book. I thank in particular John Malone, Nancy Innis, Jennifer Higa, Max Hocutt, Kent Berridge, Geoffrey Hall, Eugene Moss and Peter Killeen. I thank the late Peter Harzem for the long Pavlov quotation in Chapter 16 and for detailed comments on the draft of the first edition. I am especially grateful to Armando Machado (for the first edition) and Jérémie Jozefowiez (for both editions), whose thoughtful comments made me think very hard about many tricky points. I thank the five commentators on the first edition in the July 2004 issue of the *Journal of the Experimental Analysis of Behavior* and also two friends, Charles Hosler and Ralph Heinz, who read and commented on the book. I also thank Sheri Sipka and Apex CoVantage for their meticulous, efficient and thoughtful help with the production of this book. I gratefully acknowledge research support from the Alexander von Humboldt Foundation, the National Institutes of Health and the National Science Foundation. Without the long-term support provided by a Senior Research Scientist Award from NIMH, and Duke University's willingness to cooperate by relieving me of most teaching and administrative responsibilities, this work could never have been undertaken. Needless to say, all errors and misjudgments are entirely my responsibility.

Part I
History

1 Early Behaviorism

Behaviorism was once the major force in American psychology. It participated in great advances in our understanding of reward and punishment, especially in animals. It drove powerful movements in education and social policy. As a self-identified movement, it is today a vigorous but isolated offshoot. But its main ideas have been absorbed into experimental psychology. A leading cognitive psychologist, writing on the centennial of B. F. Skinner's birth, put it this way: "Behaviorism is alive and I am a behaviorist."[1]

I will describe where behaviorism came from, how it dominated psychology during the early part of the twentieth century, and how philosophical flaws and concealed ideologies in the original formulation sidelined it—and left psychology prey to mentalism and naïve reductionism. I propose a new behaviorism that can restore coherence to psychology and achieve the scientific goals behaviorism originally set for itself.

Psychology has always had its critics, of course. But at a time when it occupies a substantial and secure place in university curricula, when organizations of psychologists have achieved serious political clout, and when the numbers of research papers in psychology have reached an all-time high—more than 50,000 in 1999 by one count[2] and several times that number in 2012—the number of critics has not diminished nor have their arguments been successfully refuted.[3] The emperor is, if not unclothed, at least seriously embarrassed.

Many eminent psychologists, beginning with philosopher and proto-psychologist William James (Plate 1.1), have tried to sort out the divisions within psychology. James's suggestion, before the advent of behaviorism, was to divide psychologists into "tough" and "tender minded." He would have called behaviorists tough minded and many cognitive, clinical, and personality psychologists tender minded. James might also have mentioned the division between practice (clinical psychology) and basic research (experimental psychology), between "social-science" and "natural-science," or between "structural" and "functional" approaches—not to mention the split between mentalists and realists. Drafters of multiple-choice tests should consult R. I. Watson's (1971) list of eighteen psychological slices and dices for a full list.[4] But the main division is still between those who think *mind* is the proper subject for psychology and those who plump for *behavior.*

Plate 1.1 William James (1842–1910), philosopher, pioneer psychologist, and promoter of the philosophy of pragmatism, at Harvard during the late 1890s. There were two James brothers. One wrote delicate convoluted prose; the writing of the other was vivid and direct. Surprisingly, it was the psychologist, William, who was the easy writer (e.g., his *Principles of Psychology*, 1890), and the novelist, Henry (e.g., *The Golden Bowl*), who was hard to follow.

The nineteenth-century ancestor of the mentalists is Gustav Fechner (1801–1887), the "father" of psychophysics. Fechner was the co-discoverer of the Weber-Fechner law, which relates the variability of a sensory judgment to the magnitude of the physical stimulus.[5] This is one of the few real laws in psychology. For very many sensory dimensions, variability of judgment, measured as standard deviation or "just-noticeable difference" (JND), is proportional to mean. For example, suppose that people are able to correctly detect that weights of 100 g and 105 g are different just 50% of the time—so the JND is 5%; then the Weber-Fechner relation says that they will also be able to tell the difference between 1,000 g and 1,050 g just 50% of the time.

The Weber-Fechner relation is a matter of fact. But Fechner went beyond fact to propose that there is a mental realm with concepts and measurements quite separate from biology and physics. He called his new domain *psychophysics*. Many contemporary cognitive psychologists agree with him.

On the other side are biological and physiological psychologists. Biological psychologists believe that the fact of Darwinian evolution means that the behavior of people and nonhuman animals has common roots and must therefore share important properties. Physiological psychologists—neuroscientists—believe that because behavior depends on the brain, and because the brain is made up of nerve cells, behavior can be understood through the study of nerve cells and their interactions.

Behaviorism is in the middle of the mental-biological/physiological division, neither mentalistic nor, at its core, physiological.[6] Behaviorism denies mentalism but embraces evolutionary continuity. It also accepts the role of the brain, but behaviorists are happy to leave its study to neuroscientists. As we will see, behaviorists seek to make a science at a different level, the level of the whole organism.

Since its advent in the early part of the twentieth century, behaviorism has been a reference point for doctrinal debates in psychology. Until recently, many research papers in cognitive psychology either began or ended with a ritual paragraph of behaviorist bashing—pointing out how this or that version of behaviorism is completely unable to handle this or that experimental finding or property that "mind" must possess.[7] Much cognitive theory is perfectly behavioristic, but the "cognitive" banner is flourished nevertheless. No cognitivist wants to be mistaken for a behaviorist!

The behaviorists, in their turn, often protect their turf by concocting a rigid and idiosyncratic jargon and insisting on conceptual and linguistic purity in their journals. Theories, if entertained at all, are required to meet stringent, not always well-defined and sometimes irrelevant criteria. The behaviorists have not always served their cause well.

Behaviorism has been on the retreat until very recently. In 1989 a leading neo-behaviorist (see Chapter 2 for more on these distinctions) could write,

> I have . . . used a parliamentary metaphor to characterize the confrontation . . . between those who have taken a stimulus-response [S-R] behavioristic approach and those who favor a cognitive approach . . . and I like to point out that the S-R psychologists, who at one time formed the government, are now in the loyal opposition.[8]

In a critical comment on English biologist J. S. Kennedy's behavioristically oriented book *The New Anthropomorphism*,[9] one reviewer—a distinguished biologist—assumed that behaviorism is dead:

> If anthropomorphism produces results that are, in the normal manner of science, valuable, it will be persisted with; if it does not, it will be abandoned. It was, after all abandoned once before. The only danger . . . is that scientists can be enduringly obstinate in their investigations of blind alleys. Just think how long behaviourism lasted in psychology.[10]

As recently as 1999, a philosopher blessed with the gift of prophecy could write, "Not till the 1980s was it finally *proved beyond doubt* that although a clockwork toy [i.e., computer] may emulate a worm or do a fair imitation of an ant, it *could never* match a pig or a chimpanzee."[11] Evidently all those artificial intelligence types toil in vain, and behavioristic attempts to reduce human behavior to mechanical laws are foredoomed to failure. And of course, this particular critic wrote before an IBM computer[12] beat the champions on the television quiz show *Jeopardy!* On the other hand, to be fair, computers aren't doing too well with worms and ants either (see comments on *C. Elegans* in Chapter 16). But computers cannot yet be counted out as tools for modeling animal behavior.

Behaviorism is frequently declared dead. But although services are held regularly, the corpse keeps creeping out of the coffin. A naïve observer might well conclude that vigorous attacks on an allegedly moribund movement are a sure sign that behaviorism is ready to resurrect.

What is behaviorism, and how did it begin? The word was made famous by flamboyant Johns Hopkins psychologist John Broadus Watson (1878–1958, Plate 1.2). Watson, a South Carolina native, after some rambunctious teenage years, was a prodigious academic success until he had problems with his love life. Divorced in 1920 after his wife discovered he was having an affair with his research assistant Rosalie Rayner (a scandalous event in those days), Watson was fired from Johns Hopkins on account of the resulting publicity. *Plus ça change*—but nobody would notice nowadays, especially as Watson soon married Rosalie. The next year he joined the large advertising agency J. Walter Thompson, at a much-enhanced salary, where he very successfully followed

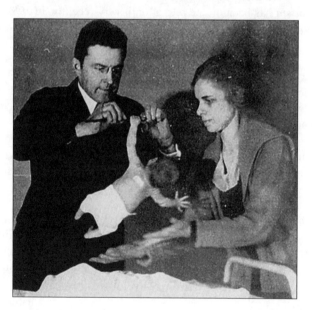

Plate 1.2 J. B. Watson and assistant (and wife-to-be) Rosalie Rayner studying grasping in a baby.

the advertising version of the *Star Trek* motto: boldly creating needs where none existed before.[13]

His success in this new field was no accident. The major figures in the softer sciences have almost invariably been people with a gift for *rhetoric,* the art of verbal persuasion. They may have other skills (Skinner was a wonderful experimenter, for example), but their ability to found schools usually owes at least as much to their ability to persuade and organize as to their purely scientific talents.

Watson's impact on psychology began with a nineteen-page article in the theoretical journal *Psychological Review* in 1913,[14] although the basic idea had been floating around for a decade or more.[15] In the next few years, Watson followed up with several books advocating behaviorism. He was reacting against the doctrine of *introspection,* the idea that the basic data of psychology could be gathered from one's own consciousness or reports of the consciousness of others. Émigré German behaviorist Max Meyer (1873–1967) made this distinction between private and public events explicit in the title of his introductory text, *Psychology of the Other One* (1921).

The idea that people have access to the causes of their own behavior via introspection has been thoroughly discredited from every possible angle. Take the "tip-of-the-tongue" phenomenon. Everyone has had the experience of being unable to recall the name of something or someone that you "know you know." The experience is quite frequent in older people—that's why old folks' groups often sport nametags, even if the members are well known to one another. Usually, after a while, the sought name comes to mind—the failure to recall is not permanent. But where does it come from and why? And how do you "know you know" (this is called *metacognition,* discussed in more detail later on). Introspection is no help in finding an answer to either question.

The great German physicist and physiologist Hermann von Helmholtz (1821–1894) pointed out many years ago that perception itself is a process of *unconscious inference,* in the sense that the brain presents to consciousness not the visual image that the eyes see, but an inferred view of the world. A given image or succession of two-dimensional images can always be interpreted in several ways, each consistent with a different view of reality. The brain picks one, automatically, based on probabilities set by personal and evolutionary history.[16] I will show later on that this view of the brain as a categorizer provides a simple alternative to mentalistic accounts of consciousness.

Perhaps the most striking illustration of the inferential nature of perception is the Ames Room (Plate 1.3).[17] Viewed through a peephole (i.e., from a fixed point of view), the girl in the room appears to be large or small depending on where she is in the room. The perception is wrong, of course. Her size has not changed. The reason she appears to grow as she moves from one side of the room to the other is that the brain assumes the angles are all right angles and the floor is level. Neither is true. But given these assumptions, the conclusion that the girl is growing follows inexorably. The inference happens unconsciously and automatically. Surprisingly, perhaps, this unconscious inference seems to be largely learned. It's not innate. People brought up in primitive

Plate 1.3 The Ames Room, viewed through a peephole.

cultures where they are not daily exposed to rectangular buildings fail to show the related Muller-Lyer illusion,[18] and there are reports of a similar dependence for the Ames Room.[19]

The power of the unintrospectable unconscious is especially striking in creative activities like mathematics. The Indian mathematician S. Ramanujan (1887–1920),[20] a poor prodigy from southern India who taught himself mathematics from an encyclopedia, is a particularly dramatic example. Ramanujan's mathematical imagination was legendary. He was brought to England just before World War I after corresponding with G. H. Hardy, a famous Cambridge mathematician. But even Hardy had difficulty understanding where Ramanujan got his ideas. Ramanujan would come up with profound theorems but had difficulty proving them and could not say where his inspiration came from (he often attributed it to Namagiri, his Hindu house goddess!). Hardy wrote,

> Here was a man who could work out modular equations and theorems of complex multiplication, to orders unheard of, whose mastery of continued fractions was, on the formal side at any rate, beyond that of any mathematician in the world. . . . All his results, new or old, right or wrong, had been arrived at by a process of mingled argument, intuition, and induction of which he was entirely unable to give any coherent account.[21]

Many less mystical mathematicians report similar experiences. J. E. Littlewood, a brilliant colleague of Hardy's, wrote that "my pencil wrote down" the solution to a particularly tough problem: "[I]t happened as if my subconscious knew the thing all the time."[22] Something of which the individual is completely unaware—something creative and vitally important—is happening in the brains of these people.

Experiences like this are not restricted to mathematicians. Here is example of memory retrieval written a few years ago by a British television quiz-show contestant:

> There was a moment on University Challenge when the [quiz] host . . . was asking about a President of the American Confederacy. I buzzed, assuming that I knew the answer, but all I could think of was "Richmond, Virginia," which I knew was wrong. The camera zoomed in, so I had to say something and when I opened my mouth I heard "Jefferson Davis" come out, but at no point was I conscious of that information before I spoke.[23]

Finally, famously, but least interestingly from a scientific point of view, is psychiatrist Sigmund Freud (1856–1939), whose vivid picture of the unconscious is known to everyone. The mysterious forces of ego, id and super-ego battle to drive human action, according to Freud. Well, maybe. Unconscious drives certainly exist. That they take the form of latter-day Greek myth is less certain. What is certain is that people are often completely unaware of their real motives. British scientist, novelist and public figure C. P. Snow (1905–1980), for example, wrote that everyone has a "secret planner" that guides actions, but whose motives are concealed. Watson alluded to something similar with his unconscious "unfulfilled wishes." People often do not know why they do what they do.

Astrophysicists now tell us that more than 80% of the matter in the universe, so-called *dark matter,* cannot be observed. The unconscious is the dark matter of psychology. Its processes are responsible for all creative activity and most recollection. But it is hard to study, and we still know very little about it. Introspection, once the standard tool for studying consciousness, turns out to be both incomplete and unreliable. But if not introspection, then what? The behaviorist solution is to look at a person's past history—what have they experienced and how have they acted?—as clues to future behavior. This also is often incomplete. But at least it is a method that points us in the right direction. More on history and the origins of novel behavior later in the book.

Watson was right to be skeptical of introspection as a source of information about the causes of behavior. Less happy was his idea of theory. Notice that Watson expressed his *theoretical* goal as "the prediction and control of behavior." Good theories do predict and often permit us to control the world. Fashion models are all tall and thin. But not every tall and thin woman can be a fashion model and "prediction and control" is not the same as theoretical understanding. You may be able to predict your spouse's behavior and even control it, but that doesn't mean you have a theory about it. You know he or she is likely to say this or that in a given situation, but you are unlikely to know why or through what process. And controlling something is not the same thing as understanding it. The Chinese bred fancy goldfish, and dog breeders many varieties of dog, long before Augustinian friar Gregor Mendel made the first step to understanding genetics in 1865. Breeders knew that "like breeds like" and not much else about the mechanism of heredity. But this was good enough to create an astonishing variety of animals and plants via artificial selection—no theory required. Watson equated theory with prediction and control, even though real scientific theories are much more than that. He burdened behaviorists with a cartoon version of "theory" that has left them open to criticism ever since.

The idea of *objectivity,* defined in terms of consensual agreement among external observers,[24] was emphasized most strongly by the Vienna Circle positivists but had its origins much earlier and was very much in the air as Watson wrote his first paper. Behaviorism (for Watson) is the redefinition of psychology as the objective study of behavior (Box 1.1).[25] Unfortunately, he got a little carried away with the apparent simplicity of this idea. He thought he understood much more than he did, as did Skinner a few years later.

Behaviorists of nearly all varieties, early as well as contemporary, agree on the following reasoning: Psychology is a science; and because it is a science, its data are *public.* Physicist John Ziman much later popularized this idea and used it as a definition of all science, which he called "public knowledge."[26]

Obviously introspective feelings, ideas, visions and images—what you or I feel or see in our "mind's eye"—are not public in Ziman's sense. The subjective aspects of consciousness, private events in Skinner's terminology, therefore (according to Watson and Meyer), cannot be the subject matter of a science. In a bizarre philosophical break, radical behaviorist Skinner tried to make private events into public ones, as we'll see later.

The public-private issue is still contentious. For example, British physicist Brian Pippard—neither a behaviorist nor even a psychologist—wrote in the leading scientific weekly *Nature,*

> All too rarely do I find colleagues who will assent to the proposition (which I find irresistible) that the very ground-rules of science, its concern only for public knowledge, preclude its finding an explanation for my consciousness, the one phenomenon of which I am absolutely certain.[27]

Box 1.1   Watson on Behaviorism

Psychology as the behaviorist views it is a purely objective experimental branch of natural science. *Its theoretical goal is the prediction and control of behavior.* Introspection forms no essential part of its methods, nor is the scientific value of its data dependent upon the readiness with which they lend themselves to interpretation in terms of consciousness. The behaviorist, in his efforts to get a unitary scheme of animal response, recognizes no dividing line between man and brute.

—John Broadus Watson (emphasis added)

Since psychology was at one time defined as the study of consciousness, and since the so-called cognitive revolution has once more legitimized speculation about mind, consciousness and theories derived from intuitions about consciousness, it is obvious why behaviorism is a source of controversy in present-day psychology.

My consciousness (or yours) is revealed to others through *speech,* of course. And my speech (as opposed to the *meaning* of my speech) *is* public. Since Watson, behaviorists have been very happy to take language (renamed "verbal behavior") as one of their domains (more about consciousness in Chapter 16).

So far I have described little more than what has come to be known as *methodological* behaviorism, with which most general experimental psychologists would agree. But Watson went well beyond insistence on third-person objectivity to argue against any kind of theory that did not explicitly refer to observables, either "real" observables, or things like "covert responses" that sound like observables, even though they cannot be measured directly. Thus, *thought,* for Watson, was nothing but "covert speech," measurable, perhaps, by imperceptible movements of the vocal chords. Other aspects of consciousness were similarly reduced to muscular movements or the perception of such movements. This emphasis drew the attention of experimenters to hitherto unexpected physiological accompaniments of conscious experience, such as rapid-eye-movement (REM) sleep as a signal of dreaming, or the direction of gaze as an indicator of the contents of thought.[28] But it was theoretically much less productive. Watson's preoccupation with the sensations of movement left a legacy of obsession with *proprioception* that was to constrict behavioristic theorizing for several decades.

Watson is not generally credited with paying much attention to the unconscious. Yet in his early years he was sympathetic even to Sigmund Freud:

> If the followers of the Freudian school of psychologists can be believed . . . we are daily betraying the presence of unfulfilled wishes. Many of these wishes are of such a character that we ourselves cannot put them into words.[29]

But his emphasis was on the motor system, "covert speech" and so on. As we will see in later chapters (especially Chapter 16), the limitations of consciousness are amply balanced by the autonomy of the unconscious.

Skinner, the predominant behaviorist of the twentieth century, was less preoccupied with proprioception. But he nevertheless claimed that psychological theory should not include any "explanation of an observed fact which appeals to events taking place somewhere else, at some other level of observation, described in different terms, and measured, if at all, in different dimensions."[30] This a very odd view, since it would exclude science atomic theory, quantum theory, and genetics. For example, the law of multiple proportions, a good behavioristic observation from nineteenth-century chemistry, is explainable by reference to atoms and molecules, which are not directly observed. The breeding patterns of peas were explained by Mendel as a reflection of the random combination of discrete hereditary particles—genes—unobserved at that time and for many decades thereafter. Much of physics is still a quest for entities postulated by theory but hitherto unobserved. The recent detection of the Higgs boson is just the most recent in a series of such efforts.[31] It is a testimony to Skinner's rhetorical skill, and the dedication of his followers, that he managed to get away with a scientific position that in effect separates psychology from the most developed of the "hard" sciences.

***

In summary, behaviorism arose in reaction against introspection as a scientific method. Watson and those who followed him were correct in this. Introspection sheds only a very dim light on the true causes of behavior. Inaccessible to conscious thought is the vast "dark matter" of the unconscious, responsible for recollection, creativity and that "secret planner" whose hidden motives complement conscious motivation. But behaviorism also went too far in its attempts to simplify psychology. Watson's claim that thought is nothing but covert speech and Skinner's nonsensical objection to theoretical concepts that cannot be directly observed have hobbled the development of behaviorism and allowed the rest of psychology to backslide slowly into mentalism—easy to understand and readily compatible with "folk psychology," but rich in philosophical error, and a probable scientific dead end.

Notes

1. Roediger, R. (2004, March). What happened to behaviorism? *American Psychological Society Observer, 17*(3), www.psychologicalscience.org/index.php/uncategorized/what-happened-to-behaviorism.html.
2. Machado, A., Lourenço, O., & Silva, F. J. (2000). Facts, concepts, and theories: The shape of psychology's epistemic triangle. *Behavior and Philosophy, 28*(1/2), 1–40.
3. Dawes, R. M. (1994). *House of cards: Psychology and psychotherapy built on myth* (New York: The Free Press); Horgan, J. (1999). *The undiscovered mind* (New York: The Free Press); "Psychology as a scientific discipline can be seen as wallowing, perhaps slowly disintegrating," writes one commentator (Marc Branch, unpublished manuscript), noting the fissiparous state of the American Psychological Association, which, as of 2013, had fifty-nine almost independent divisions. This Balkanization is mirrored in introductory psychology textbooks.
4. Watson, R. I. (1971). Prescriptions as operative in the history of psychology. *Journal of the History of the Behavioral Sciences, 7*, 311–322.
5. See, for example, Dehaene, S. (2003, April). *The neural basis of the Weber-Fechner law: A logarithmic mental number line.* Retrieved from www.sciencedirect.com/science/article/pii/S136466130300055X.
6. See O'Donohue, W., & Kitchener, R. (Eds.). (1999). *Handbook of behaviorism* (New York: Academic Press), for a collection of papers on the varieties of behaviorism.
7. For examples of this kind of debate, check out http://psycrit.com/Targets/2007-Fodor and www.ncbi.nlm.nih.gov/pmc/articles/PMC2755371/pdf/behavan00003-0119.pdf.

8. Amsel, A. (1989). *Behaviorism, neobehaviorism and cognitivism in learning theory* (Hillsdale: Erlbaum), p. 1.
9. Kennedy, J. S. (1992). *The new anthropomorphism* (Cambridge: Cambridge University Press).
10. Ridley, Mark. (1992). Animist debate: *The new anthropomorphism* by J. S. Kennedy, *Nature, 359*, 280.
11. Tudge, C. (1999, August 2). Chimps don't talk, but they do cry. *The New Statesman.* www.newstatesman.com/node/135337 (italics added).
12. See http://en.wikipedia.org/wiki/Watson_(computer). The "Watson" here refers to an IBM pioneer, not J. B. Watson, the founder of behaviorism.
13. See Todd, J. T., & Morris, E. K. (Eds.). (1994). *Modern perspectives on John B. Watson and classical behaviorism* (Westport, CT: Greenwood Press), for an account of Watson's life and work. For an account of his advertising career, see Kreshel, P. J. (1990). John B. Watson at J. Walter Thompson: The legitimation of "science" in advertising. *Journal of Advertising, 19*(2), 49–59.
14. Watson, J. B. (1913). Psychology as the behaviorist views it. *Psychological Review, 20*, 158–177.
15. Mills, J. A. (1998). *Control: A history of behavioral psychology* (New York: New York University Press).
16. See, for example, www.purveslab.net/publications/pnas-2011-purves-et-al.pdf.
17. Named after its inventor, American ophthalmologist Adelbert Ames Jr., and first built in 1934. See http://psylux.psych.tu-dresden.de/i1/kaw/diverses%20Material/www.illusionworks.com/html/ames_room.html.
18. See http://en.wikipedia.org/wiki/M%C3%BCller-Lyer_illusion.
19. For a survey, see Gregory, R. L. (2005). The Medawar Lecture 2001: Knowledge for vision: Vision for knowledge. *Philosophical Transactions of the Royal Society B, 360*, 1231–1251.
20. A comprehensive biography is Robert Kanigel's (1981) *The man who knew infinity* (New York: Macmillan).
21. Kanigel (1981), p. 216.
22. Kanigel (1981), p. 288.
23. Lance Haward; *UCL Magazine*, Autumn 1999.
24. Consensus is a flawed definition of "objectivity" or "truth," of course. The scientific majority is sometimes wrong, as in the initial rejection of Alfred Wegener's theory of tectonic drift and (according to some critics) the allegiance of the majority to the idea of anthropogenic climate change (e.g., Matt Ridley, "Cooling Down the Fears of Climate Change," *The Wall Street Journal,* December 18, 2012).
25. Watson (1913), p. 158.
26. Ziman, J. (1968). *Public knowledge: The social dimension of science* (Cambridge: Cambridge University Press).
27. Pippard, B. (1992). Review of *Counsel of despair: Understanding the present: Science and the soul of modern man* by Bryan Appleyard. *Nature, 357*, 29.
28. Here are Watson's rather inconsistent comments on proprioception: "The behaviorist . . . has never really held the view that thinking is merely the action of language mechanisms." *But then, in the next paragraph*:

   > A whole man thinks with his whole body in each and in every part. If he is mutilated or if his organs are defective or lacking, he thinks with the remaining parts left in his care: but surely he does everything else in exactly the same way. . . . [E]veryone admits that [a tennis] player is using every cell in his body during the game. Nevertheless if we sever a small group of muscles in his right arm his playing is reduced practically to that of a novice. This illustration serves us very well in explaining why one emphasizes laryngeal processes in thinking. Surely we know that the deaf and dumb use no such laryngeal processes, nor

does the individual whose larynx has been removed. Other bodily processes have to take on the function of the larynx. Such functions are usually usurped by the fingers, hands, arms, facial muscles, muscles of the head, etc. I have in another place emphasized the extent to which finger and hand movements are used by the deaf and dumb when they are engaged in silent thinking. . . . It would be an easy experiment, but so far as I know not hitherto tried, to bind the fingers and arms of such an individual and then give him a problem in arithmetic, memorizing simple stanzas, and the like, which have to be worked out without exteroceptive aid. It would be necessary probably to tie down eye movements, were such a thing possible, and to restrain even the head and intercostal muscles.

Watson, J. B. (1920). Is thinking merely the action of language mechanisms? *British Journal of Psychology, 11*, 87–104.
29. Watson, J. B. (1916). The psychology of wish fulfillment. *The Scientific Monthly,* quoted in Malone & Garcia-Penagos, *Journal of the Experimental Analysis of Behavior* (in press), who make a persuasive case for Watson's early sympathy for Freud's views on the unconscious.
30. Skinner, B. F. (1950). *Science and human behavior* (New York: Macmillan), p. 193.
31. See www.sciencenews.org/view/generic/id/341993/description/Higgs_found.

2 Behaviorism and Learning Psychology

Cognitive psychologists are interested in thought, but behaviorists are concerned with *action*—and not just observing action but *controlling* it. The behaviorist emphasis on the forces that change behavior meant that behaviorism, as an approach to psychology, was almost coextensive with the psychological study of *learning,* particularly learning in animals, for its first fifty years or so. A history of behaviorism features many of the same stars as a history of learning psychology.[1]

The budding behaviorist movement was strongly influenced by the studies of *conditioned reflexes* by the Russian physiologists Bekhterev, Pavlov and their associates at the turn of the twentieth century. Ivan P. Pavlov (1849–1936) was a gastric physiologist. He ran a large institute in the Military Medical Academy in St. Petersburg, beginning in 1895 and for the next several decades—well into the Soviet era. In 1904 Pavlov won a Nobel Prize for his contributions to gastric physiology, but he is of course much better known for his work on what he called "psychic secretions"—the salivation of dogs in response to a bell, a tone or some other neutral stimulus that has been paired with the presentation of food.[2] Vladimir Bekhterev (1857–1927) is not as well known, but his motor conditioning method is closer to *operant conditioning,* the method so named and later exploited by B. F. Skinner.

Since René Descartes (1596–1650), philosopher, mathematician and all-around genius, in the seventeenth century, physiologists and psychologists had been familiar with the idea of the *reflex,* the inborn, almost automatic elicitation of a response, such as an eye blink, by a suitable stimulus, such as a puff of air to the eye. This apparently simple phenomenon, so similar to the intuitive idea of cause and effect, was very attractive to Cartesians, who wanted to understand animal behavior in mechanical terms. But *learning* always posed something of a problem because as an organism learns, previously ineffective stimuli become effective, and previously effective stimuli may cease to be so. Pavlov's *conditioned reflex,* in which a neutral stimulus acquires the power to elicit a response, seemed to resolve this contradiction.[3] Here was an apparently mechanical process that nevertheless allowed stimuli to have different effects at different times. The reflex model could be preserved, but learning could be accommodated.

As experimental work progressed in the twentieth century, it became increasingly obvious that Pavlovian or *classical* conditioning (*respondent* is the Skinnerian term) is in fact a rather poor model for much of what humans and animals do. Classical conditioning is automatic, usually involves the autonomic (unconscious, involuntary) nervous system and is not goal directed like voluntary behavior. Indeed, as we'll see, classical conditioning can sometimes interfere with adaptive, goal-directed behavior. Instrumental or operant conditioning (about which more in a moment) provides a much better model for directed action, but at the cost of abandoning the simple cause-effect, stimulus-response (S-R) behavioral building block.

But none of this was apparent in the early part of the twentieth century, when Watson first saw the potential of Pavlovian experiments and analyses. Under the Pavlovian influence, Watson placed heavy emphasis on stimulus-response learning. Despite, or perhaps because of, his early experience studying the instinctive behavior of seabirds—terns—on the Dry Tortuga islands in the Florida Keys, Watson thought that most human behavior is not instinctive. In this he differed from William James, who thought that humans have not fewer but more instincts than other animals. Watson's biological training had given him faith in the essential simplicity of all behavior. He therefore believed that despite its apparent complexity, human behavior is basically unmysterious and comprehensible. Seeking a simple alternative to instinct, he hit upon stimulus-response learning, exemplified by Pavlovian experiments, as a suitably plastic means for the development of adaptive behavior during the lifetime of the individual. Since the mechanism of stimulus-response learning was presumed to be well understood and common to many species, Watson's view led him to give priority to the environment as a determiner of behavior. Nurture, not nature, was the key. This emphasis on the environment—as opposed to the constitution of the organism through which the environment must act—has continued in the varieties of behaviorism that grew out of Watson's original manifesto.

In addition to the Pavlovian and positivistic influences, Watson's approach to psychology also owed a debt to biologist Jacques Loeb (1859–1924), who was one of his teachers. Loeb was a Jewish-intellectual émigré from Germany who came to the United States to escape from discrimination in his native country (anti-Semitism in Europe didn't begin with Adolf Hitler). Loeb did well in the United States, spending most of his career at the University of Chicago. His work at that time was with invertebrates and plants, and, as might be expected, he found their behavior to be relatively simple. He invented a theory of what he called *tropisms,* which are simple orienting mechanisms that allow these primitive organisms to approach or avoid light, find food or a mate and so on.

These processes are rather wonderful because they achieve apparently intelligent results by very simple means. For example, bacteria like *Salmonella* (food poisoning) and *Escherichia coli* (human gut) have only two ways to move: either swimming relatively straight, or "tumbling," in which they constantly move a short distance in a more or less random direction. Yet these literally brainless creatures can move up a nutrient gradient, moving—inefficiently, but eventually—from low to high concentration.

How do they do it? The answer is very simple. When they sense a positive change in nutrient concentration, they switch from their "resting" state, which is tumbling, to straight swimming. When nutrient concentration ceases to change or begins to decrease, they revert to tumbling. In other words, when things are getting better, *go*; when there is no change or things are getting worse, *look around* (tumble). This process, called a *kinesis,* is the prototype for behavioristic theory, deriving apparently complex behavior from very simple rules.[4] Figure 2.1 shows a simulated track generated by the tumble-and-swim process. By taking large steps up the gradient and only small steps down, the kinesis eventually takes the organism to the highest point. *Hill climbing,* as this process is called, is perhaps the simplest kind of adaptive learning.

Kinesis-type strategies are common in evolution and in some human situations. Natural selection tends to favor any improvement and, genetics being what it is, most changes from generation to generation are small. Hence, natural selection is a sort of hill climbing. Hill climbing usually finds a maximum in what has been called the *adaptive landscape*[5] but it may be a local maximum. An organism may find a small hill nearby but miss the mountain further on.

A kinesis is a mechanism—a simple rule or algorithm that in the right circumstances generates adaptive behavior in real time. That is the sense in which I use the term. An equivalent term, used in physics, is *model*—a well-defined and usually simple process that mimics some aspect of the natural world.

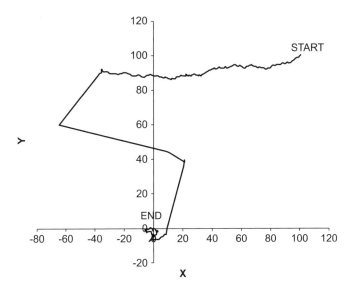

Figure 2.1 Tumble-and-swim orientation. Nutrient concentration peaks at the intersection of the two axes.

Mechanism is used in at least one other sense in psychology: to refer to the *physiological processes* that underlie behavior. An example would be *lateral inhibition,* the process that describes how simple eyes, such as the eye of *Limulus* (horseshoe crab), detects contours. If adjacent visual receptors inhibit each other, receptors on either side of a light-dark boundary will be especially excited (on the light side) or inhibited (on the dark side), allowing the visual system to respond selectively to edges.[6] Learning, which usually involves a large part of the nervous system of any animal that shows it, has not yet been (and may never be) reduced to physiological details like this, simply because the processes involved often seem to be exceedingly complex.

A mechanism in the abstract sense of a rule of operation may acquire physiological significance, but identification with physiology is not necessary to its usefulness. Feeding is an example. Feeding involves both learning and regulation. The learning aspect still awaits an adequate theory, but the regulatory part can be explained to a large extent by a simple process in which the satiating effects of food are delayed after ingestion. Food is ingested and generates an inhibitory "satiation signal" that rises with time after each bit of food. Eventually, the signal rises above a threshold, and the animal ceases to eat for a while until the satiation signal again declines below the threshold. So far, so behavioral: The model explains why eating takes place in meals, how eating changes after an interruption and some aspects of how animals adapt to schedules of food reinforcement. But once the details of the model are identified with physiological structures, the model moves from being a mechanism, in an abstract sense, to a physiological process.[7]

Watson never followed Loeb's lead in looking for mechanisms. He was interested in human behavior and in learning, which could not easily be handled by tropisms in the Loeb style—hence Watson's fascination with conditioning. Nevertheless, he took from Loeb a preference for simple, mechanistic explanations—a good idea, in principle. Unfortunately, Watson's idea of "simple" was too simple. I will show in Chapters 13–15 that the impoverished psychology endorsed by the radical behaviorism that came after Watson is inadequate to describe even behavior as simple as habituation—the diminishing response to a repeated neutral stimulus.

The Next Generation: Methodological Behaviorism

Watson's target was the target of all psychologists: human behavior. But his disavowal of consciousness, his inability to cope with the complexities of verbal behavior, as well as his training as a biologist, meant that the immediate future of behaviorism lay with animal experiments.

Psychological work with animals had already been pioneered by Edward L. Thorndike (1874–1949), first at Harvard and then at Columbia University. Thorndike was not then and never became a behaviorist. But the young Thorndike was interested in animal behavior. In the basement of William James's house, he studied the behavior of cats escaping from puzzle boxes. The animal had to push a pole or pull a chain to allow it to get out and eat a little food. Thorndike discovered that his cats seemed to learn this task in a rather simple way. At first they behaved more or less randomly, pushing the pole by accident. But then they would tend to repeat on the next trial exactly the behavior that had been followed by reward on the previous trial.

Why did Thorndike do his experiments in William James's basement rather than in a Harvard building? Because there was at that time no psychology department at Harvard. James was in the philosophy department, and the philosophers didn't want animals in their building. Once psychology became a separate discipline, this bias disappeared, but it has returned in recent years. One reason is the hostility of cognitivists to anything that reminds them of behaviorism. Another reason is the huge regulatory-compliance costs that now burden even noninvasive research with animals. Laboratory animal research is now inordinately expensive. And the third reason, which is not unrelated to the second, is the dominance of neuroscientific research with animals over purely behavioral work.

Thorndike summarized his observations in what he called the *law of effect* (see Box 2.1).[8] Thorndike's puzzle-box experiments were later repeated and the cats' behavior photographed[9] by Guthrie and Horton, who interpreted the behavior in a very simple, associative way. More recent work has raised a number of questions about their interpretation,[10] but the law of effect is true, although exactly how it works is not as simple as Guthrie and Horton thought.

Thorndike had a second law: the law of exercise. This law is familiar to everyone. It is simply that practice makes perfect. With very few exceptions, every learned skill improves with practice.

Thorndike did not consider himself a behaviorist; he is best known for his work on education. The law of effect was not original to him. The Scot Alexander Bain (1818–1903) had come to very similar conclusion more than forty years earlier. But Bain did no experiments and Thorndike's version is the one in all the textbooks. The law of effect formed the basis for the development of *reinforcement theory,* which has been the main theoretical preoccupation of the behaviorist movement. Following the lead of Thorndike and Watson, the next generation of behaviorists were the founders of the "rat psychology" that was to dominate the American academic scene for the next several decades.

Box 2.1   The Law of Effect

Of several responses made to the same situation, those which are accompanied or closely followed by satisfaction to the animal . . . will, other things being equal, be more firmly connected with the situation . . . ; those which are accompanied or closely followed by discomfort . . . will have their connections with the situation weakened. . . . The greater the satisfaction or discomfort, the greater the strengthening or weakening of the bond.

—Edward L. Thorndike (1898)

Table 2.1 The Varieties of Behaviorism

Classical: The behaviorism of Watson; the objective study of behavior; no mental life, no internal states; thought is covert speech.

Methodological: The objective study of third-person behavior; the data of psychology must be intersubjectively verifiable; no theoretical prescriptions. Has been absorbed into general experimental and cognitive psychology. Two popular subtypes are

   Neo-: Hullian and post-Hullian, theoretical, group data, not dynamic, physiological, and

   Purposive: Tolman's behavioristic anticipation of cognitive psychology.

Radical: Skinnerian behaviorism; includes behavioral approach to "mental life"; not mechanistic; internal states not permitted.

Teleological: Post-Skinnerian, purposive, nonphysiological, close to microeconomics.

Theoretical: Post-Skinnerian, accepts internal states (the skin makes a difference); dynamic, but eclectic in choice of theoretical structures, emphasizes parsimony.

Note: There is no generally agreed classification, and some would add to or modify this list. But it helps organize discussion.

The three names usually associated with the behaviorism of the 1930s, 1940s and 1950s are Edwin Guthrie, Clark Hull and Edward Tolman. However, Watson's real heir was Skinner, who rose to prominence a little later. Skinner invented new experimental methods for studying learning in animals. On the philosophical front, he applied behavioristic ideas to every aspect of human experience, including consciousness. Skinner's *radical behaviorism* is Watson's most influential legacy. Because of Skinner's influence, and his willingness to speculate about every aspect of human experience, his work is a major topic of this book. But the context and the mainstream of behavioral psychology was set by Hull and Tolman, to whose work I turn next. (Table 2.1 summarizes the varieties of behaviorism that arose in the United States after Watson.[11])

Clark L. Hull

Watson was one of the first to put rats through mazes, but the technique was exploited most extensively by Yale psychologist Clark L. Hull (1884–1952) and his followers, most notably his chief disciple, the tough-minded Kenneth Spence (1907–1967). Hull was a late developer in psychology, but in his middle years he became acquainted with, and was excited by, the theory of physics, in its classical, Newtonian form. His major contribution was a book, *The Principles of Behavior* (1943), in which he proposed a cumbersome mathematical formulation to explain learning in the white rat.

Hull was a catalyst rather than a great teacher. His weekly seminars at Yale became famous, and his ideas were spread by those who attended them to many other universities across the United States. But his most prominent followers were supervised by others, and few of his own students made names in academic psychology.

Hull's experimental method is still the norm in much of psychology. Groups of subjects are exposed to different conditions. Control and experimental groups are then compared. For Hull and his co-workers, the subjects were rats and the conditions usually related to the amount type or probability of reward—rats running, one at a time, down a straight runway to food pellets of different sizes, for example. The performances of the individuals (e.g., their running speeds) are then averaged, and compared statistically to see if the independent variable (pellet size, for example) has an effect. The method, as a way of understanding processes that take place in individuals rather than in the group, rests on assumptions about the essential uniformity of the subjects that were not understood for many years. Indeed, the limitations of what has come to be termed *between-group* methodology are yet to be grasped fully by the psychological community (see Chapter 9). The limitations of the competing *within-subject* method are somewhat better understood, as we will see shortly, but its advantages are yet to be fully exploited.

Like all the early behaviorists, Hull was a philosophical descendent of the British Empiricist philosophers, John Locke, Bishop Berkeley and the great Scot, David Hume, and inherited their belief in *associations* as the primary psychological units. He was for a while much impressed by *logical positivism,* the position of the Vienna Circle[12] of philosophers—Moritz Schlick, Rudolph Carnap and others. He had earlier been influenced by the formalism of Isaac Newton's *Principia Mathematica* (1687). The latter two influences led him to prefer a mathematical, highly formal approach to theory, despite his own quite limited mathematical capabilities. Like Skinner and many other American scientists in the Edison tradition, he was a gifted gadgeteer; but unlike Skinner, he admired abstract theory more than practical machinery.

It is helpful to organize the theoretical ideas of Hull and Tolman in terms of three questions: What *data* did they attempt to explain? Where did their theoretical *concepts* come from? What *form* did their theories take?

Hull was interested in explaining data from experiments with groups of rats learning simple tasks under the action of food reward and with groups of people learning to recall lists of nonsense syllables (i.e., trigrams such as JIV that do not correspond to actual words) under verbal instructions. In the rat experiments, the data to be explained were not the moment-by-moment behavior of individuals, but "functional relations" based on data from groups of subjects. Much was made, for example, of the negatively accelerated *learning curve* that relates a measure of performance on a learning task to learning trials. A measure such as average percentage of correct responses in a two-choice task typically increases rapidly at first, then more slowly as it approaches 100%. Another standard function was the *delay-of-reinforcement gradient,* which showed how performance declines as the time between the rewarded (reinforced) response and the reinforcement is increased.

Hull's theoretical concepts came from an associationist view of the causal chain between stimulus and response and a Watsonian notion of "ideas" as manifestations of overt or covert motor activity. "Association of ideas" derives originally from ancient Greek philosopher Aristotle, who suggested that ideas that occur close together in time are automatically linked in the mind, as are things that are similar. Temporal *proximity* and *similarity* are long-established principles of association.

For Hull, each "response" was characterized by a final "strength," called *reaction potential,* which was in turn determined by *intervening variables* (a term from Tolman, about whom more in a moment) such as *habit strength* and *generalization.* The variability characteristic of behavior was accommodated by the assumption of *behavioral oscillation* of reaction potential—what would now be termed a *stochastic* (variable-in-time) process. Each of these intervening variables was assumed to be linked in some way to observables. Experimental results were deduced as formal predictions from this rather lumbering system.

Some of Hull's theoretical elements were drawn from Pavlov, many of whose ideas were based on his conjectures about brain function. The basic "glue" that allowed learning to occur was assumed to be Pavlovian conditioning, conceived of as a process by which stimulus and response become causally linked. This usage of the term *conditioning*—which has become standard among Hull's intellectual descendants—goes well beyond Pavlov's. Pavlov used a Russian word better translated as "conditional," so that his account is descriptive rather than theoretical. He implied nothing more than the observation that elicitation of salivation (the *conditioned response* [CR]) by the tone (*conditioned stimulus* [CS]) is conditional upon pairing between the CS and the *unconditioned stimulus* (US), food (see Figure 2.2). But for Hullians,

Pavlovian Conditioning Procedures

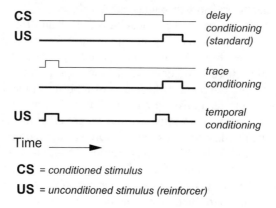

CS = *conditioned stimulus*

US = *unconditioned stimulus (reinforcer)*

Figure 2.2 Time relations between conditioned stimulus (e.g., a tone, CS: light lines) and unconditioned stimulus (e.g., food, US: heavy lines) in some Pavlovian conditioning procedures. In delay conditioning, for example, after one of these pairings has been repeated a sufficient number of times, the response reliably made to the unconditioned stimulus (e.g., salivation: the conditioned response, or CR) comes to occur when the CS is presented. In trace conditioning, the CR usually occurs after the CS, and close to the time when the US will occur. In temporal conditioning, each US presentation is the effective CS for the next US.

"conditioning" was not just a description but rather a *process.* Conditioning was a theoretical atom, which could be used to explain more complex behavior.

Generalization, the idea that training with one stimulus and response will increase the tendency to respond to similar stimuli and to make similar responses, was another idea from Pavlov. Other concepts came from Sherringtonian reflexology (Plate 2.1): For example, the idea of *reception,* a process modeled on what was then known of receptor physiology. The idea of *interaction* between stimulus effects, which was added to accommodate "whole-greater-than-sum-of-parts" effects made famous by the German Gestalt ("form") psychologists. And finally the idea of a stimulus *trace* that persists after the physical stimulus has ceased.

How were these ideas put together to explain learning? A detailed exposition would take me well beyond the confines of a short survey—and would in any case be of largely historical interest. But some of the basic ideas can be conveyed simply. Hull tied *reinforcement,* the strengthening effect of reward on a response that produces it, to the reduction of *physiological need.* This turned out to be a hard assumption to prove: Many rewarding events, especially in humans (fame, money, art, fashion), have no obvious

Plate 2.1 C. S. Sherrington (1856–1952) was an English physiologist whose book, *The Integrative Action of the Nervous System* (1906), summarized most of what was then known about the reflex and exerted a strong influence on the evolution of American psychology, especially behaviorism. But, like some other famous neurophysiologists, he ended up as no behaviorist—writing, in his eighties, a Cartesian, dualist philosophical rumination, *Man on His Nature* (1940).

link to physiology. Even food, the prototypical reinforcer, is effective as a reinforcer long before it has any nutritional consequences. The rat may well repeat his bar press after he gets the very first food pellet, long before his blood sugar or any other gross physiological measure shows any change. So much for physiological need. Moreover, the theoretical effects of reinforcing events can be described without specifying their physiological concomitants. The concept of conditioned or *secondary reinforcement* was invented to bridge the gap between physiologically effective reinforcers and "neutral" stimuli, which acquire reinforcing properties, but this idea is still problematic.[13]

How did Hull conceive of the effects of reinforcement? One effect was to "condition" events occurring at the time the "goal" (e.g., food at the end of the maze) is reached. The basic idea was that any pair of events, A-B, that regularly occur in succession somehow become linked (just as the CS and the US become linked) so that the occurrence of A will come to call up B. This is just a physiological interpretation of Aristotle's notion of association through succession and temporal contiguity, interpreted as *post hoc, ergo propter hoc*—B follows A, hence A caused B. Thus, stimuli near the goal, traces of earlier stimuli and stimuli generated by movements, or "fractional anticipatory" movements (proprioception again) may become conditioned to the "goal response." In this way, the goal response will "move forward" and occur earlier and earlier. This improvement in performance is the visible evidence that learning has occurred.

Hull defined parts of this complex process in a quantitative way, but the details were never fully specified by Hull or by his several successors, most of whom filled in theoretical gaps as best they could with verbal arguments. Numerous flaws in the system were pointed out,[14] and Hullians increasingly abandoned quantitative modeling in favor of enthusiastic data gathering. The mathematical approach was carried forward largely by the so-called *mathematical learning theorists*.[15] A single very influential theoretical paper by two neo-Hullian Yale psychologists, Robert Rescorla and Alan Wagner,[16] also led to several elaborations by Wagner and others and something of a theoretical revival. Models in the Hullian tradition continue to appear in the literature on classical conditioning (also known as *associative learning*).

Hull's other direction was the study of verbal learning. The nonsense-syllable method he used was pioneered by German experimental psychologist Hermann Ebbinghaus (1850–1909), the founder of the field of verbal learning. Hull and several co-workers in 1940 put together an extraordinary volume describing their theory of how people learn nonsense syllables. The title of this book, *Mathematico-Deductive Theory of Rote Learning*, shows its allegiance to positivistic philosophy of science, and the theory was presented in a highly formal way, using the calculus of symbolic logic (Fitch, one of the book's co-authors, was a logician). Hull defended the book as follows: "Its chief value consists in the large-scale pioneering demonstration of the logico-empirical methodology in the field of behavior."[17]

To a modern reader, the "logico-empirical methodology," with its rhetoric of mathematical theorems and corollaries, makes the work almost unreadable. Nevertheless, the assumptions of the theory are relatively simple—and important, because these ingredients, in various combinations, are part of most subsequent psychological theories. The theory explains the patterns of learning of nonsense syllables in a serial anticipation procedure: Each syllable in a short list of 5–20 syllables is presented for a couple of seconds, and the subject's task is to anticipate the next syllable. Data of interest are the patterns of errors—such as the so-called *serial-position effect,* which is that syllables at the beginning (primacy) and end (recency) of the list are better remembered than syllables in the middle—and the effects of the temporal spacing between list presentations (e.g., in comparisons of spaced versus massed practice).

The serial-position effect was discovered by Ebbinghaus. A modern version of his experiment looks like this.[18] Subjects are shown a series of fifteen words, and are then tested for recall of the words immediately or after 30 s. When tested immediately, people remembered items at the beginning and end of the series better than those in the middle. This is the serial-position effect. Memory for words at the end of the list fades when the test is delayed for 30 s or more. As a methodological footnote, although modern experiments always use groups and averaged data, Ebbinghaus used just one subject—himself. His pioneering experiment would not be publishable in a contemporary psychological journal. The reader can decide whether this reflects poorly on Ebbinghaus or on modern journal practices.

The chief theoretical ingredient in explaining results like this is the quasi-physiological idea of a *memory trace,* supposedly left by each trigram as the subject attends to it. Thus, the recency effect fades after 30 s because the trace of the last item fades to the point that there is interference with the traces of earlier items, which are now, relatively, as almost recent as the last item. This works because memory traces fade rapidly at first and then more slowly,[19] so that the traces of two successive items become more similar as time elapses.

Traces are of two kinds, excitatory and inhibitory. "Response strength," the tendency to recall a particular syllable, is proportional to the algebraic sum of these two tendencies. A correct anticipation is presumed to occur when the summed strength exceeds a threshold, which is subject to some intrinsic variability. Thus, as the trace strengths of two items approach each other, confusion between them will increase. These ingredients, a decaying trace, excitatory and inhibitory contributions to a strength variable, stochasticity and the idea of response threshold, were to form a permanent part of the theoretical toolbox used by later learning theorists.

Edward Chace Tolman

Most of the rat experiments by Hull and his students were concerned with *reinforcement learning*—that is, the change in behavior observed when one or another aspect of behavior is rewarded or punished. The focus on reinforcement learning was forced by the behaviorists' experimental subject: The rat is a species poorly suited to verbal instruction. Nevertheless, the leading behaviorist in the inter–World War years, Edward Chace Tolman (1886–1959), was notable for his rejection of a simple reward-and-punishment view even of rat learning. It was said of the great Irish wit and playwright Oscar Wilde that "[h]is art was in his life" because his writings are often less impressive than the anecdotes about him. Something similar may be said of Tolman. His theories now seem awkward or vague and sometimes naïve, but his openness and integrity, his eclectic approach, his personal warmth and the inspiration he offered to numerous graduate students—plus the fact that he was on the winning side in the infamous California loyalty oath controversy—assure his place in the history of psychology.

The California loyalty oath controversy is an interesting political footnote in the history of psychology. As part of post–World War II anti-communism, in 1949 the Regents of the University of California required all state employees, including university faculty, to sign an oath affirming nonmembership and nonbelief(!) in any organization advocating overthrow of the U.S. government. This stricture included communist organizations, of course. Tolman, at Berkeley, was one of the leaders of the opposition to this requirement. In the end, the Regents were forced to withdraw it.[20]

Tolman's views are somewhere in between Watsonian behaviorism and what is now called cognitive psychology. Indeed, apart from the fact that he worked almost exclusively with the white rat, it is not really clear why Tolman should be placed in the behaviorist camp at all. Perhaps the reason is that he identified himself as a behaviorist, albeit a *purposive* behaviorist, in his major systematic work, *Purposive Behavior in Animals and Men.*[21] Another reason may be that behaviorism was in effect "the only game in town" for an experimental learning psychologist at the time when Tolman was active.

Tolman was interested in explaining data on rats finding their way through mazes of different types. He believed that rats are smart—almost as smart as people in many ways. He said in his 1937 presidential address to the American Psychological Association that everything of importance in human psychology ("except perhaps . . . such matters as involve society and words") can be understood through the behavior of a rat at a choice point in a maze. His thinking, like his experimental subject matter, was highly spatial. He and his students devised a number of clever experiments to show that the simple stimulus-response reinforcement-learning psychology of Watson, Hull and Thorndike could not account for the spatial behavior of rats. Two examples are *latent learning* and *insight.*

Latent Learning

The demonstration of learning in the apparent absence of explicit reward—termed *latent learning*—is straightforward. If all learning depends on explicit reinforcement, then hungry rats allowed to wander unfed around a novel maze should learn nothing. This is a ridiculous idea, one might think, but much advance in psychology often still consists in turning common sense into scientific fact. So, to test the idea, one of Tolman's students[22] looked at what happens when rats are given a number of opportunities to explore a maze before reward (food) is introduced. He ran three groups: A, rewarded (in the goal box) every time they were in the maze; B, rewarded after two unrewarded days and C, rewarded only after six unrewarded days.

Group C, the latent-learning group, soon caught up with the other groups once reward was introduced. Group C reached the performance of Group A after only a couple of rewarded days, much faster that Group A, which took four days or more to learn the maze. Hence, Group C's six days of unrewarded experience was not wasted. The rats learned something, which showed up as soon as they were rewarded for getting to the goal box. Tolman and another student, Honzik, did a similar experiment the next year and confirmed this conclusion.

These results provoked much discussion. Tolman and his students contended that they reflect real unreinforced learning. One set of critics attributed the results to what would now be called "noncognitive" factors, such as habituation by the latent-learning group. The latent-learning group does better, these critics argued, not because they have learned anything, but because the unreinforced exposure allowed the rats to get over their fear of the novel apparatus (a kind of habituation). Presumably the improvement in performance of the reinforced group must then also partly reflect habituation, which should perhaps be perceived as a component of the learning process. The critics wished to argue that *real* learning is more than just habituation—but no proof was offered. There was also little basis for the tacit assumption that habituation itself is a primitive process.

Other critics argued that although food reinforcement was lacking for the latent-learning group, other, unspecified reinforcers might have been operative. A completely unrewarded group in Tolman and Honzik's experiment traversed the maze faster on successive days, despite absence of explicit reward, suggesting to some that "being taken out of the maze" (when a trial is over) might be a reinforcer. The ad hoc invocation of reinforcers like this, no matter how plausible, makes the reinforcement-learning view impossible to disprove, of course, so this line of argument gets us no closer to understanding how the rats learn the maze.

The work of Tolman and his students soon led to an explicit distinction between *performance,* the measured change in behavior in a learning task, and *learning,* the process or processes that are supposed to underlie this change. The learning-performance distinction is another commonplace: Every hung-over exam taker knows more than he shows. Learning—what the student might have done on the most searching exam under the best possible conditions—is not coextensive with performance on this exam under these conditions. The performance of Group C in Blodgett's experiment showed no evidence of learning on nonreinforced trials. But they *were* learning, and it showed up as soon as they were rewarded. The learning-performance distinction aroused controversy among psychologists. It was eventually accepted by most behaviorists—the single, striking exception being Skinner.

Insight

Tolman and Honzik[23] did another experiment, which showed that rats in some sense understand spatial constraints. Their results were cited as an example of spatial *insight*. The configuration of their maze is shown in Figure 2.3. It allows three paths from the START box to the box where food is available (GOAL). The paths differ in length: Straight-line path 1 is shorter than path 2, which is shorter than path 3.

In preliminary training, the rats were allowed to become familiar with all three paths to the food box, and the rats had experience with a block at point A, which permits access to the goal only via paths 2 and 3. In the test condition, the block was moved to point B. Now only path 3 remained open. The question was: Will the rats choose path 3 as soon as they encounter the block at B, or will they choose path 2 (normally preferred to path 3), indicating they do not know that paths 1 and 2 share a common, blocked, segment? Tolman and Honzik's rats acted intelligently, and usually went straight to path 3 after encountering the block at B, indicating that they knew something of the topology of the maze, and were not just operating on a fixed hierarchy of preferences. Tolman considered this behavior to be an example of "insight," though exactly what that might mean was not spelled out.

What data did Tolman attempt to explain? Where did his theoretical concepts come from? What form did his theory take? Tolman explained "insight" behavior and latent learning by a theoretical system that drew freely on folk psychology. Tolman's theoretical emphasis was almost entirely on the way in which rats represent their world. His rats were also well supplied with "purposes," "expectations" and "means-end readinesses" (loosely speaking: knowledge of what leads to what in a maze or an instrumental task). Their knowledge of the maze was represented as a *cognitive map*—a phrase now

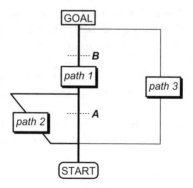

Figure 2.3 A diagram of the elevated maze used by Tolman and Honzik. Path 1 is the shortest path from start box to goal box, path 2 the next shortest and path 3 the longest. Blocks were placed at points A and B during different phases of the experiment. The question was: After encountering block B for the first time, will the rat pick path 2 (previously preferred to path 3, but now blocked) or path 3, the only effective route to the goal?

permanently associated with Tolman. Cognitive maps were never specified in any detail, but Tolman assumed they were a rich store of information about what leads to what, adjacencies and relative distances, and so on.

Tolman's last major paper[24] was a try at what would now be called a computer simulation, although usable computers were not yet available to psychologists. It is an attempt to inject *action* into his rather static theoretical picture. Cognitive maps are all very well, but a map is useless without a map *reader,* a route finder, something to translate all the information into action. Later workers did suggest theoretical mechanisms capable of translating a cognitive map into directed action.[25] But Tolman's chief contribution has clearly been his emphasis on what computer scientists and cognitive psychologists now term *knowledge representation* (i.e., the abstraction from reality that organisms are presumed to use to guide their overt behavior).

This emphasis on representation was not shared by other behaviorists. It was explicitly rejected by Skinner who, like Watson, consistently disparaged what Watson called "structuralism": "Behaviorism is founded upon natural science; structural psychology is based upon a crude dualism, the roots of which extend far back into theological mysticism."[26] (Don't sugarcoat it, Broadus!)

Tolman's contemporary legacy is research on *animal cognition,* a topic that has become very popular since the early 1980s.[27] Interest in spatial behavior has revived, encouraged by David Olton's introduction of a novel type of maze, the *radial-arm maze* (Plate 2.2).[28]

Plate 2.2 An eight-arm radial maze. The rat begins in the center and bits of food are hidden at the ends of the eight arms. Typically, the animal checks out the eight arms without repeating any.

Rats in the radial-arm maze show a type of behavior unsuspected by standard reinforcement theory. At the beginning of a trial, the goal boxes at the end of the eight arms are all baited with food, and the rat is placed in the center of the maze. The rat will then visit the eight arms, usually in no particular pattern. Note that naive reinforcement theory—"repeat what was just reinforced"— would predict that the rat should return to the first rewarded arm. This almost never happens in practice.

Control experiments have shown that the rats use some kind of spatio-temporal representation of the maze to perform accurately: They know where they are in relation to their surroundings. They are very accurate (i.e., rarely revisit an arm before exploring all arms), even if interrupted after visiting four of the eight arms. If they are returned to the maze as long as an hour or more later, they nevertheless pick up where they left off and reliably select the four unvisited arms first. The radial maze has turned out to be an important tool for the investigation of memory in animals.

More recently, the inferential and memory capabilities of dogs have been explored. They turn out to have surprising talents. A small number of dogs (usually Border collies) have been trained so that they show extremes of memory, learning the names of 200 or even more than 1,000 objects (Plate 2.3).[29] They also can learn a primitive syntax—the difference between proper nouns and verbs, for example—and to retrieve a toy by category. Pilley and Reid's

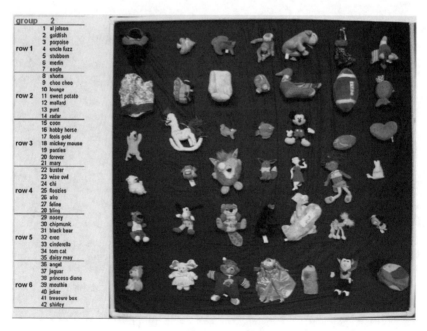

group	2	
	1	al jolson
	2	goldfish
	3	porpoise
row 1	4	uncle fuzz
	5	stubborn
	6	merlin
	7	eagle
	8	shorts
	9	choo choo
	10	lounge
row 2	11	sweet potato
	12	mallard
	13	punt
	14	radar
	15	coon
	16	hobby horse
	17	fools gold
row 3	18	mickey mouse
	19	panties
	20	forever
	21	mary
	22	buster
	23	wise owl
	24	chi
row 4	25	floozies
	26	afro
	27	feline
	28	bling
	29	nosey
	30	chipmunk
	31	black bear
row 5	32	croc
	33	cinderella
	34	tom cat
	35	daisy may
	36	angel
	37	jaguar
	38	princess diane
row 6	39	mouthie
	40	joker
	41	treasure box
	42	shirley

Plate 2.3 Forty-two of the 1,022 objects used in Pilley and Reid's Experiment 1, along with their names.

female Border collie, Chaser, could learn three verbs: paw, take and nose, and act appropriate when asked to "paw goldfish" or "nose joker" and so on, in any combination. She could also retrieve toys in one of three categories: "ball," "toy" and "Frisbee."

And this is not just memory. The dogs can also do something called *fast mapping,* which is also shown by human children. It works like this: The dog is tested by being asked to retrieve a named object from a small collection of perhaps eight at a time, in another room or behind a screen (no possibility of being cued by the experimenter). Then, on a given trial, a new object is added to the set. After being asked to get a couple of known items, the dog is asked to retrieve something she has never heard of before—say, "Darwin." Almost always, she will bring back the new object, matching up the new word with the new thing. Tolman would have called this "insight," although the term is no more than a label for something not easily explained by standard principles.

The reward in these experiments was usually something other than food—mainly pleasing the experimenter. The aim of the experiments was not just to show the cleverness of Chaser, but also to explore and understand her cognitive capacities, which turn out to be considerably more extensive than previously thought.

Another major theme in animal cognition is less obviously valuable than the ones I just discussed. It is animal behavior as entertainment—or perhaps as "Dr. Dolittle"[30] research: Experiments that explore the extent to which animals can do things that previously seemed unique to people (e.g., talk, solve abstract problems, form concepts, be embarrassed or deceive others). This work is not theoretically motivated, for the most part. The emphasis is on what the animals can do rather than how they do it. The positive aspect is that it is natural history: It explores the limits of what animals can do, an essential preliminary to adequate theory. (YouTube is a great source of data of this kind!) The negative aspect is that it has led some commentators to denigrate behaviorism and embrace a dead-end anthropomorphism: "The much-despised anthropomorphism could thus give deeper insight than the apparent rigours of behaviourism," writes one critic,[31] forgetting that showing resemblances between animals and people is only the first step toward a deeper understanding of both. Let us concede that animals "think" and people also "think"—but what *is* "thinking"?

***

Classical behaviorism grew out of an increasing impatience with the limitations of introspection. J. B. Watson, an energetic pop-psychology guru and social improver squarely in the American tradition, proposed an apparently simple view of psychology that proved irresistible in the early part of the twentieth century. When Watson left academic psychology for advertising, neo-behaviorists Hull and Tolman added a theoretical component and competed for dominance with Skinnerian radical behaviorism for several decades until the rise of cognitive psychology in the late 1960s.

Tolman's chief interest was in cognitive representation. Hull was interested in the process of learning. Both sought the mechanisms that underlie behavior, even if their emphases were different. Hull thought that relatively simple, quantitative principles could provide a complete explanation. Tolman enjoyed showing that simple stimulus-response (S-R) accounts are false. His best-remembered experiments demonstrate that rats seem to have sophisticated spatial understanding, as opposed to learning through the formation of chains of S-R links. In place of a quantification that he thought premature, Tolman provided metaphorical and impressionistic frameworks out of which he hoped more powerful theories would grow. But neither Hull's simplistic quantitative principles nor Tolman's metaphors have led to the comprehensive understanding of behavioral mechanisms that both desired.

Not all behaviorists accept the conventional scientific proposition that the aim of science is to *explain* the phenomena of nature. "Explanation" for most scientists means "theoretical explanation." Hull and Tolman agreed on this point, at least. Their efforts had only limited success; but for Watson, and later Skinner, the aim of psychology was different: "prediction and control," essentially unaided by theory. A good theory will usually imply prediction and control as an outcome, but many good theories fail to predict very much, and some things are not amenable to control, no matter how well they are understood. A theory may be persuasive simply because it summarizes much that is already known, like Darwin's theory of evolution by natural selection. A theory like quantum theory or chaos theory may even show that certain kinds of prediction are impossible. Conversely, we may predict the motion of the planets without being able to control them. And a theory is more than the sum of its predictions. The early version of Copernicus's heliocentric theory did not predict better than the Ptolemaic theory, and the calculations required were apparently no easier. Nevertheless, the Copernican theory is better because it is fundamentally simpler, and because it led to more powerful theories. There is more to theory than prediction and control.

Watson's research agenda was essentially atheoretical, and is thus scientifically eccentric. Watson's successor, Skinner, also provided an alternative to theory that was part Baconian fact gathering and part pragmatic epistemology. It also was a scientific outlier. Nevertheless, in his hands this mixture turned out to be enormously influential. I turn next to Skinner and his discoveries.

Notes

1. See Boakes, R. (1984). *From Darwin to behaviourism: Psychology and the minds of animals* (Cambridge: Cambridge University Press) for an engaging history of learning and animal psychology. See also Rachlin, H. (1991). *Introduction to modern behaviorism,* 3rd ed. (New York: Freeman), for an excellent review of behavioristic animal-learning research.
2. You can check out Pavlov's dogs at http://blogs.smithsonianmag.com/smartnews/2013/02/what-kind-of-dog-was-pavlovs-dog.
3. Pavlov, I. P. (1927). *Conditioned reflexes* (New York: Oxford University Press).

4. See McNab, R. M., & Koshland, D. E. (1972). The gradient-sensing mechanism in bacterial chemotaxis. *Proceedings of the National Academy of Sciences, USA, 69*, 2509–2512; see Berg, H. C. (2000, January). Motile behavior of bacteria. *Physics Today*, 24–29, for the rather wonderful mechanical, biochemical and genetic details. (These authors use the term *chemotaxis* for what I am calling a *kinesis*, following the classic work of Fraenkel & Gunn [1940]. *The orientation of animals: Kineses, taxes and compass reactions* [Fair Lawn, NJ: Oxford University Press, 1940. (Dover edition: 1961)].) These processes are also reviewed in Staddon, J.E.R. (2001). *Adaptive dynamics: The theoretical analysis of behavior* (Cambridge, MA: MIT/Bradford).

5. See http://en.wikipedia.org/wiki/Fitness_landscape.

6. See http://en.wikipedia.org/wiki/Lateral_inhibition.

7. Silvano Zanuto has suggested a physiological basis for the regulatory process: Zanutto, B. S., & Staddon, J. E. R. (2007). Bang-bang control of feeding: Role of hypothalamic and satiety signals. *PLoS Computional Biology, 3*(5), e97. doi:10.1371/journal.pcbi.0030097.

8. Thorndike, E. L. (1898). Animal intelligence: An experimental study of the associative processes in animals. *Psychological Review Monographs, Suppl., 2*(8).

9. Guthrie, E. R., & Horton, G. P. (1946). *Cats in a puzzle box* (Oxford, England: Rinehart).

10. Moore, B. R., & Stuttard, S. (1979, September 7). Dr. Guthrie and *Felis domesticus* or: Tripping over the cat. *Science, 205*(4410), 1031–1033:

> The principal reactions described in Guthrie and Horton's classic learning monograph appear to have been caused by the mere presence of the experimenters. Neither escape nor food reinforcement is necessary for the establishment of such responses. They are species-typical "greeting" reactions, readily elicited by the sight of human observers.

See also Moore, B. R. (2004). The evolution of learning. *Biological Reviews, 79*, 301–335, for a comprehensive review of types of learning and their possible evolution.

11. An influential compendium of classical behaviorism is Osgood, C. E. (1956). *Method and theory in experimental psychology* (Oxford: Oxford University Press).

12. See http://en.wikipedia.org/wiki/Logical_positivism.

13. Williams, B. A. (1994). Conditioned reinforcement: Neglected or outmoded explanatory construct? *Psychonomic Bulletin and Review, 1*, 457–475.

14. See, for example, the chapter on Hull in Bower, G. H., & Hilgard, E. R. (1981). *Theories of learning* (Englewood Cliffs, NJ: Prentice-Hall), for some years the standard textbook on theories of learning.

15. See, for example, Luce, R. D., Bush, R. R., & Galanter E. (Eds.). (1963). *Handbook of mathematical psychology* (Oxford, England: Wiley).

16. Rescorla, R. A., & Wagner, A. R. (1972). A theory of Pavlovian conditioning: Variations in the effectiveness of reinforcement and nonreinforcement. In A. Black & W. F. Prokasy (Eds.), *Classical conditioning: II—Current research and theory* (New York: Appleton-Century-Crofts). See also the Pearce-Hall theory: www.scholarpedia.org/article/Pearce-Hall_error_learning_theory#References.

17. Hull, C. L., Hovland, C. I., Ross, R. T., Hall, M., Perkins, D. T., & Fitch, F. G. (1940). *Mathematico-deductive theory of rote learning* (New York: McGraw-Hill), p. xi.

18. Glanzer, M., & Cunitz, A. (1966). Two storage mechanisms in free recall. *Journal of Verbal Learning and Verbal Behavior, 5*, 351–360.

19. Rubin, D., Hinton, S., & Wenzel, A. (1999). The precise time course of retention. *Journal of Experimental Psychology: Learning, Memory & Cognition, 25*(5), 1161–1176. See also Staddon, J. E. R., Machado, A., & Lourenço, O. (2001). Plus ça change . . . : Jost, Piaget and the dynamics of embodiment. *Behavioral and Brain Sciences, 24*, 63–65.

20. For a history of the controversy, see http://bancroft.berkeley.edu/collections/loyaltyoath/; for commentary, see Innis, N. K. (1992). Lessons from the controversy over the loyalty oath at the University of California. *Minerva, 30*(3), 337–365.
21. Tolman, E. C. (1932). *Purposive behavior in animals and men* (New York: Appleton-Century).
22. Blodgett, H. C. (1929). The effect of the introduction of reward upon the maze performance of rats. *University of California Publications in Psychology, 4*, 113–134.
23. Tolman, E. C., & Honzik, C. H. (1930). "Insight" in rats. *University of California Publications in Psychology, 4*, 215–232. See also Ciancia, F. (1988). Tolman and Honzik (1930) revisited or the mazes of psychology (1930–1980). *Psychological Record, 41*, 461–472.
24. Tolman, E. C. (1959). Principles of purposive behavior. In S. Koch (Ed.), *Psychology: A study of a science. Study 1: Conceptual and systematic. Vol. 2. General systematic formulations, learning, and special processes* (New York: McGraw-Hill), pp. 92–157.
25. Deutsch, J. A. (1960). *The structural basis of behavior* (Chicago, IL: University of Chicago Press); see also Reid, A. K., & Staddon, J. E. R. (1997). A reader for the cognitive map. *Information Sciences, 100*, 217–228; and Reid, A. K., & Staddon, J. E. R. (1998). A dynamic route-finder for the cognitive map. *Psychological Review, 105*, 385–601. See also Staddon, J. E. R. (2001). *Adaptive dynamics: The theoretical analysis of behavior* (Cambridge, MA: MIT/Bradford), p. xiv, for this and many other such models.
26. Watson, J. B. (1929). *Psychology from the standpoint of a behaviorist,* 3rd ed. (Philadelphia: Lippincott), p. vii.
27. Roitblat, H. L., Bever, T. G., & Terrace, H. S. (Eds.). (1984). *Animal cognition* (Hillsdale: Erlbaum); Shettleworth, S. (2012). *Fundamentals of comparative cognition,* 1st ed. (Oxford: Oxford University Press).
28. Olton, D. (1977, August). Spatial memory and radial arm maze performance of rats. *Learning and Motivation, 8*(3), 289–314.
29. Kaminski, J., Call, J., & Fischer, J. (2004). Word learning in the domestic dog: Evidence for "fast mapping." *Science, 304*, 1682–1683; Pilley, J. W., & Reid, A. K. (2011). Border collie comprehends object names as verbal referents. *Behavioural Processes, 86*, 184–195. See www.wofford.edu/psychology/chaser/.
30. After the doctor who could understand the speech of animals in Hugh Lofting's wonderful books for children.
31. Tudge, C. (1999, August 2). Chimps don't talk, but they do cry. *The New Statesman,* www.newstatesman.com/node/135337.

Part II
Radical Behaviorism

3   Radical Behaviorism, I

Method

The experimental innovations and discoveries that sparked radical behaviorism were due to B. F. Skinner. At its peak, Skinner's fame probably exceeded Sigmund Freud's, at least in the United States.[1] His popular writings made him both the most influential and the most controversial psychologist during the latter part of the twentieth century. First, a little history.

Born on March 20, 1904, in Susquehanna, in rural Pennsylvania to middle-class parents, Burrhus Frederick Skinner early showed a talent for mechanical construction. He went to Hamilton College for his undergraduate degree. Aspiring to be a writer, after graduating, he spent a year in Greenwich Village in New York. He recounts this "dark year" in his strangely monochromatic three-volume autobiography.[2] But his attempts to write fiction were unsuccessful: "[T]he literary method had failed me," he wrote, disarmingly. In due course he turned to psychology as a field better suited to his particular mix of abilities and his undergraduate preparation in biology.[3] At age twenty-four he was admitted to graduate study in the psychology department at Harvard. His supervisor was the physiologist William Crozier, who was apparently very hands-off and allowed young Fred to do whatever research he wanted—which is always the best way to handle a talented student. From Crozier, and physiology, Skinner got a preference for working with individual organisms rather than groups. Skinner got his Harvard PhD in 1931 and left to teach first at Minnesota and then at Indiana before returning to Harvard in 1958, where he remained until his death in 1990.

There are three aspects to Skinner. First, and most important from a scientific point of view, is his brilliance as an experimental innovator. He invented new methods and used them to discover unsuspected phenomena. Second is his radical behaviorist philosophy, a variant of the pragmatism invented by C. S. Peirce and promoted by William James, earlier Harvard colleagues. And third is Skinner's social meliorism, his utopian wish to improve society through the application of behaviorist principles. These three aspects are not totally separate, of course. Skinner constantly appealed to his laboratory science as support for his ideas on social and educational reform. His philosophy of science guided, and limited, his approach to theory.[4] But his science is the most important aspect and I begin with that.

Skinner's Experimental Method

Skinner consistently avoided advocating or employing standard "scientific method." His justly famous paper *A Case History in Scientific Method* was in fact a slap on the wrist to Sigmund Koch, editor of the mighty set of American Psychological Association (APA)-sponsored tomes wishfully entitled *Psychology: A Study of a Science,* in which it first appeared.[5] Koch had asked for a positivistic "systematic formulation" (recall Hull's "logico-mathematical" book that set the tone a few years earlier) defined as "any set of sentences formulated as a tool for ordering knowledge with respect to some specified domain of events." What Skinner (and a few others, such as physiological psychologist Donald Hebb) gave him was a down-to-earth, readable—and more accurate—counterexample to Koch's view of scientific discovery. Koch had prescribed a formal approach naïvely derived from Vienna-Circle positivism. Skinner told a story of insight and happy accident.

Skinner turned his mechanical skill to great practical advantage in his Harvard PhD dissertation research, which was on the "eating reflex" in rats.[6] The research apparently developed in an entirely inductive fashion, guided by a combination of efficiency ("Some ways of doing research are easier than others") and a lesson from Pavlov: "[C]ontrol your conditions and you will see order." Skinner began by looking at the force exerted by a hungry rat as it ran down a runway to get food. Tired of picking up the rat and placing it at the beginning of the eight-foot runway after each feeding, Skinner added a return path so the rat could return itself. But then he was frustrated by the long waits that developed after each feeding. At this point the gadget instinct intervened and he modified the square-loop runway so that every circuit by the rat would cause the runway to tilt and operate a primitive automatic feeder. Thus, the rat fed itself by going round the loop. Each rat still sat for a long time at the feeding place before going around again for another run, but Skinner noticed a regularity in the pattern of increasing "waits" as the animals became satiated. The rotating disk that allowed food pellets to drop had an axle. Seeking a way to record the apparently orderly pattern of delays, Skinner attached a cord to the axle. As the cord unwound with each successive feeding, it moved a pen across a steadily turning drum, tracing out the first *cumulative record* of eating behavior (Figure 3.1). Skinner had taken the first step to move learning psychology away from static statistics to the *real-time* domain of natural science.

The slope of the curve shows the rate (1/time) of eating: The more rapidly the response is repeated, the steeper the slope. Thus, the rats ate rapidly at first, but then the waits became longer; they ate more and more slowly as they became satiated. Skinner's serendipitous development of the Skinner box and his informal approach to science generally are grippingly described in the *Case History* paper and others in a collection titled *Cumulative Record.*[7] His dissertation research and the theoretical system he based on it are described in his most important technical book, *The Behavior of Organisms* (1938).

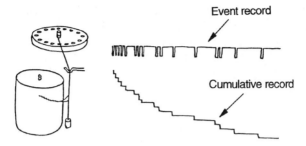

Figure 3.1 First cumulative recorder.

In the cumulative record, Skinner thought he had found an automatic, behavioral method for measuring the progress of "hunger." With the behavior directly recorded, the concept of "internal state" could be dispensed with, or so he believed. Skinner and his collaborators carried this principle further, developing experimental procedures to render measurable a few other internal (actually, *subjective*) states like *anxiety* and *fear.* A little later, the Hullian neobehaviorists Dollard and Miller tried to apply behavioristic ideas to clinical and personality issues, and later still Hobart Mowrer attempted to capture many other emotional states in behavioral terms.[8]

The evolution of the rat apparatus continued. Eventually, of course, Skinner saw that the runway was redundant and discarded it. The rat was allowed to produce food by moving a cover over a food tray. In the final adaptation of what had become the *Skinner box* (Skinner always preferred the term "operant chamber," but only dyed-in-the-wool behavior analysts use it), the rat simply pressed a little metal lever that then operated the feeder electrically.

Skinner was not the first to come up with a lever-pressing apparatus for dispensing food reward—the Briton G. C. Grindley invented something similar, for guinea pigs, at about the same time[9]—but he must be credited with the discovery of the cumulative record and of schedules of reinforcement as a separate topic for experiment. As a result of experience gained during a research project he did for the Department of Defense during World War II—using pigeons to guide missiles (the project was abandoned when the advent of the atomic bomb suggested that "pinpoint accuracy was no longer necessary"!)—Skinner subsequently abandoned rats for pigeons, which are longer lived, with better vision and more easily controlled by visual stimuli.

Operant Behavior

Lever pressing is an example of what Skinner termed *operant behavior*: "operant" because it operates on the environment, and is *guided by its consequences.*[10] The rat will continue to press so long as food is forthcoming. Other behaviorists used the term *instrumental* behavior for the same thing, but Skinner always insisted on his own terms. Operant behavior was said to be *emitted,* in contrast to *respondent* behavior (the behavior subject to classical, Pavlovian conditioning), which was said to be *elicited* by a stimulus. Skinner contrasted "voluntary" operant behavior with the kind of "involuntary" respondent behavior, such as salivation, studied by Pavlov and other students of classical conditioning. The terms "voluntary" and "involuntary" are in quotes because it is hard to give exact meaning to the notion of voluntariness when the subject is a rat. The point is that the kinds of activity that are amenable to operant conditioning (i.e., modification by consequences) are those that in people are thought of as voluntary: usually, movements of the skeletal musculature, whereas respondent behavior refers to things like salivation, heart rate or the galvanic skin response, which may occasionally be altered by indirect voluntary means (imagining a tragedy to induce crying, for example), but are not directly susceptible to operant reinforcement.

The concept of "emission" of operant behavior is important. It represents Skinner's recognition that operant behavior must occur spontaneously before it can have consequences or be guided by them. But apart from a few general comments about engineered environments that might conduce to "novel repertoires" (e.g., in his 1974 book *About Behaviorism*), Skinner never inquired systematically into the nature of the process that generates operant behavior in advance of any opportunity for reinforcement. Apart from his discussion of *shaping,* he assumed that variation would usually be adequate to allow for not just some act, but the correct, adaptive act to be rewarded and strengthened. I say a bit more about shaping in later chapters. Nevertheless, Skinner's acknowledgment of behavioral *spontaneity,* no matter how incompletely he analyzed it, was a critical advancement in our understanding of the process of instrumental learning.

Reinforcement Schedules

Just as Hull's research depended on, and was to some extent shaped by, statistical techniques, Skinner's grew out of the cumulative recorder.[11] It records first of all the behavior of just one animal.[12] It also requires a repetitive response, like eating, lever pressing or pecking a disk; it draws attention to the temporal spacing of behavior, represented as a *local rate*—the slope of the record. And a cumulative recorder operates unattended. In conjunction with automated methods of presenting food and stimuli, it allowed for very long-term experiments.

All these tendencies were further encouraged by Skinner's next discovery, which arose from his first principle: Some kinds of research are easier than others. As he tells it in *A Case History,* one weekend he ran out of food pellets (which had to be laboriously made by hand at that time). Unwilling to interrupt his research until more could be bought on Monday, he decided to abandon the standard practice of giving food to the rat for every response. Instead, he delivered a pellet only once a minute; that is, for the first successful "response" (cover displacement) a minute or more after the previous one (this would now be termed a *fixed-interval schedule of reinforcement*). Rather to his surprise, his rats continued to respond, and their responding stabilized (apparently) at a steady rate. The responding probably was not yet stable because typical behavior for animals long trained on a fixed-interval schedule is not a steady rate, but a pause after each food delivery followed by responding at an accelerating rate until the next food delivery. But the steady rate is what impressed Skinner, and response *rate*—number of lever presses or key pecks averaged over times ranging from a few minutes to several hours—was to play a central role in Skinnerian psychology. Skinner believed rate to be a measure of response *probability* and thought it of fundamental importance. This emphasis took the field in unanticipated directions that did not please Skinner, as we will see.

In this way, beginning with the study of reflex-like eating behavior, Skinner, his students and collaborators were led to devote the next few years to the study of *reinforcement schedules,* showing the real-time behavior of many individual animals. A massive, compendium of the early work, *Schedules of Reinforcement,* written with collaborator Charles Ferster, was published in 1957.[13] In rather haphazard fashion, it presented hundreds of cumulative records from dozens of pigeons trained often for many hundreds of hours under various schedules. Details of presentation may have seemed unimportant at the time because of the striking regularities visible in the cumulative-record patterns the pigeons produced.

Schedules of Reinforcement is organized atheoretically: not in terms of processes, but in terms of *procedures.* Indeed, I can still recall my surprise, as a graduate student in Skinner's pro-seminar at Harvard, at his insistence that our first task was to learn the names for the different schedules: terms like "multiple schedule," "concurrent chain" and the like. He seemed much less interested in exploring the conceptual basis for the approach, or even in analyzing specific data.

Time-based schedules are termed either *fixed* or *variable interval,* according to whether the time between food opportunities is fixed or determined by some irregular rule. In both fixed- and variable-interval schedules, the time is usually initiated by a feeding episode (for which the term positive *reinforcement* was now mandated). In more complex time-based schedules, the initiating event might be a *time-out*—a darkened no-reinforcement period of a few seconds. In *differential-reinforcement-of-low-rate* or *spaced-responding* schedules, the timer is reset by each response—so that the animal must wait a fixed number of seconds between each response if it is to get food—rats and pigeons find this very difficult for delays longer than 20 or 30 s. In *ratio* schedules, the first response after a fixed or variable *number* of responses since the previous reinforcement is reinforced. Ratio schedules typically generate high rates of responding.

Pigeons easily learn to attend to the color of the transilluminated disk they must peck to get food. Skinner very quickly found that if food is delivered only when the pecking disk (termed a *response key*) is GREEN (for example) and not when it is RED, pigeons will soon cease to respond when the RED light comes on. More interestingly, if the schedule of reinforcement when the key is GREEN is different from that when it is RED, pigeons will eventually come to

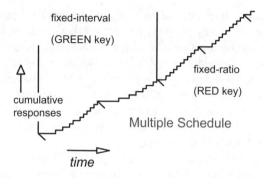

Figure 3.2 Schematic cumulative record of performance on a multiple fixed-interval, fixed-ratio schedule. Hash marks indicate food deliveries.

display in the presence of each color the cumulative-record pattern typical of each schedule: In the FI component, a wait after food followed by accelerating responding. In the FR component, a much shorter wait followed by a high rate of responding. This is an example of stimulus *discrimination,* although the Skinnerian term *stimulus control* was preferred. The successive-discrimination procedure was termed a *multiple* schedule. Figure 3.2 is a schematic of a multiple schedule, and Figure 3.3 shows some actual records.[14]

Pigeons will learn to peck a key if pecks change the color of the key to a color that has been paired with food. For example, in the presence of a RED key, pecks may be paid off on a fixed-interval schedule by a change in the key color to GREEN. In the presence of GREEN, pecks are paid off on a fixed-ratio schedule with food. After food reinforcement, the key changes to RED once again and the cycle is repeated. After experiencing several hundred repetitions of this procedure, usually spread over many days, the pattern of behavior in each of the two *links* will begin to look like the standard pattern for each schedule, obtained after extended training with food reinforcement alone. A procedure like this is termed a *chain* schedule, and the number of "links" can be extended to five or six, with the final link the only one to end with food, before responding in the early links begins to fall off (i.e., to *extinguish*).

The discovery of reinforcement schedules was enormously exciting for those who participated in it. The older, between-groups method separated the experimenter from his subject matter.[15] The experimenter dealt not with animals and actions, but with averages and statistical tests. In this context, the power of Skinnerian techniques and the direct contact they offered with individual experimental subjects was immensely rewarding. The visible and orderly output generated moment by moment by each subject, the lack of any need for inferential statistics, the possibility of easy replication, the amplification of research effort made possible by automation (Skinnerian experiments were soon run automatically by a system of electromagnetic relays,

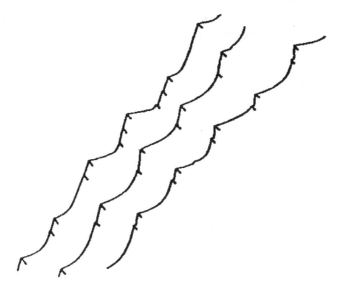

Figure 3.3 Cumulative records of steady-state performance on a multiple fixed-interval fixed-ratio schedule. Each curve is from a different species. In his 1959 *Cumulative Record* Skinner wrote: "Pigeon, rat, monkey, which is which? It doesn't matter" (p. 95). A few years later, in an article for *Science,* he wrote: "No reputable student of animal behavior has ever taken the position that . . . species' differences are insignificant" (p. 1205), but he never explained how they are significant.

timers and counters) and the new world of possibilities opened up by the reinforcement-schedule idea generated a heady atmosphere among operant conditioners in the 1950s and 1960s. The fact that many different species, from mice and monkeys to men, seemed to show essentially the same response patterns on a range of schedules (see Figure 3.3) just underlined the evident power of reinforcement schedules as universal determiners of behavior.

In 1960, Murray Sidman, a student of Fred Keller and Nat Schoenfeld (discussed more later in the chapter) at Columbia, published an influential methodological book, *The Tactics of Scientific Research,* which provided a systematic rationale for the whole approach.[16] Sidman's provocative book was a landmark. It gave a reasoned justification for what came to be known as "within-subject" research, as opposed to the "between-group" approach of Hull, all other behaviorists and almost all other experimental psychologists. Sidman emphasized the behavioral *reversibility* displayed by most reinforcement-schedule behavior. For example, the distinctive pattern of responding that can be observed on fixed-interval (FI) schedules—a pause in responding after food, followed by responding at an accelerating rate until the next food reinforcement (Figure 3.2)—can usually be recovered even after intervening training on some other procedure. The "FI scallop" is a *reversible* property of behavior.

Once this concept was accepted, it became possible to carry out extensive experiments on reinforcement learning with a handful of subjects. So long as the experimenter was careful to restore behavior to the "baseline" in between experimental conditions, the effect of different independent variables, such as stimuli, drugs or other schedules, could be repeatedly measured in the same individual subject. This is sometimes called an ABAB design, in which the two conditions to be compared, A and B, are presented repeatedly, in succession to the same organism. In recent years, the limitations of the reversibility idea have become more apparent.[17] But at the time, it was a liberating notion that permitted a vast simplification of research design and a new directness in the experimental analysis of behavior.

As the automation of schedule experiments grew increasingly easy, emphasis shifted from the cumulative record to elapsed-time measures and counter totals of responses and reinforcers. Soon a whole industry arose to study the topic of *choice,* defined as the relative *rates* (number of responses divided by elapsed time) of pecking on two or more simultaneously available response keys, each associated with a different intermittent schedule of reinforcement. (Such arrangements are termed *concurrent* schedules.)

In the early 1960s, Skinner's best-known student, Richard Herrnstein,[18] by then an assistant professor at Harvard, discovered that under many conditions, animals long exposed to choice between a pair of intermittent (VI) schedules tend to stabilize at rates of response such that the average payoff probability (total reinforcers divided by total responses, counted over a few hours) is the same for both choices: $x/(R(x) = y/R(y)$, where x and y are total responses to each choice in an experimental session, and $R(x)$ and $R(y)$ are the reinforcers obtained for each. Alternatively, $x/y = R(x)/R(y)$. In other words, if the reinforcers received are in a 2:1 ratio, so will be the ratio of responses to the two alternatives.

This relation is known as the *matching law* (see Box 3.1). Relations between averages like this are termed *molar* laws, as opposed to *molecular* laws that deal with individual responses. Herrnstein's matching-law paper in 1961 started a decades-long search for the quantitative principles of rewarded choice.[19] Many years after his discovery of the matching law, Herrnstein died prematurely—just before the publication of a book (co-authored with sociologist Charles Murray) that became famous in a circle much wider than Skinnerian operant conditioning. *The Bell Curve* (1994) is a powerfully argued discussion of the role of intelligence, class and race in American life.[20]

The *experimental analysis of behavior,* as the Skinnerian movement now called itself, grew exponentially during the 1950s and 1960s. Two new journals were founded, the *Journal of the Experimental Analysis of Behavior* (for basic research, largely with animals, in 1958) and *The Journal of Applied Behavior Analysis* (for clinical research, largely with people, in 1968). A little later, a general journal, *The Behavior Analyst,* and a philosophical journal, *Behaviorism* (now *Behavior and Philosophy*), appeared. Skinnerian research became a microcosm of psychology in general, dominated by the ideas of one man.

Box 3.1   On Notation

Notation is very important in mathematics. Behaviorists have been rather careless about it. For example, in his 1961 paper, Herrnstein wrote the matching equation thus:

$$\frac{P_L}{P_L + P_R} = \frac{R_L}{R_L + R_R}$$

meaning, "proportion of pecks on the left matches proportion of reinforcement for pecks on the left." Unfortunately, this notation makes no distinction between dependent and independent variables. In the canonical equation $y = F(x)$ it is clear that it is y that is dependent on x according to some function F; x is the independent variable and y the dependent. The problem with matching is that the two variables, x (response rate) and R (reinforcement rate) are dependent on each other. For this reason, I write matching as

$$\frac{x}{y} = \frac{R(x)}{R(y)}$$

to indicate at least that reinforcement for x, $R(x)$, depends on x. ($R(x)$ is called a schedule or *feedback function*.)

For completeness, the matching equation should really be written

$$\frac{X(R(x))}{Y(R(y))} = \frac{R(x)}{R(y)}$$

where X and Y are the (unknown) *response functions*, characteristics of the organism that translate reinforcement, as input, into responding, as output. I have chosen the halfway point just for simplicity. But it should always be understood that neither responding nor reinforcement is a truly independent variable in matching.

A substantial body of experimental work was produced, but rather little theory. The matching-law people were interested in molar *functional relations*—that is, steady-state relations between aggregate measures such as response and reinforcement ratios. But, in accordance with Skinner's strictures, there was little interest in "underlying processes." The discovery of orderly functional relations was assumed by many Skinnerians, now increasingly calling themselves *behavior analysts,* to exhaust the possibilities of the scientific study of behavior (more on the matching law in Chapter 4). Powerful experimental methods were developed, and many such orderly relations were discovered.

This growing body of empirical work was put to polemical use, however. Skinner's assertions on the general topic of a "technology of behavior" grew increasingly bold in the 1960s, culminating in his 1971 best seller, *Beyond Freedom and Dignity.* The book made recommendations about the criminal justice system, education and the "design of a culture." Laboratory research on operant behavior was held up in support of these expansive claims. I look at the validity of these arguments in subsequent chapters.

Skinnerian techniques and ideas were spread all over the world by Skinner's students, postdoctoral associates and the foreign scientists who visited the laboratories at Harvard or Columbia. The Columbia lab was especially important. Fred Keller (1899–1996), a close friend and fellow graduate student with Skinner at Harvard in the early 1930s, went on to Columbia and was a major force in spreading the behavior-analytic word. Keller, an amiable, gentle man and much-beloved teacher, together with a younger and somewhat less lovable colleague, William "Nat" Schoenfeld, wrote the first Skinnerian text in 1950.[21] Keller visited Brazil for a year in 1961 (the first of several such visits), learned Portuguese and helped found the Department of Psychology in Brazilia in 1964. The approach was carried forward by Carolina Bori and by Rodolfo Azzi until a military takeover a few years later, which devastated the universities and destroyed the lives of many academics.

Skinnerian psychology in Brazil has radiated into niches occupied elsewhere by other intellectual species. Thus, in Brazil we can find behavior-analytic cognitive psychology, behavior-analytic developmental psychology, behavior-analytic personality psychology and so on. It is a sociological version of the evolutionists' "founder effect," the founder in this case being Fred Keller. Skinner and Keller were not the only influences on Brazilian psychology, of course. But the role of radical behaviorism as the founding approach has produced interesting intellectual conjunctions—between Skinnerian and Piagetian approaches, for example—not seen in the United States.

Other early Skinnerian colonies were established in Britain at Birkbeck College in the University of London and Bangor, University College of North Wales; at Liège in Belgium and Lille in France; at Keio University in Japan and, later, at the University of Auckland in New Zealand. Two behaviorist groups were formed in Mexico City, one in the Harvard tradition (Coyoacan), the other influenced more by Columbia (Iztacala). Although the number of nonclinical radical behaviorists has probably declined from a peak in the mid-1970s in recent years, they are to be found in very many psychology departments, large and small, throughout the world. Radical behaviorist ideas have diffused widely into other areas, particularly psychotherapy and in education, where Keller's work has been especially important.

What has *not* happened (outside Brazil) is any significant fusion of radical behaviorism with other psychological approaches (although a few attempts have been made). We'll see why in a moment.

Notes

1. See, for example, www.time.com/time/covers/0,16641,19710920,00.html.
2. *Particulars of My Life* (1976b), *The Shaping of a Behaviorist* (1979) and *A Matter of Consequences* (1983).

3. For accounts of Skinner's life and work see Bjork, D. W. (1993). *B. F. Skinner: A life* (New York: Basic Books); for Skinner in social context, see Smith, L. D., & Woodward, W. R. (Eds.). (1996). *B. F. Skinner and behaviorism in American culture* (Bethlehem, PA: Lehigh University Press), which includes an excellent article by Laurence Smith on the Baconian roots of Skinner's social meliorism.

4. For a more extensive bibliography on radical behaviorism than I have space for here, check out William Baum's rather acerbic review of a book by Jay Moore and Moore's response: Baum, W. M. (2011). What is radical behaviorism? A review of Jay Moore's *Conceptual Foundations of Radical Behaviorism. Journal of the Experimental Analysis of Behavior, 95*(1), 119–126; Moore, J. (2011). A review of Baum's review of conceptual foundations of radical behaviorism. *Journal of the Experimental Analysis of Behavior, 95*(1),127–140.

5. The first two volumes in the series are Study 1: Conceptual and systematic, and Vol. 2: General systematic formulations, learning, and special processes. In Koch, S. (Ed.). (1959). *Psychology: A study of a science* (New York: McGraw-Hill). Sadly, fields that feel a need to label themselves "science" often aren't.

6. Eating isn't a reflex, of course. It is a regulated homeostatic system, like temperature or water balance. The term just reflects the philosophical biases of the field in the early 1930s.

7. Skinner, B. F. (1959). *Cumulative record* (New York: Appleton-Century-Crofts).

8. Dollard, J., & Miller, N. E. (1950). *Personality and psychotherapy* (New York: McGraw-Hill); Mowrer, O. H. (1960). *Learning theory and behavior* (New York: Wiley).

9. Grindley, G. C. (1932). The formation of a simple habit in guinea pigs. *British Journal of Psychology, 23,* 127–147.

10. For a comprehensive collection of videos showing operant conditioning and many other animal conditioning paradigms, see www.youtube.com/playlist?list=PLE5F 4237A9D17A5C2.

11. Skinner, B. F. (1976). Farewell, my lovely! *Journal of the Experimental Analysis of Behavior, 25,* 218.

12. A single abortive attempt was made to create an average cumulative record from a group of animals—a truly pointless exercise in information obliteration that has not (to my knowledge) been repeated: Heron, W. T., & Skinner, B. F. (1939). An apparatus for the study of animal behavior. *The Psychological Record, 3,* 166–176.

13. Ferster, C., & Skinner, B. F. (1957). *Schedules of reinforcement* (New York: Appleton-Century-Crofts).

14. Skinner, B. F. (1972). *Cumulative record,* 3rd ed. (New York: Appleton-Century-Crofts); Skinner, B. F. (1966). The phylogeny and ontogeny of behavior. *Science, 153,* 1205–1213.

15. For simplicity, euphony and historical continuity, I use the masculine pronoun. No disrespect to women is intended.

16. Sidman, M. (1960). *Tactics of scientific research: Evaluating experimental data in psychology* (New York: Basic Books).

17. See, for example, Davis, D. G. S., Staddon, J. E. R., Machado, A., & Palmer, R. G. (1993). The process of recurrent choice. *Psychological Review, 100,* 320–341; Staddon, J. E. R. (1993). The conventional wisdom of behavior analysis. *Journal of the Experimental Analysis of Behavior, 60,* 439–447.

18. Herrnstein, R. J. (1961). Relative and absolute strength of response as a function of frequency of reinforcement. *Journal of the Experimental Analysis of Behavior, 4,* 267–272; Herrnstein, R. J. (1970). On the law of effect. *Journal of the Experimental Analysis of Behavior, 13,* 243–266.

19. See Davison, M., & McCarthy, D. (1988). *The matching law: A research review* (Hillsdale, NJ: Erlbaum); Rachlin, H., & Laibson, D. I. (Eds.). (1997). *The matching*

law: Papers in psychology and economics (Cambridge, MA: Harvard University Press); Williams, B. A. (1988). Reinforcement, choice and response strength. In R. C. Atkinson, R. J. Herrnstein, G. Lindzey, & R. D. Luce (Eds.), *Stevens' handbook of experimental psychology: Vol. 2. Learning and cognition* (New York: Wiley), pp. 167–244.

20. Herrnstein, R. J., & Murray, C. (1994). *The bell curve: Intelligence and class structure in American life* (New York: The Free Press). See also R. J. Herrnstein. (1973). *IQ in the meritocracy* (New York: Little Brown); and http://en.wikipedia.org/wiki/The_Bell_Curve.

21. Keller, F. S., & Schoenfeld, W. N. (1950). *Principles of psychology* (New York: Appleton-Century-Crofts).

4 Radical Behaviorism, II

Explanation

Clark Hull and his neo-behaviorist successors favored what is called *hypothetico-deductive* explanation. As Charles Darwin put it in a slightly different context: "How odd it is that anyone should not see that all observation must be for or against some view if it is to be of any service!"[1] In other words, much of science consists of testing some hypothesis, some idea about what causes what or how something works.

So was Darwin a hypothetico-deductive guy? Well no, not really: "I cannot remember a single first-formed hypothesis which had not after a time to be given up or greatly modified. This has naturally led me to distrust greatly deductive reasoning in the mixed sciences." And in any case, where do those hypotheses come from? His answer: "The line of argument often pursued throughout my theory is to establish a point as a probability by induction and to apply it as hypotheses to other points and see whether it will solve them."[2] So, there you have it. First, *induction*—open-minded observation. After that, if you're lucky or creative—or more possibly, both—you may have an idea about what is going on. Then, deduction: what consequences—data—does your hypothesis predict? Finally, experiment: Test your idea, and modify it if necessary. First, induction, then hypothesis, deduction, and test. As Darwin points out, a hypothesis will nearly always need to be modified, at least in biology—and behaviorism is part of biology.

The radical behaviorists have done a great job at step 1, induction. The discovery of reinforcement schedules was rather like the invention of the microscope in Holland in the seventeenth century. B. F. Skinner and Ferster resemble underappreciated Isaac Newton rival Robert Hooke (1635–1703), whose great work *Micrographia* (1665)[3] exploited the new invention to reveal a new world of the invisibly small (Plate 4.1). In much the same way, Skinner's discovery of reinforcement schedules opened up a whole new world of orderly and largely unsuspected relations between patterns of reward and animals' adaptation to them. *Schedules of reinforcement* was Skinner's *Micrographia.*

This work started out in two directions. One followed Ferster and Skinner[4] and focused on cumulative records, looking at real-time patterns of behavior under various schedules. But this basically analog methodology has obvious limitations. It is not easy to go from a collection of cumulative records to a quantitative law, for example. So more and more researchers began to move

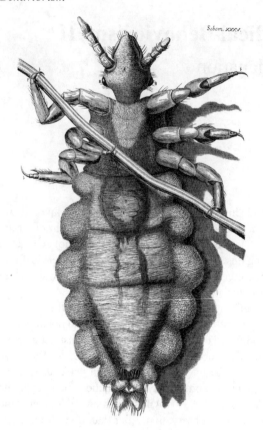

Plate 4.1 Hooke's drawing of a louse.

in another direction, inspired by three of Skinner's claims. First, that response rate—key pecks per unit time—is a measure of response probability. Second, that predicting and controlling response probability is the proper aim of a science of behavior. And finally that the aim of science is the discovery of "order." Averaging—across individuals or over time—always reduces variability and so increases "order," albeit in a way that loses some information. Recording and programming technology was improving at a rapid pace in the 1950s and 1960s (Plate 4.2). All these forces pushed the field increasingly in a statistical direction, looking at individual animals, yes, but at average response rates and times rather than real-time behavior.

Skinner himself later lamented a change for which he was in fact partly responsible. In his 1976 article "Farewell, My Lovely!" he wrote:

> Evidently we have not long to wait for an issue of JEAB without a single cumulative record! . . . What has happened to experiments where rate changed from moment to moment in interesting ways, where a cumulative

Plate 4.2 A corner of the Harvard pigeon lab in the basement of Memorial Hall, circa 1962. Cumulative recorders on the right, bottom, and center; electro-mechanical timers and relays connected by a spider web of wires on each relay rack, one per experiment. The pigeons are in another room. The whole lab, twenty experiments or so, could easily be handled by a single laptop in 2013.

record told more at a glance than could be described in a page? Straight lines and steady states are no doubt important, but something is lost when one must reach a steady state before an experiment begins.[5]

The need for reversibility, essential to within-organism comparison, meant that the focus was increasingly on steady-state or asymptotic behavior—behavior that shows no systematic change from day to day. The movement toward averages and away from cumulative records was accelerated by the discovery by Herrnstein and his students of orderly relations between average response and reinforcement rates in choice experiments.[6] The matching law (Chapter 3) and its theoretical and experimental extensions provided a major topic for operant research over the next several decades.

Matching

It is worth spending a little time on Herrnstein's influential matching-law experiment to see what we can learn from it. What does it tell us about the workings of the subject—pigeon, rat or human? And what does it miss? The procedure is less simple than it appears. The major ingredient is the variable-interval schedule: Reinforcers are "set up" by a timer that produces random intervals with a fixed average. A "VI 60" will set up reinforcers on average every minute. But individual intervals can be as short as a second or as long as 3 or 4 min. Only the average is 60 s. The actual time between reinforcements depends of course on the subject's rate of responding, because a set-up reinforcer is not delivered until the subject actually responds.

A reinforcer set-up is almost certain after a long enough wait. So, on a VI 60-s schedule with a time between responses greater than 10 min, say, almost every response will be reinforced. Under these conditions, reinforcement rate will be the same as response rate—in effect, fixed-ratio 1. But this simple relation is the inevitable byproduct of a response rate that is low in relation to the programmed reinforcer rate. Given a choice between two VI schedules (termed concurrent VI VI), and an organism that responds very slowly, matching will result. But matching under these conditions tells us nothing more than that the subject responds slowly relative to the programmed rate of reinforcement.

If response rate is the more usual 40–100 per minute, with the same VI 60 s, not only will most responses be unreinforced, but reinforcement rate will also be more or less independent of response rate. If we see matching under these conditions, therefore, it will seem more interesting because it is not forced by the reinforcement contingency. Do we in fact get matching when pigeons must choose between two VI schedules? Sometimes. But more commonly we see what is termed *undermatching*. This just means that the ratio of reinforcement rates, $R(x)/R(y)$—using the notation of the previous chapter—is more extreme than the ratio of responses x/y. For example, if $R(x)/R(y) = 0.25$, x/y might be 0.3. Undermatching is when the ratio of responses is closer to unity (indifference) than the ratio of reinforcements.

So far, so uninteresting: Undermatching is not too exciting. The function relating x/y to $R(x)/R(y)$ can always be fitted by a suitable power function: $x/y = a[R(x)/R(y)]^b$. Unless the parameters a and b can be related to some procedural feature, or at least are invariant in some way—the same across subjects, for example—all we have done is fit a smooth and totally plausible curve by a very flexible function. If Herrnstein had reported undermatching in 1961, we should probably have heard little more about it.

But Herrnstein got simple matching, $x/y = R(x)/R(y)$. He did so by making a modification to the concurrent VI VI procedure called a *changeover delay* (COD). "Each time a peck to one key followed a peck to the other key, no reinforcement was possible for 1.5 s. Thus, the pigeon never got fed immediately after changing keys."[7] The rationale for this addition was in effect a cognitive one, to do with the way the pigeon represents the situation. The idea is that in a two-choice situation, there are in fact three responses: to key A, to key B, and *switching* from one key to the other. Matching is only obtained when switching is suppressed by the COD: "The precise correspondence between relative frequency of responding and relative frequency of reinforcement broke down when the COD was omitted."[8]

Notice that the response of "switching" is hypothetical in the sense that although the pigeons do switch, we have no independent justification for treating switching as a third response type. After all, they would switch even if the process that generates pecks just allocated them randomly to each key, or if each key generated its own random pecking. The only justification for Herrnstein's argument is: It works. When he added the COD, choice behavior showed a simple invariance.

So, although matching is not forced by the concurrent VI VI procedure, to get it, you need a pretty complex arrangement involving not just two independent schedules but also a changeover delay. How long should the COD be? Luckily, just long enough: A COD greater than a second or two is sufficient to shift performance from undermatching to matching; further increases have little effect. It would have been bad news if further increases in COD shifted the behavior from matching to *over*matching, making matching as much a byproduct of the COD as an effect of relative reinforcement rate.

The matching relation is in fact pretty robust. Consequently, it has been the focus of a huge amount of empirical and theoretical research in the fifty years since Herrnstein's original paper.

How did Herrnstein explain matching? He might have gone in any one of three directions. First, he might be able to explain behavior in a two-choice experiment by a simple function that relates amount of responding to rate of reinforcement for a single response. Second, he might follow the path trodden by economists and behavioral ecologists and look at choice behavior as an example of *rational behavior*; that is, behavior that maximizes something—the organism's *utility* (for economists) or *reinforcement rate* (for behavioral psychologists), or its *Darwinian fitness* (for behavioral ecologists). (More on rationality in Chapter 8.) Or, third, he might have tried to find a *learning process,* a real-time dynamic model of some sort that would produce matching as a steady state.

The optimality approach did not come on the behaviorist scene until the early 1970s, and learning models were not favored by Skinner and his followers.[9] So Herrnstein chose the first option. He looked at the relation between rate of response to each key considered separately, as a function of reinforcement rate for that key, and found a very simple relation. Response rate was proportional to reinforcement rate on each key: $x = kR(x)$, and similarly for y, where k is a positive constant. These two linear relations of course imply matching of response and reinforcement ratios as the ks cancel.

Just how general is this result? Is it restricted to each of the two choices in Herrnstein's experiment? Or are response and reinforcement rates proportional even when there is only one choice (i.e., in a single-response situation)? The latter seems very unlikely because there is a physiological limit to the pigeon's rate of pecking. The most natural relation in the single-choice situation is therefore what is called a *negatively accelerated* function: As reinforcement rate increases, response rate at first is proportional but then increases more and more slowly until it reaches its limit. And indeed, when Catania and Reynolds

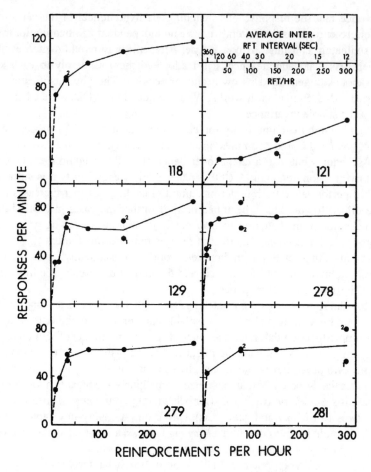

Figure 4.1 Rate of key-pecking as a function of rate of reinforcement for six pigeons.

From A. C. Catania & G. S. Reynolds. (1968). A quantitative analysis of the behavior maintained by interval schedules of reinforcement. *Journal of the Experimental Analysis of Behavior, 11,* 327–383, Figure 2.

did the relevant experiment a few years later,[10] that's exactly what they found (Figure 4.1). When reinforcement rate is low, response and reinforcement rates are proportional, but as reinforcement rate increases further, response rate increases more slowly.

How can the negatively accelerated function that relates response and reinforcement rates in the single-choice situation be reconciled with matching in the two-choice situation? Herrnstein came up with a very clever solution by making a modest additional assumption: that even when there is only one explicit reinforcement—the single-choice situation—there must be *unmeasured* reinforcers to sustain the behavior other than key pecking that the pigeon engages in when it is not pecking.

Here is Herrnstein's argument.[11] In his 1961 experiment, the two VI schedules were chosen so that overall reinforcement rate for the two choices was approximately constant. As one value increased the other decreased, so that $R(x) + R(y) =$ constant. Hence, the simple single-choice equation $x = kR(x)$ could not be distinguished from the equation

$$x = k'R(x)/(R(x) + R(y)) \tag{4.1}$$

where $k = k'/(R(x) + R(y))$. Herrnstein then extended this equation to the single-response case in the following way:

> [A]t every moment of possible action, a set of alternatives confronts the animal, so that each action may be said to be the outcome of a choice. . . . No matter how impoverished the environment, the subject will always have distractions available, other things to engage its activity.[12]

These "other sources" of reinforcement, Herrnstein labeled R_0 and added them to Equation 4.1 to come up with a new equation for the single-choice case:

$$x = \frac{kR(x)}{R(x) + R_0} \tag{4.2}$$

where k and R_0 are constants. It is easy to see that this equation, a negatively accelerated function, is a much better fit for the data in Figure 4.1 than the simple linear relation $x = kR(x)$. When $R(x)$ is small relative to R_0, x is proportional to $R(x)$. When $R(x)$ is large, x approaches an asymptote, k.

In the two-choice experiment, Equation 4.3 becomes

$$x = \frac{kR(x)}{R(x) + R(y) + R_0}.$$

In Herrnstein's (1961) experiment, because $R(x) + R(y)$ is constant, the denominator is constant, and the equation therefore predicts matching.

Equation 4.2 was extended by Herrnstein and others to cover a wide range of other schedules, including successive discrimination (multiple schedules) as well as variations on the choice theme. I have shown that Herrnstein's Equation 4.2, and some apparently unrelated matching functions from a parallel theoretical development owing to J. A. Nevin, can all be derived from a very simple model analogous to Boyle's law.[13] Several other such generalizations have been proposed.[14]

The work of many investigators has established beyond any doubt that there are some very orderly principles relating average response and reinforcement rates of individual subjects in a wide range of operant conditioning experiments. Psychophysics has its Weber-Fechner law (Chapter 1). Herrn-stein's formidable senior colleague S. S. "Smitty" Stevens had his version of Weber-Fechner, known as the power law.[15] Now behavior analysis (as it was increasingly termed) had the matching law and its extensions.

What is missing? Skinner complained that "something is lost when one must reach a steady state before an experiment begins." What has been lost, of course, is *learning,* the dynamic (real-time) process by which these steady states are achieved. Another omission is any idea of *adaptive function.* Does the matching law, and performance on reinforcement schedules generally, have any kind of fitness benefit?[16] If matching usually leads to maximizing rein-forcement, for example, then it might represent an evolutionary adaptation. I deal with maximizing in Chapter 8. Here I want to discuss learning.

Learning

Learning involves change in behavior over time. The only way to study operant learning is first to look at it: How do cumulative records change as reinforce-ments occur? And second—and this is where the task becomes difficult—to come up with a dynamic model that underlies what we actually observe. There is no substitute for imagination. We must guess at the process that drives behavior. But to test our guess, we have to construct a model and see if it gen-erates cumulative records like the ones we actually see.

Amazingly little theoretical research of this kind has been done.[17] Indeed, there has been much less research on models for operant learning in general than for classical conditioning (associative learning). Part of the reason is sheer complexity. In classical conditioning, the experimenter has complete control: He presents the stimulus, which controls the conditioned response. Stimuli are presented in fixed trials. In operant conditioning, on the other hand, a response can occur at any time, and the response is affected both by antecedent events (*discriminative stimuli*), like the conditioned stimulus (CS) in classical condi-tioning, and also by a consequential one, the reinforcer. And then there is the problem of response *selection.* How does the organism know which activity is being reinforced? This is the problem of *assignment of credit,* which I get to later. How should the researcher define the response? Herrnstein's treatment of switching illustrates the problem and one solution to it. For now, and to illus-trate the modeling problem, I will look at a very simple approach to operant learning in the single-response situation.

The "atom" in learning theory is something called a linear operator.[18] It is an ingredient of almost every associative learning theory. Let's see how we might apply this atom to operant behavior. And then let's see how far this gets us toward explaining behavior on a reinforcement schedule.

First, some simplifying assumptions. Time is discrete, not continuous. We will talk of time steps, rather than time as such. The equations are all discrete-time equations—no calculus.

I begin with the simplest possible assumptions.

1. Response x in each time step occurs with a probability $p(x)$.
2. $p(x)$ does not change unless a response, x, occurs.
3. If x is reinforced, $p(x)$ increases according to Equation 4.3. If x is not reinforced, $p(x)$ decreases according to Equation 4.4.

REINFORCED: $$p(x) \to p(x) + k_R[(1 - p(x))]$$ (4.3)

UNREINFORCED: $$p(x) \to k_U p(x)$$ (4.4)

where $0 < k_R, k_U < 1$.

Equations 4.3 and 4.4 are a law-of-effect (LOE) type of rule for learning. Reinforcement increases the probability of response; nonreinforcement decreases it. And if there is no response (hence no information), then response probability does not change. The rule for increases and decreases is the standard linear operator: Increase is proportional to the difference between $p(x)$ and 1 (the maximum), and decrease is proportional to $p(x)$.

Figure 4.2 shows how this model works on a fixed-interval (FI) schedule. The record is not smooth because responses are generated probabilistically. But there is a pattern: After each reinforcement, there is a little burst

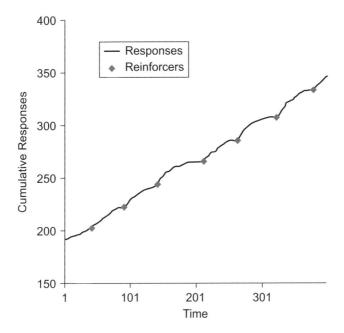

Figure 4.2 Cumulative record generated by Equations 4.3 and 4.4 on a fixed-interval 20-s schedule ($k_R = k_U = 0.9$).

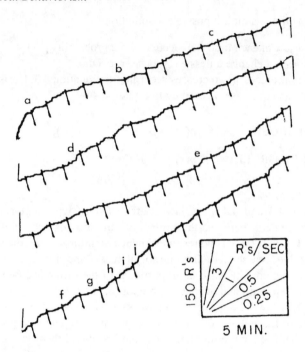

Figure 4.3 Cumulative records from an individual pigeon on first exposure to an FI
        60-s schedule. Hash marks show reinforcements.

From C.R. Ferster & B.F. Skinner. (1957). *Schedules of reinforcement.* New York: Appleton-
Century, Figure 118.

of responding.[19] Compare this pattern with what pigeons actually show when
first introduced to FI. Figure 4.3 shows some data from a pigeon first trained
with reinforcement for every peck and then shifted to an FI 60 s schedule. The
similarities are obvious. Responding is variable in both cases, but in both also
there is a burst of responding after each reinforcement.

What about the steady state? Here also this primitive model matches the
data. The function relating steady-state response rate to rate of reinforcement
is negatively accelerated, like the data in Figure 4.1. The model also shows
undermatching in a two-choice situation.

There is an obvious problem with this model, though. As everyone knows,
organisms trained on an FI schedule soon switch from the post-reinforcement
burst pattern to its opposite: a pause in responding after each reinforcement for
a time proportional to the interval value, followed by accelerating responding
up to the next reinforcement (the FI "scallop"). Pigeons are not stupid! They
soon enough learn not to respond at a time, or in the presence of a stimulus,
when they are not rewarded.

The way that Ferster and Skinner diagrammed the transition from the initial
pattern to stable *temporal discrimination* on FI is shown in Figure 4.4 (part IV

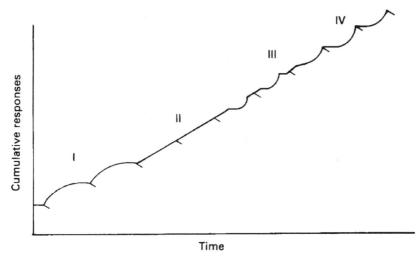

Figure 4.4 Schematic cumulative record of the changing patterns of responding as a pigeon adapts to an FI schedule.

Adapted from C.R. Ferster & B.F. Skinner. (1957). *Schedules of reinforcement.* New York: Appleton-Century, Figure 117.

shows temporal discrimination). The pattern shown in Figure 4.2 is stable, however; the LOE model never shows temporal discrimination because it has no representation of time. It *does* seem to represent accurately what naïve subjects do when first exposed to a periodic schedule. They behave exactly as the law of effect says they should: "Just reinforced? Then repeat."

But Ferster and Skinner's data show that there is a second, slower process that detects regularities in the situation. These can be either stimuli—you only get food when the green light is on, for example—or time—you only get food after 60 s, as in an FI schedule. The lack of time representation in the linear operator model is the reason it fails to shift from undermatching to matching when a COD is added in a two-choice situation. This lack also means that the linear operator model does not show the *partial-reinforcement effect* (PRE), the fact that animals take longer to quit responding, to extinguish, when reinforcement is discontinued after intermittent than after continuous reinforcement. In fact, it shows the opposite. The reason is that LOE extinction depends only on Equation 4.4. Obviously, the larger the value of $p(x)$ when reinforcement is discontinued, the longer it takes for responding to decline to zero. And in the LOE model, the steady-state value of $p(x)$ is directly related to reinforcement rate: The higher the reinforcement rate, the higher $p(x)$. So early in training, animals should show the reverse of a PRE, extinguishing faster after a lean schedule than a rich one.[20]

The PRE itself should not surprise us. If you learn to expect food only intermittently, you will be slower to recognize when it has ceased altogether.

But some sense of time is apparently necessary for this process, and the LOE model lacks it.

Learning is not a single process. The lesson from this attempt to explain learning on a reinforcement schedule with a basic law-of-effect model is that multiple processes seem to be involved. First, a rather simple law-of-effect mechanism, but then slower, more complex processes that allow the organism to detect correlations between reinforcement and time or extrinsic stimuli. Before the pigeon can show the pattern schematized in Figure 4.4, it must learn that pecking and not some other activity is what is responsible for food delivery. It must *assign credit* accurately. And this presumably involves detecting the correlation between pecking and food—and the noncorrelation between other activities and food. I discuss the way this seems to happen in Chapter 6.

Notes

1. Darwin, F. (1903). *More letters of Charles Darwin,* Vol. 1 (New York: D. Appleton), p. 3.
2. Darwin's *Notebooks*, quoted in Ghiselin, M. T. (1969). *The triumph of the Darwinian method* (Berkeley: University of California Press), p. 4.
3. See www.gutenberg.org/files/15491/15491-h/15491-h.htm.
4. Ferster, C. R., & Skinner, B. F. (1957). *Schedules of reinforcement* (New York: Appleton-Century).
5. Skinner, B. F. (1976). Farewell, my lovely! *Journal of the Experimental Analysis of Behavior, 25,* 218. (*JEAB* is the primary experimental journal for operant-conditioning research.)
6. Herrnstein, R. J. (1961). Relative and absolute strength of response as a function of frequency of reinforcement. *Journal of the Experimental Analysis of Behavior, 4,* 267–272.
7. Herrnstein (1961), p. 268.
8. Herrnstein (1961), p. 271.
9. See Skinner's influential paper: Skinner, B. F. (1950). Are theories of learning necessary? *Psychological Review, 57,* 193–216. I discussed a couple of ways that Herrnstein's equation (Equation 4.2 in the text) can be derived from dynamic assumptions in Staddon, J. E. R. (1977). On Herrnstein's equation and related forms. *Journal of the Experimental Analysis of Behavior, 28,* 163–170. Retrieved from www.ncbi.nlm.nih.gov/pmc/articles/PMC1333628/pdf/jeabehav00098–0066.pdf.
10. Catania, A. C., & Reynolds, G. S. (1968). A quantitative analysis of the behavior maintained by interval schedules of reinforcement. *Journal of the Experimental Analysis of Behavior, 11,* 327–383.
11. Herrnstein, R. J. (1970). On the law of effect. *Journal of the Experimental Analysis of Behavior, 13,* 243–266.
12. Herrnstein (1970), p. 254.
13. See, for example, Nevin, A. J., & Grace, R. (2000). Behavioral momentum and the Law of Effect. *Behavioral and Brain Sciences, 23,* 73–130; and Staddon, J. E. R. (2010). *Adaptive behavior and learning,* Ch. 12. Retrieved from http://dukespace.lib.duke.edu/dspace/handle/10161/2878.
14. Baum, W. M. (1974, July). On two types of deviation from the matching law: Bias and undermatching. *Journal of the Experimental Anlysis of Behavior, 22*(1), 231–242; Nevin and Grace (2000); Rachlin, H., & Laibson, D. I. (Eds.). (1997). *The matching law: Papers in psychology and economics* (Cambridge, MA: Harvard University Press).

15. Stevens, S. S. (1957, May). On the psychophysical law. *Psychological Review,* *64*(3), 153–181. See also Staddon, J. E. R. (1978). Theory of behavioral power functions. *Psychological Review, 85,* 305–320. Retrieved from http://hdl.handle. net/10161/6003.

16. I use the term *fitness* always in the sense of evolutionary (Darwinian) fitness—that is, reproductive success. A behavior contributes to fitness if it favors reproductive success—via access to food, mates, and so on.

17. A rare exception is Catania, A. C. (2005). The operant reserve: A computer simulation in (accelerated) real time. *Behavioural Processes, 69,* 257–278. See also Lau, B., & Glimcher, P. W. (2005). Dynamic response-by-response models of matching behavior in rhesus monkeys. *Journal of the Experimental Analysis of Behavior, 84,* 555–579. Their model is far from simple, however, and deals with averaged data.

18. The sourcebook is Bush, R. R., & Mosteller, F. (1955). *Stochastic models for learning* (New York: Wiley). See also Luce, R. D., Bush, R. R., & Galanter, E. (1963). *Handbook of mathematical psychology,* 3 vols. (New York: Wiley).

19. The size of the post-reward burst depends to some extent on the values of the two parameters in Equations 4.3 and 4.4, but the pattern shown is the most common.

20. The data on this issue are confusing. There is even some evidence that there is no, or a reverse, PRE with free-operant key pecking: Nevin, J. A. (1988, January). Behavioral momentum and the partial reinforcement effect. *Psychological Bulletin, 103*(1), 44–56.

5   Skinner and Theory

The line of argument in the previous two chapters began with B. F. Skinner's experimental discoveries. I noted the divergence of the field. The branch that looked at cumulative records and real-time behavior faded. The branch that looked at the steady state and found formal laws—matching—blossomed. But something was lost. For Skinner it was the details of behavior as it changed in time. But also lost was much attempt at explaining these processes, at understanding the dynamics of behavior. I tried to show by example how this might be done. But the task is incomplete; indeed, it has hardly begun.

Skinner became a controversial figure, which sometimes makes it difficult to isolate what he actually said from what has been said about him. His position has often been misrepresented. He was not, for example, a stimulus-response theorist of the conventional sort. Nor did he dismiss mental life: He termed mental events "private events" and treated them like publicly measurable behavior. How successful this was we will see later. He did not define behavior as "uninterpreted physical movements"[1] or stimuli as simple physical events. He did not sympathize with or advocate totalitarian regimes. But his frequent use of the word "control" encourages this interpretation and his "design for a culture" is closer to monarchy than democracy. He did not believe behavior to be exclusively a product of environment (as opposed to heredity), although he used the word "environment" very frequently and never attempted to develop a coherent view of how nature and nurture might interact.[2]

Skinner's slogan was that behavior should be studied *in its own right,* and not as a mere indicator of unspecified internal mechanisms or processes. This is an eccentric view. One might as well say that sulfuric acid should be studied in its own right and not as a compound of sulfur, oxygen and hydrogen. But perhaps he meant just that we should "sit down before facts [of behavior] as a little child":[3] Just look at the data before imposing myths from folk psychology and introspection upon it. This is *induction* and it is perfectly reasonable—as a first step toward understanding. The next step is to come up with an explanation, a hypothesis. This, Skinner did not like. He forcefully criticized any explanation of behavior "which appeals to events taking place somewhere else, at some other level of observation, described in different terms, and measured, if at all, in different dimensions"[4]—a very odd position, as I pointed out earlier. In short, he was completely uninterested in mechanisms of the sort that preoccupied Hull and Tolman. If there are "mechanisms," he argued, they are the province of physiology (neurobiology, as it would now be termed). He did not consider mechanisms in my sense: simple dynamic models that mimic the functioning of real-time behavior, without any necessary link to neurophysiology.[5]

Although he reviewed Hull's major book,[6] Skinner rarely cited any Hullian work and then only to criticize it. Yet his position was to some degree a reaction against the Hullian system. But the flaw in Hull's theory was not that it was a theory, but that it was a bad theory. It was, for example, not *parsimonious:* The number of assumptions equaled or, sometimes, even exceeded, the number of things predicted. The purpose of a theory is to summarize. Skinner was absolutely correct when he raised no objection to theory as "a formal representation of the data reduced to a minimal number of terms."[7]

In any event, Skinner felt no obligation to relate his work to the work of others, and almost never responded to his rivals or critics. In an interview near the end of his life, Skinner advised a young psychologist: "Never argue."[8] It was a principle he followed with almost no exceptions. Most damaging was his failure to respond to a long and largely misdirected critique of his work by linguist and political activist Noam Chomsky,[9] a polemicist at least Skinner's equal. In the absence of any response from Skinner, Chomsky's attack proved devastating. (A later rebuttal by Kenneth MacCorquodale was too little, too late.[10]) In a private letter, Skinner averred, "Chomsky simply does not understand what I am talking about."[11] True, perhaps; but by not responding, Skinner missed an opportunity to instruct both his critics and himself. Many readers concluded that Chomsky had a point.

Skinner intentionally separated himself and his followers from the rest of psychology by his use of language. That Skinnerians are isolated by vocabulary can hardly be doubted. But that it was intentional requires more evidence. First, the data: Skinner insisted on unique terms for familiar concepts: operant for instrumental/voluntary behavior, reinforcement for reward, conditioned reinforcement for secondary reinforcement, contingency for dependency, respondent for autonomic or classically conditioned, ontogenic for ontogenetic, phylogenic for phylogenetic.

Arguments can be made for each of these differences of course. But they do not withstand scrutiny: Operant/instrumental behavior is not well enough understood as a category to justify heavyweight doctrinal discussion about the use of terms. Language is still a lively issue among behavior analysts. Early in 2013, a lengthy exchange took place on a listerv for behavioral analysts about the proper usage for the term *behavior.* Yet in most sciences, behavior—of an electron, or a chemical compound, for example—is just whatever it is that you measure. If you define that, what's the problem? But Skinner's preoccupation with language lives on.

There is some evidence for intent. It is telling that in earlier writings, Skinner was perfectly happy with "phylogenetic" and "ontogenetic."[12] Only later did he use his own terms "phylogenic" and "ontogenic." As I mentioned earlier, I still recall my surprise as a graduate student at Harvard in the early 1960s that when Skinner took his three-week turn teaching the first-year pro-seminar, his main concern seemed to be about technical language. Any tendency to use earlier terms like "instrumental behavior" or "secondary reinforcement" was to be extinguished, and the appropriate Skinnerian terms—"operant behavior," "conditioned reinforcement" and the like—were to be substituted. There is nothing particularly sinister about a concern with proper technical terms, but the dominance in Skinner's brief teaching spell of what most would consider a secondary issue struck me as odd. The conclusion that this attempt to impose his own vocabulary was a self-conscious strategy became harder to resist as I learned the full list of equivalences between Skinnerian and non-Skinnerian terms for things that were objectively identical as well as for concepts that were still in flux.

Skinner had a lifelong interest in language as behavior reinforced through its effect on the behavior of others—in other words, as a way for one person to control another. Most evolutionary biologists also consider control—of the wooed by the wooer, for example—as a selective factor in the evolution of language. *Verbal Behavior* attempted to create a pragmatic vocabulary—*mands, tacts, autoclitics,* and so on—to describe language as a controller rather than as a means of transmitting information.[13] Skinner regarded it as his best book. Taken together with his almost obsessive concern with an idiosyncratic technical vocabulary, the inference that he consciously used it as a way to ensure solidarity among his disciples is hard to resist.

Skinner's focus on persuasive writing was remorseless. Because so many of his books are directed at a general audience, they lack much of the usual scholarly apparatus. His introductory textbook *Science and Human Behavior* (1953), for example, cites only a handful of contemporaries, none of them in the psychology of learning, the work's main topic. The book has no references. Several of his other influential books have no, or only a vestigial, index, an important omission in an era when all books were unsearchable hard copy. It is always hazardous to infer motive, but two things are certain. First, the absence of an index in most of Skinner's books encourages the reader to read them from front to back, as he intended, rather than looking up topics out of context, which might expose contradictions and diminish the force of his argument. And second, Skinner's combination of radical views, informally presented, is a recipe for misunderstanding.

So much for background. It should by now be obvious that Skinner consistently avoided anything approaching a real theory of learning. Although he always admitted the *possibility* of theory, his most frequent comments are highly critical. The historian Laurence Smith summarized his views as follows:

> Skinner admits that "theories are fun," but he insists that the activity of conjecturing is less efficient than that of observing. Conjecturing appeals to the investigator "whose curiosity about nature is not equal to his interest

in the accuracy of his guesses." Moreover, conjecturing is said to be "wasteful," to create "a false sense of security," and to lead to "useless" and "misdirected" experimentation, "bootless theorizing," and the necessary loss of "much energy and skill."[14]

This is a good summary. It also provides a prize example of Skinner's artful rhetoric. He contrasts a scientist's "curiosity about nature" with "his interest in the accuracy of his guesses"—as if the two are in any way opposed! Why should you be interested in the accuracy of your guess about nature if you aren't interested in nature?

In other places, Skinner acknowledged a place for theory of a limited sort. His book *Contingencies of Reinforcement* is subtitled *A Theoretical Analysis,* but the "theory" is very far from the kind of formal system favored by other learning theorists and scientists in other areas. Skinner never met a theory he really liked and never developed anything approaching a real theoretical system. His one foray into formal theory was something called the reflex reserve, but he soon abandoned it.[15] The kind of explanation for behavior favored by Skinnerians is of a very different sort.

Skinner began with the idea of reinforcement, defined more or less as Edward Thorndike defined it in the Law of Effect. Since his ultimate aim was the control of behavior, a precise specification of reinforcement, the agent of change, was essentially all that Skinner thought necessary. It is exactly as if our understandings of the mechanisms of heredity were assumed to be complete once plant and animal breeders found that "like begets like" and they could produce new varieties by selective breeding. No more research, no genetics, no epigenetics, no DNA. But we have control! That was in effect Skinner's conclusion. He began, and ended, with reinforcement; using appropriate reinforcement, we can change—control—behavior, which is what Skinner was really interested in.

Skinner defined reinforcement, as he defined most things, by experimental example. He first describes training a pigeon to stretch its head upward by reinforcing with food any movement that goes above a line that is continually adjusted upward (this general technique is known as "*shaping* by successive approximations"). He then goes on to define reinforcement as follows: "The barest possible statement of the process is this: we make a given consequence contingent [dependent] on certain physical properties of behavior (the upward movement of the head), and the behavior is then observed to increase in frequency."[16] Any event that will have this frequency-increasing effect if made contingent on behavior—on more than one type of behavior, preferably, so that the definition is not circular—is termed a *reinforcer.* Skinner appropriated the word *contingency* for the dependent, causal relation between behavior (*response*) and consequence (reinforcer) necessary for the reinforcer to have an effect.

There are two key terms in Skinner's definition of reinforcement: *contingency* and *frequency* (or probability). It turns out that the way in which behavior determines the occurrence of a reinforcer makes a very great deal of difference to the effectiveness of the reinforcer. The single term *contingency* in fact refers to at least three properties: reinforcement *probability, delay* and (in a different sense) *contingency*. The less likely a reinforcer given a response, the weaker its probability-enhancing effect (probability). The longer the time delay between the behavior and the occurrence of the reinforcer, the weaker the effect of the reinforcer (delay). And the more likely a reinforcer is to occur in the absence of the response, the less the effect of those reinforcers that are response-produced (contingency, in the Skinnerian sense) will be.

The key point is that the effect of a reinforcer is closely related to what might be termed the *predictiveness* of the response: To the extent that a response is a reliable predictor of a reinforcer, the response will tend to increase in frequency. What is not obvious is that the predictiveness of a response depends on the degree of behavioral variation. Suppose the pigeon in the superstition experiment (discussed later) happens to turn his head at the instant food is delivered. The only way the pigeon-as-experimenter can test the predictiveness of head-turning for food is to try it at arbitrary, preferably random times and try other activities as well. He has to do the relevant experiments. Otherwise, all he has are correlations, not causes. In practice, animals and people do test hypotheses, and that's how reinforcement actually works most of the time. Reinforcers act in much more complex ways than simple, automatic response strengthening.

The importance of predictiveness in Pavlovian conditioning was also beginning to be understood in the 1960s. Pavlovian conditioning, like operant conditioning, is facilitated by short delays between conditioned and unconditioned stimuli (CS and US), by high probability of CS-US pairing, and by absence of USs unpaired with the CS.[17] (The unconditioned stimulus [US] is just a reinforcer in another guise.) Thus, it was natural for Skinner to combine the two types of relation, Pavlovian (stimulus-reinforcer) and operant (response-reinforcer) into what he called a *three-term contingency* involving stimulus (now termed a *discriminative stimulus*), response and reinforcer.

True to his principles, Skinner never formalized this idea. But it implies an organization of behavior into a collection of more or less independent units, by now termed *operants,* each defined by *classes* of responses and stimuli that jointly predict the occurrence of the relevant reinforcer. Skinner changed the definition of the *response* away from either a physical movement or set of physical movements—or some kind of cognitively defined *act*—to that *class* of physical movements that are effective in producing a given reinforcer. The discriminative stimulus was by implication defined in a similar way.[18]

From an experimental point of view, this framework was very fruitful. For example, beginning with a seminal study by George Reynolds, a succession of experiments began to look at interactions between operants (i.e., at violations of the independence assumption).[19]

The concept of stimulus control was experimentally refined through various techniques for measuring stimulus *generalization*. The concept was due to

Pavlov, but he never measured generalization gradients experimentally. Skinner's discovery of reinforcement schedules was helpful here because an intermittent schedule allows for many unreinforced responses before the animal quits. A famous experiment by Guttman and Kalish exploited this property of intermittent schedules to measure generalization directly.[20]

Pigeons were trained to peck, on a variable-interval schedule of food reinforcement, a key transilluminated by monochromatic light (at a wavelength of 550 nm, spectral green). Then, food delivery was discontinued and the wavelength was changed randomly every minute. The pigeons nevertheless continued to peck for an hour or more because of the persistence built in by their training on an intermittent schedule. But the *rate* at which they pecked depended on the wavelength: the farther from 550 nm, the lower the rate. A plot of average rate against wavelength took a peaked form (with the maximum at 550 nm, the training value) that was to become familiar in subsequent years as numerous experiments were carried out with other species and stimulus dimensions (Figure 5.1). A key finding was that generalization was almost unrelated to discriminability: The generalization gradient measures *similarity,* a basically cognitive idea, not how easy it is to tell one wavelength from another.

Once again, Skinnerian methods had allowed a hypothetical process—Pavlov's notion of stimulus generalization—to be made visible. Thereafter, Skinner was frequently to evoke "generalization" as an explanation for

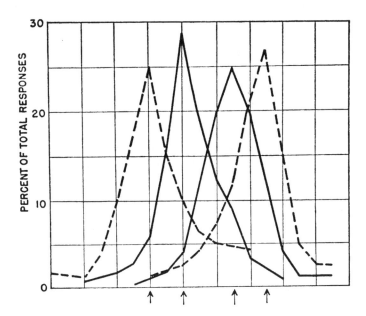

Figure 5.1 Generalization gradients of wavelength obtained from pigeons trained with four different S+ wavelengths (arrows).

From N. Guttman & H. I. Kalish. (1956). Discriminability and stimulus generalization. *Journal of Experimental Psychology, 51,* 79–88.

complex aspects of human behavior, even in situations far removed from the discrimination of wavelength.

The notion of reinforcement was also expanded, using chain schedules as a model. In a two-link chain schedule, the pigeon pecks a RED key (for example) for the reinforcement offered by a change to GREEN, in the presence of which pecks lead to food. The GREEN key was said to be a *conditioned* (or second-ary) reinforcer.[21] Although each link in the chain appears to act as a reinforcer for responding that produces it, the whole thing soon collapses if the final food reinforcement is omitted. When there is no food, pigeons soon cease to peck for conditioned reinforcement alone. A stimulus paired with many different reinforcers (food, water, sex) was said to be a *generalized* reinforcer—money was used as a human example. But there are no good examples of generalized reinforcers in the animal-research literature.

The Darwinian Metaphor

Beginning in the mid-1960s, Skinner modified his approach to learned behav-ior. In a 1966 paper titled "The Phylogeny and Ontogeny of Behavior," he turned to a view of reinforcement quite different from the "strengthening" metaphor he had adopted earlier.[22] Instead of strengthening, reinforcement was now said to "select" behavior, much as natural selection acts to favor certain individuals for survival and reproduction. And just as adaptation in nature can be traced to selection, so adaptation to contingencies of reinforcement was said to reflect the selective action of reinforcement. The idea that learned, operant behavior evolves through a process of variation and selection by consequences is at the core of the new behaviorism.

The basic idea of evolution by natural selection is that some process cre-ates a set of variants, individual organisms that differ in various ways. Some of these variants are more successful than others in giving rise to progeny. The faster horse, the taller giraffe, the cleverer chimpanzee have (for one reason or another) more offspring than their slower, shorter or dumber brethren. Now, if (and this is a big *if*) these critical differences are *heritable* (that is, if they are passed on without undue dilution), then the next generation will be that much faster, taller, smarter than the one that went before. Darwin's insight was to see that across the reaches of geological time, these small generational changes might accumulate not just to change one species but, eventually, to differenti-ate one from another, to create new species.

There are several aspects of this story that make it compelling. We can see the actual reproducing units, *phenotypes.* We know more and more about the heritable characteristics, the *genotypes,* that are associated with different phe-notypes and about the processes of *development* that translate a fixed geno-type into a range of possible phenotypes. And we can see in the way that each organism interacts with its environment, in its ecological *niche,* just why it is that faster horses do better than slower (they are less subject to predation), why taller giraffes do better than shorter (they get more food), and why smarter chimps do better than dumber (they are able to copulate with more females). We can see, in short, what *selective factors* are at work.[23]

Skinner's identification of reinforcement ("reward" in an older language) as an agent of behavioral selection was not a new idea. The Scotsman Alexander Bain (1818–1903) made a proposal very like the law of effect almost fifty years before Thorndike, and then suggested a process for generating variants that is close to Darwinian variation and selection, even though *The Origin of Species* was four years in the future:

> When there is not a sufficiency of forms within reach of the present recol-
> lection, the process of intellectual recovery must be plied to bring up others,
> until the desired combination is attained. . . . In all difficult operations, for
> purposes or ends, the rule of trial and error is the grand and final resort.[24]

The psychologist James Baldwin discussed the relations between ontogenetic selection and phylogenetic selection early in the twentieth century (the "Baldwin Effect"); Clark Hull at least mentioned the resemblances before World War II; and W. R. Ashby, D. T. Campbell and philosopher Karl Popper had elaborated on the idea in different ways in the postwar years.[25] Quite possibly, Darwin somewhere in his many works speculates along similar lines.

These parallels with evolution by natural selection are all incomplete. What is the behavioral analogue to the genotype, for example? To phenotype—how are we to compare a set of activities extending over time, a *repertoire,* to the concrete, more or less fixed phenotypes that are the units of natural selection? And what about selection? What, in the selection of behavior, corresponds to differential reproduction? What, in the selection of behavior, corresponds to selective factors in a niche? The parallel between learning and evolution *is* a metaphor. But it is an indispensable metaphor.

The Darwinian metaphor has been applied to reinforcement learning in several ways: (1) As a formal model for behavior—what I've been calling a "mechanism": "The work . . . develops a theory of the 'natural selection' of behaviour-patterns," wrote W. Ross Ashby in a brilliant anticipation of later developments in artificial intelligence.[26] J. J. McDowell has explored a gene-like selectionist learning model and shown that it can duplicate many of the standard results from animal-laboratory operant-conditioning experiments.[27] (2) As a model for the real nervous system.[28] And (3) as a way of thinking about the relation between behavioral *variation*—the processes that generate behavior in advance of reinforcement—and *selection*—the processes that favor some variants over others.[29] The idea here is that some (largely unknown) process generates an initial *repertoire* of behavior. Reinforcement then acts, largely through temporal contiguity, to select a smaller repertoire of actions, which evolve into what Skinner termed *operants,* functional units owing their existence to the history of selection by reinforcement.

Skinner's approach in his 1966 and later papers is closest to category 3. But, perhaps reflecting the centrality of the reinforcement concept to his thinking, he essentially ignored behavioral variation, placing all emphasis on the selective effects of reinforcement. Variation was deemed to be "sufficient," as I pointed out earlier. Surprisingly, perhaps, Skinner made no use of the Darwinian metaphor as an explanation for the reinforcement-schedule effects I discuss in the next chapter. He mostly cited evolution as a rather "pat" account for reinforcement itself. Food reinforcers (for example) exist, said Skinner because animals reinforced by appropriate food are favored in phylogeny (i.e., in the evolution of the species). Thus, "what is reinforcing" is determined by what Skinner termed "phylogenic" contingencies (once again, Skinner insisted on his own word: *phylogenetic* would be the usual term). "What is done" (i.e., operant behavior) is then determined by "ontogenic" (*ontogenetic*) contingencies— contingencies of reinforcement.

The account led to the usual ingenious extrapolations. Thus, obesity in the modern world is explicable, said Skinner, by the fact that high-calorie substances containing sugar taste sweet and are much preferred over low-calorie foods. In our "selection environment" in the remote past, these beneficial substances (as well as fats and proteins) were rare. Thus, individuals who were strongly reinforced by sweetness, and hence motivated to seek out sweet things, were favored in the race to reproduce. But because sugar was rare, there was no negative selection for overindulgence. (This is a variant of the supernormal-stimulus argument, discussed further on.) Today, in the developed world, sweet things are widely available, are eaten to excess by many people and cause unhealthy obesity. We are victims, says Skinner, of changes in our environment—changes too rapid for natural, phylogenetic, selection to keep up with. This is as plausible as most evolutionary "Just-So" stories,[30] but it added nothing to what was already known, and is little help in understanding the details of learning in animals.

Some efforts were made by other behaviorists to apply the evolutionary metaphor to the specifics of learning. One of the earliest was a lengthy discussion of the relations between selection and behavioral variation by Virginia Simmelhag and myself. The key point in our account is that processes of behavioral *variation* are just as important as processes of *selection*. Variation and selection were of equal importance to Darwin and his successors; they must be of equal importance in the application of the Darwinian idea to operant behavior. Variation, the process that generates behavior in advance of operant reinforcement, is often much more important than selection. In teaching difficult concepts (in mathematics, for example), the hard task for the teacher is to get the child to "understand" the concept at all, not to "increase the frequency" of some simple, repetitive behavior. It is getting the "behavior" for the very first time that is critical, not its subsequent maintenance. This problem cannot even be attacked, much less solved, without some grasp of mechanisms of variation. Much more on variation in later chapters.

Skinner made no attempt to specify the mechanisms of variation. Indeed, in his famous simile, "Operant conditioning shapes behavior as a sculptor shapes a lump of clay,"[31] he implies, as we put it, that "moment-to-moment variation is small in magnitude, and essentially random . . . in direction."[32] Like Darwin, Skinner was a gradualist. But unlike Darwin, who was well aware of the existence of large and often directional phenotypic changes from generation to generation ("sports"), Skinner never seriously considered the possibility that variation might be structured or constrained. But in fact, if operant conditioning is a sculptor, she is a sculptor in wood, with its grain and knots, rather than a sculptor in isotropic clay.

Notes

1. As described by eminent moral philosopher Alasdair MacIntyre (1984) in *After virtue: A study in moral theory* (Notre Dame, IN: University of Notre Dame Press).
2. Contemporary views of Skinner and Skinnerianism by several authors have been collected in Reflections on B. F. Skinner and psychology. (1992). *American Psychologist, 47*. See also Richelle, M. N. (1993). *B. F. Skinner: A reappraisal* (Hove, UK: Erlbaum).
3. This is a famous recommendation of English biologist and Darwin fan Thomas Henry Huxley (1825–1895).
4. Skinner, B. F. (1950). *Science and human behavior* (New York: Macmillan), p. 193.
5. Skinner never changed his view on this. Three years before his death he wrote: Whatever happened to psychology as the science of behavior? *American Psychologist* (1987), 780–786.
6. Skinner, B. F. (1944). Review of Hull's principles of behavior. *American Journal of Psychology, 57*, 276–281.
7. Skinner, B. F. (1950) Are theories of learning necessary. *Psychological Review, 57*, 193–216, p. 216.
8. A. Machado, personal communication.
9. Chomsky, N. (1959). A review of B. F. Skinner's *Verbal Behavior. Language, 35*, 26–58. Chomsky apparently wrote the review before *Verbal Behavior* was published. One hopes he actually read the book. But the review is indeed more an attack on radical behaviorism in general than a critique of the specifics of *Verbal Behavior*. Chomsky followed it up a decade later with a full-throated attack on Skinner and all his works: The Case Against B. F. Skinner. *The New York Review of Books* (December 30, 1971). See also Virués-Ortega, J. (2006). The case against B. F. Skinner 45 years later: An encounter with N. Chomsky. *The Behavior Analyst, 29*, 243–251.
10. MacCorquodale, K. (1970). On Chomsky's review of Skinner's *Verbal Behavior*. *Journal of the Experimental Analysis of Behavior, 13*, 83–99.
11. Andresen, J. (1991). Skinner and Chomsky 30 years later or: The return of the repressed. *The Behavior Analyst, 14*, 49–60.
12. See Skinner, B. F. (1961). The design of cultures. *Daedalus, 90*, 534–546. Reprinted in *Cumulative Record* (1961).
13. Skinner, B. F. (1958). *Verbal behavior* (New York: Appleton-Century-Crofts).
14. Smith, L. D. (1986). *Behaviorism and logical positivism* (Stanford, CA: Stanford University Press), p. 272.
15. See *Behavior of Organisms* (1938) and Skinner, B. F. (1940). The nature of the operant reserve. *Psychological Bulletin, 37*, 423 (abstract). A critique is Ellson, D. G. (1939, November). The concept of reflex reserve. *Psychological Review, 46*(6), 566–575, and a modern discussion is Killeen, P. (1988). The reflex reserve. *Journal of the Experimental Analysis of Behavior, 50*, 319–331. More than six decades after Skinner's original paper, A. C. Catania made a formal model showing that Skinner's idea can duplicate a number of schedule properties (Catania,

A. C. [2005]. The operant reserve: A computer simulation in [accelerated] real time. *Behavioural Processes, 69*, 257–278).

16. Skinner, B. F. (1953). *Science and human behavior* (New York: Macmillan), p. 64.

17. Rescorla, R. A. (1967). Pavlovian conditioning and its proper control procedures. *Psychological Review, 74*, 71–80.

18. Staddon, J. E. R. (1967). Asymptotic behavior: The concept of the operant. *Psychological Review, 74*, 377–391.

19. Reynolds, G. S. (1961). Behavioral contrast. *Journal of the Experimental Analysis of Behavior, 4*, 57–71.

20. Guttman, N., & Kalish, H. I. (1956). Discriminability and stimulus generalization. *Journal of Experimental Psychology, 51*, 79–88.

21. See Staddon, J. E. R., & Cerutti, D. T. (2003). Operant conditioning. *Annual Review of Psychology, 54*, 115–144, for an extended discussion of chain FI schedules.

22. Skinner, B. F. (1966). The phylogeny and ontogeny of behavior. *Science, 153*, 1205–1213; Skinner, B. F. (1981). Selection by consequences. *Science, 213*, 501–504.

23. There are many splendid books on evolution by natural selection, beginning with the first and still the best, *The Origin of Species*. More recent expositions are, for example, Ghiselin, M. T. (1969/2003). *The triumph of the Darwinian method* (Mineola, NY: Dover); Dennett, D. C. (1995). *Darwin's dangerous idea: Evolution and the meanings of life* (New York: Simon & Schuster); and Coyne, J., & Orr, H. A. (2004). *Speciation* (Sunderland. MA: Sinauer).

24. Bain, A. (1855). *The senses and the intellect* (London: John W. Parker and Son), p. 575.

25. Amsel, A., & Rashotte, M. E. (Eds.). (1984). *Mechanisms of adaptive behavior: Clark L. Hull's theoretical papers, with commentary* (New York: Columbia Press); Bain, J. M. (1902). *Development and evolution* (New York: Macmillan); Campbell, D. T. (1956). Adaptive behavior from random response. *Behavioral Science, 1*, 105–110; Popper, K. R. (1972). *Objective knowledge: An evolutionary approach* (Oxford: Clarendon Press).

26. Ashby, W. R. (1952). *Design for a brain* (London: Chapman & Hall), p. vi; Baldwin, J. M. (1911). *Mental development in the child and the race* (3rd ed.) (New York: Macmillan).

27. McDowell, J. J. (2004). A computational model of selection by consequences. *Journal of the Experimental Analysis of Behavior, 81*, 297–317; McDowell, J. J. (2010). Behavioral and neural Darwinism: Selectionist function and mechanism in adaptive behavior dynamics. *Behavioural Processes, 84*, 358–365.

28. Edelman, G. M. (1987). *Neural Darwinism* (New York: Basic Books); see also Pringle, J. W. S. (1951). On the parallel between learning and evolution. *Behaviour, 3*, 174–215; see also Palmer, D. C., & Donahoe, J. W. (1992). Essentialism and selectionism in cognitive science and behavior analysis. *American Psychologist, 47*, 1344–1358, and Donahoe, J. W. (1997). The necessity of neural networks. In J. W. Donahoe & V. P. Packard (Eds.), *Neural-network models of cognition* (New York: Elsevier).

29. Staddon, J. E. R., & Simmelhag, V. (1971). The "superstition" experiment: A reexamination of its implications for the principles of adaptive behavior. *Psychological Review, 78*, 3–43.

30. The allusion to Rudyard Kipling's justly famous stories for children is from biologist Stephen Jay Gould, who used the phrase "Just-So" pejoratively in his many critiques of adaptationist arguments.

31. Skinner (1953), p. 91.

32. Staddon & Simmelhag (1971), p. 31.

6 Variation and Selection

Biomedical researchers are interested in animals mainly as compliant experimental material, as *animal models*, worth study only as aids to better medicine. The squid attracts experimental attention because its nerve cells are larger and more accessible than human neurons and seem to function in much the same way. Rat kidney, baboon liver and sea-slug (*Aplysia*) nervous systems are all studied for similar reasons.

Although B. F. Skinner was not a biomedical scientist, his interest in rats and pigeons was of the animal-model variety. He was not much affected by the pioneering work of zoologists W. H. Thorpe, Konrad Lorenz, Niko Tinbergen, Karl von Frisch and their students on species differences and the instinctive behavior of animals. The rich findings of *ethology,* as the zoological approach to animal behavior came to be called in the 1950s, were of little interest to Skinner, or, indeed, to most of psychology. He was not interested in studying animals in their own right. In the empiricist/behaviorist tradition, Skinner paid scant attention to the genetic and evolutionary factors that differentiate one animal species from another. His main interest in individual differences was to discover procedures to minimize them.

Despite the biological differences between pigeons and people, and between pigeons in Skinner box and pigeons in real life, the animal-model idea worked well for Skinner. He was as uninterested in detailed correspondences as his popular audience was unaware of experimental minutiae. Next I describe one of Skinner's most compelling extrapolations from the experimental laboratory to human affairs, the so-called superstition experiment. I believe that the failure of this attempt shows the dangers of extrapolating without an adequate theory. This experiment also pointed the way to a new behaviorism.

The Superstition Experiment

In his middle and later years, Skinner himself did surprisingly little experimental work to test or even to exploit his ideas. He would hang out with the Harvard group in the basement of Memorial Hall at the weekly "pigeon lab" meetings in the early 1960s, but the experiments discussed there were not his. His students and disciples at Harvard, Columbia, Walter Reed Medical Center and a few other places did many experiments using the operant-conditioning method and explored the world of reinforcement schedules. Almost none of these experiments were a direct test of Skinner's theoretical position, however. Skinner's proscription of the hypothetico-deductive approach—"As to hypotheses, [my] system does not require them"[1]—seemed to make hypothesis testing unnecessary.

Increasingly, Skinner's own gaze was directed elsewhere, to human behavior, which was always his chief interest. He used experimental results from the animal laboratory largely to provide scientific support for his analysis of human problems. Skinner's classic 1948 paper "'Superstition' in the Pigeon" is one of the earliest and most dramatic examples of this strategy.[2]

The experiment was incredibly simple. Skinner took a hungry pigeon that had learned to eat from an automatic feeder (Plate 6.1) but that had received no other training. The pigeon was placed in a Skinner box and given brief access to food every 12 s. This is *response-independent* reinforcement. The procedure is in fact classical or Pavlovian conditioning, not operant conditioning (*temporal conditioning*—see Figure 2.1). After a few dozen feedings, every pigeon Skinner tried began to show vigorous, stereotyped activity. This

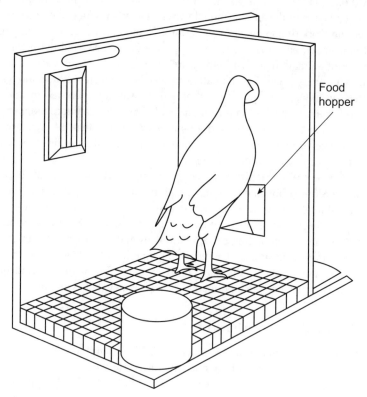

Food
hopper

Plate 6.1 A typical Skinner box for pigeons. Food—the reinforcer—is delivered via a hopper that is raised for a few seconds. The pecking key was disconnected in the "superstition" experiment.

result is surprising because the bird had no control over food delivery: All it was required to do was wait, and eat when food became available every few seconds. The pigeon's vigorous activity was completely unnecessary. No contingency, hence no reinforcement. So how come all this vigorous activity?

We'll see how Skinner turned this unanticipated and potentially damaging result to his own advantage. The "superstition" paper shows Skinner's flexibility as an experimenter. It also shows his rhetorical genius. And it shows how he could vault effortlessly from an animal-laboratory curiosity to the most rarified aspects of human culture.

The superstition experiment is almost unique in Skinner's *oeuvre* because it presents observational, rather than automatically gathered, data. Nearly all subsequent experimental papers by Skinner and other operant conditioners eschewed all but counter readings and cumulative records. Observational data were generally regarded as unacceptable. Yet the master, more adaptable than his followers, presented simple, anecdotal observations without apology. To study a classical conditioning procedure, using such an informal method to gather data, was a creative departure for someone whose whole career until that time had been devoted to automated instrumental learning experiments.

Skinner's rhetoric was brilliant because the results of the experiment—vigorous activity, despite the absence of any operant response requirement—would by most observers surely have been interpreted as contrary to his ideas about the indispensability of "consequences" as a molder of behavior. The pigeon's behavior had *no* consequences. So why did it occur? The "conditioning" of vigorous skeletal activities by response-independent food delivery might well have been taken then as strong evidence *against* Skinner's view that *contingency* (his term for *dependency* or *causal linkage*) between response and reinforcer is essential to operant conditioning. The obvious interpretation is one that draws on the principles not of operant but of *Pavlovian* conditioning. In fact, as we'll see, the behavior in the superstition experiment manifests the properties of variation rather than selection.

Skinner solved the contradiction in the first paragraph of the paper, by predicting (yes, *predicting*) the outcome of the experiment as a deduction from operant reinforcement theory (yes, *theory*). Presenting new data, whether anticipated or not, as a logical deduction from existing theory had long been standard in many areas of experimental science. But Skinner's choice of this method of presentation is surprising because he elsewhere argued repeatedly against the hypothetico-deductive approach ("As to hypotheses, [my] system does not require them") and, as far as I know, followed it in no other paper. Skinner usually advocated *induction*, not deduction. Consequently, it is hard to believe that his use of the method here was for anything but purposes of persuasion—a rhetorical device rather than an accurate account of why he actually did the experiment.

Skinner begins the paper as follows:

> To say that a reinforcement is contingent upon a response may mean nothing more than that it follows the response. It may follow because of

some mechanical connection [contingency] or because of the mediation of another organism; *but conditioning takes place presumably because of the temporal relation only,* expressed in terms of the order and proximity of response and reinforcement. Whenever we present a state of affairs which is known to be reinforcing at a given level of [food] deprivation, we must suppose that conditioning takes place even though we have paid no attention to the behavior of the organism in making the presentation. *A simple experiment demonstrates this to be the case.* (italics added)

This is a remarkable paragraph. The terms "may" and "must suppose" tend to expel from the reader's mind all sorts of inconvenient counterexamples. In hindsight, these questions pop into the foreground: To say that a reinforcement is contingent on a response does *not* mean only that it follows the response (*contiguity*). It also means at least two other things: that reinforcement cannot occur (or occurs less often) in the absence of the response and that reinforcement occurs more often if the response occurs more often. Skinner's rhetoric had the effect of focusing readers' attention on contiguity to the exclusion of the other properties of a reinforcement contingency. Persuading a behaviorist audience in this way was no mean feat because in all practical matters, causal *dependency* (the response is necessary for the reinforcer)—which implies all three properties—is the prevailing view. In clinical behavior modification, for example, an undesirable behavior is abolished by omitting reinforcers normally dependent on it, or by delivering punishment for undesirable behavior (self-injurious behavior, for example). Desirable behavior is strengthened by making reward dependent on it. In each case, there must be a real causal dependence of reinforcer or punisher on the target behavior.

Response contingency in Skinner's usual sense (i.e., dependency) is a procedural feature, not a behavioral process—contingencies must act through some proximal mechanism. Skinner's argument for the superstition paper relied on the fact that the mechanism for reinforcement was then widely thought to be nothing more than closeness in time: response-reinforcer *contiguity*. Contiguity was also thought to be the key to learning CS-US relations in classical conditioning. At this time, the inadequacy of simple contiguity theory as an account of either classical or operant conditioning was not fully understood.

Skinner explained the vigorous, stereotyped behavior of his pigeons in between periodic food deliveries by means of what he called *adventitious reinforcement*—that is, accidental contiguity between food and a behavior that originally occurs for "other reasons." His argument begins with the reasonable assumption that a hungry pigeon is not passive in a situation where it receives occasional food. Suppose it happens to be doing something toward the end of an interfood interval and food is delivered. The behavior will be contiguous with the food and so, by the reinforcement principle, will be more likely to occur again. If the next food delivery comes quite soon, this same behavior might still be occurring, and so receive another accidental pairing with food, be further strengthened, occur again in the next interval and so on. By means of this positive-feedback process, some behavior might be raised to a very high probability. Since there is no real causal relation between behavior and reinforcer, Skinner called the behavior *superstitious*—implying a parallel with human superstitions, which he believed to arise in a similar way.

This plausible account was not based on direct observation of the process. No one had actually recorded these accidental response-reinforcer contiguities or the progressive increase in response strength that was supposed to follow them. Indeed, the contiguity view, in this impressionistic form, is almost immune to disproof.

Contiguity learning was in fact generally accepted as an explanation for the effects of contingency itself. The idea had been used to explain the effect of "free" (response-independent) reinforcers on a schedule of contingent reinforcement. Even in 1948 there was some understanding that free reinforcers on a response-contingent schedule might tend to weaken the reinforced response.[3] This weakening was explained, in effect, by adventitious reinforcement. If, for some unexamined reason, a behavior other than the instrumental response should happen to occur, then by chance it would sometimes be contiguous with the occasional free reinforcers. This would tend to strengthen it and thus, by competition, weaken the reinforced response.

Few observations had been done to back up this hypothesis: Did such competing behaviors actually occur? How often were they contiguous with free food? What is the form of competition between different acts? Did the frequency of the instrumental response change before or after such accidental pairings? Skinner also offered no quantitative details: How many accidental pairings are needed to produce how much increment in strength? How often should unreinforced "other" behaviors be expected to occur? Nevertheless, the adventitious reinforcement hypothesis view was plausible enough to be accepted for more than twenty years.

The simple contiguity account of operant reinforcement poses a real methodological problem. It is a hypothesis where the putative cause is not a stimulus but a *relation* between the response (which is controlled by the animal, not the experimenter) and a reinforcing consequence. Inability to control the occurrence of the response makes it impossible to be sure of the effect of any particular pairing between response and reinforcer. For example, suppose the response occurs and we at once deliver a reinforcer, thus ensuring response-reinforcer contiguity. Suppose that a few additional responses then occur; have we demonstrated a strengthening effect of contiguity? Not at all; perhaps this response just happens to occur in runs, so that one response is usually followed by others, quite apart from any reinforcing effect. This is not uncommon—a pigeon will rarely make just one peck, for example. Suppose we reinforce a second response, just to be sure. After a few repeats, no doubt the pigeon is pecking away at a good rate; have we then demonstrated an effect of contiguity? Again, not really. By repeating the pairings of response and reinforcer, we have now established a real *dependency* between response and reinforcer. Perhaps the increase in pecking is just the result of some other process that allows the pigeon to detect such *molar contingencies* (covariation between two rate measures), as they are called.

In fact, there is little doubt that animals often learn to repeat a response after just one response-reinforcer pairing—just like the law-of-effect (LOE) model I discussed in Chapter 4. The question is whether persistent behavior that is in fact unnecessary for the delivery of the reinforcer—superstitious behavior—is the automatic consequence of a simple contiguity process. The first does not imply the second. The point, of course, is that in the absence of any proposal for a specific real-time mechanism for the action of reinforcement, the hypothesis of adventitious reinforcement is almost impossible to disprove. Unless behavior in the absence of reinforcement is highly predictable, unless a single reinforcement reliably produces an immediate enhancing effect, preferably on more than one response type, the meaning of those occasional instances where responding seems to increase rapidly following a single contiguous reinforcer is ambiguous. A few apparently confirming observations have appeared.[4] But there have been no convincing experimental proofs of the adventitious-reinforcement hypothesis as a process with anything like the generality often assumed for it.

The very obscurity of these theoretical points, along with the simplicity of his experimental method, combined to add plausibility to Skinner's simple account of the vigorous behavior induced in pigeons (not all species show such effects) by periodic free food delivery. But I believe the main reason for the success of this paper, and of Skinner's other writings, lies elsewhere: in his easy extension of dry data from the animal operant laboratory to highly salient aspects of human culture—like *superstition*. The leap here is substantial, from pigeons posturing in a box to rituals in card games and body language by bowlers and, in Skinner's later writings, to religious beliefs. It rests not so much on any convincing isomorphism between the pigeon in the box and the human situation—where is temporal contiguity and frequent reinforcement in a card game, for example?—as on the reader's empathy with the pigeon. "The bird behaves as if there were a causal relation," writes Skinner,[5] and the reader nods assent to an argument that has more in common with cognitive than behavioristic psychology.

Many possibilities are suggested by the two words "as if"! Is *reinforcement* the source of all knowledge? Is human knowledge as much an illusion as the pigeon's mistaken causal inference in the superstition experiment? Deists behave "as if" there were a God, scientists "as if" truth exists, and all of us "as if" the floor will not open up under our feet. Are all these "superstitions"? Are all to be explained by reinforcement? Skinner would probably have answered, "Yes. . . ."

Experimental Problems with Skinner's Account

Skinner's account of laboratory "superstition" stood unchallenged for twenty years. The first cracks appeared in 1968 with the publication of a paper by Brown and Jenkins on what they called *autoshaping*. A subsequent paper by Williams and Williams using the same procedure established that operant key pecking could be produced and maintained by purely Pavlovian procedures.[6] In these experiments, pigeons untrained to peck a response key are simply allowed to experience occasional pairing of a 7-s key illumination with access to food (Pavlovian delay conditioning—see Figure 2.1). The procedure reliably produces key pecking after a couple of dozen pairings—even if key pecks have no effect at all. Indeed, the pigeon will continue to peck even if pecks actually prevent food delivery, a procedure termed *omission training.*

Brown and Jenkins's result was surprising not because they got conditioning, but because of the kind of response that was conditioned. Not the usual *respondent,* like salivation in Pavlov's dogs, but the prototypical *operant* response, key pecking. This was important partly because Skinner had proposed a distinction between operant and respondent behavior—the former "controlled" by its consequences, the latter by Pavlovian pairing (see Chapter 2). But if skeletal, "operant" responses can be produced through classical conditioning procedures—as autoshaping and the superstition experiment both show—then Skinner's distinction between operant behavior (conditionable only by consequential reinforcement) and respondent behavior (conditionable only by Pavlovian means) loses its generality. Salivation, the prototypical Pavlovian response, is of course physiologically different from pecking and lever pressing (the prototypical operant responses). Salivation, a respondent, is controlled by the autonomic nervous system; lever pressing, an operant response, by the skeletal nervous system. The point is that the terms "operant" and "respondent" add nothing to these physiological differences if the terms fail to correspond to sharp differences in susceptibility to operant and Pavlovian conditioning. Pecking, and a number of other activities in other species, has both operant and respondent properties. Hence, the operant-respondent distinction becomes less useful.

A couple of years before Brown and Jenkins published their arresting results, Virginia Simmelhag and I had repeated Skinner's 1948 experiment and observed the pigeons' behavior from the very beginning of training. We looked second by second at the brief interval between feedings. A few years later we published the results in a long theoretical paper.[7] Our interest was purely exploratory; we had no hypothesis. The experiment was inductive, not hypothetico-deductive. Skinner would have approved! We wondered about two things: Would you get "superstitious" behavior even if the schedule were variable, as opposed to fixed time? (Answer: yes.) And what are the details— what is the bird doing second by second in each interfood interval?

The answer to the second question is very interesting. We found three things that differ from Skinner's account:

1. The activities that develop are of two kinds: *interim activities,* which occur in the first two-thirds or so of the interfood interval, are rarely contiguous with food and vary from subject to subject, and a single *terminal*

response, which occurs during the last third of the fixed interval. The terminal response is restricted to times of high food probability and interim activities to times of low probability.

2. The terminal response is either pecking or a stereotyped pacing activity obviously related to it. The topography (form) of the terminal response does not differ from animal to animal in the irregular way Skinner described.

3. Neither the interim activities nor the terminal response develops in the accidental way implied by the adventitious-reinforcement hypothesis (Figure 6.1). Pecking is never contiguous with food in the first few days of the procedure. It suddenly supplants the behavior that *had been* contiguous—"head in feeder"—after a few days. In other words, there is no way that the pecking that comes to predominate can be explained by adventitious reinforcement. Indeed, it behaves just like a classically conditioned response, not the standard operant response it was thought to be. The interim activities, on the other hand, occur at times of low reinforcement probability. They are almost never contiguous with food, hence they also cannot be explained by adventitious reinforcement.

These findings have been repeated many times by others, and the details are now quite familiar. In the meantime a number of other superstition-like effects had been reported.

The most dramatic is something called *instinctive drift.* Keller Breland and his wife, Marion, were students of Skinner who learned their trade training pigeons to guide missiles on "Project Pelican" during World War II and later went into the business of training animals for commercial purposes such as advertising.[8] They found, and reported in 1960, many years before the autoshaping experiment, that animal behavior is not so malleable— "reinforcement shapes behavior as a sculptor shapes a lump of clay"—as Skinner had proposed.[9] They discovered that even though an animal may be trained to get food by making Response A, it will under some conditions after a while switch to (ineffective) Response B—even though it thereby misses food deliveries. Their work was essentially ignored until autoshaping and reanalysis of the superstition experiment allowed operant conditioning to be looked at in a new way—a way that had a place for instinctive drift.

In one demonstration, the Brelands trained a raccoon to pick up a wooden egg and drop it down a chute. At first the animal readily released the egg and went at once to the feeder for its bite of food. But after a while the animal was reluctant to let go of the egg: "He kept it in his hand, pulled it back out, looked at it, fondled it, put it back in the chute, pulled it back out again, and so on; this went on for several seconds."[10] And of course during this time, the animal got no food. The Brelands called effects like this *instinctive drift.* Animals of other species—otters, pigs and squirrel monkeys—are equally reluctant to let go of an object that has become a reliable predictor of food. In another experiment, a chicken had been trained to make a chain of responses, leading at last

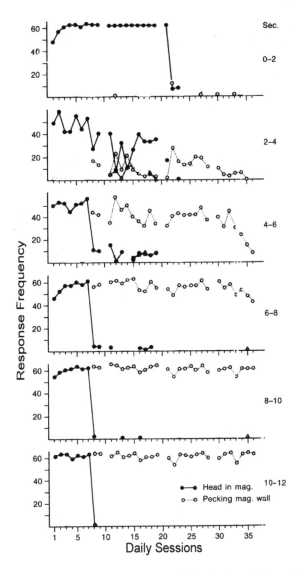

Figure 6.1 The development of "superstitious" pecking. Each panel shows the frequency
each day of two of the induced activities: *head-in-feeder* (filled circles, solid
lines) and *pecking* (open circles, dotted lines). The panels show the levels
of these two activities in the six 2-s bins that make up the 12-s interfood
interval. Notice that for the first seven days, *head-in-feeder* predominates
throughout the interfood interval, including the last 2 s—and is therefore
reliably contiguous with the food in every interval. Nevertheless, on the
eighth day, *head-in-feeder* drops to zero in the last bin and is supplanted by
pecking, which dominates from 6 to 12 s every day thereafter.

Redrawn from J. E. R. Staddon and V. L. Simmelhag. (1971). The "superstition" experiment: A
reexamination of its implications for the principles of adaptive behavior. *Psychological Review,
78*, 3–43, Figure 3, with permission.

to standing on a platform for 15 s, when food was delivered. After training, the chicken showed vigorous ground scratching (an apparently innate food-seeking activity) while waiting on the platform. The scratching was of course completely unnecessary for food delivery.

The type of instinctive drift depends on all aspects of the situation. In still another experiment, the Brelands trained a chicken to operate a firing mechanism that projected a ball at a target; a hit produced food. All went well at first, but when the animal had learned that food followed ball, it could not refrain from pecking directly at the ball. Thus, when a chicken must stand and wait for food, it ground scratches, but when it has a food-like object that signals food, it pecks at it. Information from several sources combines to determine the "instinctive" response. All these animals in some sense clearly "know" how to get food. Hence, instinctive drift poses real problems for cognitive and economic learning theories as well as for Skinner's account.

Assignment of Credit

The empirical realities of superstitious behavior are not as tidy as Skinner suggested. We also now understand better the gaps in his theoretical account. His theory is deficient in two main respects: First, he minimized the importance of the processes that originate novel (i.e., previously unreinforced) behavior— the processes of behavioral *variation.* Will the chicken try pecking or ground scratching? It depends on the situation. Skinner's exclusive emphasis was on reinforcement, as the agent of response selection.

Second, he and most other behaviorists at the time, accepted contiguity as a sufficient process for response selection. But then Rescorla and Wagner, in a very influential paper (see Chapter 2), showed in 1972, for classical conditioning, that *competition* is an essential complement to contiguity. It is the competition for a finite quantity of "associative value" that allows the R-W model to assess predictability. In operant conditioning, both contiguity and competition are necessary for the detection of cause-effect relations.

The experiments and theoretical analysis of Rescorla, Wagner and others showed for the first time the limitations of the adventitious reinforcement idea. It can work, but only if the strengthening effect of reinforcement is almost unvarying from instance to instance, and if the time between reinforcers is very short. Neither condition holds in reality: Behavior following reinforcement is often highly variable, and superstitious behavior is abolished at very short inter-reinforcement intervals.

The question that underlies all this research is this: How do organisms detect causation? In other words, how do they discover which action is effective in securing a reward? If pigeons identify cause with contiguity—*post hoc, ergo propter hoc*—then it is no wonder that they sometimes show activity even when there is no causal link between reward and anything they do. Finding causes—*assignment of credit*—is a major adaptive problem for all organisms.[11] No solution to this problem is perfect, and all organisms will therefore "misbehave" under some conditions. Skinner's logic was correct. Hypothesis: contiguity is the mechanism of reinforcement (not that he used the word "mechanism"!). Deduction: contiguity will mislead the pigeon when reinforcement is response independent and frequent. Bingo! Superstitious behavior is explained.

But his hypothesis was wrong. Contiguity alone is not adequate to assign credit. Something more is going on. But just what is it? There is as yet no general answer. Let me walk you through two simple models to give an idea of the problems the animal must solve in operant conditioning.

The simple LOE model that I described in Chapter 4 gives us a hint about how assignment of credit—response selection—in operant conditioning may work. Assume that instead of just one response there are, say, three, identical responses x, y and z.[12] The probability of occurrence of each of them is determined by Equations 4.3 and 4.4, repeated here:

1. Response x in each time step occurs with a probability $p(x)$.
2. $p(x)$ does not change unless a response, x, occurs.
3. If x is reinforced, $p(x)$ increases according to Equation 4.3. If x is not reinforced, $p(x)$ decreases according to Equation 4.4.

REINFORCED: $$p(x) \rightarrow p(x) + k_R[(1 - p(x))] \qquad (4.3)$$

UNREINFORCED: $$p(x) \rightarrow k_U p(x) \qquad (4.4)$$

Now imagine what will happen if reward is delivered only for one of the three otherwise identical responses—pecks on one of three response keys, A, B and C, for example. If all responses begin with the same probability, each will be equally likely to occur in each time step. If A (response x) is the rewarded response, then when y or z occurs, their probabilities will decrease (Equation 4.4), but if x occurs, it will be reinforced and its probability will increase (Equation 4.3). Eventually, therefore, response x will predominate. Credit will have been assigned correctly.

What if reinforcement is intermittent so not every instance of A is rewarded? Well, x will not reach such a high level, but since it is reinforced more often that y or z, it will still predominate, albeit at a lower level than under continuous reinforcement.

What if free reinforcers are delivered from time to time in addition to the response-dependent reinforcement of x? We know this should reduce the probability of x, but the model cannot make a prediction because it has no way to deal with contiguity, how close a reward is to the occurrence of a given response. Equations 4.3 and 4.4 basically just assume perfect contiguity or no contiguity at all. For this reason, the model also cannot deal with delayed reinforcement.

There is a modification of the LOE model that can deal with the problem of delay and free (noncontingent) rewards. Response probabilities are replaced with response *strengths*: V_x for response x, and so on. The response that occurs is selected through competition; the highest V wins. The new model looks like this:[13]

1. *Competition* assumption: In each time step, the response with the highest V value occurs—"winner-take-all" response selection.
2. *Noise* assumption: V values are the sum of two values: a decay component and a random (noise) component (Equation 6.1): ε is random noise with mean 1. (This assumption ensures variability and replaces the LOE assumption that reinforcement acts directly on response probabilities.)
3. *Reinforcement* assumption: A reward increases *all* V values, in proportion, so that the response that is actually occurring, which, by assumption 1, has the highest V value, gets the largest increment in strength.

REINFORCED: $$V(x) \rightarrow a_x V(x) + b_{Rx} V(x) + (1 - a_x)\varepsilon, \qquad (6.1)$$

UNREINFORCED: $$V(x) \rightarrow a_x V(x) + (1 - a_x)\varepsilon, \qquad (6.2)$$

$$0 < a_x,\ b_x < 1.$$

In summary, some response is always occurring, reward increases all V values in proportion to their value, and in the absence of reward, response strengths decay (probabilistically) according to Equation 6.2 at a rate a_x. Reward increments the activity by the fraction b_x. Because of assumption 3, the reinforced response will always be selected, just as in the LOE model.

Delaying reinforcement after the response that produces it always reduces its effect. The LOE model had no way of handling delay, but this model (the S-Z model) does because during the delay, the target response is likely to lose strength (Equation 6.2), hence receive a smaller boost when the delayed reward does occur.

A response on which reward is not contingent will sometimes, by chance, occur contiguously with reward and so will be increased in strength. Since the system is competitive, an increase in the probability of one activity will take time away from the (contingently) rewarded response. Thus the S-Z model predicts that the more frequent the free rewards, the lower the level of the contingent response, in conformity with the data.

The model also shows what looks like Skinner-type superstition. If rewards occur frequently enough, a response that accidentally occurs just before a free reward can be "captured," increasing in probability with successive closely spaced rewards. But, unlike the behavior Staddon and Simmelhag observed, this behavior shows no temporal discrimination, and there is no interim/terminal separation. What the model shows is that each behavior just occurs in longer runs when reward is frequent than when it is infrequent. If you look at a short time sample, therefore, it appears that a "superstitious" behavior is occurring, whereas all that is happening is that activities switch less frequently when reinforcement is more frequent. (Reduced behavior-switching at high reinforcement rates is a general principle: I describe an experimental example in Chapter 8.) Over a long enough time stretch, all three will occur equally often.

What about instinctive drift? Can this model show the transitions described by the Brelands? Is it possible in this system to reward an activity A and then, after a little training to see A supplanted by an apparently unrewarded response B—mistaking the egg for the drop, like the Brelands' raccoon? Well, yes, if activities are not all identical—which means, in the impoverished context of a model, just that they have different parameters a and b. In fact, if Activity B, say, has a larger (slower) decay parameter a than Activity A ($a_b > a_a$) then V_B may nevertheless eventually overtake V_A even if B, which is never contiguous with reward, gets smaller increments than A. The reason is just that the larger a_b value means that Activity B loses strength over time more slowly than Activity A. So even though B is reinforced only after a delay (because it is not the contingent response) and therefore gets smaller increments with each reinforcement than A, it can eventually build up more strength than A.

Why should an activity like handling the egg, by the raccoon, be more resistant to extinction than the activity, dropping the egg, that actually produces food? This is an interesting question because it forces us to think beyond the simple confines of reinforcement theory. There are a couple of possibilities. One is that some activities are simply more persistent and have higher a values than others. So they will often show "instinctive drift," overtaking the conditioned activity under some conditions. But then one might expect the same activity to show up with different kinds of reinforcers—water or sex as well as food, for example. There is no evidence for this. The raccoon's handling behavior seems to be food specific.

So the second possibility is that the a value is set by the type of reinforcer, so that handling has a high a value for food, but a much smaller one for other reinforcers. This sort of difference would be easy to incorporate into the model for parameter b, which affects the boost to response strength given by the reward itself. It's harder for the model to set parameter a, which affects the decay of strength in the absence of reward. How does the model, the animal, "know" what a should be, since it affects strength not at the time of reward, but in the absence of reward? The question seems to propel us reluctantly into the area of *cognition,* an approach avoided by radical behaviorists. But there is no alternative to the idea that animals and people categorize, frame, label—choose your word—situations in terms of the type of reward they can expect to receive. And this labeling limits the repertoire from which contingent reinforcement can select.

What determines the label? Pavlovian conditioning—the pairing of reward type with situational cues—is one easily identifiable process. When food is on offer, the pigeon pecks, the chicken scratches. But sometimes the process is more complex, less directly tied to simple conditioning paradigms. What is it about the animal's history that causes it to label things in the way that it does? More on this question later.

Philosophy

What of Skinner's "as if" account? In what sense do superstitious pigeons behave "as if" their responses produce food? Well, not in the sense that they cannot tell the difference. In an ingenious experiment, Peter Killeen tested pigeons' ability to detect causation.[14] He had individual pigeons peck the center key of a three-key apparatus to produce two lighted side keys. A computer was also generating pecks at about the same rate as the pigeon, so that when the side keys appeared, the cause could have been pigeon peck or computer peck. A peck to one of the side keys produced food: the left key (for example) paid off if the keys had been turned on by the pigeon, the right if by the computer. The pigeons could tell the difference very well. Pigeons can detect extraordinarily small differences in temporal contiguity—much smaller than those they experience under the fixed-time "superstition" schedule. If they continue to peck when pecking is irrelevant, it is certainly not because they are unable to discriminate pecks that produce food from pecks that don't.

On the other hand, there is no doubt that adventitious reinforcement does occur—it's nothing more than the response-strengthening effect of contiguity. A conditionable response that occurs just before reward *is* very likely to increase in strength, just as the cumulative records in Figures 4.3 and 4.4 show. But if that burst of responding is not confirmed by more reward, it will soon die out. Adventitious reinforcement is only one of several processes driving conditioning. It has nothing like the power that Skinner assumed. But it does exist. Here are two examples, one anecdotal, the other experimental.

In the early evening of November 9, 1965, I was attending a late-afternoon seminar on an upper floor of a large modern building at the University of Toronto. The room had a wall of glass and all the lights of the city could be seen. When the meeting ended, I was the last to leave and I turned out the lights. At almost the same instant, all the lights in the city below went out. The subjective impression that I had caused the Great Northeastern Blackout of 1965 (it extended from New York to Canada) was quite overwhelming.

A year or two earlier, I did an experiment with human subjects who responded on a computer keyboard on a spaced-responding schedule, rewarded with "points."[15] The schedule required subjects to press the space bar at least 20 s after their previous press in order to get a reward. A too-early press just reset the clock and required another wait. They had to discover the contingency, but most did not guess that only time was involved. Instead they developed a pattern of pressing other, and completely ineffective keys, ending with a press of the space bar. This routine served to fill the time and allowed them to get the reward. Although these other key presses were completely irrelevant, the subjects never figured it out. This is real superstitious behavior, with the partial qualification that there was a weak contingency involved. After all, suppose a subject learned to press ABCD . . . Bar as a way to space his bar presses. Suppose he omits A, say, one time. This will shorten the sequence and abbreviate the time between bar presses, costing him a reward. So this behavior is only partially superstitious. The superstition is thinking that a particular sequence is what is essential, rather than any sequence long enough to span the required delay. The only way to discover that it is the length of the sequence rather than its composition that is important is to vary the sequence. In the short time available to them, few subjects did this. The take-home: Behavioral variation is the key to optimal behavior. More on this in the next chapter.

Despite criticism and experiment, the "as if" account shows signs of outliving every other idea in Skinner's "superstition" paper. The idea suggests philosophical implications. Perhaps we do nothing from real *knowledge*; indeed the idea of knowledge is itself suspect. We do everything only because of things that have happened to us in the past, our *reinforcement history*. To the minor objection that reflexes, digestion and so forth are activities not easily traced to reinforcement history, Skinner has responded with an evolutionary argument: if not your history, then the history of your ancestors. His epistemology, as befits an intellectual descendant of William James, is just the ultimate form of *pragmatism*: "Truth" is what produces reinforcement. In his later years, Skinner was to embrace a pragmatic, evolutionary epistemology explicitly. This is not nonsense. Knowledge depends on formal or informal experiment, and experiment involves trial and error. If you don't ask the right questions, you won't get the right answers. But the pragmatism of some radical behaviorists goes well beyond this. I explore this theme in later chapters.

A distorted version of these ideas has taken root in the weedy groves of literary theory that claimed the humanities "cutting edge" a few years ago. (It seems to be on the wane now.) Abolition of the idea of *knowledge* seems to be attractive, even liberating, to a number of humanistic scholars. "The detached eye of objective science is an ideological fiction, and a powerful one. But it is a fiction that hides—and is designed to hide—how the powerful discourses of the natural sciences really work,"[16] wrote leading feminist scholar Donna Haraway in 1989. This viewpoint is useful to humanists because it elevates—*privileges*—literary theory at the expense of natural science. But its effect on language has not been good. Readers willing to brave prose that bruises the mind will find in critical theory mutated descendants of Skinner's pragmatic linguistic philosophy. See, for example, critical theorist Barbara Herrnstein Smith's best known book, *Contingencies of Value: Alternative Perspectives for Critical Theory,* which describes a quasi-Skinnerian philosophy she terms "relativism." Relativism seems to deny (it is hard to be sure) the existence of objective truth, even in principle: "[Relativism is] any more or less extensively theorized questioning—analysis, problematizing, critique—of the key elements of objectivist thought and its attendant axiological machinery."[17] Er, yes . . . More on this issue in Chapter 9.

This is not the first time that an influential psychological system has been taken up by the literati. The decline of psychoanalysis as a scientific discipline coincided with the appropriation of psychoanalytic ideas into literary criticism. Freud's "psychoanalytic method" was neither analytic nor a (scientific) method in anything but a metaphorical sense. Skinner's ideas are much better grounded in experiment than were Freud's. Nevertheless, the drift of transmogrified Skinnerian ideas into literary theory is surely not a good sign.

***

Skinner's interest in research with animals was purely analogical. He had little interest in phylogeny and species-specific behavior, the topics studied by ethologists like Lorenz and Tinbergen. For Skinner, as for the biomedical community, animals were simply convenient preparations with which to demonstrate effects that have human analogues. His approach was to take experimental results (rather than theoretical principles) from the animal laboratory and extrapolate them persuasively to human behavior. I illustrated this approach with a discussion of the so-called superstition experiment, a procedure that simply delivers predictable rewards to an animal. It nevertheless generates vigorous but unnecessary activity in pigeons and in many other animal species. By presenting this result as a prediction of the contiguity theory of reinforcement, and by invoking the reader's empathy with the pigeon in an "as-if" account, Skinner was able to convince his audience that many human superstitions, and many puzzling effects in the operant laboratory, simply reflect the ubiquitous effects of operant reinforcement.

He was wrong. Nevertheless, the superstition experiment is interesting for two reasons. First, because it illustrates the subtleties of Skinner's rhetorical method, and second, because it was a focus for a series of experiments and theoretical developments that eroded the early simplicities of reinforcement theory.

The response of Skinner and others to these developments was increased emphasis on the *Darwinian metaphor*, the analogy between reinforcement and natural (or artificial) selection. Skinner emphasized the selection aspect—reinforcement "shapes behavior as a sculptor shapes a lump of clay." But others were more even-handed and placed equal emphasis on the selective action of reinforcement and the limiting role of behavioral *variation* in providing material on which reinforcement can act. For reasons to do with his consistent emphasis on ways to *change* behavior, Skinner was apparently reluctant to take the problems of variation seriously. In his 1966 paper, Skinner seemed concerned to show evolutionists what they could learn from operant conditioning. He was much less attentive to what he might learn from the evolutionists.

Notes

1. *Behavior of Organisms* (1938), p. 44.
2. Skinner, B. F. (1948). "Superstition" in the pigeon. *Journal of Experimental Psychology, 38*, 168–172.
3. The depressive effects of free reinforcers on a contingent (reinforced) response have been repeatedly demonstrated in subsequent years—for example, Rachlin, H., & Baum, W. M. (1972). Effects of alternative reinforcement: Does the source matter? *Journal of the Experimental Analysis of Behavior, 18*, 231–241; Hammond, L. J. (1980). The effect of contingency upon the appetitive conditioning of free-operant behavior. *Journal of the Experimental Analysis of Behavior, 34*, 297–304.
4. Henton, W. W., & Iversen, I. H. (1978). *Classical conditioning and operant conditioning* (New York: Springer-Verlag).

5. Skinner (1948), p. 171.

6. Brown, P. L., & Jenkins, H. M. (1968). Auto-shaping of the pigeon's key-peck. *Journal of the Experimental Analysis of Behavior, 11*, 1–8; Williams, D. R., & Williams, H. (1969). Auto-maintenance in the pigeon: Sustained pecking despite contingent nonreinforcement. *Journal of the Experimental Analysis of Behavior, 12*, 511–520.

7. Staddon, J. E. R., & Simmelhag, V. L. (1971). The "superstition" experiment: A reexamination of its implications for the principles of adaptive behavior. *Psychological Review, 78*, 3–43; Timberlake, W., & Lucas, G. A. (1985, November). The basis of superstitious behavior: Chance contingency, stimulus substitution, or appetitive behavior? *Journal of the Experimental Analysis of Behavior, 44*(3), 279–299.

8. Bjork, D. W. (1993). *B. F. Skinner: A life* (New York: Basic Books); Skinner, B. F. (1960). Pigeons in a pelican. *American Psychologist, 15*, 28–37.

9. Breland, K., & Breland, M. (1960). The misbehavior of organisms. *American Psychologist, 16*, 661–664.

10. Breland, K., & Breland, M. (1966). *Animal behavior* (New York: Macmillan), p. 67.

11. Assignment of credit seems to have been first identified as a problem in the study of artificial intelligence—for example, Minsky, M. (1969). *Computation: Finite and infinite machines* (Cambridge, MA: MIT Press).

12. For a movie of an apparatus like this and a fascinating interview with B. F. Skinner where he describes how he would design a culture, see www.bbc.co.uk/blogs/adamcurtis/2010/11/post_1.html. This 2010 piece also traces the link between modern behavioral economics and Skinner's ideas (see also Chapter 10).

13. Slightly modified from Staddon, J. E. R., & Zhang, Y. (1991). On the assignment-of-credit problem in operant learning. In M. L. Commons, S. Grossberg, & J. E. R. Staddon (Eds.), *Neural networks of conditioning and action, the XIIth Harvard Symposium* (Hillsdale, NJ: Erlbaum Associates), pp. 279–293. See also Staddon, J. E. R. (2001). *Adaptive dynamics: Simple learning mechanisms* (Cambridge, MA: MIT/Bradford).

14. Killeen, P. R. (1978). Superstition: A matter of bias, not detectability. *Science, 199*, 88–90.

15. Nowadays these folk are called "participants," rather than the more accurate "subjects." I'm not sure why.

16. Haraway, D. (1989). *Primate visions: Gender, race, and nature in the world of modern science* (New York: Routledge), p. 13.

17. Herrnstein Smith, B. (1986). *Contingencies of value: Alternative perspectives for critical theory* (Cambridge, MA: Harvard University Press), p. 151. Herrnstein Smith was Richard Herrnstein's first wife.

7 Behavior-Evolution Parallels

Even at a time when the beautiful mechanisms of molecular genetics were unknown, Darwin was able to identify several factors that affect variation in phylogenetic evolution. We are at about the same point as far as ontogenetic evolution is concerned. We can see it happen, as the organism learns, even though the underlying details are still obscure. Darwin knew nothing of the genetics that underlie phenotypic variation.[1] We still do not understand the "[onto]genetics" of learning. But it is worth looking at the many parallels between ontogenetic and phylogenetic evolution. For example, Darwin noted that both a change in conditions and relaxation of selection can cause great increases in the range of variation.[2] There is little reason to doubt that similar effects can occur in ontogeny under the action of reinforcement. In experimental extinction (cessation of reinforcement = relaxation of selection), for example, the range of behavioral variation typically increases at first. Here are some other parallels.

Shaping by successive approximations, which has already come up a couple of times, is analogous to artificial selection for phenotypic characters by, for example, horse breeders. If fast racehorses are desired, then the fastest stallions are mated with the fastest and healthiest mares and so on for many generations. The result is faster and faster runners. The idea is to exploit any variation in the desired direction—here, faster running—by selecting the animals that show it and breeding from them. Shaping is the same method applied to behavior. Suppose you want to train your dog to, say, lift his paw. Then you reward him at first for any movement of the paw, then set the bar higher and higher until you get the full-blown movement you want. If you search "shape dog tricks" on YouTube you can find many examples of this technique.

So much, so obvious. But what about shaping a complex skill, perhaps a task involving many subtasks, or a new behavior not previously seen in the animal or perhaps even the species? A complex sequence can be trained by breaking it down into simple elements. B. F. Skinner applied this technique to educating children in elementary tasks.[3] But teaching an animal something that has never been seen before is trickier. What *is* an approximation to a completely new behavior? What, in other words, are the precursors of the end product you desire?

One very clever way to get completely new behavior is . . . to reward completely new behavior. (This is an extreme version of what is termed frequency-dependent selection, discussed more below.) Karen Pryor many years ago did this in Hawaii with two porpoises. She rewarded each day a behavior never seen before and concluded:

> A technique of reinforcing a series of different, normally occurring actions, in a series of training sessions . . . serve[d] . . . in the case of Hou, as with Malia, to establish in the animal a highly increased probability that new types of behavior would be emitted.[4]

Interestingly, some of these behaviors were entirely novel to the dolphin species with which she worked (*Steno bredanensis*), although they were seen in others (such as the more common *Tursiops truncatus*). It's also interesting that this technique doesn't seem to work with pigeons; they don't become more creative as the training is continued.[5]

Human beings are of course more complicated—or at least, via language, have more different things they can do—than dolphins. If we want to train them in a complex skill, like writing poetry, just paying them off for any new scribble won't do it! It takes countless zillions of monkeys randomly tapping keyboards to produce a single Shakespeare sonnet. Just generating variety is not, by itself, enough. Selection must also be involved.

Darwin faced the problem in applying natural selection to what he called *organs of extreme perfection and complication*, like the eye:

> To suppose that the eye with all its inimitable contrivances for adjusting the focus to different distances, for admitting different amounts of light, and for the correction of spherical and chromatic aberration, could have been formed by natural selection, seems, I freely confess, absurd in the highest degree. . . . [But] [r]eason tells me, that if numerous gradations from a simple and imperfect eye to one complex and perfect can be shown to exist, each grade being useful to its possessor, as is certainly the case; if further, the eye ever varies and the variations be inherited, as is likewise certainly the case; and if such variations should be useful to any animal under changing conditions of life, then the difficulty of believing that a perfect and complex eye could be formed by natural selection, though insuperable by our imagination, should not be considered as subversive of the theory.[6]

By meticulously describing parallels of stages of eye development within (embryology) and between existing species, from simple photocell eye-spots of primitive mollusks, to non-focusing eye-cups to compound eyes to eyes with a single, focusing lens, Darwin made a plausible case for a set of precursors along the path to the evolution of the vertebrate eye.

Much the same can be done with human behavior: Generate variation, then select. How do you get the human equivalents to Pryor's "creative porpoise"? First, behavioral variation without which you have nothing from which to select. But then, what are the behaviors that parallel Darwin's stages of eye development? What are the precursors of the behavioral end product? Indeed, what *is* the end product of a creative education? Answers to these questions are still very much a matter of intuition on the part of the creative teacher.

Behavioral Variation: Context and Pavlovian Conditioning

Context—stimuli and reinforcers—constrains, sustains and directs behavioral variation. For example, Pavlovian conditioning, which allows a neutral stimulus to acquire signal properties, will itself give rise to a repertoire of reinforcer-related activities on which operant reinforcement can act. A stimulus associated with food, or food by itself, will induce a wide range of food-related activities in a hungry animal—activities from which operant contingencies can select. Pigeons peck, chickens peck and scratch, raccoons manipulate. Pavlovian conditioning, with (say) a food US, in effect frames or *labels* the context as food related. The label then limits the emitted behavior to a food-related repertoire, which is defined partly by past history but also by the organism's evolutionary history. If the operant contingency is one rarely or never encountered by the organism's ancestors, this repertoire may be inadequate or inappropriate—and the organism will "misbehave," as in the examples discussed earlier.

How does this labeling work? This is a neglected problem, probably because it involves not behavior but cognition. Labeling is determined by how the organism "perceives" the situation given its cognitive limitations and its past history in similar situations. It would be nice to know, for a given individual and species, exactly how context limits behavioral variation and what might be done to manage these effects—for the purposes of training and education, for example. More on training and teaching in Chapters 19 and 21.

If context limits the range of induced activities, then the power of operant reinforcement to mold behavior will also be limited, in ways that may conflict with standard reinforcement accounts. Autoshaped pecking and some kinds of instinctive drift are examples. Given a highly predictive stimulus, pecking (in pigeons) may be the *only* activity induced, so that a contingency involving some other activity, particularly one that interferes with pecking, can have no effect. Recall, for example, the Williams and Williams experiment that delivered food on a Pavlovian schedule so long as no pecking occurred (omission training). The birds pecked anyway about half the time, the remaining stimulus-food pairings still being sufficient to sustain pecking as a major part of the repertoire offered up by processes of behavioral variation. Pigeons show similar misbehavior in something called the feature-negative effect[7] when they continue to peck at a stimulus that signals nonreinforcement because it shares common features with a strongly reinforced stimulus. This happens even if the pigeons can tell the positive and negative stimuli apart under other conditions.

Frequency-Dependent Selection

Over the long term, selection can affect variation. This process is well known in biological evolution. In frequency-dependent selection, for example, variability is favored if rare types have higher fitness than common types. Why should rare types be favored? One reason is the perceptual limitations of predators. As they search for cryptic (i.e., camouflaged) prey, rare types may do better because predators have to learn to see cryptic prey. Learning is quicker and

Plate 7.1 Some polymorphic examples of the snail *Cepea* (http://en.wikipedia.org/wiki/File:Polymorphism_in_Cepaea_nemoralis.jpg).

more complete when the same type is encountered frequently. Consequently, rare types are harder to recognize than common ones. There is now a fair amount of evidence in favor of this interesting idea.[8]

If each new variant has an advantage just because of its rarity, frequency-dependent selection can give rise to a population that is highly variable in form. Biology texts describe many examples. The highly variable snail *Cepea* is perhaps the best known (Plate 7.1). Reinforcement schedules with the property of frequency dependence—preferentially reinforcing response types that have occurred "least recently"—also give rise to random-appearing behavior, presumably for the same reason.[9]

Supernormal Stimuli and Asymmetrical Selection

Specific reinforcement effects have surprising parallels in phylogeny. For example, there is a phenomenon of instinctive behavior known as *supernormal stimuli.* A supernormal stimulus is a stimulus never seen under natural conditions that is nevertheless more effective than the natural stimulus. Plate 7.2 shows an example: In preference to its own egg, an oystercatcher is retrieving

Plate 7.2 An oystercatcher retrieving an artificial, super-large egg in preference to its own, smaller egg.

a much larger artificial egg. Another example is the preference of male *Argynnis paphia* butterflies for a light stimulus that flickers at a much faster rate than the natural stimulus—the wings of a female butterfly. The hugely exaggerated proportions of primitive fertility symbols like the 25,000-year-old Venus of Willendorf (Plate 7.3) may be a human example.[10]

There is a comparable phenomenon in discrimination learning (see the discussion of stimulus generalization in Chapter 5). It works like this. A pigeon is trained to respond to one stimulus, say a wavelength of 550 nm, which is alternated with another, at 500 nm, in the presence of which it never gets any food. Pigeons soon learn not to peck the 500 nm stimulus and to peck the (rewarded) 550 nm one. Yet, a test with *600* nm will usually show more enthusiastic pecking than to the 550 nm positive stimulus used in training. In other words, responding is maximal at a point on the wavelength dimension displaced away from the negative (500 nm) stimulus (*peak shift*).

These phenomena all seem to reflect *asymmetrical* selection.[11] In the operant case, the subject is trained to respond at 550 nm and to suppress responding

Plate 7.3 The Venus of Willendorf (circa 23,000 BC).

to 500 nm. It never sees 600 nm in training, so there is no selection against responding to 600 nm, which is why it is favored over 550 nm in a generalization test. In the phylogenetic case, the normal egg is favored, but retrieval of smaller-than-normal eggs may be selected against because they are likely to be unviable. Larger-than-normal eggs are never encountered in nature (too big to lay, presumably); hence they may be favored when encountered under artificial conditions. A similar account also works for the butterflies. High flicker rates are not encountered in nature, but low rates are—the wings of birds that feed on butterflies. So natural selection drives preference away from low rates.

Phenotype and Genotype

Intrinsic to the Darwinian metaphor is the distinction between *phenotype* and *genotype*. The phenotype is the visible outcome of the developmental process, the whole organism with its morphology and behavior. The phenotype is what makes contact with the environment and is subject to the "contingencies of survival." (Actually, Darwinian fitness depends on *reproduction*, not just survival, but Skinner's phrase, echoing Herbert Spencer's "survival of the fittest," is catchier.) But it is the genotype that is inherited, so that only those phenotypic characteristics that have a genetic counterpart can take part in the evolutionary process.[12] The generations of spaniel pups that had their tails docked at birth have not given rise to a race of tailless spaniels.

The phenotype-genotype distinction resembles the neo-behaviorist distinction between performance and learning. Performance is what you see: measured behavior. Learning, or *competence*, is what you can see potentially. Performance is how well you do on the exam right after a night of drunken carousing. Competence is how you could have done, had you managed your evening more moderately. Skinner never accepted the competence-performance distinction. Consequently, he never admitted that the phenotype-genotype distinction might also apply to operant behavior, even though it is part and parcel of the Darwinian metaphor. The distinction nevertheless reflects well-known facts. Not all phenotypic characteristics are heritable, and hence subject to selection pressure. Only some things that animals do can be selected through operant reinforcement. Distinguishing those that can from those that cannot requires an understanding of the relations between the internal processes that generate overt actions and the actions themselves—the behavioral equivalent of the laws of development that translate genotype into phenotype. It also requires an understanding of the differences between those internal states that have successors across time (i.e., *memories*) and those internal states that leave no imprint on the future. Skinner never accepted the idea of internal states as essential elements in explanations for behavior. So: no memories, no principled way to distinguished between experiences that do have persistent effects and those that don't.

The Darwinian metaphor can be applied in many different ways—and there is often no easy way to distinguish empirically among them. What we can say is that Skinner's application was rather superficial. Even in the area of human social arrangements, much better attempts have been made. D. T. Campbell, for example, in a carefully reasoned account, identified sources of conflict between "selfish" propensities favored by individual genetic selection, and "altruistic" propensities favored by cultural evolution within groups driven by competition between them. Campbell's claims were cautious: "You are hereby warned—this talk is not hardheaded science but an exercise in quasi-scientific speculation."[13] He frequently reminds his readers that real-life social questions cannot be the subject of meaningful experiments. Campbell knew that generalizing from laboratory situations to the world at large was fraught with uncertainty. In recent years, a new field of *evolutionary psychology* has come into being, which seeks to apply the Darwinian metaphor in systematic and testable ways to human behavior.[14] It has so far had limited success, for reasons that Campbell well understood.

Notes

1. In his later years, Darwin did come up with a theory of inheritance, which he called *pangenesis*. In effect it stood modern genetics on its head. Rather than the genome dividing along with the zygote and its descendants, Darwin's gene equivalents, which he called "gemmules," migrated in the adult from every part of the body into the reproductive organs. See http://en.wikipedia.org/wiki/Pangenesis.
2. Darwin, C. (1868). *The variation of animals and plants under domestication* (John Murray). Retrieved from http://darwin-online.org.uk/EditorialIntroductions/ Freeman_VariationunderDomestication.html.
3. For a quick video summary, see Charles Osgood on the *Sunday Morning Show* around 1972 or so: www.youtube.com/watch?v=D-RS80DVvrg.
4. Pryor, K. W., Haag, R., & O'Reilly, J. (1969). The creative porpoise: Training for novel behavior. *Journal of the Experimental Analysis of Behavior, 12*, 653–661. See also Maltzman, I. (1960). On the training of originality. *Psychological Review, 67*, 229–242.
5. JERS, unpublished data.
6. Darwin, C. (1859). *The origin of species*.
7. See Staddon, J. E. R. (2010). *Adaptive behavior and learning,* Ch. 11. Retrieved from http://dukespace.lib.duke.edu/dspace/handle/10161/2878.
8. See, for example, "Search Image Formation in the Blue Jay (*Cyanocitta cristata*)" by Alexandra T. Pietrewicz and Alan C. Kamil: http://digitalcommons.unl.edu/cgi/ viewcontent.cgi?article=1065&context=bioscibehavior&sei-redir=1&referer=ht tp%3A%2F%2Fscholar.google.com%2Fscholar%3Fhl%3Den%26q%3Dsearch %2Bimage%26btnG%3D%26as_sdt%3D1%252C34%26as_sdtp%3D#search= %22search%20image%22.

    For reviews, see Davies, N. B., Krebs, J. R., & West, S. A. (2012). *An introduction to behavioural ecology* (New York: John Wiley); see also Shettleworth, S. (2010). *Cognition, evolution and behavior* (New York: Oxford University Press).
9. The original frequency-dependent experiment was done by Blough, D. S. (1966). The reinforcement of least-frequent interresponse times. *Journal of the Experimental Analysis of Behavior, 9*(5), 581–591. More recent studies are Machado, A. (1992). Behavioral variability and frequency-dependent selection. *Journal of the Experimental Analysis of Behavior, 58*, 241–263; and Page, S., & Neuringer, A. (1985). Variability is an operant. *Journal of Experimental Psychology: Animal Behavior Processes, 11*, 429–452.

10. See http://en.wikipedia.org/wiki/Venus_of_Willendorf.
11. Staddon, J. E. R. (1975). A note on the evolutionary significance of supernormal stimuli. *American Naturalist, 109*, 541–545; see also Ghirlanda, S., & Enquist, M. (2003). A century of generalization. *Animal Behaviour, 66*(1), 15–36; Reid, A. K., & Staddon, J. E. R. (1998). A dynamic route-finder for the cognitive map. *Psychological Review, 105*, 585–601. Retrieved from http://dukespace.lib.duke.edu/dspace/handle/10161/7383.
12. There are some modest exceptions to this. See, for example, Nature insight. (2007). *Epigenetics, 447*(7143), 396–440: "Genetic mechanisms alone cannot explain how some cellular traits are propagated. Rapid advances in the field of epigenetics are now revealing a molecular basis for how heritable information other than DNA sequence can influence gene function."
13. Campbell, D. T. (1975). On the conflicts between biological and social evolution and between psychology and moral tradition. *American Psychologist, 30*, 1103–1126; Campbell, D. T. (1956). Adaptive behavior from random response. *Behavioral Science, 1*, 105–110.
14. Buss, D. M. (Ed.). (2005). *The handbook of evolutionary psychology* (Hoboken, NJ: John Wiley); Stent, G. (1980). *Morality as a biological phenomenon* (Berkeley: University of California Press); Ridley, M. (1997). *The origins of virtue: Human instincts and the evolution of cooperation* (New York: Viking); Cosmides, L., & Tooby, J. (1994). Better than rational: Evolutionary psychology and the invisible hand. *The American Economic Review, 84*(2), 327–332. See http://en.wikipedia.org/wiki/Evolutionary_psychology.

8   Rationality

Economists talk about "rationality," evolutionary theorists about "optimality." Human beings are supposed to behave rationally—that is to say, in a way that maximizes their "utility." For economists, that usually means maximizing their income. Evolution by natural selection often works to produce behavior that is "optimal" in terms of reproduction—number of offspring—or some proxy for reproduction like food or access to a mate. Some theorists have claimed that much operant behavior is optimal in the sense that it maximizes rate of reinforcement. The idea in all cases is that the system—evolution or the free market or the law of effect—almost always produces the "best" result.

I need to spend some time on the idea of rationality because explanations for behavior both by behaviorists and nonbehaviorists, make some use of it. Economists, for the most part, see human action as rational. Behavioral economists, of which there are at least two varieties, tend to disagree. Radical behaviorists refer to reason only to disparage it. How useful are explanations of behavior in terms of rationality? I will argue that the term is usually more trouble than it's worth.

In economics, especially, there is much confusion about what "rational" means. Here is an example to illustrate the problem. It's from a brief article in *Scientific American*. The author, a distinguished economist,[1] discusses a game called the Traveler's Dilemma. It is a variant of the well-known prisoner's dilemma,[2] a game in which each player, following his own interest, yields a result that is worse for both players than if they had followed less selfish strategies. The article begins, "When playing this simple game, people consistently reject the rational choice." The point of the example is that the author, not alone among economists, confuses one kind of optimizing *method* with rationality itself. But, as the Darwinian metaphor should remind us, there are many ways to skin a cat, and rational behavior cannot be identified with a single process, no matter how useful. Let's see how the Traveler's Dilemma works:

> Lucy and Pete, returning from a remote Pacific island, find that the airline has damaged the identical antiques that each had purchased. An airline manager says that he is happy to compensate them but is handicapped by

being clueless about the value of these strange objects. Simply asking the travelers for the price is hopeless, he figures, for they will inflate it.

Instead he devises a more complicated scheme. He asks each of them to write down the price of the antique as any dollar integer between 2 and 100 without conferring together. If both write the same number, he will take that to be the true price, and he will pay each of them that amount. But if they write different numbers, he will assume that the lower one is the actual price and that the person writing the higher number is cheating. In that case, he will pay both of them the lower number along with a bonus and a penalty—the person who wrote the lower number will get $2 more as a reward for honesty and the one who wrote the higher number will get $2 less as a punishment. For instance, if Lucy writes 46 and Pete writes 100, Lucy will get $48 and Pete will get $44.

What numbers will Lucy and Pete write? What number would you write?

Scenarios of this kind, in which one or more individuals have choices to make and will be rewarded according to those choices, are known as games by the people who study them (game theorists). . . .

To see why 2 is the logical choice, consider a plausible line of thought that Lucy might pursue: her first idea is that she should write the largest possible number, 100, which will earn her $100 if Pete is similarly greedy. . . . Soon, however, it strikes her that if she wrote 99 instead, she would make a little more money, because in that case she would get $101. But surely this insight will also occur to Pete, and if both wrote 99, Lucy would get $99. If Pete wrote 99, then she could do better by writing 98, in which case she would get $100. Yet the same logic would lead Pete to choose 98 as well. In that case, she could deviate to 97 and earn $99. And so on. Continuing with this line of reasoning would take the travelers spiraling down to the smallest permissible number, namely, 2. It may seem highly implausible that Lucy would really go all the way down to 2 in this fashion. That does not matter (and is, in fact, the whole point)—this is where the logic leads us. (italics added)

What do people actually do? Well, they pick a number closer to 100 than 2 and thus do much better than the "rational" strategy. But then what makes the strategy "rational" if there are better ones? What's wrong is that the article has conflated a process, called *hill climbing*,[3] with rational behavior. We'll see more examples of hill climbing in a moment. But let's see how it works in this situation.

A Nash equilibrium, named after eccentric Princeton mathematician John Nash (he of the book and movie *A Beautiful Mind*), is the name for the state of a game such that neither player gains by changing his strategy. In the theory of evolution, the term *evolutionarily stable strategy* (ESS) is used for the same idea. If, for example, there are two different varieties of an organism: aggressive ones, that always fight an opponent ("hawks") and passive ones that always flee a fight ("doves") and the Darwinian fitness of each is inversely dependent on its frequency—the more they are the less fit they are—then the species will settle down at a ratio of the two that is an ESS—because if either variety increases in number, its fitness decreases. But this mix may or may not be the best for the species. As in the Traveler's Dilemma, there may be strategies that will lead to higher overall fitness for all individuals.

Here's how hill climbing works to produce a Nash equilibrium in the Traveler's Dilemma. The process proceeds iteratively, comparing the current payoff with the payoff if the chosen number is reduced by one (see the italicized passage in the previous excerpt). The result is that when both "players" get to 2, the Nash equilibrium, further reduction reduces their payoff, so they stop.

Notice how arbitrary this process is. For example, subtracting 5 each time instead of 1, for example, would fail to yield the same answer because both players would lose at the first step down. Details matter; there is nothing absolute about the 2,2 outcome, even within the hill-climbing framework.

The Nash equilibrium works in many evolutionary examples because natural selection usually (if not invariably) works through small changes from generation to generation. In other words, the Nash equilibrium is the outcome for a plausible evolutionary process, a process without foresight that proceeds by small steps. The success of the Nash analysis in the evolutionary case shows that the notion of *rationality* in the conventional sense—choosing a strategy from among a set of well-defined possibilities—doesn't even apply.

Conversely, a (truly) rational human being can understand both the Nash argument and its superior alternative, which is more complicated and involves the further step of seeing that a hill-climbing strategy leads to disaster for both parties. The player with foresight can see that 100,100 is probably the best attainable outcome. In this case, both instinct and reason converge, which is presumably why most people choose this strategy.

The logical conclusion here is that "rationality" is not, and cannot be, a simple rule, an *algorithm*. Rational behavior depends on *knowledge* and *computation*. If, in the "traveler" case, the subject can only compare the present situation (value) with values one greater or less, then hill climbing drives the value chosen down to the minimum possible. But if he knows that the best he can do in this situation is say 100 (not worrying about the fact that he might make 101 if the other person says something different), then he will do what most people do. His behavior is not so much more or less rational than the Nash guy (well, if rationality is defined in terms of outcomes, it *is* more rational), it's simply the outcome of a different process.

The Darwinian metaphor, with its emphasis on variation, allows behaviorism to explain behavior in terms of consequences without falling into the trap of algorithmic rationality. For many years, economics was dominated by two ideas: that markets are efficient and that humans usually make rational choices. The financial crisis beginning in 2008 pretty much put paid to the idea of market efficiency, which is both philosophically and empirically deficient.[4] But the idea that people act rationally persists. And economists seem to have rather simplistic ideas of what rationality is. One highly visible economist[5] was recently quoted as saying, "After all, while there is only one way to be perfectly rational, there are an infinite number of ways to be irrational. . . ." It seems to follow that rationality demands omniscience and omnicompetence. Only God is truly rational, under this definition.

The Traveler's Dilemma situation is highly contrived. Games like this are popular in economic discussions because they yield easy experiments with human subjects. But the experiments are invariably short in duration and the rewards on offer trivial. Animals, in long experiments with hefty rewards (food, for a pigeon at 80% of its free-feeding weight, for example), provide a more realistic test bed for theory. So now, let's look at three examples from the animal operant lab that involve real behavior rather than game playing. How useful is the idea that behavior is rational (= optimal) in explaining what we see there?

The first example is the matching behavior discussed in Chapters 3 and 4. A pigeon responding at the typical high rate in a two-choice situation under the conditions that Herrnstein used will match response ratios to reinforcement ratios. Because both choices pay off on variable-interval schedules, and response rate is high, the animal can vary its response ratio quite a bit without suffering much loss in total reinforcements per hour. But in fact matching is the behavior that yields the most reinforcements per hour for a given overall response rate.[6] The bird is therefore maximizing, behaving optimally—rationally.

There is still some debate about exactly what underlies matching behavior. Most believe that it is some more or less moment-by-moment hill-climbing process. All agree that the bird does not employ what I call *explicit maximizing*. In fact there is little evidence that pigeons are sensitive to average rates, to what are called *molar* variables.[7] The matching pigeon isn't varying his choice proportions, comparing the resulting overall payoff rate, and then picking the best in the "rational" way that many economists assume. This is true of all maximizing, human or animal. Optimal behavior is the result of an underlying process that is usually very much simpler than the explicit maximizing tacitly assumed by economists.

The second example is both simpler and more informative than matching: the two-armed bandit. This is also a choice situation, but choice between two variable *ratios* (VR) rather than variable-interval schedules. As with the Las Vegas–style gambling device, the pigeon is paid off after a random number of responses to each choice. For example, a VR 5 just means that on average the fifth peck in a run will get some food.

Suppose we train a pigeon with a two-armed bandit (concurrent) schedule where his two options are A: VR 5 and B: VR 20. It will shock no one to learn that after a little experience with these conditions, the pigeon will go 100% of the time for the smaller ratio, 5. This can be explained in at least two ways. The rationality/optimality theorist will say at once, "he's maximizing," because it never pays to choose the lower-probability option. The dynamic theorist will not disagree, but may point out that a simple reward-following model, like the

LOE model I introduced in Chapter 4, will also usually fixate on the alternative with a much higher payoff. The matching theorist also will be happy. The bird is still matching: 100% of payoffs, and responses, on the same side. True, but not useful, since matching doesn't say just which side will be favored.

How can we distinguish among these accounts? Well, what do they predict for the very simple situation where both choices pay off with the *same* probability, say 1 in 20? The maximizers will say either that the pigeons should be indifferent or, if it takes even a little effort to switch keys, the bird should just fixate on one key. The matchers cannot make a prediction because no matter how the bird allocates his pecks, matching is guaranteed. How about the dynamic modelers? Here the prediction is a bit more interesting. For many reward-following models, including a two-choice version of the LOE model I introduced in Chapter 4, the prediction depends on the *absolute value* of the two identical ratios. If they are small, these models predict fixation on one side or another.[8] But if the ratios are large, and the schedule is lean, they predict indifference. Why?

A little reflection suggests the reason. When the ratio is small, and the schedule is rich, probability of response ($p(x)$ in the LOE model) loses little on the relatively small proportion of nonreinforced responses (downshifts) to counter the gains on the reinforced responses (upshifts).[9] Thus, $p(x)$ hovers around a high value, which implies fixation on one of the two identical alternatives. Conversely, when the ratio is high (so payoff probability is low), $p(x)$ gets many downshifts relative to upshifts, driving responding away from both choices. The result is indifference.

Experiment supports this prediction. In one study,[10] for example, pigeons fixated on one choice when the ratio for both was VR 20, but were indifferent when it was VR 75. Figure 8.1 shows the data. Two things are worth noting.

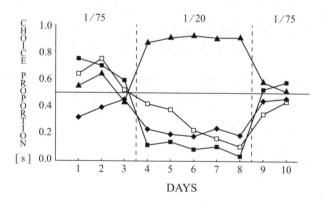

Figure 8.1 The effect of absolute reward probability on choice between identical probabilistic alternatives ("two-armed bandit"). The figure plots the proportion of choices of the right-hand alternative, *s*, across daily sessions for each of four pigeons for two conditions, $p = 1/75$ and $p = 1/20$, in ABA sequence (Horner & Staddon, 1987, Figure 1).

First, all four subjects switch from more or less indifference when the schedule is lean, 1 in 75 responses, to exclusive choice when it is richer, 1 in 20. All switch back to indifference when the ratio reverts back to 75. And second, they don't all show the same exclusive preference—there is no evidence of bias in favor of one choice.

The dynamic model also predicts that preference in the 75,75 condition could be shifted from indifference to fixation on one side or the other without changing the ratio, just by changing the size of the reinforcer, or by adding a weak shock (punishment) to every response. Alas, those experiments remain to be done.

Again, the matchers have nothing to say about these outcomes—matching is forced by the equal schedules. But maximizers must add an assumption to explain the effect of the richness of the schedule. How about assuming that there is some cost to switching? Can this explain the difference between the VR 20 and VR 75 choice patterns? No, switching cost can explain fixation on the rich schedule, but it can't explain switching away from a poor one. Given two identical schedules, it always pays to stay rather than incur the switching cost.

The rational/optimizing account can be salvaged by something called *satisficing*. This is a term coined by Nobel Prize winner in economics, H. A. Simon (1916–2001), in his discussion of what he called *bounded rationality*.[11] It means that a decision maker will quit trying once he comes up with a solution that is "good enough." If the rich schedule is OK, why switch? But if it isn't, then keep looking. The process resembles the tumble-and-swim kinesis I discussed in Chapter 2, with the addition of a parameter, the satisficing threshold. If payoff is above the threshold, the subject stays; if below, he switches.

Kinesis is another example of hill climbing, which is the simplest kind of variation/selection. The notion is that the organism samples various alternatives, one at a time, and picks the better one—like a blind man tap-tapping his way up hill. The bacterium samples various directions (tumbles) and then when the current one is better than the last, picks it (straight swim). This idea turns up in many areas—the "rational" solution to the Traveler's Dilemma is one. In the matching experiment, two versions of hill climbing, momentary maximizing and melioration, have been suggested as the underlying process.[12]

How about exploration? Organisms, even pigeons, come with a built-in tendency to explore any new environment. As we saw earlier in the discussion of latent learning, rats dumped in a maze will learn something about it even in the absence of explicit reward. If this tendency competes with the law-of-effect learning that keeps the animal responding to one choice, then the weaker the reward for that choice, the more likely that he will break away from time to time—and respond to the other choice.

Another way to say the same thing is to start with the presumption that in the absence of any selection, organisms will vary their behavior. But then, the lower the rate or amount of reinforcement—the weaker the selection—the more variability—switching—will remain. Hence switching between a pair of poor schedules is more likely than if the schedules are both rich. So a shift from fixation to indifference when the ratio shifts from rich to lean is in fact perfectly consistent with the fact that reinforcement, like natural selection, reduces variation.

So these three accounts—a dynamic model, satisficing and the analogy with reinforcement as selection acting to restrict variation—all agree. All provide a reasonably accurate account of behavior in this simple situation. But the dynamic model is obviously the most specific and powerful account.

Finally, a very simple operant example. Recall that organisms trained on a fixed-interval schedule soon develop a highly adaptive pattern of response. They learn to quit responding for the first half of the interval or so, when they are never reinforced, and then respond at an accelerating rate as the time for reinforcement approaches (e.g., Figure 4.4). Given that their timing is not perfectly accurate, it makes sense to begin responding a bit early so as not to delay food unnecessarily (and a delay affects not just the next reward, but all subsequent rewards). In other words, behavior on FI schedules is optimal/rational by almost any standard.

A small modification of this schedule causes pigeons to misbehave. Figure 8.2 shows a single cycle of a procedure called a *response-initiated-delay* (RID) schedule.[13] It's just a *fixed-time* (FT) schedule (no final peck required, but an FI works as well) with the interval started by the first peck rather than food delivery. The cycle begins with brief access to food. Then the pigeon can wait as long or as little as it likes before making his first key peck. The time it waits is labeled t. After it responds, a computer-controlled clock starts running and goes for T seconds, at which point food is delivered again.

The optimal behavior in this situation is not hard to figure out: The pigeon should respond as soon as it can after food. Time t should be set as short as possible so that the postpeck clock can begin running as soon as possible. Pigeons don't do this. Instead they set time t so that it is a fraction of the *total* interfood interval, $t + T$, that is about the same as if the *whole* time had been fixed at that value by the experimenter. For example, suppose that time T is fixed at 20 s; the pigeon's waiting time (t) will also be about 20 s (half of $t + T$), the same as if the experimenter had arranged for the total interfood time, $t + T$, to be set at 40 s, independently of waiting time (i.e., a regular FI 40). In other words, the pigeon uses the food as a time marker rather than his first peck. But by doing so, he gets food 20 s later than necessary.

The limitation here is not one of physical capacity. Pigeons are perfectly capable of responding immediately after food. It is a limitation on the process

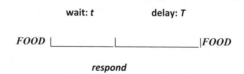

Figure 8.2 Response-initiated-delay (RID) schedule. An experimenter-controlled delay (T) is initiated by a response after post-reward delay (t), which is determined by the subject. Reward occurs again when T has elapsed.

that governs pigeon's adaptation to temporal regularities. To solve the problem poised by a RID schedule, the animal must have some way to compare two times: the time between the first peck in an interval and food, and the time between food and food. If it can detect that the first-peck-to-food time is shorter than the food-to-food time, it may learn to peck as soon as possible. Unfortunately, food is much more salient (memorable) than a peck, so that postfood time, and not postpeck time, is remembered and governs the pigeon's waiting time. The pigeon's problem is to do with memory, not with his ability to do what is required to maximize payoff.

People are a little smarter but still show remnants of the RID effect. Who hasn't attended a regular meeting run by a chair who often comes a little late? The members begin to adjust to the wait by turning up a little late; the chair, in turn, adjusts to their tardiness by turning up a little later. The meeting begins later and later until someone notices what is happening and calls a halt.

A small modification to the RID schedule causes the pigeon to show either optimal or nonoptimal behavior, depending on a parameter. The same situation also nicely illustrates the difference between *positive* and *negative feedback*. The modification is this. Suppose that instead of a fixed value, we make the delay, T (see Figure 8.2) proportional to the wait-time t that precedes it: $T_n = kt_{n-1}$, where k is a constant and n is the number of the interval. In other words, we make the pigeon wait for food after its first peck for a time proportional to how long it just waited.

This relation is a property of the schedule, but there is a corresponding relation in the pigeon. As numerous experiments have shown, for the pigeon $t_{n+1} = M(T_n + t_n)$; that is, the wait time in interval $n + 1$ is proportional (M) to the duration of the preceding interval. (Yes, the pigeon will adjust its wait time that fast under many conditions.) If you put these two equations together,[14] it is easy to see that the expected behavior depends on the value of M in relation to the value of k.

Table 8.1 shows an example. The two columns show wait times in successive intervals, starting with an initial wait of 10. The pigeon's wait proportion, k, is 0.25—he waits 25% of the duration of the preceding interval; that is, $t_{n-1} = 0.25(t_n + T_n)$. The two columns show the wait times in successive intervals predicted for two values of the schedule parameter, M: 0.2 and 4. Wait time gets shorter and shorter in the first case (column 1) and longer and longer in the second (column 2). The first column is an example of *negative* (stabilizing) *feedback* and rational behavior—*rational* because it minimizes the time between food deliveries. The second column shows *positive* (destabilizing) *feedback*. The delay to food gets longer and longer, which is irrational. But notice that *the underlying process is the same in both cases*.

Pigeons actually behave in the way predicted by this incredibly simple model. Figure 8.3 shows an example.[15] When parameter k is less than k_{crit}, the feedback is negative, wait time declines to zero, and the behavior is "rational." But when k is greater than k_{crit}, the wait time increases without limit, and the behavior is therefore deemed "irrational." But—and this is the critical point—the *process* is the same in both cases. It's the environment, the schedule, that makes the difference.

Table 8.1 Successive wait times under two
RID schedules, one with a small multiplier
(*M* value) the other with a large. The wait
times are derived from equations in the text.

Schedule:	*M* =	*M* =
Parameter *k*	**0.2**	**4.0**
0.25	Wait **1**	Wait **2**
Initial wait	**10**	**10**
	3.000	12.500
	0.900	15.625
	0.270	19.531
	0.081	24.414
	0.024	30.518
	0.007	38.147
	0.002	47.684
	0.001	59.605

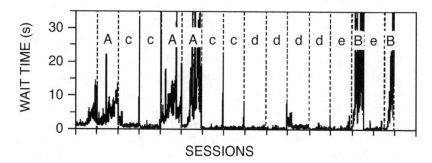

Figure 8.3 Wait time for a single pigeon in every interval throughout an experiment
with the adjusting RID schedule. Daily sessions are shown by the vertical
dashed lines (Wynne & Staddon, 1988, Figure 9). Parameter *k* was
different each day. Capital letters (A, etc.) show values of *k* that imposed
positive feedback; small letters (a, etc.) show values that imposed negative
feedback.

Maximizing vs. Model

Any choice situation—which is to say any situation, since choice is always involved—can be looked at in terms of optimizing or in terms of a model of the underlying choice process. Finding the optimum depends on two things: the goal, or the objective of his behavior, ("what is to be optimized"), and the constraints under which the agent must operate. To say, as the famous economist said, "[T]here is only one way to be perfectly rational," is to ignore uncertainty about the goal—"rational in terms of what?"—and the constraints—"how much do you know and what can you do about it?" On operant schedules with hungry animal subjects, the goal is simple: food, as much of it as possible. But when human action is involved, the goal will usually be much more complex and even uncertain—what is the purpose of education, for example, or art, or democracy, or the legal system? Yet without agreement on the goal, nothing meaningful can be said about the optimal means to achieve it.

The constraints are of two kinds: limitations on action and *cognitive* limitations—like the memory limitation that causes misbehavior on a RID schedule. For example, in a standard operant conditioning experiment, the subject is limited to pecking keys or pressing levers. But if the schedule requires a particular sequence of pecks, say LRLLRLLLRRR, to get food, the animal may fail simply because he can't remember such a complicated sequence. His problem is cognitive/computational, and not a physical inability to do what is required.

Human beings also have cognitive limits. Financial instruments—stocks, bonds, mortgage-backed securities—are nothing but complex reinforcement schedules. You buy one with the understanding that at time t with probability p you will be paid amount x (the reinforcer). One of the causes of the recent financial crash was the creation of financial instruments, derivatives, too complex to be understood by buyers. The complexity of credit default swaps, collateralized debt obligations and their like was intentional.[16] It allowed banks to take on huge amounts of risk that neither they nor their buyers understood. (However, the bankers understood at least this: They stood to win a lot, and the downside risk was likely to be borne by others!) Intentional complexification pervades the financial industry, especially at the highest levels. "Even with 40 years' experience in banking, I cannot fully understand the financial statements of Bank of America," writes one conservative banker.[17] After attempting to understand the annual report of Wells Fargo, a huge and well-regarded bank, two experts found it basically incomprehensible. It included "details about the bank's businesses that range from the incomprehensible to the disturbing,"[18] they report. None of this is accidental.

But sometimes complexity just evolves in a political system that lacks any real restraints. The result is a tax code that is currently around 72,000 pages, and the Federal Register—the code of all Federal regulations—which as of the time of writing was about 34,000 pages. No one can hope to comprehend such documents in their entirety. No one, therefore, can behave optimally—rationally—under the schedules they impose.

To understand how people deal with these complex contingencies, we need something like the models for operant behavior that I just discussed. Such an analysis would yield a prediction of the expected behavior given the schedule. We are, of course, a very long way from that in our discussions even of financial markets, where both the contingencies (financial instruments) and the reinforcer (money) are well defined. What we see instead are flawed analyses based on an ill-defined assumption of human rationality.

***

In some ways, the most revealing figure in Ferster and B. F. Skinner's seminal book is their schematic showing of how a pigeon learns a fixed-interval schedule (my Figure 4.4). It shows the transition from a simple law-of-effect process—a burst of pecking after each reinforcement—to the fixed-interval "scallop"—a wait followed by accelerating pecking until the next food. The figure tells us that learning involves *more than one process.* Psychologists (behaviorists too!) notoriously suffer from "physics envy." They want a single quantitative law to describe it all. But adaptive behavior is about *variation*—an "adaptive toolbox," as one theorist describes it.[19] Many laws/models, not one. Recall that credit assignment seems to involve a number of systems in parallel that are selectively strengthened by contiguity with a reinforcer. That's a prototype for how learning works. A multiplicity of systems running more or less in parallel—the *variation* of the Darwinian metaphor—that are *selected* from by cues like contiguity. Sometimes the available variation allows for behavior that maximizes payoff. But sometimes variation is insufficient or contiguity is an inadequate cue (as in any situation involving delayed reward), and the organism fails to do as well as possible. The organism is not "rational" in the first case and "irrational" in the second. Once we really understand what is happening, "rationality" plays no part in the account.

Notes

1. Basu, K. (2007, May 20). The traveler's dilemma. *Scientific American.* Basu is Chief Economist at the World Bank and also a professor at Cornell University. See also Basu, K. (1994). The traveler's dilemma: Paradoxes of rationality in game theory. *The American Economic Review, 84*(2), 391–395.
2. See http://en.wikipedia.org/wiki/Prisoner's_dilemma.
3. Also called *gradient ascent.* See http://en.wikipedia.org/wiki/Hill_climbing.
4. See my *The malign hand of the markets* (McGraw-Hill, 2012), Chapter 3: "The words 'efficiency' and 'rationality' are barriers to clear thinking about markets because they suggest a level of objective knowledge that does not exist. Market 'efficiency' is meaningless without an independent measure of value."
5. Paul Krugman, paraphrased in a biographical article by Larissa MacFarqhar, *New Yorker,* March 1, 2010.
6. Staddon, J. E. R., & Motheral, S. (1978). On matching and maximizing in operant choice experiments. *Psychological Review, 85*, 436–444; Baum, W. (1981). Optimization and the matching law as accounts of instrumental behavior. *Journal of the Experimental Analysis of Behavior, 36*, 387–403.

7. One experiment that tried explicitly to demonstrate an effect of a molar independent variable failed to do so: Ettinger, R. H., Reid, A. K., & Staddon, J. E. R. (1987). Sensitivity to molar feedback functions: A test of molar optimality theory. *Journal of Experimental Psychology: Animal Behavior Processes, 13*, 366–375. Retrieved from http://webs.wofford.edu/reidak/Pubs/Ettinger,%20Reid,%20and%20 Staddon%201987.pdf.

    But see also Williams, B. A. (1991). Choice as a function of local versus molar reinforcement contingencies. *Journal of the Experimental Analysis of Behavior, 56*, 455–473.

8. But with infrequent preference shifts after the occasional long run of nonreinforcement on the preferred side.

9. This conclusion depends on parameter values: The downshift must be relatively small relative to the upshift to get these effects, but choice data seem to support such a difference.

10. Horner, J. M., & Staddon, J. E. R. (1987). Probabilistic choice: A simple invariance. *Behavioural Processes, 15*, 59–92. Retrieved from http://dukespace.lib.duke.edu/dspace/handle/10161/3231.

11. Simon, H. A. (1992). *Economics, bounded rationality and the cognitive revolution* (Brookfield, VT: Edward Elgar).

12. Shimp, C. P. (1966). Probabilistically reinforced choice behavior in pigeons. *Journal of the Experimental Analysis of Behavior, 9*(4). Retrieved from www.ncbi.nlm.nih.gov/pmc/articles/PMC1338246/pdf/jeabehav00168–0134.pdf; Rachlin, H., & Laibson, D. I. (Eds.). (1997). *The matching law: Papers in psychology and economics* (Cambridge, MA: Harvard University Press); see also Staddon, J. E. R. (1988). Quasi-dynamic choice models: Melioration and ratio-invariance. *Journal of the Experimental Analysis of Behavior, 49*, 303–320. Retrieved from www.ncbi.nlm.nih.gov/pmc/articles/PMC1338815/.

13. A version of this procedure was first reported in Shull, R. L. (1970). A response-initiated fixed-interval schedule of reinforcement. *Journal of the Experimental Analysis of Behavior, 13*, 13–15. Retrieved from www.ncbi.nlm.nih.gov/pmc/articles/PMC1333651/pdf/jeabehav00145–0015.pdf.

14. A little algebra shows that the critical value for k is $k_{crit} = (1 - M)/M$. If k is less than that, the feedback is negative, and t gets smaller and smaller; if greater, t rises without limit (positive feedback). For the values in the table, the critical value is $k = 3$.

15. Wynne, C. D. L., & Staddon, J. E. R. (1988). Typical delay determines waiting time on periodic-food schedules: Static and dynamic tests. *Journal of the Experimental Analysis of Behavior, 50*, 197–210. Retrieved from www.ncbi.nlm.nih.gov/pmc/articles/PMC1338868/.

16. See, for example, my *The malign hand of the markets,* Chapter 10, and Silver, N. (2012). *The signal and noise: Why so many predictions fail—but some don't* (New York: Penguin), Chapter 1.

17. Allison, J. A. (2013). *The financial crisis and the free market cure: Why pure capitalism is the world economy's only hope* (New York: McGraw-Hill).

18. Partnoy, F., & Eisinger, J. (2013, January 1). What's inside America's banks? *The Atlantic,* pp. 60–71. http://csinvesting.org/wp-content/uploads/2013/02/What-is-inside-Americas-Banks1.pdf.

19. Gigerenzer, G., & Selten, R. (Eds.). (2001). *Bounded rationality: The adaptive toolbox* (Cambridge, MA: MIT Press).

9   Truth, Science and Behaviorism

"Behaviorism is not the science of human behavior; it is the philosophy of that science," wrote B. F. Skinner in *About Behaviorism*.[1] The Darwinian metaphor, which Skinner applied only half-heartedly to operant conditioning in animals, was put to full philosophical use in his *evolutionary epistemology* (EE). EE plays a key role in Skinner's unabashedly utopian ideas. He made some jaw-dropping epistemological claims—claims that allowed him to extrapolate without restraint from laboratory to society. In an early discussion of the philosophical basis for behaviorism, for example, he wrote:

> If it turns out that our final view of verbal behavior invalidates our scientific structure from the point of view of logic and truth-value, then so much the worse for logic, which will also have been embraced by our analysis.[2]

This bit of hubris should have been received with guffaws, but apparently went unchallenged. As George Orwell possibly said some years earlier, "There are some ideas so absurd that only an intellectual could believe them." Skinner had no hesitation in asserting the hegemony of radical behaviorism over every other type of human knowledge, even logic, the most certain.

Skinner was not a professional philosopher and avoided philosophical debate. His philosophy must usually be inferred; it is rarely explicit. As philosopher Stephen Stich has pointed out, Skinner's writings slip seamlessly between science (the facts and methods of operant conditioning) and radical behaviorism, the underlying philosophy of that science.[3] Nevertheless, we can identify three key themes: knowledge and value as the products of evolution, the illusion of free will and the radical behaviorist view of mental life. This chapter looks at knowledge.

Knowledge and Evolutionary Epistemology

Evolutionary epistemology is the notion that *knowledge* is entirely a product of our evolutionary history. *Truth* is what worked in evolution—"successful working," as some Skinnerians put it.[4] Evolutionary epistemology is thus a variant of pragmatism, the philosophy elaborated by brilliant but grumpy (he suffered from chronic neuralgia) philosopher and logician Charles Sanders Peirce (1839–1914) and promoted by his colleague and sponsor, psychologist-philosopher William James (Chapter 1).

"Thirty years ago, pragmatism was dead beyond all hope of resurrection," wrote a reviewer in 1999.[5] But it has revived, in more than one form. Political pragmatism was summarized in 1998 by disgraced presidential adviser Dick Morris in the aphorism, "Truth is that which cannot be proved wrong." (Politics has not improved since.) Cynical, and obviously false in general since we may be unable to disprove any of several mutually incompatible theses, yet all cannot be true. The nuanced pragmatist must allow for three truth categories—probably true, probably false—and "don't know," to accommodate Mr. Morris.

So what is "truth"? For all varieties of pragmatism, truth equals functional utility—truth is what works. I'll expand on "works" in a moment. Evolutionary epistemology adds the phylogenetic dimension: what works, yes, but not just during your lifetime—also during the lifetimes of your ancestors.[6]

Everything we appear to know (says EE) is the outcome of millions of years of natural selection and thousands of years of cultural selection. An essential feature of evolution by natural selection is that it is *contingent,* it depends on both *chance* and *necessity* in biologist Jacques Monod's memorable phrase[7]—on the vagaries of variation and the steady push of selection. This means that nothing is *certain*—not logic, not the hand in front of your face, not the tree you see through the window. Thus, our belief in logic is strong not because logic is "true" in some essential, Platonic sense, but because those individuals and cultures that failed to believe in logic lost out in the struggle to reproduce. We believe in tables and chairs, in other people, and in their minds, not because these things are true either, but because such beliefs have been effective in the battle of life. "Truth" is not absolute. We say that something is "true" not because it really is, but simply because it has survived in a quasi-Darwinian struggle for intellectual existence. Just like Skinner's (mistaken) version of the pigeon in the autoshaping experiment, we may believe in "superstitions" if the right variant (idea) fails to occur. If no one has the idea that the Earth circles the sun, rather than the other way around, the consequences of that idea cannot be tested and it cannot prevail—and, like Skinner's pigeon, we will misbelieve.

If the "correct" idea does not occur, it cannot be selected, so that what occurs will not represent the world accurately. A consistent evolutionary epistemologist would go on (as D. T. Campbell did) to contend that our value systems and religious beliefs have also survived a Darwinian history and should on that account be granted some degree of "truth." But this step is rarely taken, for reasons I'll explore later.

One more thing about evolutionary epistemology: Although it denies us access to absolute truth, it does believe one thing that cannot be proved. It does have faith—in the existence of some more or less stable "external reality" within which natural selection can take place.[8] There has to be something that does the selecting, and the assumption is that that "something" has fixed properties. This belief in a fixed external reality is, and must be, just that: a belief, not something provable as fact.[9] It is nevertheless a belief that can be justified in several ways. First, it is (I would argue) essential to the normal activities of science. Absent any belief in reality, the usual scientific tests lose their power to convince. After all, if the laws of nature can change capriciously from day to day; why should any test be decisive? Second, if there is no truth, contentious issues of fact will be decided by politics or force: "[T]he idea that there is no such thing as objective truth . . . [is] closely linked with authoritarian and totalitarian ideas," wrote philosopher Karl Popper,[10] paraphrasing Bertrand Russell. Perhaps the best-known expression of this fear is George Orwell's dystopian novel *1984*, with its Ministry of Truth falsifying history and bending reality to the needs of the Party. Orwell and Popper were right to be alarmed, as the genocidal histories of the Soviet Union, Nazi Germany and Maoist China have proved in blood and terror.[11]

Nevertheless, some thinkers have proposed that we give up the idea of truth. In its place they propose locutions such as "relatively permanent beliefs" or "consensually agreed beliefs." These substitutes are unsatisfactory. Consensus is an unreliable guide to truth. The Earth-centered universe and the theory of the four humors both received almost universal assent for many years. There is a better criterion than popularity. For science, the point of evolutionary epistemology is just that the "truth" of any proposition *is relative to the challenges it has successfully met.* Thus, an unquestioned belief is likely to be less "true" than one that has emerged unscathed from a variety of tests pitting it against alternatives. On the other hand, a longstanding belief, even if it has not been— or cannot be—explicitly tested, is more likely to be "true" than something you just thought of: *veritas temporis filia*. The test of time is worth something. But the fact that people agree on something adds little if it has never been challenged by any alternative. Persistence and consensus are only indirectly related to truth, as EE views it.

There are a few beliefs, like the laws of logic or arithmetic, the belief that the chair I am sitting in is real, and so on, that survive every conceivable test. Such beliefs are the best kind of truth we have. When we ask of some new proposition "Is it true?" all we mean is (says my version of EE), "Will it be as resistant to disproof as the laws of logic?" In effect, those beliefs that are most resistant to disproof become the standard by which the truth of others is judged. Since this is how scientists are supposed to judge truth anyway, evolutionary epistemology poses no threat to traditional foundations of science. Evolutionary epistemology in fact entails no real change in what scientists do, or even in what they believe, despite the attacks of the relativists.

Truth? Not True!

Skinnerian radical behaviorism is cited with approval by more than one fan of the "postmodern aesthetic,"[12] and there are indeed similarities between the views of Skinner and some Skinnerians and proposals of postmodernists/deconstructionists and relativists such as Foucault, Derrida and Latour.[13]

Skinner certainly believed in a stable reality, which is the subject of science, but he was also skeptical of reason and objectivity. In short, his views are contradictory.[14] The postmodern star is no longer in the ascendant, but it shone brightly over the humanities for a couple of decades. How seriously should we take it?

The postmodernist attack on the idea of truth is so contorted and on-its-face absurd that it is hard to know how to tackle it in a civil fashion, although a few have tried.[15] The most obvious objection is that it is self-refuting: Is it *true* that there is no such thing as truth? This proposition is either true or false. If it is true, then the proposition is false. If it is false, then we can ignore it. Case closed. Like the famous "class of all classes that are not members of themselves: Is it a member of itself?" the proposition reduces to paradox. As C. S. Lewis put it in a slightly different context, by arguing against truth, philosophers are cutting off the branch they are sitting on. Relativists disagree, of course, but most decline to debate the issue.

One of the few to take up the challenge is Skinner-influenced relativist Barbara Herrnstein Smith. Smith addresses the self-refutation problem in a chapter "Unloading the Self-Refutation Charge" (note her studied substitution of "unloading" for the more natural "refuting").[16] If we grant her that no proposition—no empirical proposition at any rate—is *certainly* true or false, the issue then becomes: What does it mean for one theory or proposition to be *better* or *worse* than another? Smith argues that "the common and unshakable conviction that differences of 'better' and 'worse' must be objective" is a fallacy.

> The supposed relativist [says] that her point is, precisely, that theories . . . can be and are evaluated in *other* non-'objective' ways. Not all theories are equal because they . . . can be, and commonly will be, found better or worse than others in relation to measures such as applicability, coherence, connectability and so forth. These measures are not objective in the classic sense, since they depend on matters of perspective, interpretation and judgment, and will vary under different conditions.

She concludes, "Thus theories, judgments, or opinions . . . may still be seen as better or worse even though not, in a classic sense, as more or less objectively valid."[17]

Smith introduces this chapter by positioning "relativism," "postmodernism," and so on, as "diverg[ing] from . . . philosophical orthodoxy"; relativists are "philosophical innovators," "demonized" by the opposition as "communally perilous" and "morally criminal." Who could be against victimized-but-innovative critics of orthodoxy? Yet what is proposed is a great deal less revolutionary than this rhetoric leads us to suppose. What Smith seems to be saying is that some theories are better than others; but the criteria by which we make these judgments are not themselves absolute, but vary depending on "perspective," "interpretation," and so on. This does not differ from pragmatism, as I have presented it: (Our belief in) the truth of a proposition is relative to the tests it has undergone. And no working scientist, or historian of science, would deny that our test criteria are far from immutable. They differ from school to school and evolve as a discipline develops.

How the "Scientific Method" Evolves

Here is a contemporary example of how standards evolve. There are thousands of published research studies every year purporting to show a curative effect of some new drug. But do they? A 2011 *Wall Street Journal* article[18] listed a slew of such "breakthroughs," reported in prestigious peer-reviewed scientific journals like *Nature, Science* and *The Lancet,* that *could not be replicated* by pharmaceutical companies that would like to profit from them.

The author cites a number of possible reasons for these failures: increased competition to publish, the proliferation of scientific journals, differing details among attempts to replicate—and fraud. But these possibilities seem inadequate to account for the prevalence of this problem, which looks like a breakdown of the scientific method. Why do so many drugs that are apparently effective in one study fail to hold up in others?

One big problem is bias in favor of publishing positive results. Unless there is already overwhelming reason to believe a drug will have an effect, a study reporting that it has no effect is not too newsworthy. Unless a negative result contradicts some widely accepted belief, it's not news. Nor will a commercial drug firm wish to save its competitors the time and money involved in testing a new drug they already know to be ineffective.[19] Conversely, a result that contradicts received wisdom will also make reviewers less willing to believe it, so it may not be published for that reason as well. Such a study is unlikely to be done, and if done is unlikely to be accepted for publication. There are many reasons why negative results have a hard time seeing the light of day.

But there is another factor that, taken together with the bias in favor of positive results, can account for the large number of failures to repeat results reported in respected scientific journals. This sentence gives a clue: "Statistically, the studies were very robust," says one scientist, describing a study that nevertheless failed to replicate. All these studies rely on statistics,[20] on comparison between a control and an experimental group, to establish their effects. A "robust" result is not robust as it might be in physics or engineering—or single-subject operant conditioning—because you can't just keep repeating the experiment to see if you get the same result again and again. Clinical trials are now very expensive. The cost of developing a new drug has risen from $100 million in 1975 to $1.3 billion in 2005.[21] Trials are rarely repeated, largely for this reason. Resources, ethics and a host of other practical considerations mean that each test is usually done just once, with a limited set of subjects, and then statistics are used to see if the difference between controls and experimentals is real or not.

The significance level used to establish "robustness" is typically 5%. That is to say, a result is accepted as real (= publishable) if statistics show that if the study were to be repeated many times, and if the control and experimental groups do not in fact differ (i.e., the drug has no effect), then no more than 5% of the differences between the two groups would be as large as what was observed in the study that was actually done. In other words, the probability of a "false positive" is no more than one in twenty.

So perhaps as many as 5% of published studies will not be replicable? Well, no, the actual number will be much larger. To see why, imagine a hundred hypothetical studies testing a hundred different drugs. Let's stipulate that for 20% of them there is a real effect of the drug. For some small percentage of these "real" effects, the outcome will nevertheless fail to reach the 5% significance level. Let's ignore these and assume that 100% of real effects show up as significant; that's twenty out of the one hundred. What about the failures, the eighty studies where there is no real effect? Well, sticking with the 5% significance-level criterion, we can expect that 5% of them—four—will show up as positive even though the drug is really ineffective. These are the 5% false positives. So seventy-six will show up (correctly) as negative. How many of these seventy-six will be published? Well, for the reasons I just gave, essentially none. So we are left with: a total of twenty-four studies (20 + 4) showing a positive effect of a drug, but of these twenty-four, four, nearly 17% of the total, will be false. So, given the understandable bias in publishing positive results, and the accepted 5% significance level, the number of published studies that are false, the result of experimental variability, not real effects, will be much larger than 5%.

The number of published false positives obviously depends on the proportion of ineffective drugs that are tested. For example, if only 5% of experimental drugs tested are actually effective, 95% will be ineffective. Thus, the number of false positives rises from four in the previous example to nearly five, and the number of correct positives falls from twenty to five. Result: Almost 49% of published studies will be unreplicable. Bayer reported in 2012 that *two-thirds* of its attempts to replicate failed.[22] This is not an academic issue.

Paradoxically, the wider researchers cast their net, the more compounds they actually investigate, the worse the replicability problem will become. On the order of 10,000 compounds are tested for every one found to be effective. Given this number of failures, the number of statistical false positives is also certain to be very large.

This problem applies to any branch of science that uses between-group statistical comparisons.[23] Experimental psychologists have been aware of the problem for several decades,[24] although practices have changed little until recently. There is beginning to be some movement;[25] I suggest below why it has been snail-like. As studies proliferate—perhaps because more money goes into science and experimenters become less choosy about their topics—there is a danger that the "signal" loses out to the "noise" as the proportion of "false positives" increases. The data in most social-science, between-group studies are generally quite bad—so variable that the temptation to engage in what might be called "low-level fraud"—massaging data, excluding outliers (always for good reason), choosing statistical methods that "work" (i.e., yield a 5% significant result)—is strong. Strong enough that one researcher has been able to identify studies that are *too* good, where replications are better than the variability of the data seem to warrant.[26]

One solution is to recognize that there is nothing magical about the 5% significance level. It has no scientific basis. It is in fact completely arbitrary. It would help, therefore, to set the standard for publication much higher, let's say 0.1% significance, which would reduce the errors (false positives) in my example from four to less than one. At a stroke, the flood of scientific papers, many of them questionable, will be reduced to a manageable flow, the number of unreplicable results will be massively reduced, and much wasted labor examining small or negligible effects will be eliminated.

But whatever value we set for the publishable level of significance will be arbitrary. What is more, there is a logical flaw at the heart of the significance-test method: Proving that a given experimental result is very unlikely if the null hypothesis (no difference) is correct is emphatically not the same as proving that there really is a difference between the two experimental conditions. As I just explained, the probability that a drug will in fact cure (just 33%, according to Bayer), given a significant trial result, is emphatically not the same as the probability of a significant result given that the drug does work (close to 100%). The problem with the standard method is that it mistakes the finger for the moon: "It views uncertainty as something intrinsic to the experiment rather than something intrinsic to our ability to understand the real world."[27]

There is a principled way to deal with this problem that has been around for more than 200 years. It is due to Thomas Bayes (1701–1761) an English Presbyterian minister and mathematician (he defended Newton's calculus against the criticisms of Irish idealist philosopher and cleric George Berkeley). In an account published after his death, Bayes pointed out a way to incorporate what are called "priors" into estimates of statistical probability. The priors, in the case of drug tests, are just the (in this case known) probability that any new compound, chosen at random, will really have a therapeutic effect and the probability that the effect may occur on its own without any drug. If only 1 in 10,000 compounds tested proves to be effective, the first prior for a new compound is very low. This means that the evidence from a test must be very strong to warrant a positive conclusion.

Nate Silver, in his excellent account of Bayes's method,[28] uses the example of the 9/11 attack. How likely was it, he asks after the second plane crashed into the tower, that a terrorist attack was happening? The evidence was very strong—a second plane—and the conclusion that it was an act of terrorism was therefore conclusive, even though the initial prior probability—of an accidental crash of a commercial airliner into a New York skyscraper on a clear day—was almost zero.

But if the experimental evidence is in fact weak, as it usually is, then a very low prior will mean that the increase in our confidence in the drug from a single test should be small—much smaller than the usual "yes, it is significant (at the 5% level). The drug works!"

Bayes's method works like this. You need three probabilities related to the experiment being evaluated:

1. probability of a positive result from a random drug, prior #1: p_0.
2. probability of a positive result in this experiment: q.
3. probability of a positive result if nothing is done (i.e., spontaneous cure), prior #2: m.

The first probability is the very low 1 in 10,000 or so probability that any old drug will be effective: $p = 0.0001$. The second probability is the result of your experiment. If it is significant at the 5% level, the probability is $q = 0.95$. The third probability is the presumably small chance of a spontaneous cure, say $m = 0.01$. These all then go into Bayes's theorem:

$$p_1 = \frac{p_0 q}{p_0 q + m(1 - p_0)},$$

where p_1 is the revised estimate of the effectiveness of the drug. With the numbers I have given, this yields $p_1 = 0.0094$, up from the even lower prior of 0.0001. Increasing p_0 from 1 in 10,000 to 1 in 1,000 just increases y to about 9%, still far from conclusive proof of the effectiveness of the new drug. Given the fact that all drugs have some side effects, my guess is that you would want at least a 50% chance that the new drug is effective before adopting it. In other words, this single experiment, with its weak significance level, is likely to add little to our faith in the effectiveness of the new drug. It should not be enough to propel it to market.

So why don't researchers use the Bayesian method? One reason is just the difficulty of estimating the prior probability, p_0. Now that we know roughly how many drugs have been tried and how many have proven effective, we can get at this number for drug trials. Not so for the hypotheses tested in between-group experiments of other kinds. There is no easy way to estimate the priors there. So Bayesian analysis is uncertain and difficult to understand. Conventional significance testing, on the other hand, is an algorithm—just follow the rules and you'll get a yes/no result.

But the main reason the Bayesian method is almost never used is probably sociological, not scientific. Bayesian analysis will yield a much lower level of confidence in most experimental results than the standard method. The alternative, using the standard method but requiring a low significance level like 0.1% would also mean that very few statistical studies would make it. The real basis for the usual method and the 5% level seems to be that it allows earnest tenure/grant/promotion seekers, with a reasonable amount of work, to achieve a publishable result. Even if their treatments really have no effect, one in twenty times they will get something publishable. A little work and all shall have prizes!

Parenthetically, notice the disparity in publication rates between the two subfields of experimental animal-learning research. The number of publications using the between-groups, significance-test method (usually termed "associative learning") now far exceeds the number of those using single animals (operant conditioning). The reason is not that the first method is better science than the second. The reason is that, given a reasonable amount of effort, it guarantees a publishable result.

But real science is a story of percipience, persistence and failure. All the great discoveries involve either accident, like Becquerel and radioactivity and Fleming and penicillin, or incredible persistence in the face of repeated failure, like Skinner's evolution of the Skinner box and discovery of reinforcement schedules (Chapter 3), Mendel's experiments with peas or, to go a little further back, Humphry Davy's dozens of experiments that finally ended with his identification of the elements sodium and potassium.[29] In any event, the drug-test story shows that our methods for evaluating scientific "truth" are, and must always be, evolving. If that is the point of science critics like Herrnstein Smith, few will disagree.

The same is true for the evaluation of scientific theory. Types of theory also evolve. Again, emulating physics is part of the problem in psychology. Everyone is impressed by the fact that quantum mechanics, incomprehensible to most and bizarre even to those most familiar with it, can nevertheless make predictions accurate to fourteen decimal places. Hence much of quantitative theoretical psychology is concerned with fitting quantitative models to data curves. Yet, aside from Weber's law and a handful of others, there may be no general laws in psychology comparable to those in physics. The most important theory in biology, evolution by natural selection, makes very few predictions and none of them are quantitative. The same is true for the science of behavior. What we have is not quantitative precision, but variation, the adaptive toolbox. Testing theory like this involves not curve fitting but qualitative comparison of the range of behaviors observed versus those encompassed by theory. The discussion in Chapter 8 of three approaches to explaining choice experiments is an example, but little research of this sort has been done.

Causation and Truth

Relativism is also subject to a more subtle error, that once you know the causes of a belief, it is drained of truth-value. There is an old Columbia University *Jester* cartoon from the heyday of Skinnerian influence that shows a rat pressing a lever in a Skinner box. "Boy have I got this guy conditioned!" the rat explains to his companion, "Every time I press the lever he gives me a pellet!" The relativist, and the Skinnerian, would say, "No, Mr. Rat, your belief is mistaken. You are simply responding as your history of reinforcement dictates." In other words, they argue that because they know the *process* by which the behavior came about, the behavior—belief—is, if not false, at least irrelevant.

But, as human beings, with a more comprehensive—privileged—worldview than the rat, we know that Mr. Rat's belief is in fact largely correct. The apparatus, if not the experimenter, is indeed "conditioned" to present a pellet every time the bar is pressed. And the way the rat "knows" this is via its history of reinforcement. In short, not only does knowing the process *not* invalidate the belief, it is the reason and justification for the belief. It is only in this rather obvious sense that science is "socially constructed." It by no means justifies the statement (a commonplace in postmodernism) that "[i]t has thus become increasingly apparent that physical 'reality,' no less than social 'reality,' is at bottom a social and linguistic construct; that scientific 'knowledge,' far from being objective, reflects and encodes the dominant ideologies and power relations of the culture that produced it."[30] Truth-value and "reinforcement history" are not antithetical; one is the product of the other. That doesn't mean a belief will always be correct. A super-Spock who bears the same relation to us as we do to the rat would no doubt find us often subject to "superstitions." But not always; nor would he be immune from the perspective of a still "higher" being. In short, some beliefs are better than others because they are truer. And we know they are truer because they pass (or have passed) our tests better. That's what *truth* means.

I think that Skinner would agree: "The truth of a statement of fact is limited to the sources of the behavior of the speaker. . . . A scientific law is . . . limited by the repertoires of the scientists involved."[31] When truth is defined in this way, there is no contradiction between tracing a belief to a particular "reinforcement history" and evaluating it as true or false. Some histories—those that involve test and evaluation—lead to true beliefs; others lead to beliefs that are either false or of unknown truth-value. Joe may believe the end of the world is nigh because he drank too much and saw it in a stupor; astronomer Janet may believe the same thing because she just measured the velocity of an approaching asteroid. Both beliefs are products of particular histories. But some histories are better than others.

Notes

1. Skinner, B. F. (1976). *About behaviorism* (New York: Vintage Books), p. 3. See also Malone, J. C., Jr., & Cruchon, N. M. (2001). Radical behaviorism and the rest of psychology: A review/précis of Skinner's *About Behaviorism*. *Behavior and Philosophy, 29*, 31–57.
2. Final sentence in Skinner, B. F. (1961/1945). The operational analysis of psychological terms. In *Cumulative record,* 2nd ed. (New York: Appleton-Century-Crofts), p. 282.
3. Catania, A. C., & Harnad, S. (1988). *The selection of behavior. The operant behaviorism of B. F. Skinner: Comments and consequences* (Cambridge: Cambridge University Press), p. 361.
4. Hayes, S. C. (1993, September). Why environmentally based analyses are necessary in behavior analysis. *Journal of the Experimental Analysis of Behavior, 60*(2), 461–463.
5. Ryan, A. (1999). Review of M. Dickstein (Ed.), *The revival of pragmatism: New essays on social thought, law, and culture (post-contemporary interventions)* (Durham, NC: Duke University Press).
6. Evolutionary epistemology is discussed in D. L. Hull's (1988) *Science as a process* (Chicago: University of Chicago Press), and in Radnitzky, G., & Bartley, W. W.

(Eds.). (1993). *Evolutionary epistemology, rationality, and the sociology of knowledge* (Open Court); Tullock, G. (1966). *The organization of inquiry* (Durham, NC: Duke University Press), provides an excellent, short survey of the epistemology of science. For historical surveys, see Bertrand Russell's (1946) wonderful *History of Western philosophy* (London: Allen & Unwin), and J. Bronowski and B. Mazlish's (1960) excellent *The Western intellectual tradition: From Leonardo to Hegel* (New York: Harper and Row).

7. Monod, J. (1971). *Chance and necessity: An essay on the natural philosophy of modern biology* (New York: Knopf).

8. Staddon, J. E. R. (1993). Pepper with a pinch of psalt: A comment on contextualistic mechanism or mechanistic contextualism. *The Behavior Analyst, 16,* 245–250. Retrieved from www.ncbi.nlm.nih.gov/pmc/articles/PMC2733655/pdf/behavan00026–0115.pdf.

9. This is just philosopher David Hume's argument against induction in a slightly different guise.

10. Popper, K. R. (1962). *Conjectures and refutations: The growth of scientific knowledge* (New York: Basic Books), pp. 4–5.

11. See Jung Chang's (1992) wonderful book *The wild swans: Three daughters of China* (New York: Anchor) for a moving autobiographical account of one family's fate in Maoist China. Her story shows more clearly than any abstract argument the truly hideous consequences when a political system abandons objectivity for ideology.

12. Andresen, J. (1991). Skinner and Chomsky 30 years later or: The return of the repressed. *The Behavior Analyst, 14,* 49–60.

13. See, for example, Hayes, L. (1993). Reality and truth. In S. C. Hayes, L. J. Hayes, H. W. Reese, & T. R. Sarbin (Eds.), *Varieties of scientific contextualism* (Reno, NV: Context Press); Latour, B. (1993). *We have never been modern* (Cambridge, MA: Harvard University Press); Smith, B. H. (1997). *Belief and resistance: Dynamics of contemporary intellectual controversy* (Cambridge, MA: Harvard University Press); Moxley, R. (1999). The two Skinners: Modern and postmodern. *Behavior and Philosophy, 27,* 97–125.

14. See Barnes, D., & Roche, B. (1994, Spring). Mechanistic ontology and contextualistic epistemology: A contradiction within behavior analysis. *The Behavior Analyst, 17*(1), 165–168.

15. See, for example, Hacking, I. (1999). *The social construction of what?* (Cambridge, MA: Harvard University Press); and Zuriff, G. (1999). Against metaphysical social constructionism in psychology. *Behavior & Philosophy, 26,* 5–28.

16. Herrnstein Smith, B. (1997) *Belief and resistance: Dynamics of contemporary intellectual controversy* (Cambridge, MA: Harvard University Press).

17. Herrnstein Smith (1997), pp. 77–78.

18. Naik, G. (2011, December 2). Scientists' elusive goal: Reproducing study results. *Wall Street Journal.*

19. Drug firms are reluctant to publicize their own negative results. See, for example, "Battle heats up over drugs data," which reports a pushback by U.S. drug companies over a European Union effort to get them to share more test data (*Financial Times,* March 11, 2013).

20. See http://en.wikipedia.org/wiki/Statistical_hypothesis_testing#Origins_and_Early_Controversy.

21. See www.manhattan-institute.org/html/fda_05.htm.

22. See www.newscientist.com/article/mg21528826.000-is-medical-science-built-on-shaky-foundations.html.

The problem is even worse in cancer studies: [S]cientists . . . in the haematology and oncology department at the biotechnology firm Amgen in Thousand Oaks, California, tried to confirm published findings. . . . Fifty-three papers were deemed "landmark" studies. . . . It was acknowledged from the outset that some of the data might not hold up, because papers were deliberately selected that described something completely new, such as fresh approaches to targeting cancers or alternative clinical uses for existing therapeutics. Nevertheless, scientific findings were confirmed in only 6 (11%) of the cases.

Begley, C. G., & Ellis, L. M. (2012, March 29). Drug development: Raise standards for preclinical cancer research. *Nature, 483*, 531–533.

23. Young, N. S., Ioannidis, J. P. A., & Al-Ubaydli, O. (2008, October 1). Why current publication practices may distort science. *PLoS Medicine.* Retrieved from www.plosmedicine.org; Branch, M. N. (n.d.). Malignant side effects of null-hypothesis significance testing. Unpublished manuscript.

24. See, for example, Meehl, P. E. (1967). Theory testing in psychology and physics: A methodological paradox. *Philosophy of Science, 34*, 103–115; Meehl, P. E. (1987). Theoretical risks and tabular asterisks: Sir Karl, Sir Ronald, and the slow progress of soft psychology. *Journal of Consulting and Clinical Psychology, 46*, 806–834; Loftus, G. R. (1996). Psychology will be a much better science when we change the way we analyze data. *Current Directions in Psychological Science, 5*, 161–171; Krueger, J. (2001). Null hypothesis significance testing: On the survival of a flawed method. *American Psychologist, 56*, 16–26 [PubMed: 11242984]; Killeen, P. R. (2005). An alternative to null-hypothesis significance tests. *Psychological Science, 8*, 345–353.

25. See, for example, Pashler, H., & Wagenmakers, E.-J. (2012). Editors' introduction to the special section on replicability in psychological science: A crisis of confidence? *Perspectives in Psychological Science, 7*(6), 528–530.

26. Francis, G. (2013). Replication, statistical consistency, and publication bias. *Journal of Mathematical Psychology, 57,* 153–169. This article evoked several comments, which appear in the same issue of the journal.

27. Silver, N. (2012). *The signal and the noise: Why so many predictions fail—but some don't* (New York: Penguin Press).

28. Silver (2012), Chapter 8. See also http://en.wikipedia.org/wiki/Bayes'_theorem.

29. Well described in Harold Hartley's excellent biography, *Humphry Davy* (London: Nelson, 1966). A wonderful paper on this general topic is the late Richard Feynman's "Cargo Cult Science," adapted from his Caltech commencement address given in 1974. Available on the Internet at www.lhup.edu/%7EDSIMANEK/cargocul.htm and several other places.

30. This quote is not in fact from a postmodernist, but from New York University physicist Alan Sokal in a paper titled, "Transgressing the Boundaries: Towards a Transformative Hermeneutics of Quantum Gravity," which has become perhaps the most famous academic hoax of the twentieth century. Sokal was upset by the misuse and misrepresentation of science by postmodernists, deconstructionists and the like. To demonstrate in irrefutable fashion the intellectual shoddiness of this movement, he constructed an article that shamelessly appealed to all their shibboleths and authority figures, while presenting an absurd argument. In his own words, "I decided to try a modest . . . experiment: Would a leading North American journal of cultural studies [*Social Text*] . . . publish an article liberally salted with nonsense if (a) it sounded good and (b) it flattered the editors' ideological preconceptions?" The answer was a deafening "yes"! The article was published without comment—indeed, without independent refereeing, which Sokal asked for, but didn't get. Nothing in the article is factually false; all the citations and quotations are accurate. Only the argument is nonsense, at a level that could be detected by an undergraduate physics major. What was the response of the deconstructionists? Not a decent embarrassment, but an attack on Sokal, an article in the *New York Times* by one of the noisier literati accusing Sokal of betraying a trust. Digging himself in deeper, this critic went on to compare the laws of science to the laws of baseball. See www.nytimes.com/books/98/11/15/specials/sokal-fish.html.

31. Skinner (1976), p. 150.

10   Free Will and Utopia

Free will is not a behavioristic or even a particularly psychological concept. It is a term from legal theory and moral philosophy. Yet it constantly intrudes into discussions of behaviorism[1] because of a fallacy. Before I get to the fallacy, let's look at a few examples. Where might a behaviorist see evidence of free will?

A company called iRobot[2] markets a gadget called a Roomba. Roomba is a robotic vacuum cleaner. When you turn it on, it moves about the room, retreating from walls and avoiding stairs, cleaning more on dirtier pieces of carpet, until it has covered the whole room. When its battery gets low, it goes back and sits on a charger. The question is, does Roomba have free will? Well, for the most part, Roomba's behavior is pretty predictable. It moves in straight lines until it either encounters an obstacle or finishes cleaning—or needs to recharge. And we know it is probably driven by a set of completely deterministic computer algorithms. So, most people would say no, of course Roomba doesn't have free will. They assume that if its behavior is predictable it must lack free will.

Well, what about a cockroach? It moves faster than Roomba and its track is less predictable; and we don't know exactly how it is "programmed," or even if it is. But it does react predictably in some situations. Enter the room or turn on a light and it will head for a dark corner, for example. It can learn the location of food or even to approach a bright light it would otherwise avoid.[3] Does a cockroach have free will? Maybe.

Finally, the humble rat. It moves unpredictably; it learns from experience. It will press a lever if leverpressing produces food; it will remember where it has found food in the past. Free will? Again, who knows?

The point is that *from a behavioristic point of view* the concept of free will is not only unnecessary, but it is also completely unverifiable. We can tell whether (we think) behavior is predictable. We can tell when it is under the control of a reinforcement schedule. But unless we are willing to equate unpredictability with free will and predictability with its absence, we cannot tell, just from studying an organism's behavior, whether it has free will or not.

B. F. Skinner thought otherwise: "Freedom is a matter of contingencies of reinforcement, not of the feelings the contingencies generate. The distinction is particularly important when the contingencies do not generate counterattack."[4]

Skinner implies, very unbehavioristically, that people may not be free even when they say they are—even when they make no attempt to escape from their situation. But then, how do you know? He claims first that schedules of negative reinforcement (punishment) limit freedom in his sense. More on this later. He goes on to describe a number of situations where people are subjected to contingencies of positive reinforcement that also, he claims, limit their freedom: bribing farmers not to produce a crop the government decides is in surplus; lotteries that, some now say, are a "tax" on the gambling addicted and statistically challenged;[5] and finally paying prisoners to be subjects in hazardous medical experiments. Of these people, Skinner asks, "Are they really free?" even though positively reinforced? His implicit answer: no, not really. But unless we are to wander into the Marxist thickets of "false consciousness," surely the correct response to Skinner's question is: Just ask them. Who are we to say that the gambler is unfree, or the prisoner volunteer free? The gambler probably feels perfectly free; the prisoner may not. He is, after all, under as much constraint as those thousands of criminal defendants every year induced to agree to a plea bargain by a prosecutor's threat of massive new charges.[6] In both cases, the prisoner and the defendant, the positive reinforcement is positive only in the sense that "Your money or your life" offers "life" as a positive reinforcement. It is positive only because the subject is offered some relief while under overarching negative contingencies: death, harsh incarceration or the threat of worse punishment. The point is that we are under no obligation to accept Skinner's view of freedom over the view of the individuals involved.

So if free will is unknowable, why care about it? Moral philosophers care about it because, some have argued, without it people cannot be held responsible for their actions. The famous British political philosopher Isaiah Berlin (1909–1997), who wrote extensively about liberty, was quite clear:

> Berlin did not assert that determinism was untrue, but rather that to accept it required a radical transformation of the language and concepts we use to think about human life—especially a rejection of the idea of individual moral responsibility. To praise or blame individuals, to hold them responsible, is to assume that they have some control over their actions, and could have chosen differently. If individuals are wholly determined by unalterable forces, it makes no more sense to praise or blame them for their actions than it would to blame someone for being ill, or praise someone for obeying the laws of gravity. Indeed, Berlin suggested that acceptance of determinism—that is, the complete abandonment of the concept of human free will—would lead to the collapse of all meaningful rational activity as we know it.[7]

If your behavior is perfectly determined, then you should not be punished for it. Berlin wrote, quite mistakenly, I believe: "[I]t is not rational both to believe choices are caused, and to consider men as deserving of reproach or indignation (or their opposites) for choosing to act or refrain as they do."[8]

I will argue in more detail in later chapters that Berlin and Skinner were both wrong in opposing determinism and the appropriateness of praise and blame. The reason is simple. Praise and blame exist as human customs because they have predictable effects on our behavior. If, in a particular case, they cease to have the usual effects, then they have no point or purpose. The assumption of nondeterminism, Skinner's "autonomous man," is not only unnecessary for the concept of personal responsibility, it is also incompatible with it. Free will is a red herring.

Skinner and many other radical behaviorists equate free will with unpredictability. There are two problems with predictability. If can predict behavior, fine. But if you can't, you don't know if the behavior is just random, hence intrinsically unpredictable, of if you just haven't figured out the rule. Predictability is just code breaking. If I show you a series of 1,000 apparently random numbers, you will have to agree that they are indeed random—unless I tell you they are just digits 2,000 to 3,000 of the transcendental number π. They may look random, but they are in fact completely determined by the formula for π. You need to know the code. In other words, apparently unpredictable behavior may, or may not, be completely determined.

Underlying this issue a fact that is less well known than it should be, namely that in the black-box world, not everything about the box (its state at the beginning of the experiment, for example) can be discovered by an outside observer, even if the box itself is perfectly deterministic.[9] No matter how many experiments you do, no matter how many questions you ask, some systems will have secrets you cannot discover. In other words, even if behavior is in fact completely determined, we may not be able to discover how.

In addition, as I just pointed out, you may be able to predict a creature's behavior, but from that nothing about free will follows (some examples below). So we can leave free will out of Skinner's argument, which then reduces to: Your behavior is predictable, therefore you cannot be held responsible for your actions. This is almost the opposite of the truth. I'll say more about why in a moment, but first some comments on Skinner's utopian recommendations.

Designing Society

There are several varieties of behaviorism but only one, Skinner's radical behaviorism, has proposed to redesign society. He explained his plan first in a utopian novel, *Walden Two,* published in 1948.[10] The little fictional community of Walden Two has a constitution and is run by a "Board of Planners" and a bunch of specialists called "managers." The constitution and legislators can be changed via votes—of the citizens or the planners. All is presided over, in a fashion not made explicit, by the founder, a man called Frazier, who seems to have almost plenary powers. The relevant principles were expounded at length two decades later in a best seller called *Beyond Freedom and Dignity* (BFAD, 1971).

Skinner thought *Walden Two* an accomplishment comparable to two science-fiction classics: Aldous Huxley's *Brave New World* (1931) and George

Orwell's *1984* (1949). He assigned all three in his introductory psychology course at Harvard. There is some irony in Skinner's choice, because Orwell's and Huxley's novels are both *dystopias*. They portray not the supposed benefits of a technological approach to human society, but the evil consequences of either coercive (*1984*) or stealthy (*Brave New World*) efforts to control or gentle human beings. On the contrary, *Walden Two* is supposed to light the technological path to utopia.

A few communities, more or less modeled on Skinner's proposals, were set up in the United States and Mexico, but most have since folded.[11] There is still some interest in his utopian ideas[12] and both BFAD and *Walden Two* are still in print. Nevertheless, it would hardly be worth discussing these ideas at length, but for the fact that much modern social policy reflects them in some way or other. Longtime New York City mayor Bloomberg's belief that we can tame obesity by reducing the size of soft drink containers, or plans to improve people's decisions by adopting "opt-out" rather than "opt-in" default options for things like organ donation and payroll pension deductions, and other such measures suggested by the recent book *Nudge,*[13] are all reminiscent of Skinner's ideas in *Walden Two* (1948) and recommended explicitly in *Beyond Freedom and Dignity*:

> [I]t should be possible to design a world in which behavior likely to be punished seldom or never occurs. We try to design such a world for those who cannot solve the problem of punishment for themselves, such as babies, retardates, or psychotics, and if it could be done for everyone, much time and energy would be saved.[14]

In other words, rather than punish people for misbehavior, it would be better to bribe or trick them into doing the right thing. BFAD is a guidebook to non-coercive ways to get people to behave according to standards set by technical experts.

Skinner's Walden proposal is in a tradition that goes back to Plato's philosopher king: a "legislator" (monarch) and a set of guardians who are wiser than the common people. The guardians "are to be a class apart, like the Jesuits in old Paraguay, the ecclesiastics in the States of the Church until 1870 and the Communist Party in the U.S.S.R. at the present day [1946]."[15] Not too different from *Walden Two*'s Managers and Planners, and Frazier, Skinner's avatar and leader of the community. Skinner was quite explicit about the need for technocratic rule: "We must delegate control of the population as a whole to specialists—to police, priests, teachers, therapies, and so on, with their specialized reinforcers and their codified contingencies."[16]

Millenia after Plato, the idea that most people need wise, even manipulative, guidance from benevolent technocrats was embraced by intellectual elites in Europe and Great Britain and the progressive movement in the United States. Here, for example, is Maynard Keynes, British intellectual and probably the most influential economist of the past 100 years—his ideas are still being applied as a solution for the recent financial crisis. Keynes comments: "I believe . . . the right solution [to the economic questions of the day] will involve intellectual and scientific elements which must be above the heads of the vast mass of more or less illiterate voters." And: "It is, therefore, not inappropriate for economic managers to resort to sleight of hand or even mild deception in order to obtain the consent of the governed for essential actions."[17] Keynes's willingness to manipulate the populace was not limited to economic matters. He, along with a long list of British and American public figures, was also a fan of eugenics, serving as director of the British Eugenics Society, and writing that eugenics is "the most important, significant and, I would add, genuine branch of sociology which exists."[18] The North Carolina Eugenics Board (one among many in several states), which oversaw enforced sterilization of criminals and the mentally ill, remained in operation until 1977, but the laws that authorized it were not repealed until 2003. This is not ancient history. Eugenicists also advocated positive reinforcement—paying "unfit" women to undergo sterilization, for example. Less controversially, Lee Kwan Yew's Singapore in 1984 introduced a tax scheme that favored well-educated mothers, as a way to encourage them to have more children. But even this plan had to be abandoned because of the taint of eugenics. Skinner was of course not involved in eugenics, which fell right out of fashion after World War II and the Holocaust, but it is hard to see why he would have objected to some of its practices.

Skinner, apparently so groundbreaking in his plans to remake society, was in fact right in tune with the intellectual *zeitgeist*. This is one reason his ideas that, when examined closely, turn out to be either wrong, simplistic and paternalistic, not to say crypto-totalitarian, have proven to be surprisingly influential.

Skinner's ideas may have been popular, but he himself was not.[19] The title of *Beyond Freedom and Dignity*[20] is an open affront to Western liberal values (should we look for a subtitle: *Towards Slavery and Humiliation!*). BFAD certainly upset libertarian icon Ayn Rand.[21] As we've seen, Skinner also upset Noam Chomsky, at the opposite end of the political spectrum. Skinner basically offended everybody except technocrats and die-hard Skinnerians.[22] Nevertheless, his general approach, though unacknowledged, lives on in modern progressive policies. Why has it been so influential, and how good are the arguments on which it is based?

BFAD is a fascinating book because it is a thoroughgoing application of essentially medical principles to the organization of society.[23] The environment is everything. If a person misbehaves, let us look, says Skinner, first at how he was raised. What measures of what might be called "behavioral hygiene" might be applied to such individuals in the future to immunize society against this kind of thing? In the case of addictions—to drugs, alcohol or whatever—we should first ask whether there is a medical cause. But then, "[H]ow fair is it to punish the alcoholic?"[24] The two approaches are placed in opposition. How much better to find the right environment or the right medication, than to subject the hapless criminal to punishment, even torture! To underline his point,

Skinner quotes almost with relish a horrific description of public torture by the French philosophe Joseph de Maistre (1753–1821).[25]

Two passages from BFAD suggest Skinner's method. The book is concerned with the application of a "technology of behavior" to improve human society. Many traditional values seem to be in the way of this desirable outcome, but Skinner believed in a sort of historical inevitability, which ensures that they must give way before a behavioral analysis:

> In what we may call the prescientific view [Skinner adds disingenuously that "the word is not necessarily pejorative"!] a person's behavior is at least to some extent his own achievement. . . . [H]e is to be given credit for his successes and blamed for his failures. In the scientific view . . . a person's behavior is determined by a genetic endowment traceable to the evolutionary history of the species and by the environmental circumstances to which as an individual he has been exposed. Neither view can be proved, but it is in the nature of scientific inquiry that the evidence should shift in favor of the second.[26]

In this passage Skinner promotes a false opposition between the process by which a behavior comes about—"In the scientific view . . . a person's behavior is determined by a genetic endowment . . . and by the environmental circumstances to which . . . he has been exposed"—which is true; and the status of that behavior as responsible or not—"a person's behavior is . . . his own achievement. . . . [H]e is to be given credit for his successes and blamed for his failures"—which is also true. I say a bit more in a moment about why these two concepts, determinism and responsibility, are not contradictory at all.

Notice that Skinner's false opposition between responsibility and determinism is just like the relativists' false opposition between the truth of a belief and the process by which we arrive at the belief. Understanding the causal chain that led to an act need not diminish the responsibility of the actor any more than understanding the causes of a belief diminishes its truth. To do otherwise is to commit the *genetic fallacy*[27]—dismissing an argument because of its source, not its merits. British showgirl Mandy Rice-Davies, a major figure in the notorious Profumo scandal of 1962, pulled this trick quite effectively when she responded to Lord Astor's denial of an affair: "Well, he would say that wouldn't he!" The tactic often works.

Skinner also attacks punishment, "feelings" and above all, the concept of what he calls "autonomous man," which is his parody of the folk psychology idea of free will. I say "parody" because when you look at just what he means by autonomous man, few actually believe it. His attack on autonomy is at the core of his opposition to traditional morality:

> Two features of autonomous man are particularly troublesome. In the traditional view, a person is free. *He is autonomous in the sense that his behavior is uncaused.* He can therefore be held responsible for what he

does and justly punished if he offends. That view, together with its associated practices, must be re-examined when a scientific analysis reveals unsuspected controlling relations between behavior and environment.[28]

These passages lead the reader down two garden paths at once. First, he is led to believe that science will inevitably identify more and more environmental causes for human behavior. Behavior will become more and more predictable. This is possible; it is far from inevitable. Second, the passage advances a totally false opposition: that only "uncaused" behavior can be justly punished. In other words, personal responsibility is incompatible with determinism. I'll show why this is false in a moment, but let's look first at Skinner's argument.

Continuing his attack on autonomy, Skinner points to conventional discussions of "influences" on the lives of the great, and notes how commentators nevertheless seem to draw back from the natural conclusion: that *all* behavior is environmentally determined.

No one is greatly disturbed when important details of works of art and literature, political careers, and scientific discoveries are attributed to "influences" in the lives of artists, writers, statesmen, and scientists, respectively. But as analysis of behavior adds further evidence, the achievements for which a person himself is to be given credit seem to approach zero, and both the evidence and the science which produces it are then challenged.[29]

Of course, for every individual who goes on to greatness, aided by whatever details of his upbringing we care to discern, there are dozens with similar advantages who achieve little, and dozens more who achieve in the face of apparently insuperable odds. And most artists counted as "great" are notable for breaking away from influences that sway their contemporaries—Pablo Picasso is an obvious case. These counterexamples do not concern Skinner. But they are not the main problem with his analysis, as we'll see.

"Autonomous man" must be preserved by society, argues Skinner, for a variety of (false) reasons that he expounds later in the book. "Autonomous man survives in the face of all this because he is the happy exception. Theologians[30] have reconciled predestination with free will"[31]—but we shouldn't believe them. Skinner recognized that determinism and predestination are closely related, although determinism acts through genetics and personal history rather than through the agency of a Supreme Being. He claims that determinism and predestination threaten free will. But he offers no arguments. He simply assumes a particular solution to the problem, namely that determinism precludes personal responsibility.

He also assumes that conventional judicial practices, especially punishment for misdeeds, somehow depend upon the free-will assumption. *All* these assertions—perfect determinism, the implication that autonomy is a myth, and the supposed dependence of judicial practices on nondeterminism—are either questionable or false.

Determinism and Autonomy

Let's look first at determinism. Is it a fact? It clearly is not a fact *now*. At present, human behavior cannot be predicted with anything like the precision required. Determinism at the required level may never be achieved. For the moment, we can certainly ignore many of Skinner's societal recommendations on the grounds that the knowledge of human behavior he presupposes does not exist. We don't know enough. Nevertheless, we must admit that as science advances, our behavior may turn out to be predictable in detail by some super-psychology of the future. So we cannot avoid indefinitely the philosophical problem of reconciling determinism with traditional notions of freedom and responsibility. That reconciliation is perfectly possible. Let's look at some of the arguments that dissolve the opposition between determinism and individual responsibility.

Suppose, impoverished reader, that a generous investment banker, rich again after the crash of 2008, offers you a choice between two piles of cash: one with ten dollars, the other with one thousand. Under almost any foreseeable set of circumstances, I predict that you will choose the one-thousand-dollar pile. This is the level of predictability that Skinner promises us we shall eventually have for all behavior, not just choices between vastly disparate outcomes. So we can reasonably ask whether, in this simple situation, your autonomy has been destroyed. The answer, surely, is "obviously not" under any generally accepted notion of "freedom." This is an example of the fact that we can choose between rewards, but not choose what is rewarding: "Bertrand Russell once quipped that we can do as we please but not please as we please."[32] Skinner quotes Voltaire along the same lines.[33] In other words, we are free to choose the $1,000 or the $10. We are not as free to be indifferent to money.

Another example: Suppose you ask a mathematician "What is the square root of 1,024?" With perfect predictability he will answer "32." Has his autonomy been destroyed? Again, obviously not. Obedience to fact is not usually construed as a limitation on free will. A mathematician does not feel that the laws of arithmetic impinge on his freedom. Why is it that in these concrete cases there seems to be no conflict between predictability and autonomy, yet many people who read Skinner's arguments end up being convinced there is a problem?

Skinner's opposition between freedom and predictability is superficially persuasive because he tacitly conflates subject and object. Freedom is an entirely *subjective* concept—a man is free if he feels free. The sense of freedom is *Domain 1* in the scheme I describe in Chapter 16.

There is no place in Skinner's philosophy for *feelings,* of course, although he uses the word freely in BFAD. But this statement could be restated in a behavioristically acceptable form—"appropriate verbal behavior" and the like—if necessary. (See Chapter 16 for an extended discussion of the differences between subjective and objective.) *Predictability,* on the other hand, whether by oneself (predicting your own behavior) or by others, is an *objective* property. It simply has no bearing on the feeling of freedom. The husband whose behavior is completely predictable by his wife is no less free than the husband whose wife is constantly surprised. What's more, an individual who cannot predict his own behavior ahead of time is likely to feel *less* free, less autonomous, than someone who better "knows himself." So, if anything, the "feeling of freedom" is more likely to coexist with predictability than with caprice.

Assuming that he attaches some value to the "feeling of freedom," a good behaviorist would go on and ask, What are the environmental conditions that cause men to give expression to this feeling: When do men feel free? This, of course, is precisely the subject matter of the "literatures of freedom and dignity" that Skinner disparages, even as he disclaims any such intention: "The importance of the literature of freedom can scarcely be questioned. . . . [It] has made an essential contribution to the elimination of many aversive practices in government, religion, education, family life, and the production of goods."[34] Nevertheless, the thrust of the book is to question the traditional view of freedom. If there is no freedom, of what use is its literature?

The next paragraph gets to Skinner's main point: "Some traditional theories could conceivably be said to define freedom as the absence of aversive control, but the emphasis has been on how that condition *feels.*" "Freedom" *is* a feeling, of course, and when his guard is down, Skinner himself says things like individuals should "enjoy the greatest sense of freedom" and the like.

Moreover, "aversive control" is not always perceived as a limitation on freedom. You learn to skate in part by avoiding painful contact with the ice. But the pain is not usually perceived as a limitation on your freedom. You are not "punished" by the ice when you fall. Karl Marx's friend and patron Friedrich Engels once wrote that "[f]reedom is the recognition of necessity" but of course it all depends on what form the "necessity" takes. Submitting to gravity is one thing, but bowing to Stalin's NKVD quite another. The fact is that Skinner has confused determinism, which is an objective property of the observer in relation to what is observed, with freedom, which is a subjective property of the observed, inaccessible to the observer. Consequently, he is forced (contrary to my claim about the ice) to consider falling on a broken stairway a "natural punishing contingency."[35] More on punishment and how it depends on the predictability of behavior in Chapter 17 on behaviorism and the law.

Many of Skinner's philosophical errors derive from his often idiosyncratic use of language. His use of the word "control" is a particular problem. He often speaks of "control by the environment," "unsuspected controlling relations" and the like. "Control" for Skinner is essentially universal: "It is a mistake to suppose that the whole issue is how to free man. The issue is to improve the way in which he is controlled,"[36] the presumption being that man is always controlled by something. Skinner simply equates "control" with "determined" or "caused." But there are two senses of the word "control." One is indeed equivalent to cause, but the other is not: "Close reading reveals that [Skinner] routinely alternates between using the verb 'control' to mean cause and using it to mean regulate, which has quite a different sense."[37]

An example will help illustrate the difference. Imagine a NASCAR driver zooming around the track at Daytona. The driver turns the steering wheel and the road wheels turn. That is control, but it is also causation: Turning the steering *causes* the wheels to turn. The driver controls the car and causes it to move, start, stop, etc. The action of the driver is what is called an *efficient cause* of the movement of the wheels. Now imagine a helicopter, hovering above the track. The pilot observes the car following the curvature of the track as if on rails. He might say: "Look, the car (driver) is controlled by his environment. I can predict his course perfectly." Or, as Skinner might say, "A scientific analysis of behavior dispossesses autonomous man and turns the control he has been said to exert over to the environment."[38] There is a sense in which the track controls the movement of the car. If we know the track, we can predict the movement. The car follows the track—usually. So does the driver not control the car? Of course he does. If another vehicle should suddenly enter the track, the driver will swerve to avoid it. Environmental "control" involves feedback; it is control by consequences (which is one of Skinner's meanings for "control"), not control by antecedents. But the consequences act through a control system, which is in the driver and not the environment.

The track is not an efficient cause of the car's movement; it is what is called a final cause. Behavior that is determined in this way is completely different from behavior like reflexes (see Chapter 2), which are stimulus-response behavior that really does operate like (efficient) cause and effect. Again, an older terminology is in many ways more useful than Skinner's idiolect.[39] Reflexive, automatic behavior is involuntary, in the sense that the individual cannot control it. It makes no sense to reward or punish such behavior because reward and punishment have no effect on it.[40] But behavior like driving a car is voluntary. It may be predictable or unpredictable, but since it is controllable by reward and punishment, it obviously makes perfect sense to reward and punish it.

Walden Two and the Philosopher King

The two most famous aphorisms about government are *quis custodiet ipsos custodes*—who shall guard the guardians?—and Lord Acton's "[P]ower corrupts and absolute power corrupts absolutely." They both mean the same thing: Even a philosopher king is likely to do bad things if left long unrestrained. Public Choice Theory[41] is a branch of economics that has tried to understand the many ways in which the incentives of politicians and bureaucrats lead them to behave in ways contrary to the common good they are supposed to serve. Francis Fukuyama, who came to public notice with a happy but premature vision of a settled world of secular democracies in his 1992 book, *The End of History and the Last Man,* recently put the problem this way:

> Undoubtedly if you have competent and well-trained bureaucrats, or well-educated technical professionals who are dedicated to the public interest,

this kind of government is better than democratic government in the short term. Having a good emperor, however, doesn't guarantee that no bad emperor will emerge. There is no accountability system to remove the bad emperor if there is one. How can you get a good emperor? How can you make sure good emperors will reproduce themselves generation after generation? There is no ready answer.[42]

The major contribution of behaviorism to our understanding of society is what it can tell us about the effects of reward and punishment—incentives in the language of economics. Yet in Skinner's utopia, the effects of reinforcement are considered only in relation to the citizens, not in relation to the "king" (Frazier, in Walden Two). What are *his* reinforcers? How can we be sure that his successor has the same? The U.S. constitution was designed to take care of this problem through "checks and balances"—periodic elections, term limits, veto and filibuster power and so on. Political philosopher Edmund Burke (1729–1797) made a similar comment about the British constitution:

> [T]he genius of the British constitution is precisely that it creates a mixed polity, in which monarchy, Lords and Commons divide power between them, and set boundaries to each other. The popular will is not unfettered, therefore: the constitution binds the people just as surely as it binds the other estates of the realm.[43]

Neither the British nor the American systems work perfectly. But at least they address the problem of "unfettered" power. Utopias like Plato's Republic and Skinner's Walden Two are designed as if the problem does not exist. It does.

In Chapter 17, I discuss in detail how Skinner's muddled view of causation affected his views on law and justice. I will show that the controllability (in Skinner's sense) of behavior does not rule out judicial punishment. On the contrary, it is essential to its effectiveness. Skinner's odd epistemology has led to flawed recommendations that have had some unfortunate effects on modern society. But first I need to say something about *values:* what's it all *for.*

Notes

1. See, for example, William Baum's (2005). *Understanding behaviorism,* 2nd ed. (Blackwell). But Skinner (1971) was first, in *Beyond freedom and dignity* (New York: Knopf) (hereafter, BFAD).
2. Presumably after Isaac Asimov's wonderful science fiction stories—or after the iPad? Maybe both.
3. Rachlin, H. (1991) *Introduction to modern behaviorism,* 3rd ed. (New York: Freeman).
4. BFAD, pp. 37–38.
5. Clotfelter, C. T., & Cook, P. J. (1987). Implicit taxation in lottery finance. NBER Working Paper No. 2246.
6. See, for example, www.pbs.org/wgbh/pages/frontline/criminal-justice/the-problem-with-pleas/, and Grant, R. W. (2011). *Strings attached: Untangling the ethics of*

incentives (Princeton, NJ: Princeton University Press), Kindle edition. The suicide of Internet maverick Aaron Swartz was probably caused by the threat of life imprisonment for his illegal downloading and distributing of hundreds of scholarly articles. See, for example, http://lessig.tumblr.com/post/40845525507/a-time-for-silence. The practice of introducing contingencies resembling either bribery or extortion into government litigators' bargaining with suspects has become a serious problem with the criminal justice system. See, for example, Harvey Silverglate's analysis of prosecutors' strategy in case of supposed financial malfeasance: http://online.wsj.com/article/SB10001424127887324100904578401000346404928.html?mod=WSJ_article_MoreIn_Opinion.

7. *Stanford encyclopedia of philosophy.* Retrieved from http://plato.stanford.edu/entries/berlin/#2.4.
8. Berlin, I. (1995). *Liberty* (New York: Oxford University Press), p. 16.
9. This was first demonstrated rigorously in a classic paper by E. F. Moore in 1956: Gedanken-experiments on sequential machines. In C. E. Shannon & J. McCarthy (Eds.), *Automata studies* (Princeton, NJ: Princeton University Press), pp. 129–153.
10. Some say that Skinner did not think *Walden Two* utopian. But in a taped address on YouTube, he comments that his intention was "to see if there isn't a better way of doing something and that after all is the essence of utopian thinking."
11. See http://en.wikipedia.org/wiki/Walden_Two.
12. See, for example, Altus, D. E., & Morris, E. K. (2009, Fall). B. F. Skinner's utopian vision: Behind and beyond *Walden Two. The Behaior Analyst, 32*(2), 319–335.
13. Wallace-Wells, B. (2010, May 13). Cass Sunstein wants to nudge us. *New York Times*; Sunstein, C. (2013). It's for your own good! Retrieved from www.nybooks.com/articles/archives/2013/mar/07/its-your-own-good/.
14. BFAD, p. 66. Skinner's approach here is reminiscent of the way that abattoirs are designed so that cattle do not get alarmed as they are led to the slaughter. See, for example, Temple Grandin's website with her tips on how to handle farm animals: www.grandin.com/index.html.
15. Russell, B. (1946). *History of Western philosophy* (London: Routledge), p. 125.
16. BFAD, pp. 154–155.
17. Quoted in Lewis, H. (2011). *Where Keynes went wrong: And why world governments keep creating inflation, bubbles, and busts* (Mount Jackson, VA: Axios Press), Kindle edition.
18. Keynes, J. M. (1946). Opening remarks: The Galton Lecture. *Eugenics Review, 38*(1), 39–40.
19. See, for example, Freedman, D. H. (2012, June). The perfected self. *The Atlantic,* www.theatlantic.com/magazine/archive/2012/06/the-perfected-self/308970/: "B. F. Skinner's notorious theory of behavior modification was denounced by critics 50 years ago as a fascist, manipulative vehicle for government control. But Skinner's ideas are making an unlikely comeback today."
20. Skinner (1971).
21. "The Stimulus and the Response: A Critique of B.F. Skinner." In Chapter 13 of her book *Philosophy, who needs it?* (Signet, 1984), Ayn Rand comments:

> The book itself [BFAD] is like Boris Karloff's embodiment of Frankenstein's monster: a corpse patched with nuts, bolts and screws from the junkyard of philosophy (Pragmatism, Social Darwinism, Positivism, Linguistic Analysis, with some nails by Hume, threads by Russell, and glue by the *New York Post*). The book's voice, like Karloff's, is an emission of inarticulate, moaning growls—directed at a special enemy: 'Autonomous Man.' And political freedom, [Skinner] declares, necessitates the use of 'aversive reinforcers,' i.e., punishment for evil behavior. Since you are not free anyway, but controlled by everyone at all times, why not let specialists control you in a scientific way and design for you a world consisting of nothing but 'positive reinforcers'?

22. I was a teaching assistant, along with several others, in Skinner's Nat. Sci. 114 introductory course at Harvard some years ago. We had to grade many essays by pissed off students. Some were quite eloquent, and we posted them on the walls of our office.

23. In this, Skinner was preceded by the extraordinary nineteenth-century writer Samuel Butler in his satirical utopian novel *Erewhon: or, over the range,* published anonymously in 1872. The Erewhonians treated crime as a disease (and, disease as a crime!)—to be treated by people called "straighteners" (behavior-analysts?). Unlike behavior analysts, however, the straighteners did not scruple to apply quite severe punishment as part of their "cure" for the criminal condition. Butler also pointed out many of the problems with the concept of free will that I discuss in this chapter and even ventured to speculate on animal rights.

24. BFAD, p. 73. In *Walden two,* Skinner has his hero Frazier say, "A moral or ethical lapse, whether in explicit violation of the Code or not, needs treatment, not punishment" (p. 159).

25. BFAD, p. 79.

26. BFAD, p. 100.

27. See http://en.wikipedia.org/wiki/Genetic_fallacy.

28. BFAD, p. 17, my italics.

29. BFAD, p. 41.

30. Not a prestigious group among psychologists!

31. BFAD, pp. 17–18.

32. Levin, M. (1997). *Why race matters: Race differences and what they mean* (Westport, CT: Praeger), p. 320. This is a thoughtful and wide-ranging book, unfairly neglected because it discusses some controversial issues.

33. BFAD, p. 37.

34. BFAD, p. 29.

35. BFAD, p. 63.

36. "I have been misunderstood": An interview with B. F. Skinner. (1972, March/April). *Center Magazine,* pp. 63–65.

37. Hocutt, M. (2012). B. F. Skinner on freedom and dignity. Unpublished manuscript. Isaiah Berlin in the quote earlier also blurs these two kinds of determinism: efficient causation, where praise and blame is irrelevant, and final cause, which involves environmental feedback, where praise and blame are completely appropriate.

38. BFAD, p. 205.

39. I thank Max Hocutt for this useful term.

40. I'm simplifying a bit here. There may well be indirect effects of reward and punishment on reflex behavior.

41. See http://en.wikipedia.org/wiki/Public_choice.

42. Quoted in Berggruen, N., & Gardels, N. (2013). *Intelligent governance for the 21st century: A middle way between West and East* (Cambridge: Polity Press), p. 47.

43. Quoted in Norman, J. (2013). *Edmund Burke: The first conservative* (New York: Basic Books), p. 148, Kindle edition.

11 Values

B.F. Skinner devoted an entire chapter in *Beyond Freedom and Dignity* to values. He was well aware behaviorism is all about action, and action requires some idea of good and bad. He has two suggestions: one a statement of what is "good," the other of why it is. In the first case, he says that "good things are positive reinforcers. . . . [T]he things we call bad . . . are all negative reinforcers. . . . To make a value judgment by calling something good or bad is to classify it in terms of its reinforcing effects" and "the only good things are positive reinforcers, and the only bad things are negative reinforcers."[1] In the second case, as for why, he says, "Things are good (positively reinforcing) or bad (negatively reinforcing) presumably because of the contingencies of survival under which the species evolved."[2]

The former sounds rather like the narcissistic hedonism—"good" is what *I* like!—that was still appealing at the end of the 1960s. But it fails as a definition for two reasons. First, what feels good may not *be* good: No doubt sobriety is better than drunkenness, but that argument has little effect on an alcoholic even though he accepts it in principle. Sobriety and scotch may both be reinforcing, but scotch is reinforcing *now!* Charity is good (according to most people), but selfishness is what people prefer most of the time. "Sin" is the term that theologians use for actions that people know to be bad but do anyway. The concept, and those internal conflicts that are part and parcel of human nature, had no meaning for Skinner.

Second, Skinner's definition provides no independent guide to "the good" because it doesn't say what *is* reinforcing. Unfortunately, the set of all possible reinforcers, for a pigeon much less a human being, cannot be specified in advance. Philosophers have made the same point: Even the most careful observation of how people actually behave fails to discover any rule that will permit us to deduce "all and only" things that they all call "good." Skinner seems to accept this, but doesn't think it a problem.[3]

Skinner, like many scientists who dabble in philosophy, seemed to believe that what *ought to be* can be inferred from *what is*—that science can guide us in all things. But eighteenth-century philosopher David Hume showed this to be a fallacy. Francis Bacon (1561–1626), Elizabethan courtier and proto-philosopher of modern science, seems to have anticipated Hume, writing: "The reason why scientific study can be a means only, not an end, is because the ultimate purpose of life is not study, but action."[4] Facts may help us decide between two courses of action—which medicine is the best cure for a given disease, for example. But the facts by themselves don't urge us to action. The wish to cure comes from somewhere else. Skinner, like contemporary *scientific naturalists*[5] does not accept Hume's conclusion. His colleague, the great biologist E. O. Wilson, for example, wrote that "ought" is just the same as "is" and "is" is the realm of empirical fact:

> If the empiricist world view is correct, ought is just shorthand for one kind of factual statement, a word that denotes what society first chose (or was coerced) to do, and then codified. . . . Ought is the product of a material process.[6]

In a 2009 interview,[7] Wilson expanded on the same theme:

> One by one, the great questions of philosophy, including 'Who are we?' and 'Where did we come from?' are being answered to different degrees of solidity. So gradually, science is simply taking over the big questions created by philosophy. Philosophy consists largely of the history of failed models of the brain.

Wilson is pretty sure that science will eventually take care of all the philosophical questions that are worth asking, moral questions included. Skinner felt much the same. "It is usually accepted that the answers [to *ought* questions] are out of the reach of science." But then he affirms, "It would be a mistake for the behavioral scientist to agree."[8] In other words, physicists and biologists don't know what should be done, but we (behavioral scientists) do. But the limitation that Hume discovered is not one of scientific knowledge. It's not that behavioral science can find things about value that biology cannot. The limitation is the difference between fact and action. Facts, any facts, behavioral or biological, by themselves cannot urge us to action, cannot confer value by themselves. The science of behavior is not exempt from this limitation.

This confusion of what *is* with what *should be* is the main problem with Skinner's approach to values. His rather diffident attempt to get out of this box is evolutionary: "The survival of a culture then emerges as a new value to be taken into account in addition to personal and social goods."[9] In other words, "survival"—of the culture or the species—is offered as a superordinate value from which all others can be deduced. This is the only ultimate value Skinner explicitly defended in his utopian writings. It is hard to quarrel with this position in the abstract. Few would defend a belief or custom that is bound to cause the downfall of the culture that adopts it. But even assuming that we can with any accuracy predict just which of our values conduces to the survival of our culture—and what is "our culture" anyway, if, while adapting and surviving, it changes beyond recognition?—even assuming we know what we should believe to survive, how are those beliefs to be reconciled with Skinner's "personal and social goods"? Suppose, for example, as seems to be increasingly, and surprisingly, true across much of the planet,[10] it is a personal good to have no or few children? Obviously, sterility, like the universal celibacy of the Shakers, is bad for cultural survival, so which good should the culture go with?

The problem with "survival" as a value is that it depends on prophesying the unknowable. It is precisely as true, and as helpful, as the advice to a young investor: "Buy low, sell high." Well, yes, but . . . what *is* "low"? What *will* conduce to the survival of the race/culture? In most cases, we do not know.[11] For example, cultures sympathetic to alcohol and tobacco are presumably less "fit" (in the Darwinian sense) than cultures that proscribe them. But this is not at all obvious. There may be hidden benefits to one or the other that we cannot now foresee. The consensus (in the United States, at least) used to be that alcohol is an unmitigated evil: bad for your body, leads to wife beating and family breakup, etc. Alcohol was prohibited by the Volstead Act from 1920 to 1933, with disastrous effects on crime and social cohesion. The social benefits associated with moderate drinking were assumed to be outweighed by its many other evil effects. Yet drinking alcohol in some form is a custom common to the majority of cultures and now, it turns out, there may even be health benefits to moderate drinking. So the evolutionary balance sheet on alcohol is not yet closed.

"Well," you may respond, "alcohol may be controversial, but smoking is certainly bad." But this isn't so clear either. Some smokers die from lung cancer and emphysema, usually in unpleasant ways (not that dying is ever a walk in the park). This is unquestionably bad—for them. But only 25% or so of U.S. smokers die because of their habit, and smoking-induced illnesses generally don't kill until their victims reach their fifties and sixties, after most of their productive life is over and before they become a burden to their children and society. Smoking does not seem to have a collective cost. It does not diminish the common good and may even add to it if we include the innocent pleasure smokers get from their habit.

It is an evolutionary truism that life history is determined by adaptive considerations. *Life-history strategy* is biologists' name for the fact that lifespan is affected by natural selection. The result is a short life for mayflies, long for Galapagos tortoises. What is the "fittest" lifespan for human beings: forty, fifty, one hundred years? Of course, we don't know. It is perfectly possible that a society which encourages smoking—which yields a generally short but productive life—would be more successful in the long run than one that discourages smoking and has to put up with a lot of costly and unproductive old people. An apparently callous—and perhaps improbable—suggestion. But not one Skinner could have dismissed out of hand.[12]

If reinforcers are set for life, what is one to do when confronted with apparently undesirable reinforcers such as recreational drugs? The Darwinian metaphor gives little guidance. If these substances formed part of our "selection environment," then presumably this behavior, despite its apparent ill effects, may have served some positive function. Should we let well alone? But if a drug is a new arrival, these habits may now be maladaptive (Skinner discusses such cases). We should desist, Skinner would say, because their negative effects are so obvious. But how obvious are they, really? At the time of painter William Hogarth's *Gin Lane* in the eighteenth century, alcohol was considered a hard drug, bound to destroy much of society. Now it is accepted as risky but tolerable. Which view is correct?

How about cherished values that most people accept as without question— like the principle of equality. Most people in developed countries assume that hierarchy is bad and democracy is good. But the most stable (i.e., evolution-arily successful) societies we know were not democratic but hierarchical. The ancient Egyptian culture survived substantially unchanged for thousands of years. The Greeks, the inventors of democracy, survived as a culture only for two centuries, and were defeated by the highly undemocratic Romans, who lasted three times as long. The oldest extant democracy is no more than 300 years old. In the animal kingdom, the ants and bees, with built-in hierarchies, have outlasted countless more egalitarian species. The attempt to base val-ues on evolutionary success very soon raises questions about many traditional beliefs.[13]

One problem with "survival of the culture" as a guide is that it requires perfect knowledge of the future. Another is that it calls many contemporary beliefs into question. While some customs, like indiscriminate homicide and poor hygiene, are clearly maladaptive under all imaginable circumstances (although there are arguments for poor hygiene under some conditions![14]), oth-ers, like respect for elders, monogamy, gender equality, monotheism, tolerance, homophobia, selflessness, democracy, the Divine Right of Kings, even belief in a single objective reality, are more contingent. The problem is that most of the prescriptions of traditional morality fall in the latter class. We simply do not know, belief by belief, custom by custom, whether our culture would in the long run be better off with or without them.

It is certain that some cultures will survive longer than others. It is also cer-tain that the ones that survive will have many beliefs that were in fact essential to their survival. But the importance of at least some of those beliefs *could not have been foreseen,* even in principle. Interestingly, a similar argument has been made in economics. Successful firms, it is argued, are not necessarily smarter or better at computing marginal utilities than unsuccessful ones; they may just have begun with a "corporate culture" that happens to be more suc-cessful under the prevailing conditions.[15] The reasons for success, of the firm or the culture, may well be clear *post hoc*, after the fact. But in many cases, they could not have been predicted in advance.

The story in biology is the same. Every organism acts in certain ways with-out foreknowledge of consequences: Trees shed their leaves in anticipation of winter; birds lay eggs in the spring. In animals, such behavior is termed *instinctive.* Much of human behavior, even, involves preferences and habits that owe little to experience. Indeed, it is hard to conceive of any adaptive entity that could succeed in the evolutionary race by relying entirely on learning. If—and this is a fairly big "if"—cultures evolve just as living organisms do, then we may expect that successful cultures will also act in certain possibly arbitrary ways whose consequences could not have been foreseen, but which nevertheless prove beneficial in competition with other cultures. It seems certain, therefore, that a culture with some unquestioned, culturally inherited beliefs is more fit in the Darwinian sense (i.e., more likely to persist) than a culture with none or only a few. From the point of view of cultural survival, it is all but certain that we should take *some* things on faith. But which things? Here, alas, evolutionary epistemology provides no real guidance—the Darwinian metaphor has failed us. Nevertheless, moralists can take some comfort from this argument, which provides a rational basis for faith, if not for any faith in particular.

Conclusion: Where science applies—the world of facts and scientific theory—we should certainly rely on it. But when it comes to unprovable beliefs, evolution—the success of a culture—cannot provide an easy guide. We must take some things on faith, although we can never be sure what they should be.

Values and Reinforcement

Skinner's descriptive approach to values gets him into another difficulty. Because he is reluctant to define "reinforcers" in advance, he often assumes that they are mostly set by the history of the species, and are not alterable within a man's lifetime. But not all reinforcers are innate, nor is it reasonable to assume that the ill-defined mechanism of conditioned reinforcement is sufficient to account for those reinforcers that are clearly acquired. This approach (termed primary and secondary drives) was tried by Hull and other early behaviorists and abandoned. It is simply not possible to link all rewards to a few inherited ones by this mechanism—or at least, no one has done so convincingly. It may be reasonable to assume that sex, hunger, thirst and perhaps things like even a love of music, are entirely innate. And clearly, "neutral" stimuli may be linked to these motives through conditioning principles. There is a character in the tenth-century Japanese novel *Tale of Genji*, for example, who is erotically stimulated by the calligraphy of his beloved— an example of Pavlovian (what Skinner terms "respondent") conditioning, perhaps. Skinner seems to agree: "[N]ew stimuli [may] become reinforcing through 'respondent' conditioning."[16] It is much less plausible to assume that being reinforced by a red sports car, James Joyce or a particular brand of sneaker can be linked in this way with innate reinforcers. The world of fashion, what is "cool" this season, proves that reinforcers (for humans) cannot be linked to invariants like our need for food and sex—because fashions, by definition, are transient. Fashion—in clothing, art and even science— provides an ever-changing set of reinforcers that are products of the social environment.[17] Why have mechanical watches—more expensive to make and maintain, and less accurate than the quartz variety—come back into to fashion to the point that some cost more than a luxury automobile? Why will Brits pay thousands of pounds for an apparently undistinguished car number plate (36KC was recently on offer for £24,000, for example)? Why can "art" that is sometimes mistaken for trash by the cleaning lady be sold for thousands of dollars?[18]

Defenders of Skinner will argue that he never embraced the conditioned-reinforcement position. Reinforcers are where you find them, according to Skinner. Well, yes—and no. In some places, Skinner loosely ties all reinforcers to primary reinforcement via the ideas of conditioned and generalized reinforcement. But in his later writings, he usually disclaimed any need to define the set of reinforcers. And as we have just seen, in *Beyond Freedom and Dignity* he comes out for an entirely Darwinian interpretation.

On yet another tack, Skinner defines the words "good" and "bad" in terms of community practice: "Behavior is called good or bad . . . according to the way in which it is usually reinforced by others."[19] This says little more than that "good acts are what people call good, and bad acts are what they call bad," which is often true but not helpful—especially when one culture reinforces what another punishes. He might have gone on to say that many reinforcers are established socially (the favored sneaker brand, for example), but this would have led into sociological complexities, which he always avoided. And the origin of this social behavior (Why this brand of sneaker? Why *sneaker* at all?) would still be unexplained.

Skinner, like many other scientific naturalists, confused description with prescription. Yes, good can be identified as "what people call good," but what do you think *is* good? What values will guide *you,* the behavioral engineer? Surely Skinner does not mean that we should all just follow the crowd?

***

Skinner's approach to the problem of value is a muddle. He vacillated between a "final-cause" evolutionary viewpoint and two versions of proximal causation: Values are just reinforcers, and reinforcers just *are,* or can be derived via respondent conditioning or conditioned reinforcement from a few primaries. There are problems with each of these approaches. As we'll see in the chapters on society, the real problem is that Skinner wasn't much interested in the problem of values because he knew what he believed and thought that the main problem was in implementation: "To confuse and delay the improvement of cultural practices by quibbling about the word *improve* is itself not a useful practice."[20] Complacency in defense of virtue is no vice, one might say.[21]

But science, even behavioral science, does *not* provide us with values, with ideas of what is good and bad. One of the aims of applied behavioral science is to control behavior for the common good. Unlike Skinner, we *should* "quibble" about "cultural practices" and their "improvement." Before we try and change anything, we should be very clear about what should be changed and why.

Notes

1. BFAD, p. 107.
2. BFAD, p. 104.
3. On the *naturalistic fallacy* see, for example, Moore, G. E. (1903). *Principia ethica* (Cambridge: Cambridge University Press).
4. Bacon, F. (1863). *Novum Organum I, Aph. LXX, Collected works* (Boston: Taggard and Thompson), pp.47–48.
5. See, for example, Timothy Williamson http://opinionator.blogs.nytimes.com/2011/09/04/what-is-naturalism/ and Alex Rosenberg's response http://opinionator.blogs.nytimes.com/2011/09/17/why-i-am-a-naturalist/. A better term for these folk is *scientific imperialists,* since they seem to believe that there is nothing else but science. See also Staddon, J. E. R. (2004). Scientific imperialism and behaviorist epistemology. *Behavior and Philosophy, 32,* 231–242. http://dukespace.lib.duke.edu/dspace/handle/10161/3389.
6. Wilson, E.O. (1998). *Consilience: The unity of knowledge* (New York: Alfred Knopf), p. 251.
7. Junod, T. (2009). *E. O. Wilson: What I've learned.* Retrieved from www.esquire.com/features/what-ive-learned/eo-wilson-quotes-0109.
8. BFAD, p. 102.
9. BFAD, p. 129.
10. See Last, J. (2013). *What to expect when no one's expecting* (Encounter Books), http://jonathanlast.com/.
11. For a fuller discussion of this issue, see Staddon, J. (2013). Faith, fact and behaviorism. *The Behavior Analyst, 36*(2), 229–238.
12. Sloan, Frank A., Ostermann, J., Conover, C., Picone, G., & Taylor, Jr., D. H. (2011). *The price of smoking* (Cambridge, MA: MIT Press), Kindle edition; Staddon, J. (2013). *Unlucky strike: Private health and the science, law and politics of smoking* (Buckingham, UK: University of Buckingham Press).
13. For discussions of alternatives to U.S.-style democracy see Berggruen, N., & Gardels, N. (2013). *Intelligent governance for the 21st century: A middle way between West and East* (Cambridge: Polity Press). See also Wilson, J. Q. (2000). Democracy for all? Commentary, March. Retrieved from www.commentarymagazine.com/0003/wilson.html.
14. Ridley, M. (2012, September 8). Dirtier lives may be just the medicine we need. *Wall Street Journal*, a review of *An Epidemic of Absence: A new way of understanding allergies and autoimmune diseases,* by Moises Velasquez-Manoff.
15. See, for example, Winter, S. (1964). Economic natural selection and the theory of the firm. *Yale Economic Essays, 4,* 225–272.
16. BFAD, p. 104.
17. See, for example, Chapter 3, "Value and Reason" in Staddon, J. (2012). *The malign hand of the markets* (New York: McGraw-Hill).
18. See www.nytimes.com/2001/10/20/arts/art-imitates-life-perhaps-too-closely.html.
19. BFAD, p. 109.
20. Skinner, B. F. (1961/1955). Freedom and the control of men. In *Cumulative record* (pp. 3–18), p. 6. (Originally published in 1955.)
21. Older readers will recall 1964 presidential candidate Barry Goldwater's much condemned "Extremism in the defense of liberty is no vice. And moderation in the pursuit of justice is no virtue."

12 Skinner and Mental Life

This is a short chapter because B. F. Skinner's view of mental life is so odd and so hard to reconcile with any other view that there is rather little to say about it. Skinner's view of thinking and consciousness is what distinguishes his radical behaviorism from methodological behaviorism and from cognitive psychology:

> Methodological behaviorism and certain versions of logical positivism could be said to ignore consciousness, feelings and states of mind, but radical behaviorism does not thus "behead the organism"; it does not "maintain a strictly behavioristic methodology by treating reports of intro-spection merely as verbal behavior"; and it was not designed to "permit consciousness to atrophy." What it has to say about consciousness is this: (a) Stimulation arising inside the body plays an important part in behavior. (b) The nervous systems through which it is effective evolved because of their role in the internal and external economy of the organism. (c) In the sense in which we say that a person is conscious of his surroundings, he is conscious of states or events in his body; he is under their control as stim-uli. . . . [A] person may continue to talk, "unconscious of the effect he is having on his listeners" if that effect is not exerting control on his behav-ior. Far from ignoring consciousness in this sense, a science of behavior has developed new ways of studying it.[1]

Skinner's epistemology of mind is not a model of clarity. Let's take first his notion of internal stimulation, which he invokes to explain "feeling" and "thinking." For example, when we answer the question, "What are you think-ing? . . . it is . . . likely that we are describing private conditions associated with public behavior but not necessarily generated by it."[2] What this seems to mean is that "we" are describing some internal state (but the word "state" is avoided). Skinner's alternative is "internal stimulation," but stimulation of what by what? And it is apparently silent: The stimulation is of a type that may lead to speech, but on this occasion occurs in the absence of speech. Since all this is internal, it presumably also includes some part of the observer, who is thus observing himself. How can we differentiate between observer and observed? And how are we to deal scientifically—behavioristically—with an internal stimulus we cannot see or measure? Skinner does not solve these problems, and when confronted directly with them could not clarify his argument so that this reader, at least, could understand him.[3]

So much for thought. But Skinner's position does seem to give a plausible account of some aspects of mental life, such as pain and reports of internal disorders. Reports of pain, particularly when referred to sites within the body, are notoriously inaccurate. Heart attack victims, for example, may report one or more of the following symptoms: pains in the left arm, the neck, even the back, as well as in the chest. Harvard psychologist Edwin Boring years ago stimulated his own esophagus and found that the place where he located the sensation was much closer to the mouth than the actual stimulus. On the other hand, people can report the location of a touch on the skin, particularly the skin of the hands or face, with great accuracy. Why this difference? Skinner gives a social answer: Internal stimuli are reported inaccurately because the "verbal community" cannot differentially reinforce accurate responding. A mother can only guess at the source of her child's "tummy ache"; neither child nor mother knows for sure. But if little Billy has fallen and grazed his knee, both know the source of the trouble very well. Since both know where the pain is, the mother can teach the child the proper label.

Skinner's account may be part of the truth. Children clearly need social support to learn the correct name for the source of the pain, even if they need no extrinsic guidance to locate it—nonsocial and nonverbal animals have no difficulty locating a touch. But stimuli from inside the body are different.

There is an obvious evolutionary reason why external stimuli are accurately located: Accuracy is essential to effective action. The animal that pricks its right paw but withdraws the left is a poor bet in the evolutionary race. Social reinforcement is not the basis for the normal sense of touch, only for the correct use of language in relation to stimulation.

Anatomical specificity is much less important in the internal milieu, however. For example, the appropriate response to the ingestion of poison does not require a rat to accurately locate the source of internal damage. What is required is a behavioral change: to stop eating, and perhaps avoid the most recently eaten or most novel food. And, in rats and several other species, this is indeed the usual reaction. A rat fed a novel and a familiar food, and then made sick by lithium chloride injection, learns on one trial to avoid the novel food (which, in nature, is obviously more likely to be the source of the problem). This is called *taste-aversion learning,* and numerous studies have shown how beautifully it is adapted to the evolutionary contingencies.[4] The feeling of nausea is vague as to anatomical locus, but goes along with the food-avoidance behavior that the natural selection has favored. It is possible that we cannot name the source of the problem not because we cannot be told the correct name, as Skinner suggests, but because we don't have the necessary physiological information.

If identifying the anatomical sources of internal problems were of consequence to natural selection, no doubt we would locate them with accuracy also, and also without need for extrinsic reinforcement—just as we can locate a touch on the skin instinctively, without training. The big difference between internally and externally caused distress is that what little can be done to remove the source of internal distress does not depend on localization. In the past, at least, nothing much hinged on accurate identification of "where it hurts" internally, so that selection pressure for accurate localization was weak. As medical science offers more possibilities for corrective action, it constitutes a selection pressure, favoring patients who can report the site of internal problems accurately. Individuals with atypical symptoms for cardiac problems or an inflamed appendix are at a slightly higher risk of dying than people who report their heart attack more conventionally. After many generations, even such a small selective effect may produce noticeable changes in the population. A future generation may report cardiac ischemia with perfect accuracy.

But notice that what selection favors in this example is not necessarily accuracy but *conformity*. The patient does best whose symptoms most closely match the most commonly reported symptoms—because that favors an accurate diagnosis. Whether these symptoms correspond to the real anatomical locus of the problem is irrelevant, so long as the connection between symptom and diagnosis is strong. I suspect that weak selection pressure, rather than inaccessibility to social reinforcement, is the likely explanation for our inability to accurately localize internal events.

Skinner prefers to label something like "seeing an object" or "hearing a tune" as a "response" rather than as a stimulus or a state. This allows him to deal with "images" and "hallucinations" as "responses," different from seeing real objects only in that the objects happen to be absent:

> After hearing a piece of music several times, a person may hear it when it is not being played, though probably not as richly or as clearly. So far as we know, he is simply doing in the absence of the music some of the things he did in its presence.[5]

There can be little doubt that a person who is "imagining" an object is in a state similar to his state when actually seeing the object. Evidence from brain activity scans shows that visual areas of the brain are indeed active when the subject is "seeing" an image, for example. Skinner's view is undoubtedly a useful antidote to the "copy" theory of perception that asserts that "imagining" an object actually recreates a "mental picture" of the object. While there is some evidence for the copy theory, Skinner is right to point out that the assumption is often unnecessary.

Nevertheless, there are a few ingenious studies that are at least consistent with the idea that some perception involves a "mental representation" with properties quite similar to the real object. For example, cognitive psychologist Roger Shepard[6] did a famous series of experiments in which subjects were asked to identify an object as the same or different from a target object. On each trial, either the target object or its mirror image was presented. Shepard found that the time taken to respond correctly is proportional to the number of degrees the test object must be rotated to bring it into registry with the target object—suggesting that subjects "rotate a mental image" in their heads (although other interpretations are possible). Modern cognitive psychology largely rests on the assumption that Shepard's result is perfectly general, that something like the "copy theory" of perception is universally valid. How true this is we will see in later chapters.

There is a problem with Skinner's alternative, identifying a "mental image" as a "response," however. The whole point about an image is that it is compatible with a whole set of potential responses, and an open-ended set at that. Thus, the person who sees an image of an apple might say, "I see an apple"; but he might also answer "yes" when asked, "Do you see what fell on Newton's head" or "Are you thinking that one a day may keep the doctor away?" In short, the *object* property of the image is lost when it is reduced to a response. Of course, Skinner was aware of all this, and dealt with it by evolving very flexible concepts of "response" and "stimulus." It is this sort of elusiveness that allows Skinnerians to deny that their hero is a stimulus-response theorist—at the same time that a literal reading of what he says allows non-Skinnerians to assert that a stimulus-response theorist is precisely what he is.

Notes

1. Skinner, B. F. (1976). *About behaviorism* (New York: Vintage Books), pp. 242–243.
2. Skinner (1976), pp. 30–31.
3. See the reprint of *Behaviorism at fifty* and commentaries, with Skinner's response, in Catania, A. C., & Harnad, S. (1988). *The selection of behavior. The operant behaviorism of B. F. Skinner: Comments and consequences* (Cambridge: Cambridge University Press).
4. See, for example, Reilly, S., & Schachtman, T. R. (Eds.). (2009). *Conditioned taste-aversion learning: Behavioral and neural processes* (Oxford: Oxford University Press).
5. Skinner, B. F. (1976). *About behaviorism* (New York: Vintage Books), p. 91.
6. Shepard, R. N., & Metzler, J. (1971). Mental rotation of three-dimensional objects. *Science, 171*, 701–703.

Part III
The New Behaviorism

13 Cognitivism and the New Behaviorism

In 1976 it was possible to write:

> [S]ince the days of Chicago functionalism and Columbia Thorndikianism, no one has seriously doubted the hegemony of behaviorism in American psychology. Cognitive psychology, considered by many the only viable option to behaviorism, has, in fact, existed more by contrast with behaviorism than as a school of thought in its own right.[1]

Yet shortly thereafter, the "cognitive revolution" displaced behaviorism from psychology's front page and, increasingly, from departments of psychology across the land. What happened?

First, some definitions. The terminology in this area is confusing. Cognitive psychology is the movement inspired by George Miller's 1962 book, *Psychology: The Science of Mental Life,* and launched in a very successful textbook, *Cognitive Psychology,* by Ulric Neisser in 1967. Cognitive science is a broader term that also includes workers in artificial intelligence, linguistics and other ancillary disciplines who share an interest in human thought. The most recent movement along these lines is cognitive neuroscience, which is dominated by the new brain-imaging technologies: functional magnetic resonance imaging (fMRI), positron emission tomography (PET), superconducting quantum interference device (SQUID), and others.

There are also several varieties of artificial intelligence. A philosopher has commented:

> Just to keep the terminology straight, I call the view that all there is to having a mind is having a program, Strong AI [artificial intelligence], the view that brain processes (and mental processes) can be simulated computationally, Weak AI, and the view that the brain is a digital computer, cognitivism.[2]

I'm not sure that is completely fair, but it does convey the feelings of many enthusiasts when all was bright and clear in the 1970s.

The Rise of Cognitivism

So why did cognitive psychology/science eclipse behaviorism? What happened was that psychologists got leave to "do what comes naturally"—leave denied to them by the unforgiving behaviorism of Watson and his successors for more than sixty years. What comes naturally to psychologists is *mentalism.* "Psychology is the science of mental life," pronounced William James in 1890, but his writ ran for only a few pre-Watsonian years. Harvard professor George Miller used James's sentence as a rallying cry in the first salvo of the mentalistic counter-revolution the title of his 1962 book *Psychology: The Science of Mental Life*.[3]

Not only do psychologists want to study mental life, they want to study the mental life of *human beings*. This was also impeded by the behaviorists, who argued from evolutionary biology that simpler, more comprehensible, antecedents of the human mind are to be found in the behavior of animals. The need for experiments in which reward and punishment may be administered freely also implied that scientific psychology must be centered on animal experiments. This was all soon to be dismissed as "rat psychology." Psychologists had been chafing against the constraints of biology and behaviorism for two generations when they were liberated by the cognitive revolution. The new cognitive psychology legitimated the study of language, mental representation and consciousness, which (it was argued) had been ruled out or trivialized by the old behaviorism. As one cognitivist commented: "[I]f mental states exist, a complete psychological explanation should give an account of them even if they could be dropped from the laws of behavior."[4]

How was this emancipation achieved? Chiefly through two things: the digital computer, and the act of theoretical *seppuku* committed by Skinnerian radical behaviorism. I discussed B. F. Skinner's antipathy to theory in Chapter 5, and I will say a bit more about it later in this chapter. But first, the computer.

The digital computer meant that theories—of mental life, perception, syntax or whatever—could be *simulated,* made up into a working *computer model*. This was heady stuff in the 1960s and 1970s. Computer-literate cognitivists boasted in the 1950s that the best chess player in the world would be a computer within ten years, automatic language translation was around the corner, and comprehensive models of thought were on the horizon. Already, in 1957, a computer program had discovered novel proofs for theorems in Russell and Whitehead's *Principia Mathematica*.[5] By the 1960s, the sunlit uplands of cognitive hegemony were in full view. Especially confident prophecies for the new cognitive psychology were made by psychologist and economics-Nobelist-to-be Herbert Simon—see, for example, his ambitiously titled collection of papers *Models of Thought*.[6]

Not only did computation offer power, it also offered respectability. Rigor and quantification had been almost a monopoly of the behaviorists. The vague, verbal theorizing of the Gestalt school and other proto-cognitive psychologists could easily be dismissed. But now, the ability to simulate mentalistic theories with quantitative precision conferred a Good Science Seal of Approval on cognitive psychology. No longer need cognitive psychologists feel embarrassed by hardheaded behaviorists. Philosophical objections to the study of subjective experience remained unanswered, but no matter: Computers could remember, perceive, even understand. The possibilities appeared boundless.

Well, not quite boundless, perhaps, but still pretty good. Now, with computers on every desktop thousands of times more powerful than the water-cooled monsters available to the prophets of cognitive science, the uplands, while still in sight, seem a little cloudy. Chess champion Gary Kasparov has finally been beaten by IBM's Deep Blue,[7] Watson (named not after J. B. but Thomas W., a founder of IBM) has defeated top Jeopardy contestants[8] and the Internet (ah, the Internet!) has pretty good language translation on offer. But Deep Blue plays chess very differently from Gary Kasparov—more exhaustive search, less remembered strategy; and the computer Watson excels in large part because of speed. Artificial intelligence, brilliant at retrieving, sorting and analyzing "big data," is still more artificial than intelligent.

Radical behaviorists were insulated from the siren song of cognitivism by Skinnerian suspicion of formal theory and by their dedication to experimental results as ends in themselves. Behaviorists trained in the traditions of Hull and Tolman were much more susceptible, however. Several of the leading cognitive psychologists of the 1970s and 1980s were re-treaded rat runners, or at least, people reared in the Hullian tradition. The few neo-Tolmanians for the most part embraced with enthusiasm the new animal-cognition movement.

How has the computer-assisted excitement of the original cognitivists panned out? Well, okay, but criticism continues. Attacks are coming from the left and the right. On the left, philosophers are arguing that cognitivism is failing because the computer metaphor is wrong—and because cognitivism is not mental enough. On the right, some artificial intelligence (AI) researchers and roboticists are arguing that the emphasis on representation and symbolic thought is largely irrelevant to the development of truly intelligent systems. I suggest that the philosophical objections to contemporary cognitive psychology merely underscore the importance of a sophisticated behaviorism. The AI objections partly define the new behaviorism. Let's look at the philosophy first.

Philosophical Objections to (Some) Cognitive Psychology

A central tenet of cognitive psychology is that the brain is like a computer and cognitive operations like a program running on that computer. This is still a very widely accepted view in cognition.[9] Its founding inspiration was Cambridge mathematician Alan Turing (1912–1954). Turing is famous on several counts: He played a key role in deciphering the German "Enigma" code during World War II. He proposed a test for artificial intelligence (AI) that has become a classic.[10] He did the mathematics that forms the basis for the general-purpose digital computer, describing what has come to be known as the universal *Turing Machine.*[11] And he died tragically by his own hand at the young age of forty-two in the aftermath of a criminal conviction for homosexual behavior,[12] which was then a criminal offense in the United Kingdom.

Although he owed no allegiance to behaviorism as a movement in psychology—indeed, he was not a psychologist at all—Turing proposed a perfectly behavioristic test for "thought." The experimenter types questions that are read and responded to either by an appropriately programmed computer or by another human being. The experimenter is not told which: His task is to decide from the responses whether his correspondent is man or machine. If he cannot tell which, within a "reasonable time," then "thought" should be conceded to the machine as well as to the man. Passing the *Turing test* is an avowed objective of modern cognitive science. Most cognitivists go beyond the possibility of mere functional equivalence to accept the idea that source of behavior, the brain, is to be thought of as a "symbol-manipulating device," just like the digital computer.

The Turing test can never be decisive because it depends on two things that are both necessary for answering the question, "Does the machine think?" The first is simply time. If the human interrogator can ask only one or two questions, even a very simple computer program can fool him. I remember in the very earliest days of microcomputers showing a NorthStar Horizon desktop PC (4K memory!) running a little program called Lisa to a clinical colleague. Lisa was a much-simplified version of a more elaborate mainframe program called Eliza, written by Joseph Weizenbaum,[13] an MIT computer scientist. Lisa simulated a Rogerian psychotherapist and responded to typed input. Question: Are you happy? Answer: I am upset about my sister. Q: How do you feel about your sister? (cued by the word "sister"), and so on. The program had no content and no real intelligence. But a couple of minutes' exposure to it convinced my colleague that it was pretty smart.

The second limitation is one with which Skinner was very familiar: the repertoire of the human interrogator: "The truth of a statement of fact is limited . . . by the repertoires of the scientists involved."[14] If the questioner doesn't ask the right questions, he may fail to detect the difference between a machine and a human being. But what exactly *are* the right questions? If you know that, you really don't need the computer to know what human intelligence is.

Philosopher John Searle[15] attacked the Turing test from another angle. Searle objects that even if the test is passed, the successful program need not be accepted as a valid theory of the human mind. Searle's main objection is that *anything* can be conceived of as a computer: A ball rolling down an inclined plane, for example, is an analogue computer that computes Newton's laws of motion; a nail driven into a plank computes the distance it must travel given the force of the hammer and the friction of the wood. The problem, says Searle, is that computational properties are not intrinsic to any system; they are interpretations imposed from outside.[16]

I don't believe that this particular objection holds water. Quantum theory, which is one of the very best theories in existence, is often associated with comments like, "If quantum mechanics hasn't profoundly shocked you, you haven't understood it yet," by iconic physicist Niels Bohr. In other words, a theory may have little or no intuitive appeal, yet work very well. If it explains much with little and makes accurate predictions, we should be happy. Whether the theory is "intrinsic to the system" or not is completely irrelevant.

Searle's second objection is to accuse cognitivism of the familiar homunculus fallacy. Sophisticated cognitivists are of course aware of this problem: There is no "little man in the head" looking at some sort of screen on which the products of sensation are displayed. An influential idea in the study of human memory is that the frontal lobes are the location of something with the homunculus-like name of the "central executive": "The central executive component of working memory is a poorly specified and very powerful system that could be criticized as little more than a homunculus," writes its co-inventor, who has defended the idea at length.[17] Nevertheless, the ways in which important problems are presented imply such a little man, says Searle: "Typical homunculus questions in cognitive science are such as the following: 'How does the visual system compute shape from shading; how does it compute object distance from size of retinal image?'"[18] The savvy cognitivist might respond by saying that what is really meant is, "How is information about object distance represented in the brain?" and "How is this information derived from the retinal input?"

He will need to add, of course, "How do we know these things?" In other words, we need to know something about how states of mind are translated into things we can measure (i.e., into behavior). This response shows that the question of representation cannot be separated from the questions of computation and action—but it often is, as these questions show. When all three are considered together, it is difficult to see how they amount to asking more than, "How does the brain work to make behavior?" which is not necessarily a computational or even a cognitive question.

Searle's case against the computer metaphor for the mind has some merit. Much of the standard cognitivist boilerplate about "information processing" and computational "levels" now looks less impressive. No information is being processed; perhaps nothing is being "represented" at all: The external world is changing, neurons are firing, chemicals are circulating and physical actions are occurring. The psychologist's job is to find the connections among these events. Rhetoric about "levels"—functional, hardware, computational and intentional—is empty in the absence of clear evidence, which can come only from a truly comprehensive theoretical system that explains behavior within a level and connects levels to one another. There is as yet no "mental chemistry" and "mental physics" to provide justification for a division between the psychological equivalents of "atomic" and "molecular" levels, for example. Until some convincing, specific justification for levels is provided, we are under no compulsion to accept the idea. It's just another plausible conjecture.

To these criticisms I would add five more. First, there is the distinction between *competence* and *performance*. This distinction has both an innocent and a sinister meaning. The innocent meaning is just the one I discussed in Chapter 7. The student often knows more than she shows on this exam on this day. The sinister meaning is more theoretical and arose in connection with language. Like the "levels" just discussed, it is another "trust me" distinction that depends for its validity on the reader's acceptance of the theorist's view of the subject. The subject in this case is language, and the theorist is mathematical linguist Noam Chomsky,[19] who we have already encountered as Skinner's most virulent critic. The idea is that language follows certain syntactic "rules," but that actual examples—speech as she is spoken or writing as she is writ— fall short of perfection because of constraints such as memory limitations. The competence/performance distinction is less conspicuous now than it used to be—it has run into empirical problems, for one thing:

> Although there is plenty of evidence that humans use language creatively (saying and understanding things that have never been said before) and well (with very low error rates), there is very little evidence for the claim that "perfect" knowledge underlies our (occasionally) imperfect behavior.[20]

Nevertheless, the Platonic thinking represented by the competence-performance distinction still permeates cognitive psychology.

The arbitrariness of this distinction is obvious from a thought experiment. Suppose someone gives you a device of unknown function with a numerical keypad. You try it out by typing in various combinations, and you get the following set of outputs: $2 \times 2 = 4$, $20 \times 20 = 400$, $25 \times 25 = 625$, $30 \times 30 = 900$. "Great!" you think. "I've figured it out. It's a calculator that multiplies." But then you try: $40 \times 40 = 999$—whoops! It turns out that the calculator multiplies fine, so long as the answer is less than 1,000. Anything greater, and it just gives the largest number of which it is capable: 999. How shall we describe the behavior of this device? The competence-performance people would say, "Well, the deep rule underlying this behavior is multiplication, but because of memory limitations, answers greater than 999 cannot be produced." There is an exactly parallel argument in linguistic theory to account for the fact that people are limited in their ability to understand and produce deeply embedded, but perfectly grammatical, sentences. "Fine," you may well say, "what's wrong with the competence-performance account of the behavior of this 'constrained' calculator?" The answer is: "nothing, so far." The problem is that there are alternative accounts, and deciding among them demands additional information.

For example, one alternative is that the device doesn't multiply at all, but rather just consults a fixed lookup table, which comprises all the three-digit (or fewer) products of two-digit numbers. A "brain lesion" (i.e., damage to the device memory) would support this view if it simply knocked out certain answers, but left others involving the two multiplicands unaffected. More general effects might support the competence-performance alternative. The point is that the competence-performance idea, which implies an organization involving a rule-following engine limited by memory and other constraints, represents just one kind of model for what is happening in the linguistic black box. We are under no obligation whatever to accept it without knowing both the exact nature of the rules that are being enforced and the precise constraints that limit their output. Without the details, we are simply invited to accept as a matter of fact what is nothing more than a self-imposed limitation on theoretical inquiry.

Second, cognitive psychology is all steering and no motor. As Edwin Guthrie pointed out in his criticism of cognitive behaviorist Edward Tolman many years ago, Tolman's purely representational approach left the maze-running rat "buried in thought" at the choice point. Things have not improved much since: "Psychology is the science that investigates the representation and processing of information by complex organisms," says the supposedly authoritative MIT Encyclopedia of Cognitive Sciences,[21] dismissing in an act of silent imperialism not just behaviorism but any nonrepresentational, non-information-processing view of the human mind.

Motivation, the motor, is not intrinsic to cognitive psychology. It is an add-on. Yet for most organisms, the motor is by far the most important component. The cognitive, "computational" component is for many simple organisms almost trivial. As the great dramatists show us, motivation and emotion are major contributors to human behavior also. Every politician and pollster knows that the emotional freight of words and phrases like "extreme," "risky," "working families" (Americans, people), "children," "our future," "family values," etc., is much more important than their syntactic arrangement. In other words, what is important is that the voters hear these words. What is almost irrelevant is the meaning of the sentence in which they are used (so long as it doesn't provoke hostility or provide ammunition for critics). Much behavior even of human beings is not very "cognitive" at all.

A related objection is that the term *cognition* derives from an old view of psychology that includes two other divisions of the soul: *conation* (the will—motivation), and *emotion.* It is far from certain that this division corresponds to a natural line of behavioral or physiological fracture. Motivational and cognitive elements are intertwined in the behavior of simple organisms and are not certainly separable even in human behavior. And the brain does not divide up neatly into three areas either. But in any case, if one is willing to settle for a Kantian psychology, why not buy the whole package?

Fourth, in early days, the more thoughtful cognitivists seemed to offer a robust view of "mental life" that differs not one whit from a pragmatic behaviorism:[22]

> If Watson had not been so inept as a philosopher, he might have offered behaviorism as a pragmatic theory of mind, comparable to Peirce's pragmatic theory of meaning, James's pragmatic theory of truth, and Dewey's pragmatic theory of value. The mind—the other chap's mind, at any rate—is something whose existence is inferred entirely from the behavior we observe. "John is conscious" must be translated into the hypothesis, "If I

call to John, he will answer," or, "If I stand in John's way, he will detour round me," and so on. In short, if I present him with such-and-such stimuli he will make such-and-such responses. To paraphrase Peirce, "*Consider what effects, which might conceivably have practical bearings, we conceive the mind to have. Then, our conception of these effects is the whole of our conception of the mind.*"[23]

This commonsensical view has been largely lost in the self-congratulatory mentalism of latter-day cognitive psychology.

Let me give just two more examples, one general and one specific, of how the cognitive approach can mislead. First, two eminent cognitive neuroscientists contrast what they call the "associative" view (which is what I have been calling neo-behaviorism in the Hull-Spence tradition) with the information-processing (cognitive) view, as follows:

> The distinction between the associative and information-processing frameworks is of critical importance: By the first view, what is learned is a mapping from inputs to outputs. Thus, the learned behavior (of the animal or the network, as the case may be) is always recapitulative of the input-output conditions during learning: An input that is part of the training input, or similar to it, evokes the trained output, or an output similar to it. By the second view, what is learned is a representation of important aspects of the experienced world. This representation supports input-output mappings that are in no way recapitulations of the mappings (if any) that occurred during the learning.[24]

Notice that no actual models are being compared here. The comparison is between descriptions of two possible kinds of models. It is telling us, soothsayer-fashion, what kinds of model are likely to work. This is not theory, but metatheory, which is something much less productive. I suggest that this approach to behavioral science is simply befuddling. If you have a model, and want to call it cognitive (or behavioral), okay. But let's see it. Let's see how well it deals with the data. What does it assume? How much does it explain? What does it predict? Where does it fail? You might want to label the model "associative" or "information-processing" according to taste. But what really matters is how well it handles the existing data; what new data it suggests you look for; and how well it predicts.

This kind of prescriptive thinking, plus the fact that cognitive categories are so familiar, can lead cognitive commentators to overinterpret relatively simple, and often skimpy, experimental findings. Consider, for example, this discussion of some interesting data on the sequence of events that take place in the brains of patients instructed to memorize a series of twelve words presented on a computer screen and then recalled after a delay.[25] The researchers separated electrical brain-recording data for words that were later recalled correctly versus words that were not recalled. In recordings from rhinal cortex and hippocampus, they found small differences in the time pattern of recalled versus nonrecalled words. What commentators Schachter and Wagner say is,

> Now, Fernandez et al. track the serial encoding of memories . . . within the medial temporal lobe (MTL) of the brain. . . . They report on . . . an attempt to answer the fundamental question: Where and when are memories formed in the brain?

And, later,

> The Fernandez study brings into bold relief a critical and as yet unanswered question: exactly what computations do each of the MTL regions perform, and how is the later encoding activity in the hippocampus influenced by, or dependent on, earlier activity in the MTL? . . . However, additional evidence is necessary to determine whether these structures support encoding of the same or similar types of information.

Pretty impressive! Or is it? What Fernandez at al. showed is that after a certain experience with visual stimuli, some stimuli have a measurable effect later (the words are recalled) and others do not (they are not recalled, under these conditions). The brain recordings of event-related potentials suggest that at the time they were presented, the recalled words had a different effect on (some parts of) the brain than the others. Interpreting this result in terms of "encoding," "information" goes well beyond what was observed without suggesting any new experiment or interpretation beyond the raw experimental result. Who says there are (spatially localized) "memories" at all? In what sense is "encoding" taking place? In what sense is "information"—which means something only when defined in a technical way not attempted here[26]—involved?

Unfortunately the cognitive approach makes this kind of over-interpretation all too easy. Because it is so intuitive, so close to folk psychology, the cognitive story tends to block out all others. It obscures the fact—obvious on disinterested examination—that the data in question are often modest, hence consistent with a wide variety of other interpretations. The real question addressed by this study is not, "Where and when are memories formed in the brain?" but "How (and to some extent, when) is the brain changed by experience?"—a much broader question to which the data necessarily contribute only a very modest answer: Verbal stimuli that are recalled or not recalled after a certain time have slightly different initial effects on two brain areas. Big whoop, as the students might say.

AI Objections to Cognitivism

John Searle ends his attack on cognitive psychology by writing,

> One of the unexpected consequences of this whole investigation is that I have quite inadvertently arrived at a defense . . . of connectionism. Among

their other merits, at least some connectionist models show how a system might convert a meaningful input into a meaningful output without any rules, principles, inferences or other sorts of meaningful phenomena in between. This is not to say that existing connectionist models are correct. . . . But it is to say that they are not obviously false or incoherent in the way that traditional cognitivist models . . . are.[27]

Connectionists use simplified models of nerve cells (neurons) and their connections to simulate behavior such as learning, pattern identification, associative memory and (the example Searle had in mind) the perception of grammatical regularities such as the rule for plural forms. The elements in such an account, the neurons and their connections, are completely unmental and unintelligent. The brain is seen not as an "executive" and a set of subordinates, but as a *self-organizing system.*[28] A little thought shows that the brain must be this kind of system because even if we could identify an "executive," we would then be left with the problem of how *it* operates. Ultimately, there is nothing left but self-organization.

The seminal connectionist paper was written by eccentric MIT psychiatrist-turned-philosopher-turned-neuroscientist Warren McCulloch and his mathematician collaborator Walter Pitts, with the typically obscure McCulloch title "A Logical Calculus of the Ideas Immanent in Nervous Activity."[29] McCulloch and Pitts showed that networks of highly simplified neuron-like elements had computational power similar to the universal Turing machine—the digital computer. The neural-network idea was taken up later and extended by several notable figures such as Hungarian American mathematician John von Neumann and engineer Frank Rosenblatt.

The idea of neural nets was introduced to psychology by Donald Hebb in his 1949 book, *The Organization of Behavior,*[30] but Hebb's approach was very informal and couched in strictly physiological terms (rather than in terms of associations or mathematical neurons). Few unequivocal predictions about behavior could be derived from it. His idea about how connections between neurons are strengthened by synchronous activity lives on in neural-network theory, however.

The most persistent and comprehensive effort to extend the reach of neural nets was made by mathematician Stephen Grossberg and his students and colleagues. Beginning in the 1960s, he attempted to explain all the standard phenomena of animal learning in terms of formal neural networks. Unfortunately, his papers were for the most part long and difficult and his intended audience inadequately trained, and philosophically unprepared, to absorb them. His work had little influence on behaviorist thinking, but was eventually recognized by the formation of the new field of neural network theory of which he has become one of the leaders.[31] The sourcebook in psychology is McClelland et al.[32] The history of the rise, fall and rise again of the neural-network approach is described in a special issue of *Daedalus.*[33]

This theme, intelligence through the collective action of many unintelligent agents, has been carried forward by researchers in *robotics,* the engineering of intelligent, autonomous artificial creatures. In 1991, robotics researcher Rodney Brooks wrote critically of the state of cognitive science at its peak:

> No one talks about replicating the full gamut of human intelligence any more. Instead we see a retreat into specialized subproblems, such as ways to represent knowledge, natural language understanding, vision or even more specialized areas. . . . I . . . believe that human level intelligence is too complex and little understood to be correctly decomposed into the right subpieces at the moment. . . . we will never understand how to decompose human level intelligence until we've had a lot of practice with simpler level intelligence.[34]

He concluded, perhaps cynically, "Representation has been the central issue in artificial intelligence work over the last 15 years only because it has provided an interface between otherwise isolated modules and conference papers." Not much has changed since this was written.

Brooks provides a plausible biological argument for this position. He notes that language and symbolic communication generally are very recent arrivals on the evolutionary scene. Most of evolutionary time was taken up developing creatures that could simply find their way about. Distinctively human abilities like speech and writing arrived only during the last few ticks of the evolutionary clock.

> This suggests that problem solving behavior, language, expert knowledge and application, and reason, are all pretty simple once the essence of being and reacting are available. . . . This part of intelligence is where evolution has concentrated its time—it is much harder.

It is perhaps no accident that the abilities that are hardest to simulate—motor coordination, object perception, the survival skills necessary to sustenance and reproduction—are the ones over which evolution labored longest.

Another MIT researcher has summarized the conflict between old- and new-style AI as "knowledge-based vs. behavior-based artificial intelligence."[35] Knowledge-based AI is just the engineering equivalent of mainstream, symbolic, cognitive psychology. Fundamental to both knowledge-based AI and cognitive psychology is the idea of representation. The working assumption is that once you get the representation right, you have solved the problem—either of artificial intelligence, or of human cognition. Behavior-based AI is a more recent development, which denies both these ideas. Brooks and his colleagues argue instead that complex behavior arises from the combined actions of a multiplicity of stupid agents. There is no special internal representation of the external world. Or, at least, the representation is a byproduct of the unintelligent action of more or less independent, simple processes. These objections to representation are similar to John Watson's objections to structuralism (see Chapter 1).

So, my impression is that the standard AI approach has stalled.[36] It is still too early to know whether the arguments for a behavior-based approach to AI are valid. What does seem clear is that the commitment of the early behaviorists to research on animals was abandoned prematurely. To get psychology moving again, it looks as if we might do better to return to simpler systems—to animals. Slowly, as the contributions from the old approach begin to wane and those from the new begin to accelerate, a new behaviorism, combining ideas from psychology, biology and engineering, is beginning to crystallize around these ideas. Cognitive science has enjoyed the usual "high" induced by the appearance of a new technology (the digital computer). A few years earlier, operant conditioning was comparably energized by the technology of the Skinner box and schedules of reinforcement. But the most recent advances in the study of cognition have come from artificial neural networks, a technology explicitly derived from biology and completely congenial to classical behavioristic associationism, if not to atheoretical radical behaviorism.

The irony is that work on neural nets *should* have emerged from behaviorism, not cognitive psychology. The idea of stimulus-response associations was central to early behaviorism, and a network merely adds internal "nodes" that can be associated with one another, as well as with external stimuli and responses. In the 1960s and 1970s, a few attempts were made to extend neural-network ideas to rat-runner data, but the anti-theoretical bias of the radical behaviorists proved too strong and, in the end, neural-net ideas found more fertile ground among cognitive psychologists.

Connectionism is in fact the name that Edward Thorndike gave to his approach to reinforcement learning more than a hundred years ago. The same name, *connectionism,* has been independently adopted by contemporary proponents of parallel-processing techniques loosely derived from the properties of real nerve cells. But the new connectionists are generally unaware that their field is an example of what the biologists call *convergent evolution:* a return to an earlier form via a different evolutionary path. Not a few traditional cognitive psychologists are properly uneasy about these new developments, which they correctly perceive as a resurrection of behaviorism under a new guise. Connectionism has therefore gotten a mixed reception, with many cognitive psychologists attempting to prove that connectionist systems are incapable of modeling one or more of the "higher mental processes" that interest them.[37] None of these refutations has yet stuck. Let's take a look at some of the ingredients of the new behaviorism.

Contemporary Behaviorism

The clearest division within contemporary behaviorism is between those who continue to believe in a fundamentally purposive (teleological) approach to reinforcement learning, and those with a renewed commitment to behavioral mechanisms. I believe that the division is not fundamental. The teleologists are relative pessimists. They believe that the true behavioral or physiological mechanisms for behavior are so complex that we will never be able to unravel them in detail. On the other hand, behavior *is* adaptive and more or less goal oriented. We can therefore understand it (they argue) by understanding its goals: how they are weighed and how the subject's strategies for attaining them are constrained. This view is quite close to folk psychology, the nonscientific way we attempt to understand the "motives" of our spouses, children and colleagues, and to neoclassical microeconomics, which is to a large extent a formalization of folk psychology.

Howard Rachlin has provided the most developed statement of teleological behaviorism.[38] He summarizes his view thus:

> Efficient-cause psychology is designed to answer the question of how a particular act is emitted; final-cause psychology is designed to answer the question of why a particular act is emitted. . . . [F]inal-cause psychology, a development of Skinnerian behaviorism, is . . . called teleological behaviorism.

Rachlin's ideas are an explicit blend of some aspects of Skinner with some aspects of Aristotle.[39] Although couched in terms of individual acts, teleological behaviorism defines "response," "stimulus" and "reinforcement" (the Skinnerian trinity) in temporally extended terms that go well beyond their usual definitions:

> Skinner's original concept of reinforcement [is expanded] from a single event dependent on a single operant [response] (for example, a single food-pellet delivery immediately after a single lever press) to a pattern of environmental events perhaps only vaguely contingent on an overlapping pattern of operants.[40]

The Aristotelian elements are the notion of teleology itself, a rejection (*contra* Skinner) of the private nature of mental events and equating (*pro* Skinner) mental states with action: "For Aristotle, imagining was acting and not dreaming: Vividness of imagination was not vividness of interior image but of overt behavior."[41] The *final causes* in the system are the economist's utility functions, discovered through behavioral methods. The scheme is very close to the economic idea of revealed preference. It is therefore open to some of the objections to "rationality" I discussed in Chapter 8.

Teleological behaviorism, like Watsonian behaviorism and (according to Rachlin) Aristotle, but unlike Skinner, rejects private events: "If the individual himself reports 'I have had the idea for some time but have only just recently acted upon it,' he is describing a covert response which preceded the overt."[42] "For Aristotle, the idea would not be a covert response at all but a pattern of wholly overt responses including the individual's verbal report as one part of the pattern."[43] I will argue in a moment that this way of dealing with internal events, as temporally extended patterns of stimuli and responses, amounts to defining internal states in terms of equivalent histories.

The Darwinian Metaphor, Again

There is another way of looking at the problem of complex outcome-guided behavior that avoids the trap of rationalism implicit in the utility functions of teleological behaviorism. The pessimist's alternative to what Rachlin calls "efficient-cause" psychology is the Darwinian metaphor. If things are complicated, so that the search for mechanisms is futile, then the focus must be on selection, and the approach is close to Rachlin's or to classical microeconomics. But if we have some hope of understanding mechanisms, so that a causal account is possible, the emphasis is on variation: the mechanisms that generate behavior.

The Darwinian metaphor has practical consequences. Consider, for example, the problem of teaching a dull or depressed child who has simply "given up." Neither economics nor Skinnerian reinforcement-as-selection provides much help. The child is passive, hence there is no behavior and nothing from which to select. Reward is ineffective if the behavior on which it is contingent fails to occur. The economist's utility functions are empty if the behavior of the subject makes no contact with them. The point is to get *some* behavior. The Darwinian metaphor has some suggestions. Variation is increased by changing conditions, for example. "Free" (i.e., response-independent) reinforcers generate a repertoire of behavior through Pavlovian mechanisms of variation discussed in Chapter 3. These treatments are simply what folk psychology would call "encouraging the child" or "raising his self-esteem." But they are an improvement over folk psychology because they entail a temporal order: *First* you encourage; *second* you reward more selectively. "Self-esteem" is not an unqualified good but a transitional state induced only to provide conditions that prepare the child to gain rewards by meeting objective criteria. More on this issue in Chapter 21.

A slightly different version of teleological behaviorism has been proposed by George Ainslie:

> Economics is the original theory of goal-directed choice . . . self-defeating behavior is best understood in terms of an economic marketplace within the individual. . . . [T]he recent burgeoning of "behavioral economics" has shown how nearly congruent reinforcement theory is with economics.[44]

Ainslie's idea is that each individual acts not as a single, rational agent, but rather as a set of competing agents, each sensitive to the outcomes of the act it represents. The agents compete through a "demon" that chooses among them according to a version of Herrnstein's matching law (see Chapter 4). The structure of Ainslie's system is not identical to the set of independent, stupid agents favored by the behavior-based AI people. It is perhaps closer to the distributed-cognition approach of AI guru Marvin Minsky in his "society of mind."[45] What does seem to be clear is that theorists of all persuasions seem to moving away from the idea of the person as a single executive decision maker toward parallel systems of more or less unintelligent entities that compete for control of overt behavior. Unlike Skinner, these folk acknowledge the possibility of internal conflict. But all agree in rejecting a homunculus central executive.

Notes

1. Wispé, L.G., & Thompson, J.N. (1976). The war between the words: Biological versus social evolution and some related issues. *American Psychologist, 31,* 341–347.
2. Searle, J. (1992). *The rediscovery of the mind* (Cambridge, MA: MIT/Bradford), pp. 201–202.
3. Miller, G.A. (1962). *Psychology: The science of mental life* (New York: Harper & Row).
4. Johnson-Laird, P.N. (1988). *The computer and the mind* (Cambridge, MA: Harvard University Press), pp. 17–18.
5. Newell, A., Shaw, J.C., & Simon, H.A. (1957, February). Empirical explorations of the logic theory machine: A case study in heuristic. *Proceedings of the Western Joint Computer Conference* (Institute of Radio Engineers), pp. 218–230. Reprinted in Feigenbaum, E., & Feldman, J. (Eds.). (1963). *Computers and thought* (New York: McGraw-Hill), pp. 109–133.
6. Simon, H.A. (1979). *Models of thought* (New Haven, CT: Yale University Press).
7. See http://en.wikipedia.org/wiki/Deep_Blue_versus_Garry_Kasparov.
8. See http://en.wikipedia.org/wiki/Watson_(computer).
9. See, for example, Johnson-Laird (1988); Pylyshyn, Z. (1984). *Computation and cognition: Toward a foundation for cognitive science* (Cambridge, MA: MIT/Bradford); Eckert, M. (Ed.). (2006). *Theories of mind: An introductory reader* (New York: Rowman & Littlefield).
10. Turing, A.M. (1950). Computing machinery and intelligence. *Mind, 59,* 433–460.
11. Turing, A.M. (1936). On computable numbers with an application to the *Entscheidungsproblem. Proceedings of the London Mathematical Society,* Series 2, *42,* 230–265.
12. See the website maintained by Andrew Hodges: www.turing.org.uk/turing/.
13. Author of a fascinating early critique of AI: *Computer power and human reason: From judgment to calculation* (San Francisco: W.H. Freeman, 1976).
14. Skinner, B.F. (1976). *About behaviorism* (New York: Vintage Books).
15. Searle (1992); Searle, J. (2004). *Mind: A brief introduction* (New York: Oxford University Press).
16. See also Dreyfus, H.L. (1972). *What computers can't do* (New York: Harper and Row); and Penrose, R. (1989). *The emperor's new mind* (New York: Oxford University Press), for other influential attacks on "strong AI."
17. Baddeley, A. (1996). Exploring the central executive. *The Quarterly Journal of Experimental Psychology, 49A*(1), 518–528; Parkin, A.J. (1998). The central executive does not exist. *Journal of the International Neuropsychological Society, 4,* 518–522; Baddeley, A. (1998). The central executive: A concept and some misconceptions. *Journal of the International Neuropsychological Society, 4,* 523–526.
18. Searle (1992), p. 214.
19. For example, in Chomsky, N. (1964). *Current issues in linguistic theory* (The Hague: Mouton).

20. Bates, E., & Elman, J. (1996). Learning rediscovered. *Science, 274*, 1849–1851, p. 1849.
21. Holyoak, K. (1999). Psychology. In *MIT encyclopedia of the cognitive sciences* (Cambridge, MA: MIT Press).
22. See also Zuriff, G. (1985). *Behaviorism: A conceptual reconstruction* (New York: Columbia University Press).
23. Miller (1962), p. 66 (italics added).
24. Gallistel, C. R., & Matzel, L. D. (2013). The neuroscience of learning: Beyond the Hebbian synapse. *Annual Review of Psychology, 64*, 169–200.
25. Schacter, D. L., & Wagner, A. D. (1999). Remembrance of things past. *Science, 285*, 1503–1504.
26. Shannon, C. E., & Weaver, W. (1963). *The mathematical theory of communication* (Chicago: University of Illinois Press).
27. Searle (1992), p. 247.
28. The first major collection of papers on this important topic seems to be *Principles of self-organization,* by Heinz von Foerster and George W. Zopf (Eds.) (Pergamon Press, 1962), a report on a conference at the University of Illinois in 1961.
29. See the collection of papers: McCulloch, W. S. (1965). *Embodiments of mind* (Cambridge, MA: MIT Press).
30. Hebb, D. (1949). *The organization of behavior: A neurophysiological theory* (New York: John Wiley).
31. For examples of Grossberg's work, see *Studies of mind and brain* (Dordrecht, Holland: Reidel, 1982); and *The adapted brain, Vols. I and II* (Amsterdam: North-Holland, 1987). Another early voice out of the behavioristic mainstream was Air Force researcher Harry Klopf. For a summary of some of this work, see his book Klopf, H. (1982). *The hedonistic neuron: A theory of memory, learning and intelligence* (New York: Hemisphere). See also Nestor Schmajuk's (2010). *Computational models of conditioning* (Cambridge: Cambridge University Press).
32. McClelland, J. L., Rumelhart, D. E., & the PDP Research Group. (1986). *Parallel distributed processing: Explorations in the microstructure of cognition, Vols 1 & 2* (Cambridge, MA: MIT Press); McCulloch, W. S. (1965). *Embodiments of mind* (Cambridge, MA: MIT Press). See also Hertz, J. A., Krogh, A., & Palmer, R. G. (1989). *Neural computation* (Reading, MA: Addison-Wesley); Donahoe, J. W., & Dorsel, V. P. (Eds.). (1997). *Neural network models of cognition: Biobehavioral foundations* (Amsterdam: North-Holland Elsevier).
33. *Daedalus* (1988), *117*(1).
34. Brooks, R. A. (1991). Intelligence without representation. *Artificial Intelligence, 47*, 139–159.
35. Maes, P. (1992). Behavior-based artificial intelligence: From animals to animats, II. *Proceedings of the Second International Conference on the Simulation of Adaptive Behavior* (Cambridge, MA: MIT Press), pp. 2–10.
36. See also Uttal, W. R. (1998). *Towards a new behaviorism: The case against perceptual reductionism* (Hillsdale, NJ: Erlbaum), for a book-length critique; and Machado, A. (1999). Of minds, brains, and behavior—A review of Uttal's (1998) *Towards a new behaviorism: The case against perceptual reductionism. Behavior & Philosophy, 27*, 51–74, for an essay review.
37. See, for example, Pinker, S., & Mehler, J. (Eds.). (1988). *Connections and symbols* (Cambridge, MA: MIT Press).
38. Rachlin, H. (1992). Teleological behaviorism. *American Psychologist, 47*, 1371–1382.

39. For a lively behavioristic look at Aristotle and other classical philosophers, see John C. Malone's *Psychology: Pythagoras to present* (Cambridge, MA: MIT/Bradford, 2009).
40. Rachlin (1992), p. 1377.
41. Rachlin (1992), p. 1372.
42. Skinner, B. F. (1953). *Science and human behavior* (New York: Macmillan), p. 279.
43. Rachlin (1992), p. 1375.
44. Ainslie, G. (1992). *Picoeconomics* (Cambridge: Cambridge University Press), p. xii. See also Ainslie's (2001). *Breakdown of will* (Cambridge: Cambridge University Press).
45. Minsky, M. (1986). *Society of mind* (New York: Simon & Schuster).

14 Theoretical Behaviorism

The optimistic approach to behaviorism is to look for efficient causes: the antecedent environmental factors that determine behavior, and the mechanisms through which they act. B. F. Skinner seemed to favor this view. He constantly emphasized the organism's *history* as the determinant of its behavior. His emphasis was almost entirely on *reinforcement* history—Skinner had little interest in nonreinforcement effects of great concern to other behaviorists such as habituation and latent learning, for example (see Chapter 1). Because he was uninterested in models, Skinner also provided no way to interpret the effects of complex histories: no way for the effects of events in the remote past to combine with the effects of more recent events—as in the memory-trace account for the serial-position effect that I described in Chapter 2, for example.

Perhaps for this reason, the experimental emphasis of single-organism research on operant conditioning has been overwhelmingly on what are known as *reversible* effects (see Chapter 3). For example, a pigeon might be trained for many experimental sessions to peck a key for food reinforcement on some intermittent schedule of food reinforcement. After twenty or more daily experimental sessions, its response rate, the average number of key pecks over an hour period, will stabilize at some value such as 65 per minute. This value will be largely determined by the average rate (food deliveries per hour) at which the bird gets food, which in turn is determined by the parameters of the schedule (e.g., the average minimum interfood interval for a variable-interval schedule). The pigeon's rate of responding is largely independent of the bird's history prior to this particular protracted experimental condition. If the schedule parameter is changed, from 1 food delivery per minute to 2 per minute, for example, the bird will settle down at a higher peck rate of, for example, 75 per minute. But if the schedule parameter is changed back again to 1 per minute, the rate of pecking will eventually return to 65, its pre-change value. Thus, the relation between schedule parameter and response rate is a *reversible* property of behavior. The problem is that the same behavior on these two occasions does not mean that the pigeon is in the same *state*. Observed behavior is often reversible; but the state of the organism rarely is. Hence, by restricting their attention to reversible properties of behavior, radical behaviorists avoided dealing with the deeply historical nature of learned behavior in higher organisms.

I will give two examples of historical effects, the first hypothetical, and the second involving actual data. Imagine an experimental situation with pigeons that involves not one but two response keys. Pecks on each key are paid off like a Las Vegas–style one-armed bandit, probabilistically (I discussed a setup like this in Chapter 8). Let's look at two different experimental histories. Pigeon A is trained at first to peck on the *left* response key and paid off on the probabilistic schedule; pecks on the *right* have no effect. After fifty or so reinforcements for pecking *left*, bird A is trained to peck only on the *right;* pecks on the *left* go unrewarded. After 300 reinforcements for *right* pecks (this might take four or five daily experimental sessions), pecks on neither key are rewarded (this is termed *extinction*). Pigeon B is trained throughout (350 reinforcements) to peck the *right* key only for food, then extinguished, like A.

There are two things to notice about this simple experiment: On the last day of rewarded training, the behavior of the two pigeons will be indistinguishable—both will be pecking exclusively on the *right* key. But in extinction, their behavior will be very different: Bird B, which has never gotten food for pecking *left*, will simply peck more and more slowly on the *right*, with maybe one or two pecks on the left, until pecking ceases altogether. But Bird A, with its history of a few rewards for pecking *left*, will show many pecks to both keys before quitting entirely. This is usually called *regression*.[1] What can this difference in behavior in extinction mean? If behavior is all that matters, the two birds were in the same state at the end of *right* training. So why did they behave differently when conditions changed?

There are two ways to deal with this divergence. The solution adopted by teleological behaviorism is to redefine behavior in a temporally extended way. *Behavior* becomes *behavioral history.* Since our two pigeons have different histories, the fact that their response to a new condition (extinction) is not the same is no longer a puzzle. The limitation of this view is that is provides no compression of the data. If each history is unique, there is no way to predict the effect of a novel history. More than one history produces the kind of divergence I have just described. It would be nice to understand why, to have some rationale for similarities among histories.

It is possible, in principle and to some degree in practice, to group together histories that are *equivalent,* in the sense that the future behavior of the animal (in response to new conditions) will be the same after any history in the set. For example, in a version of the experiment I have described, we might find that an animal with the history (number of rewards in parenthesis) *right*(10), *left*(10) behaves the same in extinction as an animal whose history is *left*(10), *right*(15), *left*(5). The usual way to describe this equivalence is to say that the two animals are in the same *state* after these two *equivalent histories.* It might be possible to go further, and find some formula or process that would allow us to say that all histories of the form *left*(x), *right*(y), *left*(z) are equivalent (yield the same subsequent behavior) so long as some function $f(x,y,z)$ is the same.

My second example presents just such a formula and shows how it works to account for many aspects of behavior in the two-armed bandit situation. First, the experiment, which is on what is called reversal learning: a single pigeon getting his daily food (a total of sixty cracks at the food magazine, plus an after-experiment supplement to maintain his weight) by pecking at one of two response keys. The schedule on each key is either extinction (i.e., pecking is ineffective) or a variable-ratio schedule with a payoff probability of 1/8. Which key is "hot" changes from day to day according to some rule.

Now just look at two data points. After a history during which the bird gets food for pecking both keys, but never from both on the same day, on day N he gets food for pecking, say, left (L). He does well: Ninety percent of responses are correct (on the left). Now on the next day, the situation is reversed. He gets food only for pecking on the right (R). Again, he does very well: around 90% correct. Now look at what happens a little later in the experiment, say on day $N + 20$. Again, we begin with food just for L pecks; again responding is pretty accurate, around 90%. Again, the situation is reversed the next day, but now the bird does less well: only about 80% correct.

Why this difference? The reason is of course the animal's history. The first data point was taken after a history of daily reversals: LRLR. . . . The second was taken after reversals on every fourth day: LLLLRRRRLLLL. . . .

From a commonsense point of view, it's pretty obvious what is happening here. When reinforcement alternates every day, the pigeon learns to quickly reverse its preference. Not spontaneously—it needs one or two reinforcers before it switches—but quite quickly. But when reinforcement alternates only every fourth day, the pigeon is more cautious. He waits for several reinforcers before switching, hence the poor performance on each switch day—80% when reversal is every fourth day versus 90% when it is every day.

The cognitive account for this behavior parallels common sense. It just adds a label. The pigeon is said to have developed a *reversal learning set* when alternation happens every day. But of course, he might have developed such a set when reinforcement alternates every fourth day. Why doesn't he? Or, at least, why doesn't he do it as well?

One way to answer this question is to try and summarize the bird's history in a way that allows us to predict on each day how well he will do in this experiment. What seems to be required is a model that reflects two separate aspects of "response strength." One is simply performance: "percent correct," or how well the organism is doing on a particular day. The second aspect, which might be called "stickiness,"[2] is a measure of how quickly performance changes when conditions change. Stickiness captures the difference between performance after four days of payoff on the left (four-day alternation) followed by a day on the right versus performance after just one day on the left (daily alternation). Performance clearly becomes stickier day by day, so long as conditions do not change: stickier—slower to change—after four days of left reward than after just one day.

A model that captures these two properties of choice behavior is as follows:[3]

1. Assume that the animal's tendency to peck left or right is determined by response strength, V_{Left} or V_{Right}, according to a winner-take-all rule. In other words, in each discrete time step, the strongest response wins.
2. Assume that V_{Left} = (total reinforcers on left)/(total responses on left)—in other words: that V_{Left} = average payoff probability on the left, and similarly for the right.
3. All that remains is to decide *over what time period* these two totals are to be computed. A simple possibility that turns out to work surprisingly well is the following:

$$V_{Left} = \frac{(R_{Left} + R_{L0})}{(x_{Left} + x_{L0})}, \tag{14.1}$$

and similarly for the Right response. R_{Left} is the total number of reinforcements received for the left response in the experiment, and x_{Left} is the total number of responses on the left. These totals are updated with every left response (and similarly for the right). x_{L0} and R_{L0} are constants representing the animal's initial tendency to respond left and right.

No matter what the values for x and R, each unreinforced response reduces V (because x, the denominator, increases) and each reinforced response increases it (because the numerator, R, increases[4]), the exact amount depending on the current values for $x_{Left} + x_{L0}$ and $R_{Left} + R_{L0}$.

This is called the *cumulative effects* (CE) model. It is another variant of the Law of Effect model I discussed in Chapter 4. In the CE model, all histories that yield the same set of values for x_{Left}, x_{L0}, R_{Left} and R_{L0} (and similarly for the right) are equivalent in terms of the future behavior of the model. It describes quite accurately the performance of individual subjects in a long series of daily, two-day, or four-day reversals. (See Figure 14.1.)

It works in a very simple way. The more experience the model accumulates, the larger the numerator and denominator of Equation 14.1 become, hence the smaller the change in V produced by each response. Also, the more the schedule rewards, say, the left choice, the greater the difference between the strengths of the left and right responses, $V_{left} - V_{right}$, becomes. Thus, it takes longer for the model to reverse its preference after four days of left reinforcement than after just a single day, just as the data show. It is stickier after four days of training on one side than after just one. What the model does not do is learn the rule "reverse every day"; it does not show a real "learning set." On the other hand, there is no evidence that pigeons do either, although smarter animals—monkeys, dogs, children—may.

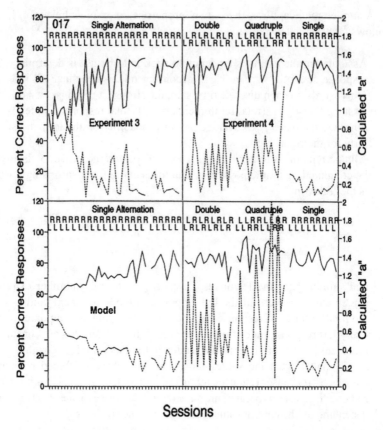

Figure 14.1 (Top panel) The entire course of a discrimination-reversal experiment with
a single pigeon. The solid line shows the proportion of responses each
day on the key that currently produced food (with probability 1/8) when
those conditions were alternated every day, every two days, or every four
days, as shown by the staggered letters at the top: L = only left responses
reinforced; R = only right responses reinforced. The dotted line shows
the rate of learning from Day *N* to Day *N* + 1: the higher the "a" value,
the smaller the change in performance from day to day—the "stickier"
the pigeon's behavior. (Bottom panel): Simulation of these data by the
cumulative effects model with initial conditions 1,000, 2,000. (From
Staddon, 1993, "Conventional wisdom . . ." op. cit.; see Davis et al., 1993,
for more details.)

The model also explains the response-based spontaneous recovery (regression) in my first example. Recall: Train first with left-only reinforcement then
with right-only—enough that performance is close to 100% correct at the end of
each phase. Then extinguish. The result is regression to an intermediate preference that reflects the total amount of training on left and right. But if the bird's history includes no left reinforcement, this regression will not happen: In extinction,
most responses will be on the right. The CE model easily duplicates this pattern.[5]

The model doesn't capture every aspect of reversal learning, even in pigeons, however. The CE model is response based, not time based. Hence, it cannot explain time-based phenomena like spontaneous recovery and something called Jost's law[6]—weakening of newer memories relative to older ones with passage of time. Despite the fact that the model is not time based, it can nevertheless duplicate matching in the interval-schedule concurrent VI VI procedure (see Chapter 4),[7] which is yet another demonstration that the matching result is both robust and overdetermined—in the sense that almost any law-of-effect learning process in the *conc* VI VI situation will conform to it.

The CE model illustrates my main point: how past histories can be summarized by a formula that has predictive value. The study of learning can do better than just make lists of particular histories and particular results. The aim of *theoretical behaviorism* (TB), therefore, is to understand the internal states of the organism by discovering rules that allow us to group together sets of histories that are equivalent in terms of its future behavior.

Theoretical behaviorism shares some features of both classical and Hullian behaviorism. It gets from classical behaviorism the conviction that we learn about the organism only through its behavior. It rejects, however, the view shared by Watson and Skinner that psychology need refer only to stimuli and responses. *Contra* Skinner, it argues that the skin does make a difference: Events inside the organism (e.g., the changes wrought by past history) are *state* variables, not stimuli or responses. *Contra* cognitivism, internal states are not necessarily conscious—mental, introspectable. *Contra* Hullian behaviorism, internal states are not necessarily physiological.[8] In other words, theoretical behaviorism respects the distinction between *intervening variables,* which claim no necessary relation to brain physiology, and *hypothetical constructs,* which do.[9] TB models may make contact with physiology eventually, but the first priority is to explain behavior. TB sees internal states as purely theoretical constructions based on historical information from behavioral experiments. Nevertheless, it shares with Hullian behaviorism the idea that the ultimate aim of behavioral study is the derivation of mechanisms or models. As these models evolve, they will surely make some connection with brain physiology.

Theoretical behaviorism is interested in mechanisms for entirely practical reasons. The argument runs like this: Classes of equivalent histories must be discovered by putting together the results from the appropriate set of experiments. But real organisms are very complicated and historical experiments take time. There is no way that the full set of internal states of a real animal can be fully enumerated experimentally. Theoretical creativity is necessary, and theories arise not just from "orderly arrangement of data," but also through invention. In practice, therefore, the main way to specify sets of equivalent histories is through dynamic theories that define how moment-by-moment experience changes the state of the organism. These theories can be compared with data, tested (if they do well enough with what is already known), overthrown (all theories are eventually overthrown), revised, and tested again, in the usual scientific way.

How does theoretical behaviorism differ from cognitivism? Both are theoretical and both assume internal states. One difference is that theoretical behaviorism is explicitly historical and dynamic. It is not concerned directly with representation, but instead with the way that the organism is changed by its experience. A second difference is that theoretical behaviorism makes no presumptions about either its subject matter or its theoretical constructs. Cognitive psychology is "the [computational] study of mental life"; theoretical behaviorism is not committed to a prejudged view of what theory must do. It looks for models/mechanisms of behavior, where *mechanism* is whatever works to account for behavior; and *behavior* is whatever can be usefully observed or measured, including reports of conscious experience (see Chapter 16). Theoretical behaviorism assumes in advance neither that mental categories are inevitable ingredients of any valid theory, nor that they must be immediately explicable by such a theory.

And, finally, TB contends that the sole purpose of science *is* to frame parsimonious laws, and *not* to "explain mental phenomena" in terms of familiar mentalistic ingredients like "expectations," "representations" and the like. An early advocate of the view that science is simply the simplest possible description of nature was Isaac Newton, who famously wrote "hypotheses non fingo" ("I make no hypotheses"), by which he meant that he intended not to "explain" phenomena but simply to discover their rules of operation. To questions such as, "But what do you *mean* by force?" and the like, he could simply respond by pointing to the appropriate law.

So why theoretical *behaviorism?* What is specifically behavioristic about this approach? Pure behaviorism, a psychology constructed entirely of physical stimuli and "uninterpreted physical movements," is impossible. Why? Because the same physical act can mean many different things: "Not waving, but drowning"—or saying "No!" or "Goodbye!" or whatever. The fact that perception interprets rather than records means that the same physical stimulus can look very different under different conditions. And different physical stimuli can look the same: "Red" is not just a wavelength. The sensation "red" can be produced in many ways, some involving no red wavelengths at all.[10] The question, therefore, is not *should* we focus just on behavior and stimuli, defined in a physical way—the answer is "no"—but *how* should we interpret physical movements and stimuli? My suggestion is that we do so through parsimonious dynamic models. These models then *are* the "behavior," interpreted in the simplest way that makes sense. This is what the organism is "doing," described in the simplest possible way. And in a way that assumes as little as possible about the relation between subjective experience and observed activity. This is where TB differs from cognitivism—which happily assumes "expectations," "representations," "information" and the like, all with only a tenuous connection to observables. Theoretical behaviorism also assumes as little as possible about brain-behavior relations. What it does attempt is to provide an accurate real-time description of *what the organism is doing*. It is this—not the "behavior" *tout court*—that the neurophysiologist must explain.

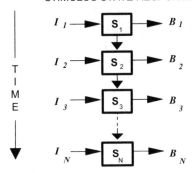

Figure 14.2 The view of the organism in theoretical behaviorism. For simplicity, time is divided into discrete instants (down arrow). At each instant, a *stimulus* (which may be "no stimulus"), I_t, can have either or both of two effects: It can produce a *response, B_t,* and change the organism's *state* from S_t to S_{t+1}. The states are defined by two tables: one that shows the effect of each stimulus on the response, the other that shows the effect if each stimulus on the subsequent state. This notation is just the standard way of describing a finite-state machine.

Figure 14.2 shows the standard framework for representing a finite-state machine.[11] It is a perfectly general picture. It just describes the logic of any process whose future behavior depends on its current input and its state, where *state* just summarizes the effect of all its past inputs. Since this is how we must think logically about the behavior of historical systems, it is an obvious place to begin. Figure 14.2 is also the framework for theoretical behaviorism. It tells us nothing about how stimuli and responses are to be defined. It does not specify the properties of the states: how many there are, the rules by which they change, and so on. These are the concern of specific theories, and I refer the reader to technical sources for more details.[12] One emerging theme is the idea that many of the properties of simple learning can be explained by interactions among independent agents ("integrators"), each of which retains a memory of its past effectiveness in a given context. I summarized one version of this idea in Chapter 6. This theme recurs in the earlier discussion of behavior-based AI. Models along these general lines can describe the basic properties of operant learning, for some properties of complex choice, for temporal properties of habituation, the progressive decrease in responding to repeated "neutral" stimulation and for some properties of the kind of interval timing seen on fixed-interval reinforcement schedules. I discuss in more detail in the next chapter a model for habituation.

***

Behaviorism was once the dominant movement in American psychology. It was eclipsed by the "cognitive revolution" in the late 1970s. Two things seem to have favored the cognitive movement: First, the digital computer, which for the first time allowed mentalistic ideas to be simulated and overcame behavioristic criticisms that cognitive theories were inexact and anecdotal. Second, the takeover of behaviorism by Skinnerian radical behaviorism with its strong bias against formal theory and its belief that psychology is little more than the collection of orderly experimental data. Radical behaviorism blocked theoretical advances within behaviorism so that connectionism, a natural "next step" in the associationistic tradition of the early behaviorists, was forced to find an uneasy home in cognitive, rather than behavioristic, psychology.

In recent years, cognitivism has come under attack. The computer metaphor has been criticized as fundamentally inadequate, and workers on behavior-based artificial intelligence have suggested that the cognitive-science approach through representation has failed to achieve real intelligence. Lower-level, nonsymbolic tasks, they argue, are more fundamental to biological intelligence, evolved earlier, and are more difficult to re-create by artificial methods. At the same time, a new theoretical behaviorism is emerging that shares the behavior-based-AI emphasis on intelligent behavior as the outcome of self-organizing interactions among independent, unintelligent agents.

Notes

1. This can also be called *resurgence*. *Spontaneous recovery* is yet another name for effects like this.
2. In a slightly different context, the term "resistance to change" has been used for what I am calling "stickiness": Grace, R. C., & Nevin, J. A. (1997). On the relation between preference and resistance to change. *Journal of the Experimental Analysis of Behavior, 67*, 43–65; see also AB&L, op. cit., Chapter 12. The term "fragility" was proposed in an early exploration of the idea of a two-dimensional memory strength: Wickelgren, W. (1974). Single-trace fragility theory of memory dynamics. *Memory & Cognition, 2*(4), 775–780.
3. See Davis, D. G. S., Staddon, J. E. R., Machado, A., & Palmer, R. G. (1993). The process of recurrent choice. *Psychological Review, 100*, 320–341; Staddon, J. E. R. (1993). The conventional wisdom of behavior analysis. *Journal of the Experimental Analysis of Behavior, 60*, 439–447.
4. The denominator also increases, of course. But because payoff probability is less than 1, unit increase in the numerator always increases V more than unit increase in the denominator decreases it.
5. Davis et al. (1993), Figure 8.
6. See Staddon, J. E. R., Machado, A., & Lourenço, O. (2001). Plus ça change . . . : Jost, Piaget and the dynamics of embodiment. *Behavioral and Brain Sciences, 24*, 63–65. Example of Jost's law: You usually leave your keys in a drawer in front hall. You move them to a drawer in the bedroom just before you go away on a trip. When you return, you look first, in vain, in the front hall.
7. Davis et al. (1993), Figure 13.
8. Staddon, J. E. R., & Bueno, J. L. O. (1991). On models, behaviorism and the neural basis of learning. *Psychological Science, 2*, 3–11.

9. MacCorquodale, K., & Meehl, P. E. (1948). On a distinction between hypothetical constructs and intervening variables. Retrieved from http://psychclassics.yorku.ca/MacMeehl/hypcon-intvar.htm.

10. See, for example, http://en.wikipedia.org/wiki/Color_constancy.

11. An early and excellent account of the logic of finite-state machines, on which this analysis is based, is Minsky, M. (1969). *Computation: Finite and infinite machines* (Cambridge, MA: MIT Press). For a philosophical analysis, see Staddon, J. E. R. (1973). On the notion of cause, with applications to behaviorism. *Behaviorism, 1,* 25–63.

12. See, for example, Staddon, J. E. R. (2001). *Adaptive dynamics: The theoretical analysis of behavior* (Cambridge, MA: MIT/Bradford), pp. xiv, 1–423.

15 Internal States

The Logic of Historical Systems

The big break between theoretical behaviorism and two of B. F. Skinner's other offspring, radical and teleological behaviorism, is the idea of internal state. Theoretical behaviorism claims that internal states—whether they are called hidden variables, intervening variables or some other such term—are essential to any theory of behavior. The other two behaviorisms do not.

The methodological behaviorism of Hull and Tolman was comfortable with internal states. In Hull's case they were hypothetical constructs, terms like "drive," "reaction potential" and "habit strength," loosely modeled on contemporary reflex physiology. Tolman was more "cognitive" and less physiological. Concepts like "means-end-readiness," "expectation" and "cognitive map" were merely intervening variables not explicitly tied to physiology[1]—and, it must be admitted, not a million miles from folk psychology. These are all ideas with which contemporary cognitive psychologists are comfortable. It is no surprise, therefore, that most Hullians and Tolmanians embraced the cognitive revolution when it blossomed in the early 1970s.

But the original selling point of John B. Watson's behaviorism was stimulus-response simplicity. After the neo-behavioristic interregnum of Hull and Tolman, Skinner attempted to turn the tide in 1938, returning to a deceptively simple stimulus-response (S-R) analysis. The only "third term" allowed was *reinforcement,* as part of Skinner's *three-term contingency.* But Skinner's S and R are not Hull and Tolman's S and R. Skinner retained only the surface appearance of Watsonian simplicity. He defined stimuli and responses in such a broad way that Skinnerian accounts could plausibly be offered for the whole range of human and animal private and public behavior.[2] I have analyzed the limited success of this endeavor in earlier chapters. But still, for radical behaviorism, as well as for the earlier Watsonian variety, "internal states" are a no-no.

I believe that both Skinner and Watson were wrong. Some idea of internal state, of so-called hidden variables, is not just desirable, it is essential to the theoretical understanding of any historical system. The behavior of no organism above a bacterium[3] can be understood without this concept. This chapter shows how the properties of the simplest kind of learning, habituation, cannot be understood without assuming at least one hidden variable. It follows that more complex learning also involves hidden variables.

John Maynard Keynes, a philosopher and economist noted for his shrewdness in practical matters, says somewhere that hardheaded men of business invariably embody the views of some long-dead economist. By ignoring theory in general ("Just the facts, ma'am!"), their unconscious embrace of some particular theory is assured. So it is with those who concentrate on action, on the prediction and control of behavior to the exclusion of understanding. By refusing to think theoretically, they are likely to accept an unexamined, and probably erroneous, theoretical and philosophical position.

Most behaviorists in the Skinnerian tradition take "prediction and control" as the be-all and end-all of psychology and happily assume that stimuli and responses are all we know, or need to know, about behavior. They are mistaken. Even if prediction and control are our ultimate aim, the apparently direct route is not always the best. By aiming directly at controlling nature—at a technology rather than a science—we may miss fundamental laws that will, in the long run, give us more power than we could have dreamed possible (see Box 15.1).[4] The practical man who in 1830 might have proposed to Michael Faraday, fiddling with wires and magnets, that he give it all up and concentrate on ways to make cheap steam engines "to bring power to the masses" would have been well intentioned, but ill advised. In the next year, Faraday discovered the principle of the electric dynamo, which accomplished the same result more simply—and led to an infinity of other improvements besides.[5] Gregor Mendel, messing about with algebra and counting peas in the 1860s, may well

---

Box 15.1   A Computer Too Far?

Computer pioneer Charles Babbage and his "difference engine" provide a salutary example of premature exploitation of an immature technology. In 1833 Babbage had this great idea for a mechanical computing device. It was to be constructed out of hundreds of precisely machined brass levers, pinions and ratchets. He tried to get government funding for it and in the end got £17,000 (about $6.6 million in today's money) but still failed to finish his difference engine. Not enough funding, perhaps? Genius thwarted by shortsighted bureaucracy? Apparently not because two Swedish engineers in fact succeeded by 1853 in building the engine, for much less money. But their business venture failed because the lumbering and expensive device was little more use than conventional mathematical tables. Babbage, meanwhile, continued to complain because the government would not fund his much more ambitious analytical engine, a forerunner of the digital computer.

The whole idea was in fact impractical because mechanical computers are much too slow. A stored-program digital computer was not feasible until the science of electronics had developed to the point that fast-switching devices could be made. The British government would have done better to spend its money on Faraday's basic science than on Babbage's apparently useful, but premature, computing engines.

have been a disappointment to the monastery gardener, anxious to improve his blooms by traditional crossbreeding methods. But Mendel turned out to be right, although only now, after more than 150 years, can we see that the science he started goes vastly beyond the imaginings of plant breeders of his own age. No amount of selective breeding can match the achievements of genetic engineering based on well-understood principles of molecular biology.

A good theory, gained through a search for *understanding,* will in the end yield much more "prediction and control" than premature exploitation of a half-baked technology. Along the same lines some 400 years ago, proto-scientist Francis Bacon said,

> For though it be true that I am principally in pursuit of works . . . yet I wait for the harvest-time, and do not attempt to mow the moss or to reap the green corn. For I well know that axioms once rightly discovered will carry whole troops of works along with them.[6]

There is always danger, of course, in trying to go beyond the immediate data. The history of science is littered with theories that came to naught: phlogiston, Johannes Kepler's religiously inspired obsession with regular solids, Tycho Brahe's lifelong adherence to Ptolemaic epicycles. Even the great Isaac Newton, "voyaging through strange seas of thought, alone," spent enormous amounts of time on theological studies, which now seem like an aberration. They were not, of course. Newton's God was rational, and the Judaeo-Christian world was given to man as a beautiful puzzle to be solved. Newton's religion inspired rather than inhibited his natural curiosity. The point is that the route of theory—even though it is almost synonymous with science—is not without risk. Every field of science is strewn with the bones of extinct theories. No knowledge process can escape the imperatives of natural selection. To find one true theory, many wrong ones must first be discarded. The fact that theories can be wrong is not a reason to give up theory. It is a reason to find better ways to eliminate wrong theories, because to abandon theory is to abandon science itself.

It is also worth remembering that if theories are fallible, so are "facts." The history of social science is full of failed experiments—studies that asked questions that turned out to be irrelevant or studied phenomena now known to be imaginary or factitious. Even if the facts are true, because they are established under highly controlled conditions, their application to real life is usually problematic. Psychology is particularly prone to misinformation and premature extrapolation from lab to society. For example, many years ago, simple experiments with African American children choosing (or not) to play with brown and white dolls were thought to show that black children suffer from lowered self-esteem because of their color.[7] The study, which has been contradicted by later research and added little or nothing to the daily experience of teachers and parents, was taken to mean that black kids would do better if educated alongside white kids. It was later cited in the 1954 Supreme Court decision that led to the nationwide system of enforced busing to end racial segregation in schools. Busing may or may not have been a good idea; but this highly artificial study just added spurious science—"noise"—to what was at bottom a moral and political issue.

Another example: Generations of misbehaving U.S. schoolchildren continue to receive "timeouts" or "ADHD" drugs in lieu of real punishment because psychologists are thought to have shown that punishment is ineffective and intrinsically more damaging than positive reinforcement. Punishment may or may not be damaging; that would be almost impossible to prove scientifically. It is not ineffective, as I point out in Chapter 17.

An example of catchy extrapolation from the animal lab that has entered the vernacular is so-called learned helplessness, a phenomenon originally demonstrated by giving dogs severe electric shocks under very restricted conditions, but promoted as an "animal model" for the varied manifestations of human depression.[8] In this case, the facts are well established, their applicability to human depression much less so.

A decade or so ago, a couple of studies purported to show an increase in spatial-reasoning performance immediately after children were exposed to a Mozart piano sonata—the so-called Mozart Effect. This beneficial effect of classical music led many parents—and even school systems—to make expensive investments in music stuff. Except that the "Mozart Effect" isn't: A careful study failed to find any difference between the performance of groups exposed to nothing at all, or music by melodious Mozart or the atonal Philip Glass.[9] (The effects of rap are yet to be tested.) These are just a handful of examples from a much longer list of premature extrapolations from lab to life.

The problem seems to be that when it comes to psychological research, plausibility, or a catchy name, often trumps validity. The media, and the public, love a good story, whether it's true or not. And there is a serious sociology-of-science problem: It is almost impossible to publish a study that merely replicates an already-published study—especially if the result is negative (I discussed this problem in connection with drug-study data in Chapter 9).

"Facts" always depend on theory. Hence, the less certain the theoretical framework, the more questionable the "facts." As our theoretical understanding changes, old data are seen in a new light and old "facts" are replaced by new. So the aim of basic-science psychology must be not prediction and control, but theory. But what theory?

Parsimony

Let's look at what three great minds have said about theory. The first is, once again, Francis Bacon. Bacon wrote before Darwin, before Newton, even:

> The axioms now in use, having been suggested by a scanty and manipular experience and a few particulars of most general occurrence, are made for

the most part just large enough to fit and take these in: and therefore it is no wonder if they do not lead to new particulars. And if some opposite instance, not observed or not known before, chance to come in the way, the axiom is rescued and preserved by some frivolous distinction; whereas the truer course would be to correct the axiom itself.[10]

Beware of a theory that just fits the known facts. Don't be surprised if it fails to predict new facts. Bacon grasped an essential feature of all scientific theorizing: Don't rescue a failed theory by tweaking, adding *ad hoc* assumptions to deal with unexpected deviations. These are remarkable insights at a time when modern science was still in embryo.

So what should we look for? In physics there is general agreement. J. Willard Gibbs, one of America's greatest home-grown physicists, commented: "One of the principal objects of theoretical research in any department of knowledge is to find the point of view from which the subject appears in its greatest simplicity."[11] This is *parsimony* or *Occam's razor*: The simplest theory is the best. How about biology? Here one great mind expressed some skepticism: "While Occam's razor is a useful tool in the physical sciences, it can be a very dangerous implement in biology. It is thus very rash to use simplicity and elegance as a guide in biological research", so wrote another Francis, Francis Crick, co-discoverer, with James Watson, of the double-helix structure of DNA. In biology, evidently, the simplest theory may not be the best.

Crick himself experienced what he thought was a failure of parsimony. After the structure of DNA was discovered, there remained the problem of deciding how the four bases out of which it is built, G, T, A and C (never mind their chemical names) encode the sequence of amino acids which specify each protein. There are twenty amino acids, but only four bases, so you need more than one base to specify each amino acid. Crick showed that the simplest possible code needed just three bases and so proposed an elegant three-base code. It turned out that he was wrong. The real code is more complex. Crick concluded (partly from this experience, I expect) that parsimony is an unreliable guide to theory in biology.

But he was probably wrong about that. In the DNA case, the actual code seems to have properties in addition to just coding for proteins. Its redundancy serves an error-correction function. In other words, if a particular DNA molecule is damaged, it may nevertheless come up with the right set of proteins. So perhaps Crick's simple code is not the one that fits *all* the functions that DNA must perform. The real code may be the simplest one that does all it needs to do.

My conclusion is that the safest guide to theory in psychology is indeed parsimony: to explain much with little. The ratio of facts explained to assumptions made should be as large as possible. But what about other criteria, such as introspection and felt experience, biological plausibility, close relation to neurobiology, or, for radical behaviorists, limiting theory to statements about directly measurable entities? Let's deal with the first three and then I'll come back to parsimony and the radical behaviorist attitude to theory.

Felt experience—phenomenology—has always had a privileged status in psychological explanation. That's why Freud's supposed discovery of the unconscious—mental activities of which we have no conscious awareness—seemed so revolutionary, even though it had significant predecessors, as I pointed out in Chapter 1. Shouldn't we agree with a recent discussion group e-mail posting that: "The cognitive position, then, is not that conscious experience should be accepted at face value, but rather that concepts thrown up by introspection are worth exploring"? Perhaps they are. But has the effort paid off? I don't think so. In fact, this approach has not been anywhere near as successful as the effort devoted to it would suggest. Attempts to use folk psychology terms like "expectations," "memories" (as locatable physical entities), "craving" and the like as ingredients for theories of behavior have not revolutionized psychology. Moreover, by focusing on phenomenological concepts, simpler ideas not easily related to introspection have been overlooked.

But perhaps the strongest objection to building theories of behavior out of ingredients from felt experience is that felt experience is often wildly and provably *wrong*. For example, brain damaged patients will often *confabulate,* discuss at length experiences they have never had and sights they have never seen, with no consciousness of error at all. Most dramatic are the stories of split-brain patients—patients with cut cerebral commissures, hence almost no communication between the two sides of the brain. These patients usually know the nature of their defect and the errors to which it leads when different stimuli are presented to each half of the visual field. Yet, when they make mistakes, they invariably cover them up with some palpably false story, rather than attribute them, as they should, to their physical condition.

> Some of the most famous examples of confabulation come from 'split-brain' patients, whose left and right brain hemispheres have been surgically disconnected for medical treatment. Neuroscientists have devised clever experiments in which information is provided to the right hemisphere (for instance, pictures of naked people), causing a change in behavior (embarrassed giggling). Split-brain individuals are then asked to explain their behavior verbally, which relies on the left hemisphere. Realizing that their body is laughing, but unaware of the nude images, the left hemisphere will confabulate an excuse for the body's behavior ("I keep laughing because you ask such funny questions, Doc!").[12]

These patients believe their own stories and do not intend to deceive. There is no reason to suppose that the insights of intact, "normal" people into the causes of their own behavior are very much more accurate than these dramatic failures of the brain damaged. The easy deceptions of professional magicians, for example, depend on predictable misperception by normal people.[13]

How about biological plausibility? Well, first it is very much in the eye of the beholder. For one thing, there are at least two kinds of plausibility: *structural* and *functional.* Structural plausibility just means that the structures in the theory must map onto real neural structures. Problem: Real neural structures are very complex; no comprehensible, computable theory can begin to approach this kind of realism. (Nor would there be much point, for the theory would be as incomprehensible as that which it purported to explain.) Functional plausibility, the idea that the processes in the theory are processes for which we have biological counterparts, is better, but it's not very restrictive. Just look at a diagram of the chemical pathways in a single cell and you can see that biology has processes and to spare. Functional plausibility limits us little.

What about restricting our theories to known neurobiology? The problem with this criterion is that it is too severe. Fitting behavioral theory to neurobiology demands that we know *all* the essentials—because the bit we don't know may be vital. The brain is a highly connected system, a missed inhibitory link can completely reverse effects. It simply isn't true that knowing 99% of the neurophysiology will allow us to make predictions that are 99% correct. If the 1% we don't know is critical, our predictions may be 100% wrong.

Work on feeding models is a good illustration. Beginning in the early 1970s, numerous theorists attempted to construct computer models to explain the essentials of feeding behavior in rats: regulation in response to different kinds of challenge, the temporal pattern ("eating in meals") and the relation between eating patterns and body weight.[14] The effort peaked in the early 1980s, but then fizzled to the point that an eating model rarely makes its way into print anymore, despite the great boost in computer power and the growth of computer modeling in general. Why this decline? My guess is that it is because all the models focused on physiology; every element of every model had to *represent something physiological*. But we don't know *all* the physiology that is relevant for feeding. Neurobiology is a shifting target; we find out more about the brain every day. If we don't know it all, a model built only out of what we *do* know is likely to fail.

On the other hand, if you just look at feeding *behavior,* it *is* possible to come up with a very simple model that can duplicate feeding regulation and the basic patterns of feeding under challenge.[15] The model is parsimonious: It has very few assumptions and explains quite a lot of facts. But the ingredients of the model are designed to explain the behavioral data, not to match up with known physiology. Physiology is not irrelevant, of course. But now the ball is in the other court: It's up the physiologists to figure out how the brain can behave in the way our model says it does. Skinner would have been pleased, as this is just the role he set out for behavioral psychology.

The key to the theoretical approach is parsimony. The reason for emphasizing parsimony is not because biology is always parsimonious. It is not. On the contrary, many biologists, from Darwin to Crick, have pointed out that evolution is frequently a kludge: Bits are added on to other bits, organs originally selected for one function assume another, and so on. Processes that result from this complex history can sometimes be understood in physiological terms, but often they resist understanding and order must be found elsewhere. The reason for parsimony is simply that *that is what science is all about.* Science is reducing the multiplicity and particularity of raw experience to a limited number of principles. in Bacon's words:

> [A]nd since truth will sooner come from error than confusion I think it expedient that the understanding should have permission after the three Tables of First Presentation (such as I have exhibited) have been made and weighed, to make an essay of the Interpretation of Nature in the affirmative way.[16]

In more modern words, after you've looked at the data, have a guess at the mechanism. The working hypothesis of theoretical behaviorism is that the simplest mechanism is probably closest to the truth. At least, it's the place to start.

Notice that this approach will almost invariably require the postulation of "events taking place somewhere else, at some other level of observation [or none], described in different terms, and measured, if at all, in different dimensions."[17] Skinner's bizarre proscription would have ruled out genes, atoms, electron, quarks, the DNA double helix, indeed every great theoretical advance in modern science.[18] It even conflicts with his own view of legitimate theory as "a formal representation of the data reduced to a minimal number of terms"—a formulation not far from theoretical behaviorism. Skinner chose not to notice that such a formal representation may—indeed, usually will—contain terms that refer to "events . . . at some other level of observation."

I argue in the next section that internal states (hidden variables) are absolutely essential to the economical description of even the simplest behavioral phenomena. As an example, I choose the simplest possible kind of learning: habituation.

Internal States in Habituation

Habituation is the waning of a reflex response to repeated stimulation. Here's a very simple example. You're observing through a dissecting microscope a petri dish full of 1-mm-long nematode worms called *Caenorhabditis elegans. C. elegans* is a creature very popular with molecular biologists, who have mapped out every cell and its progeny, from zygote to adult. The worms swim in more or less straight lines through the culture medium. Every now and then, you tap the side of the dish. Some of the worms turn in response to the tap. You measure how many turn. You plot the average response as a function of successive taps and find something like what is shown in Figure 15.1.[19] The number of worms that turn declines—*habituates*—with successive taps (stimuli); and the decline is slower and less complete when the taps are widely spaced (60 s apart) than when they are more closely spaced (10 s apart).

How can we explain habituation like this in this simplest of creatures? The definition by itself does not explain why long interstimulus intervals (ISIs) produce less habituation than short ones. We cannot predict the effects of novel patterns of stimulation. We cannot predict how the system recovers after a period without stimulation.

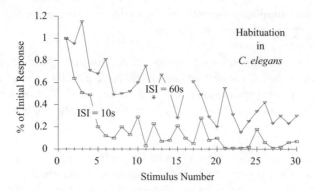

Figure 15.1 Habituation in *C. elegans*. The plot shows the proportion of worms in a group turning in response to thirty brief stimuli presented at either 10 s or 60 s interstimulus intervals.

Data from C. H. Rankin & B. S. Broster. (1992). Factors affecting habituation and recovery from habituation in the nematode *Caenorhabditis elegans*. *Behavioral Neuroscience, 106*, 239–249.

If you wait some time after the training series and then present a stimulus, the response will be greater than at the end of the series. *Spontaneous recovery,* as it is called, shows something called *rate sensitivity.*[20] Even though the level of habituation after training with a long ISI (e.g., 60 s) is lower than after the same number of stimuli at a short ISI (e.g., 10 s; see Figure 15.1), the habituation may be *more persistent* after the long-ISI training. You will often find more recovery after the short-ISI series than after the long-ISI series, even though the absolute level of responding was lower at the end of short-ISI training than after long-ISI training.

Apparently it is not sufficient just to take the level of responding at the end of training as a simple measure of "strength." By this measure, responding after short-ISI training is "weaker" than responding after long-ISI training. Yet the short-ISI behavior recovers faster than the long-ISI behavior, hence it must have been stronger not weaker. Obviously the unidimensional behavioristic idea of reflex strength is not sufficient to explain what is happening here.

Explaining rate sensitivity requires a model that goes beyond observables. It *cannot* be explained by referring to stimuli and responses alone. It cannot even be explained by referring to environmental and behavioral *histories* because there are an infinite number of possible histories. Once we attempt to reduce this infinity to a manageable number by grouping together histories that have similar effects, we are dealing with *internal states* in the sense described in the last chapter.

Memory

Habituation clearly requires some kind of memory, a persisting effect of past stimuli that somehow weakens the habituated response. As the strength of memory increases, the response to a stimulus decreases. But this memory is

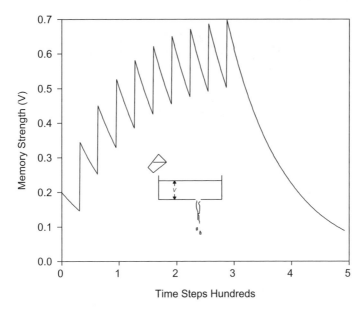

Figure 15.2 Properties of a simple memory. Memory strength increases with each stimulus presentation and decays thereafter. When no stimuli are presented, the memory eventually decays to zero. *Inset*: A physical system that has these properties. As each cup of water is emptied into the leaky bowl the water level (V) rises, and then falls at a constant rate afterward.

not permanent—at least in nematodes. If you wait long enough after the training experience, a new stimulus will produce the response at full strength (spontaneous recovery). Let's look at the simplest kind of memory process and then at a slightly more complicated version.

The simplest kind of transient memory is illustrated in Figure 15.2. The graph shows the effect of repeated stimulation on the memory. Memory strength rises with each stimulus presentation and then decays. The inset shows a physical system with the same properties: a leaky bucket into which a glass of water is periodically emptied. As in the graph, water level in the bowl rises with each glassful, and then declines. Obviously, the more frequently the glass is emptied, the higher the water level. Also obvious is the fact that the rate of "forgetting" (decline in water level) is constant: The level declines by a fixed fraction of its current value in each time step.

The "leaky-bucket" memory is a one-dimensional system that fits in well with naïve behaviorism, because the "strength" of the memory depends only on the level of the response. It does show the same effect of stimulus spacing. It is pretty obvious that the less frequent the stimuli, the less the habituation. But it does not show rate sensitivity, because the rate of memory decay (i.e., the rate of recovery from habituation) is constant, not dependent on the training history as in real organisms. What's needed is a memory system at least as complex as in Figure 15.3.[21]

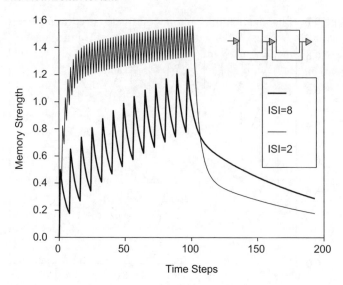

Figure 15.3 Rate sensitivity in a two-stage habituation system. The curves show the change in memory strength of the system when stimuli are presented at intervals of two or eight time steps. With the second-stage memory suitably slower than the first, memory strength is lower after the 8-TS series than after the 2-TS series, but it also decays more slowly.

A system with at least two simple memories, one that forgets more slowly than the other, is necessary for rate sensitivity. Figure 15.3 shows how this works. There are two integrators. The first decays quickly (fast) the second more slowly (slow). The output of the first is input to the second—the first is in effect a low-pass filter. Widely spaced inputs (stimuli) pass through with little reduction to the second integrator, but closely spaced stimuli keep the first integrator charged up, so the second, slow, integrator gets little input. The strength of response is the sum of the values of both integrators.

Memory strength increases more rapidly in the 2-TS series than in the 8-TS series, but it also decays more quickly. The reason is that after the short-ISI series, most of the memory strength is in the fast-decaying memory, whereas after the long-ISI series, most is in the slow-decaying memory. Hence memory strength (the sum of the two memories) decays rapidly after the short-ISI series and slowly after the long-ISI series. A system like this does show rate sensitivity.

The point of this analysis is that in this system, response strength is not sufficient by itself to tell you how the system will behave in the future. The state of the system is defined not by one number but by two (or more). But, knowing those two (the strengths of the two memories), the future behavior of the system after any stimulus history is perfectly predictable.

Even habituation, the simplest kind of learning, cannot be explained solely in terms of stimuli and responses. At least one hidden variable is necessary.

The properties of habituation imply an internal state (strictly speaking, a *state space*) defined by at least two numbers. Other kinds of learning clearly require a state space defined by many more numbers. Just how many, and what form of model is appropriate, is still for the most part unknown.

***

We understand how nature works only through models. The models may be very simple, like our model of the visual world or Copernicus's model of the solar system. Or they may be very complex, like the model of DNA. The issues for behaviorists are whether they need models at all (perhaps some kind of unidimensional "strength" notion is sufficient?), and if so, what kind they should be. Using habituation in nematodes as an example of the simplest kind of learning, I have shown that response "strength" by itself is not sufficient: A model with at least two dimensions is needed to explain experimental results. We cannot explain habituation without postulating an internal state, which, in this case, is defined by two numbers. Obviously the much more complex kinds of learning shown by higher animals—rats, pigeons, behaviorists—will require models at least as complex as this. The necessity of modeling means that sticking to observables, to behavior, is not an option. The concept of internal state cannot be avoided.

What kinds of model should we look for? I argue here that a ruthless parsimony is our best guide. Neither subjective experience, nor biological plausibility, nor a kind of erector-set approach using neurobiological ingredients, is a reliable guide. The unique contribution of the theoretical behaviorist is to find the simplest possible process to explain behavioral data.

Notes

1. Tolman didn't always agree, sometimes writing as if he expected his constructs to correspond to physiological reality. See, for example, Smith, L. D. (1986). *Behaviorism and logical positivism* (Stanford, CA: Stanford University Press), p. 118.
2. Rachlin, H. (1991). *Introduction to modern behaviorism,* 3rd ed. (New York: Freeman); Staddon, J. E. R. (1967). Asymptotic behavior: The concept of the operant. *Psychological Review, 74,* 377–391.
3. And maybe not even bacteria. More detailed data on the dynamics of kineses/taxes (see Chapter 2) are also likely to require explanation in terms of internal states. Indeed, hypothetical constructs, in the form of biochemical mechanisms, have already been proposed (see Berg, H. C. [2000, January]. Motile behavior of bacteria. *Physics Today, 24*–29).
4. Kealey, T. (1996). *The economic laws of scientific research* (New York: St. Martin's Press). A reconstructed version of Babbage's engine is on display at the London Science Museum. See www.sciencemuseum.org.uk/onlinestuff/stories/babbage.aspx.
5. Famous *pensées* along these lines are Hermann Helmholtz's, "Whoever, in the pursuit of science, seeks after immediate practical utility, may generally rest assured that he will seek in vain." Or, more pithily, Richard Feynman's, "Science is a lot like sex. Sometimes something useful comes of it, but that's not the reason we're doing it."

6. Bacon, F. (1863). *Novum Organum I, Aph. LXX, Collected works* (Boston: Taggard and Thompson).
7. Clark, K. B., & Clark, M. P. (1947). Racial identification and preference in Negro children. In *Readings in social psychology* (New York: Henry Holt), pp. 169–178.
8. Petersen, C., Maier, S. F., & Seligman, M. E. P. (1995). *Learned helplessness: A theory for the age of personal control* (New York: Oxford University Press).
9. Steele, K. M., Bella, S. D., Peretz, I., Dunlop, T., Dawe, L. A., Humphrey, G. K., . . . Olmstead, C. G. (1999). Prelude or requiem for the "Mozart effect"? *Nature, 400*, 827; Chabris, C. F. (1999). See also www1.appstate.edu/~kms/research/Steele.htm.
10. Bacon (1863), *Aph. XXV*, Bk. I.
11. Comment in a letter to the American Academy of Arts and Sciences, January 1881.
12. See www.edge.org/response-detail/11513.
13. For a good survey, see Randi, J. (1997). *An encyclopedia of claims, frauds, and hoaxes of the occult and supernatural: James Randi's skeptical definitions of alternate realities* (New York: St. Martin's Press).
14. Booth, D. A. (Ed.). (1978). *Hunger models* (London: Academic Press).
15. Staddon, J. E. R., & Zanutto, B. S. (1997). Feeding dynamics: Why rats eat in meals and what this means for foraging and feeding regulation. In M. E. Bouton, & M. S. Fanselow (Eds.), *Learning, motivation and cognition: The functional behaviorism of Robert C. Bolles* (Washington, DC: American Psychological Association), pp. 131–162. Zanutto suggested a physiological implementation of this model later (Zanutto, B. S., & Staddon, J. E. R. [2007]. Bang-bang control of feeding: Role of hypothalamic and satiety signals. *PLoS Computational Biology, 3*[5], e97), as I pointed out in Chapter 2.
16. Bacon (1863), *Aph. XX*, Book 2.
17. Skinner, B. F. (1950). *Science and human behavior* (New York: Macmillan), p. 193.
18. Williams, B. A. (1986). On the role of theory in behavior analysis. *Behaviorism, 14*, 111–124.
19. Rankin, C. H., & Broster, B. S. (1992). Factors affecting habituation and recovery from habituation in the nematode *Caenorhabditis elegans. Behavioral Neuroscience, 106*, 239–249.
20. Staddon, J. E. R. (1993). On rate-sensitive habituation. *Adaptive Behavior, 1*, 421–436; Staddon, J. E. R., & Higa, J. J. (1996). Multiple time scales in simple habituation. *Psychological Review, 103*, 720–733.
21. See Staddon & Higa (1996), for more details.

16 Consciousness and Theoretical Behaviorism

There is a famous paper by philosopher Thomas Nagel called "What Is It Like to Be a Bat?"[1] Nagel complains that materialist—behaviorist—accounts of behavior leave out the subjective "what does it feel like . . ." aspect—what most people mean by conscious experience. True, but, from an epistemological point of view, there is simply no way I or anyone else can know what it is like to be a bat, any more than you can know whether the color green looks to me just like what red looks like to you (and vice versa). If you want to know what it is like to be a bat, there really is no alternative to actually being a bat—or perhaps asking one. There is also no way that a politician can literally "feel my pain." There is of course something that the father of economics, Adam Smith, called "sympathy" and we now call "empathy." Perhaps Mr. Clinton feels that. But my pain is mine alone, although an observer might be able to measure its effects. The *qualia* of consciousness, as they are called, are strictly private. More on qualia in a moment.

At a commonsense level, there is nothing mysterious about consciousness—human consciousness, at least. It simply refers to experiences you can talk about. For example, there are a number of experiments in which words are flashed on a screen and people are asked later to recall them or say if they recognize them. It is easy to show that under some conditions, the subject may fail to recognize a word—he isn't conscious of having seen it—yet he shows by his reaction time, or speed of relearning or some other measure that the word on first exposure did have some effect. In short, he was not conscious of seeing it, but it did affect his behavior. Patients with hippocampal brain damage, which causes short-term memory loss, show even more striking effects. Repeatedly exposed to a manual puzzle, like the "Tower of Hanoi," they claim each time not to have seen it before, yet their performance improves with practice.[2]

Even normal people show similar, if less dramatic effects. For example, suppose that human subjects are presented with a number of lists of nine digits (say), with every third list being identical. The subjects are not told about the repeated list. When asked to recall the lists, they recall the repeated list better than the others (no surprise!). But many subjects also fail to notice the repetition.[3] Data like this have led to a distinction between *episodic* memory (memory for events) and *semantic* or *implicit* memory (memory for a skill).

Other data have led to still other distinctions and the subject is still in flux.[4] But clearly, learning doesn't have to be conscious.

Sleepwalking is another example of the dissociation between memory and consciousness. Awake, sleepwalkers have no recollection of their nocturnal activities. An English newspaper story a few years ago described a young man, sleepwalking, who fell out of a second-floor window on to the bonnet (this was England, not the United States) of his mother's Mercedes. Bruised but still asleep, he picked himself up and walked down the street. He woke up only after knocking on his grandmother's front door. Was he "unconscious" as he walked? Presumably, although some sleepwalkers, like this one, seem conscious as they sleepwalk, even though they cannot recall what happened when they awake. This dissociation shows that consciousness and the unity of consciousness are two different things. Being able to report on an experience requires some kind of memory. Clearly "normal" memory has failed here— although possibly the sleepwalker, while still asleep, may remember what happens in that state. We don't know whether the unfortunate young Englishman would have responded accurately to a question about his fall while still sleepwalking, even though he was unable to do so afterward.

There is a similar phenomenon in psychopharmacology called *state-dependent* learning,[5] in which an animal under the influence of a drug learns a task but cannot perform it in the absence of the drug. Does this denote divided consciousness like the sleepwalker, or something less interesting, like stimulus control (see Chapter 5) by the drug? And then there is the phenomenon of "blindsight."[6] Humans with brain lesions in the visual area cannot "see," yet sometimes avoid obstacles and show in other ways some effect of their visual environment. Their seeing is "unconscious."

Finally there is the horrific image of the "brain in a bottle," a conscious individual completely unable to communicate with the outside world. Close to the brain in a bottle is so-called locked-in syndrome: "The locked-in syndrome (pseudocoma) describes patients who are awake and conscious but selectively deefferented, i.e., have no means of producing speech, limb or facial movements."[7] Are these unfortunates conscious or not? Maybe. If progress in brain recording gets to the point that we can reliably identify, say, functional magnetic resonance imaging (fMRI) or electroencephalography (EEG) patterns with the existence of consciousness in normal (i.e., able-to-speak) individuals, then a suitable signature in pseudocoma patients would be sufficient to infer consciousness. Or, if the pseudocoma patient recovers and can remember his experience while apparently comatose, we might come to the same conclusion.

These examples are all interesting but not, I think, unduly mysterious. You are conscious when you, or your brain, says you are.

William James defined psychology as the science of mental life. He also wrote, in apparent contradiction, that "[consciousness] is the name of a non-entity, and has no right to a place among first principles."[8] But he went on to say, "Let me then immediately explain that I mean only to deny that the word stands for an entity, but to insist most emphatically that it does stand for a function." What is that function? James called it "knowing." Does the brain-damaged person who learns the Tower of Hanoi without knowing he has done so qualify as conscious, at least in that respect? James would probably say "no." So how might knowing be measured?

How Good Is the Turing Test?

These examples illustrate the Turing-test view of consciousness: If a subject can make the appropriate verbal report, we will grant him consciousness. I said something about the limitations of the Turing test as an experiment in Chapter 13. But assuming that the limitations as to time and variety of questions asked can be overcome, surely the test is conclusive? A good behaviorist will accept the Turing-test: If you act conscious, you *are* conscious.

But this view is not accepted by everyone. A creature that acts conscious but really isn't sounds like a "zombie," which is not the Haitian creation, but an imaginary creature discussed by philosophers who looks and talks like you and me, but lacks *qualia.* The zombie image is a recurring theme in fiction—*The Stepford Wives* and *Invasion of the Body Snatchers* are two modern examples (the replicants in *Blade Runner* had feelings, so perhaps they don't qualify). A zombie has no *qualia,* but behaves otherwise perfectly normally. It could presumably pass the Turing test.[9]

Philosopher John Searle is suspicious of the Turing test and made his objection in the form of his famous Chinese Room allegory:

> Simply imagine that someone who understands no Chinese is locked in a room with a lot of Chinese symbols *and a computer program for answering questions in Chinese.* [my italics] The input to the system consists in Chinese symbols in the form of questions; the output of the system consists in Chinese symbols in answer to the questions. We might suppose that the program is so good that the answers to the questions are indistinguishable from those of a native Chinese speaker. But all the same, neither the person inside nor any other part of the system literally understands Chinese.[10]

There are several objections to Searle's argument. Most important, I think is the *system response:* Of course, the man in the room doesn't understand Chinese. No part of the system "understands" Chinese, any more than any neuron in your brain understands English. *You,* the system as a whole, understand English; the room-plus-program understands Chinese. And as for that computer program: Where is it written that such a program *could* be constructed? Yet without proof that it is possible, the argument is moot.

There are at least two other objections. First is the obvious behaviorist question, "If it acts conscious, how do you know it isn't?" If you answer, "I don't," then you disagree with Searle, accept the Turing test and disbelieve in zombies. My second reaction is: Wait and see. If a "conscious" robot is ever created, you can be just about certain that people will soon treat this new R2-D2 just like another human being.

It's worth noticing that the very limited success of numerous attempts to get chimps and other great apes to talk in some way has nevertheless already led to vigorous legal efforts to get them treated like human beings.[11] If they are conscious, the argument goes, we need to treat them much better than we do. If we are willing to grant consciousness to an ape, a parrot, or to someone as impaired as deaf and blind Helen Keller, are we likely to withhold it from a device that speaks and responds indistinguishably from a human being?

These comments apply *a fortiori* to the zombie who, after all, even looks normal. If he looks and talks the same as everyone else, on what basis do we say he is different?

"Conscious" robots can at least talk. Because animals cannot communicate with anything like human facility, attributing consciousness to them is much trickier, however. The search for clever ways to get around the speech limitation continues. One possibility is a phenomenon, first discussed in connection with human cognition but now, apparently, observed in animals, called *metacognition*. Metacognition is "thinking about thinking": It

> refers to one's knowledge concerning one's own cognitive processes. . . . For example, I am engaging in metacognition if I notice that I am having more trouble learning A than B; if it strikes me that I should double check C before accepting it as fact.[12]

When navigating in strange territory you may weigh your confidence in turning left versus right at an intersection. You assume that your confidence in your choice is related to its likely accuracy. But some people are always sure and others are always hesitant. It is not clear that the confident ones are more often correct than the hesitant ones. But all this deliberation sounds pretty conscious, and some have even suggested that showing something like it in animals proves that they are also conscious.

Here is an experiment with animals that shows metacognition like this. Rats were trained to discriminate the duration of a burst of noise. There were two classes of noise duration: short (four stimuli, 2–3.62 s)—press the left (for example) lever, or long (four stimuli, 4.42–8 s)—press the right lever.[13] Correct responses got them six pellets, a large reward. On test trials the animals were allowed to choose between a third option, a small reward (three pellets) sure thing, versus one of the two test levers (a possible six pellets). Their choice was (1) choose the sure thing; (2) choose one of the two choice levers: long or short. Notice that the expected average reward if the animal cannot tell the difference between long and short is the same for the two choice levers as for the sure-thing lever: 3 versus $(0 + 6)/2$. The idea is that if the animals are unsure, "they think they don't know the right answer," they will settle for the weakly rewarded "sure thing" rather than guess and maybe

get nothing. Unsurprisingly, perhaps, when the test duration was on the bor-
derline between "short" and "long," stimuli 3.62 s or 4.42 s, the rats tended to
choose the sure thing. Even more striking was the fact that the animals were
more accurate on test trials, when the sure thing was available, than on regular
trials when it was not.

So, are these rats conscious? Should we on this account grant them full civil
rights, as at least one commentator seems to suggest?[14] Again, maybe; but the
data can also be explained in a simple, behavioristic way that leaves consciousness out of the account entirely. The explanation has three parts:[15]

1. The rats cannot discriminate time perfectly. Consequently, on the borders—
    long "short" stimulus or a short "long" one—they will make errors.
2. Rats are *risk averse,* that is, they will prefer a reward of size x to a 50%
    chance of reward of size $2x$. There is independent evidence for risk aver-
    sion in rats, but not in pigeons.[16]
3. Thus, on test trials when the choice is difficult, the rats will avoid choos-
    ing and go for the sure thing. When the sure thing is not available, and
    they must choose, they will therefore make more errors on difficult tri-
    als. Overall, therefore, they will do better when permitted the sure-thing,
    "metacognition," option.
4. Pigeons, who do not show risk aversion, should not, therefore, show better
    performance when the sure-thing option is available than when it is not.
    And indeed, there is no metacognition in pigeons.[17]

Is this explanation correct? It is perhaps too early to say, but it does fit the
facts and offers no support for a hypothetical process, metacognition, whose
properties are unspecified and which exists largely because of a kind of latent
anthropomorphism, a wish to see in the rat the richness of understanding we
believe resides within us.

Now let's look at a phenomenon of human perception that was thought to
pose a real problem for behavioristic understanding of consciousness. How is
it treated by cognitivists and by theoretical behaviorism?

Three Domains and Color Phi

When you watch a movie, your retina is stimulated twenty-four times each
second with twenty-four static images. An object that takes up adjacent positions in each successive image is perceived as moving smoothly. The effect can
be demonstrated experimentally with a single bright spot that is successively
presented at one place and then at an adjacent place (see Figure 16.1). If the
delay between the two presentations is short, the spot appears to move, rather
than disappear and then reappear. This is termed the *phi phenomenon.* There
is a related effect in which the two spots are different colors. What is seen is a
single moving spot that changes color at about the midpoint of its travel.

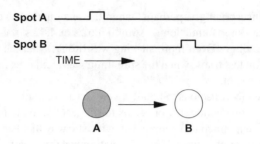

Figure 16.1 The phi phenomenon. Spot A is briefly lit; then after a short delay, spot B
is lit. If the delay is short enough, the lit spot appears to move from right
to left.

This is a puzzle for some cognitivists. A philosopher and a psychologist
conjecture as follows:

> [Philosopher Nelson] Goodman wondered: "How are we able . . . to fill in
> the spot at the intervening place-times along a path running from the first to
> the second flash *before that flash occurs?*" . . . Unless there is precognition,
> the illusory content cannot be created until *after* some identification of the
> second spot occurs in the brain. But if this identification of the second spot
> is already "in conscious experience" would it not be too late to interpose
> the illusory color-switching-while-moving scene between the conscious
> experience of spot 1 and the conscious experience of spot 2? . . . [Other
> experimenters] proposed that the intervening motion is produced retro-
> spectively, built only after the second flash occurs, and "projected back-
> wards in time." . . . But what does it mean that this experienced motion is
> "projected backwards in time"?[18]

Presented in this way, the color-phi effect certainly seems baffling, at least
to philosopher Goodman. Dennett and Kinsbourne describe, rather pictur-
esquely, two standard cognitive ways of dealing with this effect. One, which
they term "Orwellian," is that we experience things in one way, but then revise
our memories, much as Minitruth in Orwell's *1984* revised history. The color-
phi effect thus becomes a *post hoc* reinterpretation: Two spots are experienced,
but a smoothly moving, color-changing spot is reported. Dennett and Kinsbourne term the other standard approach "Stalinesque," by analogy with Stalin's show trials, in which false evidence is created but reported accurately. In
this view, what is reported is what was actually experienced, though what was
experienced was not what (objectively) happened.

Dennett and Kinsbourne dismiss both of these accounts in favor of what
they term a "multiple-drafts" model:

> Our Multiple Drafts model agrees with Goodman that retrospectively the
> brain creates the content (the judgment) that there was intervening motion,

and that this content is then available to govern activity and leave its mark on memory. But our model claims that the brain does not bother "constructing" any representations that go to the trouble of "filling in" the blanks.[19]

In the multiple-drafts model, consciousness becomes a distributed construct, like "The British Empire" (their analogy), which is not uniquely located in time or space.

Theoretical behaviorism has a much simpler way of looking at the color-phi effect. First, note that like all other psychological phenomena, the effect involves three conceptually separate domains:

Domain 1

The first is the domain of felt experience, the *phenomenological* domain. There is a certain quality (philosophers call this *quale*) associated with the color-phi experience. This is subjective and *science has nothing to say about it*. From a scientific point of view, I cannot say whether "green" looks the same to you as to me; I can only say whether or not you make the same judgments about colored objects as I do. This point used to be a commonplace in philosophy, but apparently it needs to be reiterated from time to time. Friedrich Hayek wrote:

> That different people classify external stimuli in the 'same' way does not mean that individual sense qualities are the same for different people (which would be a meaningless statement), but that the systems of sense qualities of different people have a common structure (are homeomorphic systems of relations).[20]

The same idea was on the table at the dawn of behaviorism:

> Suppose, for example, that I introspect concerning my consciousness of colors. All you can ever really learn from such introspection is whether or not I shall behave towards those colors in the same ways that you do. You can never learn what those colors really "feel" like to me.

(This from that most cognitive of behaviorists, Edward Tolman.[21])

What this means is that if you and I are standing in the same place, we see the same chair to the left of the same table, we judge these two greens to be the same and the red to be different from the green, and so forth. What we *cannot* say is that my green is the same as yours, What we *can* say (unless one of us is color-blind), is that my green bears the same relation to my yellow as your green does to your yellow.

I can also know if you say the same things about color-phi-type stimuli as I do. Note that this is a behavioristic position, but it is not the version of behaviorism dismissed by Dennett and Kinsbourne, when they say "One could, then, 'make the problems disappear' by simply refusing to take introspective reports seriously."[22] As we will see shortly, the question is not whether phenomeno-logical reports should be ignored—of course they should not—but how they should be interpreted.

Domain 2

The second domain is physiological, the real-time functioning of the brain. The color-phi experiment says nothing about the brain, but another experiment, which I will discuss in a moment, does include physiological data.

Domain 3

The third domain is the domain of behavioral data, "intersubjectively verifi-able" reports and judgments by experimental subjects. The reports of people in response to appropriate stimuli are the basis for everything objective we can know about color phi.

Much of the muddle in the various cognitive accounts arises from confusion among these three domains. For example, an eminent neuroscientist writes: "The qualia question is, how does the flux of ions in little bits of jelly—the neurons—give rise to the redness of red, the flavor of Marmite or paneer tikka masala or wine?"[23] Phrased in this way we don't know and can't know. But phrased a little differently, the question can yield a scientific answer: What brain state or states corresponds to the response "it tastes like Marmite"? As Hayek and many others have pointed out (mostly in vain), the phenomenology question—which always boils down to "how does red look to you?"—is not answerable. All we can know is whether red, green, blue, and so forth, enter into the same relations with one another with the same results for you as for me—Hayek's "homeomorphic relations."

Color phi provides yet another example of the same confusion. Dennett and Kinsbourne write, "Conscious experiences are real events occurring in the real time and space of the brain, and hence they are clockable and locat-able within the appropriate limits of precision for real phenomena of their type."[24] Well, no, not really. What can be clocked and located are *reports* of conscious experiences and *measurements* of physiological events. Conscious experiences are *Domain 1,* which has neither time nor space, but only inef-fable *qualia*. The only evidence we have for these *qualia* (at least, for some-one else's) is *Domain 3*. And we can try and correlate *Domain 3* data with *Domain 2* data and infer something about the brain correlates of reported experiences. But that's all. Dennett and Kinsbourne's confident claim just confuses the issue.

All becomes much clearer once we look more closely at *Domain 3:* What did the subjects see? What did they say about it, and when did they say it? The real-time events in the color-phi experiment are illustrated in Figure 16.2, which is a version of the general framework of Figure 14.2 tailored to this

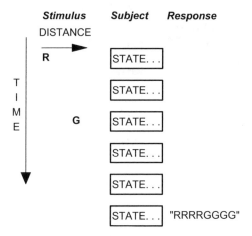

Figure 16.2 Event history in the color-phi experiment. A red spot (R) is briefly lit at time 0, and a little later a green spot (G) is lit. After an additional short delay, the subject responds that he has seen a moving spot that changes color ("RRRRGGGG"). The events are shown in discrete time, instant by instant. The discreteness is not theoretically necessary, but makes the sequence easier to illustrate.

experiment. Time goes from top to bottom in discrete steps. At time 0 the red spot is lit and goes out; there is a delay; then the green spot is lit; there is another delay and then the subject reports what he has seen, namely a continuously moving red spot that changes to green half way through its travel, which I will represent by "RRRRGGGG." Stimulus and response are both *Domain 3*. The properties of the states are as yet undefined. Defining them requires a *theory* for the effect, which I'll get to in a moment.

Confusion centers on the subject's response "RRRRGGGG". What does this response *mean?* This seems to be the heart of the puzzle, but the unknowable *quale* here is scientifically irrelevant. We do not, *can not,* know what the subject "sees." That doesn't mean the subject's response is meaningless. What it can tell us is something about other, "control" experiments that might give the *same* quale. Figure 16.3 shows one such control experiment. In this experiment, a single spot really is moving and changing color at the midpoint: RRRRGGGG, and the subject's report is, appropriately, "RRRRGGGG." The similarity between the responses to the really moving stimulus and to the color-phi stimulus is what the statement "the color-phi stimulus looks like a continuously moving spot that changes color" *means.* The point is that we (i.e., an external observer) cannot judge the subject's quale, but we *can* judge if his response is the same or different on two occasions. And as for the subject, he can also judge whether one thing looks like another or not. These same-different judgments are all that is required for a scientific account.

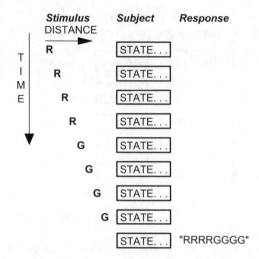

Figure 16.3 Event history in a control experiment. A smoothly moving illuminated spot changes color midway from red to green. After a delay, the subject reports, veridically, ("RRRRGGGG").

A Theory of Color Phi

The comparison between these two experiments suggests an answerable scientific problem, namely: "What kinds of process give the same output to the two different histories illustrated in the two figures?" More generally, what characterizes the class of histories that give the response "RRRRGGGG"? The answer will be some kind of model. What might the process be? It will be one in which the temporally adjacent events tend to inhibit one another, so that initial and terminal events are more salient than events in the middle of a series. Thus, the input sequence RRRRGGGG might be registered[25] as something like *RrrrggggG*—a sort of *serial-position effect* (i.e., stimuli in the middle of a series have less effect than the stimuli on the ends; see Chapter 2). In the limit, when the stimuli are presented rapidly enough, stimuli in the middle may have a negligible effect, so that the input RRRRGGGG yields the registered sequence *R . . . G,* which is indistinguishable from the color-phi sequence. It would then make perfect sense that subjects makes the same response to the complete sequence and the color-phi sequence.

The same response, yes, but just what response will it be? Let's accept the existence of a perceptual process that gives the same output to two different input sequences: RRRRGGGG and R . . . G. The question is, Why is the response "RRRRGGGG," rather than "R . . . G"? Why do people report the abbreviated sequence as appearing like the complete sequence? Why not (*per contra*) report RRRRGGGG as R . . . G? Why privilege one of the two possible interpretations over the other? It is here that evolution and personal history comes into play.[26] Just as in the Ames Room (Chapter 1), the visual system takes the processed visual input (in this case R . . . G) and *infers,* unconsciously, the most likely state of world that it signifies. Since alternating on-and-off spots are rare in our evolutionary history, the inference is that a single moving spot is changing color.

Thus, by responding "RRRRGGGG," rather than "R . . . G," we may simply be playing the evolutionary odds. Given that these two sequences produce the same internal state, the most likely state of the *world* is RRRRGGGG—the moving, color-changing spot—rather than the other. So RRRRGGGG is what we report—*and perceive* (the subject isn't lying).[27]

This approach to the color-phi effect applies as well to nonhuman as human animals. As far as I know, no one has attempted a suitable experiment with pigeons, say, but it could easily be done. A pioneering experiment very similar in form was done many years ago by Donald Blough when he measured pigeons' visual threshold, something that also raises "consciousness"-type questions. After all, only the pigeon knows when he ceases to "see" a slowly dimming stimulus. Blough's solution was a technique invented by his colleague, sensory physiologist Georg Békésy, to measure human auditory thresholds.[28] Blough describes his version of the method in this way:

> The pigeon's basic task is to peck key A when the stimulus patch is visible and to peck key B when the patch is dark. The stimulus patch, brightly lighted during early periods of training is gradually reduced in brightness until it falls beneath the pigeon's absolute threshold.[29]

As the patch dims and becomes invisible, so the pigeon's choice shifts from key A to key B. Blough's experiment tracked the pigeon's dark-adaptation curve—the change in threshold as the light dimmed—which turned out to be very similar in form to curves obtained from people.

Exactly the same procedure could be used to see when a pigeon shifts from seeing on-and-off lights to a continuously moving-and-color-changing light. The pigeon is confronted with two choice keys, on the left (A) and the right (B). In between is a digital display that can show either a continuously moving[30] dot that changes color from red to green in mid-travel (*continuous*), or two dots, a red on the left and green on the right, that alternate (*alternating;* see Figures 16.1 and 16.3). The animal would first be trained to peck key A when *alternating* is presented (with an alternation rate slow enough to make the two dots easily visible as separate events); and to peck key B when the continuously moving light is presented. The rate of the *continuous* display would need to match the alternation rate of the *alternation* display. As the experiment progresses, the alternation rate is slowly increased just as, in Blough's experiment, stimulus brightness was slowly decreased. I very much expect that the animal will at some point change its preference from key A, indicating that it sees the two dots as separate stimuli, to key B, indicating that they look like the *continuous* stimulus.

The point is that consciousness can perfectly well be studied using methods that require no verbal report—merely a response signaling that sequences are perceived as similar to one thing or the other. The attempt to interpret phenomena like color phi in terms of "consciousness" usually leads to a muddle. It's a scientific hindrance rather than a help.

This story of the color-phi problem parallels exactly the history of research on another perceptual phenomenon: color vision. An early discovery was that people sometimes see "red" (for example) when no spectrally red light is present— just as people sometimes see movement when nothing is actually moving (in movies, for example). Later research expanded on this theme through the study of after-effects, color-contrast and Land effects,[31] eventually showing a wide range of disparities between the color seen and the wavelengths present. The solution to the problem was the discovery of processing mechanisms that define the necessary and sufficient physical-stimulus conditions for a person to report "green," "red" or any other color. "Consciousness" forms no part of this account either.

My analysis of the color-phi effect sheds some light on a pseudo-issue in cognitive psychology and artificial intelligence: the so-called binding problem. A philosopher describes it this way:

> I see the yellow tennis ball. I see your face and hear what you say. I see and smell the bouquet of roses. The binding problem arises by paying attention to how these coherent perceptions arise. There are specialized sets of neurons that detect different aspects of objects in the visual field. The color and motion of the ball are detected by different sets of neurons in different areas of the visual cortex. . . . Binding seeing and hearing, or seeing and smelling, is even more complex. . . . The problem is how all this individually processed information can give rise to a unified percept.[32]

What does "unified perception" amount to? We report a unified percept "cat." When confronted with a cat, we can say "cat," can identify different aspects of the cat, can compare this cat to others like it, and so on. The cognitive assumption is that this requires some sort of unity in the brain: "The answer would be simple if there were a place where all the outputs of all the processors involved delivered their computations at the same time, a faculty of consciousness, as it were. But . . . there is no such place."[33]

There is no such place. Yes, that is correct. But why on Earth should there be? From a behavioristic point of view, "binding" is a pseudo-problem. We report continuous movement in the color-phi effect, but nothing moves in the brain. All we have is a functional equivalence between the brain state produced by a moving dot and the brain state produced by two flashing dots. The same is surely true for the cat percept. There is a state (probably a large set of states) that the subject reports as "cat." This state can be evoked by the sight of a cat, a sketch of a cat, the sound of a cat, and so on. We have no idea about the mechanism by which this comes about—perceiving a cat is more complex than perceiving movement of a dot—but there is no difficulty in principle in understanding what is happening.

Why does there seem to be a problem? *Because of a conflation of Domain 1 with Domain 2.* The percept "cat" is real and unified in Domain 1, but that has no bearing on Domain 2, the underlying physiology. Recall Kinsbourne and Dennett's erroneous claim that "[c]onscious experiences are . . . are clockable and locatable." No, they're not. Reports, or electrochemical brain events, are "clockable," but qualia are not. The "cat" percept is just one of a very large number of brain states. It is the one evoked by the sight of a cat, the word "cat," the sight of dead mouse on the doorstep, etc. But the phenomenology of that state has no relevance to its physical nature[34]—any more than there needs to be any simple relation between the contents of a book and its Dewey decimal number. The point is that the brain is (among other things) a *classifier*. It classifies the color-phi stimulus and a moving-color-changing stimulus in the same way—they have the same Dewey decimal number. That's what it means to say that we "see" two physically different things as the same. That's *all* it means.

The only objective "unity" that corresponds to the phenomenal unity of the percept is that a variety of very different physical stimuli can all yield the percept "cat." People show a sophisticated kind of stimulus generalization. There are simple mechanical equivalents for this. *Associative memories* can "store" a number of patterns and recreate them from partial inputs. Physicists describe their function in this way:

> Associative memory is the "fruit fly" or "Bohr atom" of this field. It illustrates in about the simplest possible manner the way that collective computation can work. The basic problem is this: Store a set of p patterns ξ_i^μ in such a way that when presented with a new pattern ζ_i, the network responds by producing whichever one of the stored patterns most closely resembles ζ_i.[35]

Given parts of one of the patterns as input, the network responds with the complete pattern (Plate 16.1). So, given a picture of a cat, a poem about a cat, cat's whiskers, or a meow, the result is the percept "cat." But neither cat nor any other percept exists in recognizable form in the network (Domain 2). Nothing is "bound." Nothing needs to be.

Don't be misled by the fact that in this kind of network, the output looks like the input. An even simpler network will just activate a particular node when all or part of the target stimulus is presented. The basic idea is the same. The network has N stable states; when a stimulus is presented to it, it will go to the state whose prototype, the stored stimulus, is most similar to the presented stimulus.

Plate 16.1 Examples of how an associative memory can reconstruct a whole image from a part. (*Right*): Reconstructed images. (*Left*): Incomplete input images. (*Center*): Intermediate states during image reconstruction.

From J. A. Hertz, A. Krogh, & R. G. Palmer. (1991) *Introduction to the theory of neural computation.* Westview Press, Figure 2.1, by permission.

Consciousness and the Brain

[When] the physiologist turns to higher levels of the central nervous system, a sudden and abrupt change takes place in his research. He no longer concentrates on the connection between the external phenomena and the animal's reactions to them; instead of dealing with these actual relations he begins to make suppositions about the internal states of the animals modeled on his own subjective state. So far he has based himself on the general concepts of natural science. But he now resorts to concepts that are utterly alien to him and in no way related to his earlier, physiological concepts; in short, he makes the leap from the measurable world to the immeasurable. This, obviously, is a step of extraordinary importance. But what caused it? What profound reasons impelled our physiologist to do this? What conflict of opinions preceded it? A totally unexpected answer must be given to these questions: in the world of science absolutely nothing preceded this extraordinary step. The natural scientist . . . investigating the higher parts of the central nervous system has, so to speak, unconsciously and imperceptibly for himself, yielded to the common habit of regarding the animal's activity as analogous to his own and of explaining it by the same intrinsic causes which he feels he recognizes in himself. This, then, is the first point at which the physiologist departed from the firm position of natural science.

—Ivan Pavlov[36]

In short, "hard" scientists often lose the plot when they try to relate their work to consciousness. For example, the Cambridge Declaration on Consciousness in Human and Non-Human Animals states, "Evidence that human and non-human animal emotional feelings arise from homologous subcortical brain networks provide compelling evidence for evolutionarily shared primal affective qualia."[37] The Declaration was signed by the participants (one of whom was the distinguished physicist Stephen Hawking) at a prestigious conference in memory of Francis Crick in Churchill College Cambridge in the summer of 2012. But, as I have argued, nothing, neither behavior nor neurophysiology, can prove the identity of qualia, even between two human beings, much less humans and animals.[38] But the confusion continues.

Benjamin Libet has studied conscious effects of electrical brain stimulation that have caused astonishment among susceptible commentators.[39] In a provocative series of experiments, Libet looked at the relation between recorded and applied brain electrical events and reports of consciousness. For example, in one experiment, Libet studied the tingling sensation that can be produced by a brief electrical pulse to the hand (the *left* hand, say). He found that a similar sensation could be produced by stimulating the subject's cortex (say, the *left* cortex, so that the sensation is referred to the *right* hand). Libet has reported instances in which the subject's left cortex (sensation in *right* hand) was stimulated *before* his *left* hand, yet the subject's reported sensations in the reverse order: first *left* hand, then *right*. Libet himself views these results as a challenge to materialism, and several respected neuroscientists agree with him.

It's hard to see why these results amaze. The subject's report in every case comes *after* the stimulating events have ceased; no time reversal has occurred, as some have suggested. An electrical stimulus to the cortex that is quite different from any naturally generated brain event might well take longer to interpret—that is, take longer to yield a verbal output—than a stimulus applied to sensory end organs expressly adapted to receive stimuli. Hence, it should not surprise us that the brain-induced sensation is reported as occurring after the peripherally produced one. The reversal of temporal order is puzzling only if we have some idea that consciousness is a sort of driving force, rather than a property of our system for self-report.[40]

Libet reported other results that puzzle some commentators. In one experiment, he asked subjects to make "spontaneous" decisions to move one hand while looking at a clock and noting the precise time they "formed the intention" to move. Libet recorded the movement, the judged time of the intention, and the time of the pre-intentional EEG "readiness potentials" on the surface of the subjects' scalps. He found that times subjects reported for the genesis of their intentions lagged behind the readiness potentials by almost half a second. This seems to rule out a real "executive" role for consciousness.

This result is interesting, but not in any way paradoxical, unless one has a naïve view of consciousness as a prime mover—a "first cause" of action.[41] The control scheme illustrated in Figure 16.4, for example, is perfectly consistent with Libet's result. The idea is that the "consciousness" functional subsystem receives input from the outside world and passes on instructions to "everything else" (i.e., the unconscious) to produce the desired behavior according to the required "spontaneous" rule. Libet's "readiness potentials" come from everything else, not from "consciousness." In turn, whenever "everything else" (following the rule as instructed) initiates an action, it reports its behavior to "consciousness." Each of these steps takes some time. Thus, the action of "everything else," reflected immediately in its readiness potential, occurs before "consciousness" has time to process the incoming report that an action is imminent and to note the real time coming in on the "stimulus" line. No doubt there are many other functional arrangements that can duplicate the time delays that Libet found.

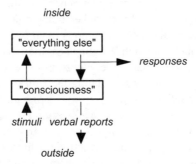

Figure 16.4 The suggested relation between two brain subsystems: the part devoted to "consciousness," and "everything else" (i.e., the unconscious). Consciousness communicates with the outside world and also receives input from the unconscious, which makes nonverbal responses. Each step—from outside world to consciousness, from consciousness to everything else, and back, and the response—takes some time. In such a system, brain signals directly from the unconscious may precede the verbal report of recognition from consciousness.

Dissociations of the sort just described can be observed without EEG paraphernalia. If you have ever participated in a quiz under time pressure you know that very often you *know that you know* the answer to a question quite some time before the answer itself arrives in consciousness. This is a sort of metacognition, I suppose. Sometimes, of course, the delay is very long indeed. In the so-called tip-of-the-tongue phenomenon, for example, you may have the "feeling of knowing" days before the answer pops into consciousness. If something corresponding to Libet's readiness potential could be measured, perhaps it would occur more or less contemporaneously with the "feeling of knowing" and thus some time before the actual answer becomes available. According to the scheme illustrated in Figure 16.4, the feeling of knowing is transmitted to consciousness from "everything else" in advance of the actual information desired—and in response to an environmentally prompted "request" for the information from consciousness.

The idea that there is a separation between the conscious and unconscious parts of the brain; that both have some degree of autonomy; and that consciousness is essential to episodic memory (memory for events, as opposed to skill memory, etc.) receives support from surprising anecdotes of people who must react in an emergency. A colleague reports two separate instances, involving himself and another person. In both cases, the individual was attacked by a supposedly peaceful bonobo chimpanzee—a formidable creature compared to an unarmed human being. In both cases, the victim of the attack took appropriate evasive action and was rescued by co-workers. In neither case did he have *any recollection whatever* of what happened. In one case, the victim assumed he had fainted; the other simply had no recall. But the facts (in one case, recorded on videotape) are indubitable. Evidently, the brain has evolved to deal very efficiently with emergencies that require rapid action. The unconscious operates on its own and doesn't always take time to tell the "consciousness" bit what is happening—so the victim, like the amnesic Tower-of-Hanoi patient, has no memory for the event. But his skill at avoiding chimpanzee attacks was doubtless improved by the experience.

Scotomata

The place where the optic nerve enters the back of the retina is perfectly blind. Yet a bright line flashed across it is perceived as unbroken. Even a plaid pattern is apparently "filled in" so that what we perceive is complete. We never "see" the blind spot. The same thing is true of many neurological injuries that leave people blind in some part of their visual field (there are interesting differences between scotomata and the blind spot, which I'll get to in a moment).

Our unawareness of the blind spot has long been a puzzle. Behavioristic analysis of color phi demystifies the blind-spot problem. All this "filling-in" business is of course Domain 1, phenomenal experience. There is no Domain 2 filling in, any more than there is real "moving and color changing" in the color-phi effect. All that is happening is that the brain is classifying as "same" complete and incomplete plaid patterns—so long as the "gap" falls on the blind spot. The phenomenal experience and the label we attach to it come from evolutionary considerations, as I described earlier. We see the line as continuous and the plaid as whole because the system has evolved to treat a line that extends across the blind spot the same as a continuous line. The inputs from retina to the brain are the same for the whole and (suitably) broken line: Why should they not be classified as the same? Indeed, how could they be classified in any other way?

A scotoma is a blind spot in the visual field, usually caused by illness or injury. The blind spot is a built-in scotoma, but other scotomata behave a little differently. People still (after a while) "fill in" figures across a scotoma, just as they do with the blind spot. But, because of the change from "before" the injury to "after," they are often aware of a scotoma, at least at first or if it is large. But, very different from the blind spot, clever tests often show that although the subject may not be conscious of it, visual stimuli that fall in a scotoma can have an effect. Presented with a word flashed on the scotoma, then asked to guess between that word and another, subjects will disclaim any knowledge but guess better than chance nevertheless. The particular properties of a scotoma depend on the source of the injury. If it is retinal, the scotoma is treated more or less like the blind spot—the brain cannot be affected by visual stimuli falling on the damaged area. But if the scotoma arises from damage to higher centers, the effects depend on what centers and how much damage.

At the heart of the muddled cognitive view of consciousness is a persistent conflation of the subjective (*Domain 1*) and objective (*Domains 2 and 3*). (I discussed a similar conflation of subjective and objective in Skinner's analysis of freedom and responsibility in Chapter 10.) This conflation has led to endless puzzlement about experiments like these. Moreover, the naïve and dismissive view of behaviorism shared, in a fashionable "cognitive correctness," by much of the psychological community, has prevented serious consideration of the kind of analysis I have just offered. The lack of a behavioristic perspective on these problems has allowed views that often verge on the mystical to gain a respectful audience.

But, surely, phenomenal experience is worth *something?* Surely it won't do to compare perception of a rainbow or a beautiful woman to a Dewey decimal number? After all, percepts seem to be so rich, so detailed, so *real*. About the vividness, we can say (scientifically) nothing. But about the richness of detail, we can say at least this: If the brain is a classifier, it is a very capacious one. The phenomenal properties of a percept must at the very least differentiate it from all other percepts. Otherwise the mind would be like the philosophy department of the Oz University of Woolloomooloo in the Monty Python sketch, in which every newcomer is called "Bruce" (to avoid confusion). Since we can distinguish a great many "states of the world," the Dewey decimal for most of them must be a very long number. Some percepts must be very detailed indeed.

***

Common sense, and theoretical behaviorism, makes a sharp division between three domains: *Domain 1* is the entirely private domain of *qualia*. *Domain 2* is the public domain of brain physiology. *Domain 3* is the public domain of intersubjectively verifiable whole-organism behavior. Science, which is public knowledge, can only deal with Domains 2 and 3. But this does not mean that phenomena commonly labeled as "conscious" lie outside behavioristic psychology. I have shown by example that many apparently puzzling effects, from color phi, through visual blind spots to the so-called binding problem either vanish or pose answerable scientific questions when regarded in this way. I cannot prove that behavioral science should confine itself to Domains 2 and 3, but I believe that the distinction will prove more useful in practice than the cognitive alternative. As C. S. Peirce once pointed out, besting the competition is, after all, the pragmatic definition of truth.

Theoretical behaviorism can deal with mentalistic problems like "consciousness" without either ignoring them, obscuring the distinction between what is inside versus what is outside the organism (like radical behaviorism), or confusing what is felt with what can be measured (like some cognitive discussions). Theoretical behaviorism promises to provide theoretical links between behavior and the brain that rest on real understanding, rather than on mentalistic presumptions about how brain-behavior relations "must" be arranged.

But *qualia* are hard to abandon. The late and great English psychologist Jeffrey Gray, in his commentary on the 1991 Ciba Foundation Symposium,[42] wrote,

> I once asked a radical behaviourist[43] what, in his view, is the difference between two awake individuals, one of them stone deaf, who are both sitting immobile in a room in which a record-player is playing a Mozart string quartet? His answer: their subsequent verbal behavior. Mercifully, there were no radical behaviourists at the symposium.

The behavioristic response is, "Do you mean 'What do I *know* about the difference?' or 'What can I *infer* about it?'" "What I know" is only the different verbal reports, before and after the experience. "What I can infer" is something about the physiology of hearing. What none but the deaf person knows is "what it is like" to be deaf.

Postscript to Parts I–III:
Alchemy of the Mind

Why was alchemy a scientific dead-end? Its aim is attainable and potentially profitable. Lead *can* be turned into gold, albeit not at a profit. And yet the whole enterprise was in fact a waste of time. It failed because it assumed something that isn't so: that because a problem is important and can be clearly posed, it should also be attacked directly. In fact, the alchemists understood too little of physics and chemistry to have any hope of achieving their aim. Instead of tackling a big, practical question, what was needed was a couple of hundred years of boring and apparently irrelevant experiments on pendulums and balls rolling down inclined planes, meticulous tables cataloguing the elements according to properties, experiments on chemicals other than lead and gold—and a lot of thought by some talented and often odd people, all aimed for the most part not at solving obvious, practical problems, but at understanding physics and chemistry.

Contemporary psychology is in many respects the alchemy of the mind. Both the two major movements in psychology, behaviorism and cognitivism, have their own shibboleths. In the case of behaviorism, it was the practical objective that dominated. From Watson to Skinner, whether they studied rats, pigeons or people, the leading behaviorists were all preoccupied with practical results. Their facts were at least real facts: running speed in a maze, key pecks in a Skinner box and so on. But their interests were utopian—to change the world, not to understand it—so they vaulted from fragmentary knowledge to sweeping recommendations about social policy and private action. Its weak philosophy and grandiose claims made behaviorism a soft target, even for the misguided missiles directed against it by Chomsky and other critics.

Contemporary cognitive psychology is not so dominated by practical objectives. Its errors are preoccupation with the *human* mind, with information rather than action and taking ordinary language at face value. Human memory, thought, ideas and consciousness, like lead and gold, are the currency of daily discourse. Who can doubt that they are the things psychology—or cognitive (neuro)science—should attempt to explain? Just as the alchemists studied gold because gold is what they were after, so the cognitive scientists study human beings because human beings are what they wish to understand. Even though animals are simpler and more tractable experimental subjects than humans, even though the facts of animal psychology are real, reliable facts, unlike many of the "findings" of other kinds of psychology, animal psychology is now an endangered species.

But several decades of increasingly well-supported research into the psychology and neurobiology of human mental life have yielded disappointingly little. A sympathetic commentator could write in 1999:

> Investigations of the mind have . . . failed to generate the kinds of applications that compel belief in a particular paradigm. Physicists can talk about lasers, transistors, radar, jets, nuclear bombs. Biologists can show off vaccines, antibiotics, cloning, and other marvels. The by-products of mind-science are rather less impressive: cognitive behavioral therapy, Thorazine, Prozac, shock therapy, alleged genetic markers for homosexuality, IQ tests.[44]

He goes on to conclude, "Theories of human nature never really die; they just go in and out of fashion." The book offers trenchant criticism of cognitive neuroscience, artificial intelligence, Freudian psychology and evolutionary psychology. Behaviorism escaped unscathed, not because it is invulnerable, but because it was invisible. Horgan accepted uncritically the dismissal of behaviorism by his cognitively inclined interviewees. Consequently, he failed to notice that the main technological accomplishment of psychological science is in fact behavioristic and based on animal research: the technology of reinforcement schedules. But his indictment of contemporary mind-science is mostly on the mark, even today.

So what is the solution? The argument of this book is that the best way forward in the quest to understand how human beings work is *not* through the study of the human mind, but through the study of the behavior of animals. I suggest that theoretical behaviorism will prove a useful guide not just for psychology but also for cognitive neuroscience. What neuroscience must explain is *not* the mind or consciousness, but the process that drives behavior. If, for example, habituation is most parsimoniously explained by a cascade of fast and slow integrators, then those are what we should probably look for in the brain—not a "habituation module." If we want to understand "memory," then we should first look at its dynamics and the processes we need to infer to duplicate those dynamics—not for brain areas that subserve "episodic" versus "procedural" memory—and whatever other categories are currently in fashion. If we cannot even fathom the neural basis for the behavior of a completely gene-mapped, 302-neuron nematode worm ("We still don't understand how *C. elegans* works," said Nobelist Torsten Wiesel in an interview more than ten years ago, and I heard a similar sentiment expressed in 2013 by one of Charlie Rose's Brain Series panelists), then what on Earth are we doing speculating on consciousness and brain-behavior relations in human beings? This is alchemy indeed!

The solution offered by theoretical behaviorism is simply to lower our sights. Don't reach for the stars; reach for a telescope. Study the dynamics of simple animal behavior. Maybe the stars will arrive in due course.

Because behaviorism deals with action, not mentation, it can shed some light on human activities that respond to incentives. These are also the domain of economics. But economics until recently was not an experimental science. Now there are experimental economists,[45] but they work almost exclusively with human subjects, short-term experiments and weak rewards and punishments. Animal experiments are not so limited—experiments can last for months or even years, and rewards and punishments can be nontrivial. In the last five chapters, I look from a behavioristic point of view at three areas of human action where the incentives are large and their effects extend across a lifetime: the judicial system, the health-care system and teaching.

Notes

1. Nagel, T. (1974, October). What is it like to be a bat? *The Philosophical Review, 83*(4), 435–540. Several reviewers point out that the "like" in "what is it like" does not imply any kind of comparison. It is hard to know, therefore, what it does imply. In the text, I do my best.
2. See, for example, Xu, Y., & Corkin, S. (2001). H.M. revisits the Tower of Hanoi puzzle. *Neuropsychology, 15*(1), 69–79.
3. Hebb, D. O. (1961). Distinctive features of learning in the higher animal. In J. F. Delafresnaye (Ed.), *Brain mechanisms and learning* (Oxford: Blackwell), pp. 37–46. Recent research is summarized in Thorn, A., & Page, M. (Eds.). (2009). *Interactions between short-term and long-term memory in the verbal domain* (New York: Psychology Press).
4. Schachter, D. L., & Tulving, E. (Eds.). (1994). *Memory systems* (Cambridge, MA: MIT Press); Baddeley, A. (2012). Working memory: Theories, models and controversies. *Annual Review of Psychology, 63*, 1–29.
5. Overton, D. A. (1996, September). State-dependent learning produced by depressant and atropine-like drugs. *Psychopharmacologia, 10*(1), 6–31.
6. Weiskrantz, L. (1996). Blindsight revisited. *Current Opinion in Neurobiology, 6*, 215–220.
7. Laureys, S., Pellas, F., Van Eeckhout, P., Ghorbel, S., Schnakers, C., Perrin, F. . . . & Goldman, S. (2005). The locked-in syndrome: What is it like to be conscious but paralyzed and voiceless? *Progress in Brain Research, 150*, 495–511.
8. James, W. (1943). *Essays in radical empiricism* (p. 2). Page numbers are from the Longmans, Green and Co. edition of *Essays in radical empiricism and a pluralistic universe* in one volume, published in 1943.
9. The only real zombies seem to be those rare humans who actually believe they are dead, so-called Cotard's syndrome, discovered by a French neurologist in 1880.
10. Searle, J. (1992). *The rediscovery of the mind* (Cambridge, MA: MIT/Bradford), p. 45.
11. See, for example, Glaberson, W. (1999, August 18). Legal pioneers seek to raise lowly status of animals. *New York Times.* See also The Francis Crick Memorial Conference: "Consciousness in Human and Non-Human Animals." Churchill College Cambridge, United Kingdom, July 2012 (http://fcmconference.org/). The Cambridge Declaration on Consciousness, signed by many eminences at this meeting, avers: "Evidence of near human-like levels of consciousness has been most dramatically observed in African grey parrots," referring to Irene Pepperberg's many years of work teaching simple language skills to a single parrot—Alex—whose obituary appeared in *The Economist* in 2007 see www.economist.com/node/9828615). And "[T]he chimpanzee overwhelmingly displays so many aspects of what we originally considered human nature, that the idea of humankind

being in any way special or separate from the rest of the animal kingdom is surely dead"—so concluded a review of ape fan Frans van De Waal (2013). *The bonobo and the atheist* (New York: W. W. Norton) in *The Independent*, April 20, 2013.

12. Flavell, J. H. (1979). Metacognition and cognitive monitoring: A new area of cognitive-development inquiry. *American Psychologist, 34*, 906–911.

13. This account is slightly simplified: see Foote, A. L., & Crystal, J. D. (2007). Meta-cognition in the rat. *Current Biology, 17,* 551–555, for more details.

14. "These species demonstrate an advanced form of consciousness that in humans is definitive evidence of our awareness," writes one commentator on the basis of results like this: "The New Science of Consciousness Informs Abortion, Animal Rights Debates" by Daniel Bor (Slate.com), posted Tuesday, September 4, 2012, at 3:41 AM. Well, not really.

15. For a fuller account, see Jozefowiez, J., Staddon, J. E. R., & Cerutti, D. T. (2009). Metacognition in animals: How do we know that they know? *Comparative Cognition and Behavior Reviews, 4,* 19–29.

16. Rats: Roche, J. P., Timberlake, W., & McCloud, C. (1997). Sensitivity to variability in food amount: Risk aversion is seen in discrete-choice, but not in free-choice, tri-als. *Behaviour, 134*(15–16), 1259–1272; pigeons: Staddon, J. E. R., & Innis, N. K. (1966). Preference for fixed vs. variable amounts of reward. *Psychonomic Science, 4,* 193–194.

17. Sutton, J. E., & Shettleworth, S. J. (2008, April). Memory without awareness: Pigeons do not show metamemory in delayed matching to sample. *Journal of Experimental Psychology: Animal Behavior Processes, 34*(2), 266–282.

18. Dennett, D., & Kinsbourne, M. (1992). Time and the observer: The where and when of consciousness in the brain. *Behavioral and Brain Sciences, 15*, 183–247, p. 186.

19. Dennett & Kinsbourne (1992), p. 194.

20. Hayek, F. A. (1979). *The counterrevolution of science: Studies in the abuse of reason* (Indianapolis: Liberty Press), p. 37 (reprint of the 1952 edition). Friedrich Hayek (1899–1992) won the Economics Nobel in 1974 but also made important contributions to sensory psychology.

21. Tolman, E. C. (1922, January). A new formula for behaviorism. *Psychological Review, 29,* 44–53, pp. 47–48.

22. Dennett & Kinsbourne (1992), p. 187.

23. Ramachandran, V. S. (2004). *A brief tour of human consciousness* (New York: PI Press), p. 96.

24. Dennett & Kinsbourne (1992), p. 235.

25. What exactly do you mean by "registered," a critic might reasonably ask? "Register" just refers to the properties of the internal state. Another way to pose the problem is to say that we need a model such that the inputs RRRRGGGG and R . . . G yield the same internal state.

26. Roger Shepard has discussed the role of evolution in the perceptual process: Shepard, R. N. (1987). Evolution of a mesh between principles of the mind and regularities of the world. In J. Dupré (Ed.), *The latest on the best: Essays on evolution and optimality* (Cambridge, MA: Bradford/MIT Press), pp. 251–275.

27. But how can you be actually seeing what isn't there (as opposed to simply reporting what is)? Answer: That's what you always do. Sometimes what you see corresponds more or less closely to physical reality, sometimes it's an approximation and sometimes it's wholly imaginary (see, for example, Oliver Sacks's [2012]. *Hallucinations* [Borzoi]).

28. Hungarian émigré Békésy won the Nobel Prize in Physiology or Medicine in 1961. See www.nobelprize.org/nobel_prizes/medicine/laureates/1961/bekesy-lecture.html.

29. Blough, D. S. (1955). Methods of tracing dark adaptation in the pigeon. *Science, 121*, 703–704. See also www.ncbi.nlm.nih.gov/pmc/articles/PMC1403870/?page=1.

30. Obviously with a digital display, this "continuous" movement will be a succession of separate images. But if the refresh rate is high enough and the spatial resolution fine enough, the movement will appear continuous to any man or animal.

31. See http://en.wikipedia.org/wiki/Color_constancy.

32. Flanagan, O. (1992). *Consciousness reconsidered* (Cambridge, MA: MIT/Bradford).

33. Flanagan (1992), p. 171.

34. Britain's Princess Anne, an avid horsewoman, fell at a jump a few years ago and suffered a concussion. She reported seeing herself from above lying on the ground. If brain states are "clockable and locatable," just how high above the ground was Princess Anne? Could she see an ant on top of a nearby post?

35. Hertz, J. A., Krogh, A., & Palmer, R. G. (1989). *Neural computation* (Reading, MA: Addison-Wesley), p. 11.

36. Pavlov, I. P. (1909). Natural science and the brain. *Journal of the Congress of Naturalists and Physicians*. English translation in Koshtoyants, K. S. (Ed.). (1955). *I. P. Pavlov: Selected works* (Moscow: Foreign Languages Publishing House), pp. 206–219, 207.

37. Glaberson (1999, August 18), p. A1.

38. The conference was clearly motivated by a shared concern for the proper treatment of animals. But that is an ethical issue for which science can provide data, but which is not scientifically decidable. No demonstration of psychophysiological isomorphism between the brains of people and, say, parrots, can by itself compel us to give parrots the vote.

39. See http://en.wikipedia.org/wiki/Benjamin_Libet. For thoughtful critiques and additional experiments, see Dehaene, S., & Christen, Y. (Eds.). (2011). *Characterizing consciousness: From cognition to the clinic?* (Berlin/Heidelberg, Germany: Springer); and Dehaene, S. (2009). Conscious and nonconscious processes: Distinct forms of evidence accumulation? *Séminaire Poincaré, 12*, 89–114. Retrieved from www.bourbaphy.fr/dehaene.pdf.

40. Nørretranders, T. (1998). *The user illusion: Cutting consciousness down to size* (New York: Viking).

41. Many do. Even eminent philosopher Thomas Nagel could write, in the famous "bat" paper, "I do not deny that conscious mental states and events cause behavior." But he should–because the evidence from Libet and others suggests that consciousness is not a cause but an effect.

42. Gray, J. (1992). Consciousness on the scientific agenda. *Nature, 358,* 277, a report of the Ciba Foundation Symposium "Experimental and Theoretical Studies of Consciousness."

43. Rachlin, H. (1995). The elusive quale. *Behavioral and Brain Sciences, 18*, 692–693.

44. Horgan, J. (1999). *The undiscovered mind* (New York: The Free Press), pp. 6–7.

45. See www.nobelprize.org/nobel_prizes/economics/laureates/2002/.

Part IV
Behaviorism and Society

17 Law, Punishment and Behaviorism

What can behaviorism tell us about the way society works? Does it urge us to change society, and in what ways? Behaviorism has always been concerned with how organisms learn through reinforcement. The Darwinian metaphor has expanded our understanding of reinforcement beyond selection alone. Behavioral variation and the effects of context must also be taken into account. I have discussed elsewhere financial markets, which are fiercely driven by large reinforcements and punishments.[1] The last five chapters of this book show how reinforcement, and the context in which it occurs, affects three other functions of society: law and punishment, health care, and education. I begin with law and punishment.

B. F. Skinner thought that predictability and determinism somehow invalidate the idea that people are responsible for their actions. In fact, logic alone shows that the predictability of human behavior is essential for the effectiveness of traditional practices that Skinner attacked. I explain why in a discussion of judicial punishment. But first, let's look at two kinds of *justice*.

Determinism and Justice

Determinism is often used to exonerate wrongdoers. If criminal behavior is perfectly predictable from a man's personal history, punishment for wrongdoing does seem unjust. "He could not help himself, so how can you punish him?" Defense attorneys will frequently argue that a defendant who was the child of abusive parents should not be held responsible for his violent actions as an adult. In the notorious Menendez case[2] in California, for example, the Menendez brothers murdered both their wealthy parents in an unprovoked attack. The defense introduced testimony about a history of child abuse as a supposed mitigating factor. This ploy worked in one case arising from these crimes, yielding a "hung" jury—but not in the next, when both brothers were convicted and sent to prison for life. Nevertheless, the assumption that behavior is causally determined by an individual's past history has gradually led to a widespread feeling that the concept of personal responsibility is a holdover from a more primitive age, when people lacked scientific insight into the springs of human action. Some legal scholars have criticized the "abuse excuse"[3] but generally not for the reasons I will shortly describe.

The abuse excuse shares some aspects with the *insanity defense,* which is usually governed by the outcome of a 170-year-old case in England. In 1843, Daniel M'Naghten murdered Edward Drummond, secretary to British Prime Minister Sir Robert Peel who was M'Naghten's intended victim. M'Naghten claimed that his mission was guided by the "voice of God." The jury believed him, and so he was found not guilty by reason of insanity. His trial yielded the *M'Naghten Rule:* Insanity is proved if the defendant was "labouring under such a defect of reason, from disease of the mind, as not to know the nature and quality of the act he was doing; or if he did know it, that he did not know he was doing what was wrong."[4] Clearly, the M'Naghten Rule implies that the perpetrator cannot help himself, either because he doesn't realize what he doing is wrong, or because he doesn't realize what he is doing, period. Some forms of the abuse excuse imply that because of his upbringing, the perpetrator did not realize his behavior was wrong. Others imply that his upbringing made him unable to act in any other way. Still others affirm that although the perpetrator knew his act was wrong (*contra* M'Naghten), his upbringing rendered him incapable of resisting an evil impulse. In practice the insanity defense is rarely invoked as such and rarely works when it is. But it is frequently used in pretrial hearings and many defendants are thus found unfit for trial. As we will see, a behavioristic analysis provides a scientific basis for the M'Naghten Rule.

Another Kind of Justice

Since his approach is technological, not legal or humanistic, Skinner's work does not deal with the concept of justice directly. When he does mention it, he usually equates it with *fairness* and efficiency. Recall his comment that much "time and energy would be saved" by applying behavioral methods. Evidently *efficiency* is one of Skinner's values. In similar vein, he writes that "the issue of fairness or justice is often simply a matter of good husbandry. The question is whether reinforcers are being used wisely."[5]

Equating "justice" with "fairness" is the theme of moral philosopher John Rawls (1921–2002), Skinner's colleague at Harvard and author of the highly influential *A Theory of Justice,* published the same year as BFAD. There is no evidence that Skinner and Rawls knew each other. But, *zeitgeist* rules! More on Rawls in a moment.

Technology is neither just nor unjust; it either works or it doesn't; it is about means, not ends. This is Skinner's view of a "technology of behavior" also. The 400-pound gorilla in the room, of course, is that the "ends" of behavioral control are much less obvious than the ends of other kinds of technology. Engineering human beings raises issues that engineering a toaster or a hubcap does not. A toaster should make toast—safely and one hopes quickly and cheaply. Not much argument there. But what about a child: Should he be industrious and obedient, or creative and willful? Should he respect authority, or challenge it? And what about adults? Any attempt to apply behavioral science must begin with values. What are you changing behavior for? What change do you intend and why?

Marxist-Leninists thought they could create by Pavlovian means a Soviet "new man"—and millions perished in the attempt. Pavlov's reported response was, "If what the communists are doing with Russia is an experiment, for this experiment I would not spare even a frog." What kind of new man was Skinner after? *Walden Two* suggests that he had in mind someone rather like himself, a freethinking version of the U.S. academic, circa 1960. Many scholars will agree with this ideal. But the Skinnerian new man, whose behavior is a product of technology, not character, gathers no kudos. He is a mirror image of the abused child, who can't help doing wrong. The product of effective behavior analysis can't help doing right. Neither requires praise or blame, says Skinner, since neither is really "responsible" for his actions.

It's worth wondering whether we should be seeking to create a "new man" at all. Aristotle thought that the purpose of government was to produce a virtuous citizenry. But the Founding Fathers thought that individual "life, liberty and the pursuit of happiness" should be the only goals. Law breaking apart, the virtue of citizens was thought to be their own business, in theory if not in practice. Even though not a few current laws are aimed at promoting virtue rather than happiness—think drug and alcohol laws, "sin" taxes, laws against various forms of sexual license—society was not supposed to serve any purpose beyond the freedom and happiness of individual citizens.[6] Radical behaviorism provides little guidance as to ends, although Skinner's idea that behavioral control is capable of producing citizens who "can't help behaving well" resembles in some respects Aristotle's wish for a virtuous populace. My own feeling is that there is always something dangerous in a philosophy that is discontented with human beings as they are and wishes them improved according to some model. But, as we've seen, Skinner had few doubts: "To confuse and delay the improvement of cultural practices by quibbling about the word *improve* is itself not a useful practice."[7] The ends of control were silently supplied by his own unexamined mid-twentieth-century liberal intuitions.

The most influential figure in reflecting, and forming, those intuitions was Skinner's Harvard colleague John Rawls. While an undergraduate at Princeton, Rawls "became deeply concerned with theology and its doctrines" and even considered becoming an Episcopal priest.[8] His masterwork, *A Theory of Justice* (TOJ), is not concerned with judicial practice. It does not deal with the individual whose good and bad actions receive appropriate positive or negative consequences—justice in the sense of "just deserts." In other words, it is not about the civil and criminal legal system. The book is about distributive or *social justice,* an idea that arose in a religious context.[9]

Many writers seem unaware of, or uninterested in, the fact that individual and social justice are incompatible with each other. If people differ in their energies and abilities (and they do), then individual justice requires that some will acquire more than others—which is contrary to Rawls's social-justice goal of general equality. This is not a novel insight. The great German polymath Johann Wolfgang von Goethe commented more than 160 years ago, "Legislators and revolutionaries who promise equality [social justice] and liberty [individual justice] at the same time are either psychopaths or mountebanks."[10]

Social justice is about how society's resources are to be allocated. It is confusing that the same word, *justice,* is used for these two very different things. But it is good public relations for believers in equality and redistribution because it seems to make social justice, like individual justice, a *right,* not a matter of political contingency. But there is a big difference. If an accused man is treated justly by the court, nothing is taken from anyone else. But if, in the interests of social justice, wealth is taken from one person and redistributed to another, the rights of the donor may be violated, even as those of the receiver are asserted. Individual justice is no-lose; social justice is never win-win.

Rawls thought that the goals of society should be a sort of "fairness" that is in effect very similar to Karl Marx's "from each according to his ability, to each according to his need." Rawls takes no account of incentives—the psychological and economic factors that generate wealth. He is about the cutting of the pie, not the making of it. Nor does he accept as a matter of right that a person has first call on the fruits of his own energy and talent. This has been taken to its logical conclusion by some writers, who argue that social justice should have priority over all other objectives of the state. In its service, the government has the first claim on everything you earn.[11]

Rawls's central assumption is equality, which he calls fairness. He contends that everyone cannot but "acknowledge as the first principle of justice one requiring an equal distribution [of all resources]. Indeed, this principle is so obvious that we would expect it to occur to anyone immediately."[12] Claims like this are common in moral philosophy. But they are astonishing to most scientists. What on Earth makes Rawls's "first principle of justice" obvious? The answer, obviously, is the social milieu of an elite northeastern-U.S. university at the end of the self-righteous, hedonistic and egalitarian 1960s. But Rawls proclaims his thesis as if it were as unquestionable as a theorem of Euclid. Even more astonishing, a large community of like-minded humanists and social scientists accepted his proposal without demur.

Sometimes moral claims come disguised as puzzles. Here is one where three versions of justice are contrasted. Distinguished social-choice theorist Amartya Sen asks us to imagine three children quarreling over a flute.[13] One says: Give it to me, I have nothing. The next says: Give it to me, I'm the only one who knows how to play it. The third says: I made it, I should have it. Who should get it: The one who can play it, the one who has nothing else, or the one who made it? This is presented as a "difficult decision" for the grownup supervising the children. Sen concedes that some will find the decision easy: Utilitarians will give it to the player; "economic egalitarians" to the poorest child. I guess I am what Sen would call a "no-nonsense libertarian," which sounds rather extreme. But it seems to me utterly obvious that the child who made it should keep it. To do otherwise would be to commit theft and undermine the basis for a productive society. How extreme is that? After all, who would make anything if the product of his labor could be snatched from him? And yet for Sen and Rawls and many like-minded others, owning what you make is not obviously just at all. For these folk, egalitarian values usually win.

Rawls proposed that a person situated behind a "veil of ignorance"—not knowing his talents or his future place in society—will naturally prefer a society in which all are equal. In other words, confronted with two lotteries, one where you are assured of the same reward as everyone else, the other where you can win big or lose completely, everyone will prefer the first. The problem is, they don't. Many would prefer the second lottery: They are risk seeking rather than, as Rawls assumes, risk averse. So Rawls's highly influential book, and the movement to which it gave rise, rests on two rather shaky propositions: that universal equality is both desirable and universally desired.

Skinner's and Rawls's approaches are at opposite poles: Skinner shows how to control people's behavior, but is vague about why we should bother. Rawls knows ends, but says little about how to achieve them. The Western university, committed to the idea of universal truth, began in Bologna almost 1,000 years ago. The U.S. university had drifted far enough from this ideal by 1971 that two distinguished Harvard professors could publish in the same year books on the same topic—the nature of society—and fail to address not only each other but even the same issues.

Most people are reluctant to labor for nothing or to give their stuff to strangers. Rawls's well-intentioned and apparently benign ideas therefore imply coercive action by the state if they are to become a reality. This alarming conclusion soon led to several alternative views. Most are close to the principles of the Founding Fathers, who emphasized the rights of the individual, particularly his rights to property and the fruits of his labor. Robert Nozick's *Anarchy, State and Utopia* appeared in 1974. It emphasized individual rights and a minimal state. More thoroughgoing is Murray Rothbard's *The Ethics of Liberty* (1998), in which the individual reigns supreme and the state withers away entirely.[14] The debate continues, but radical behaviorism never participated in it.

Punishment and Law

All agree that only the guilty should be punished. But there is disagreement about the purpose of punishment and its usefulness—should it be designed to *deter* or simply as *retribution;* and about its effectiveness—does it really deter or not? And some—Skinner—think that in a properly designed culture, there should be no punishment. Not because it's wrong but because, says Skinner, it doesn't work. Let's look first at guilt: What does it take to ensure that all and only the guilty are punished?

I have already discussed this kind of question in Chapter 6. It is an example of the assignment-of-credit problem: an injury (a loss, a death) has occurred; who, or what, caused it? The law adds another dimension, of course. You may have caused my injury, but you are only *guilty* in a legal sense if you either intended the injury (*mens rea*) or behaved in a way that you should have known was likely to cause injury. If the injury was truly accidental, then you may be the cause, in a physical sense, but you are not guilty in law.

Justice thus has two components. The first is *causation:* The accused must have caused the potentially criminal act—this known as a "simple" or "material" fact. The second is *culpability:* The event was not an unavoidable accident.

Suppose causation and culpability has been proved. Should the law inflict punishment, or no? Should we accept Skinner's view that personal determinism eliminates personal responsibility? Our response depends on what we mean by "just" and on the purposes of punishment. A position that is behaviorist but not Skinnerian is that a punishment is "just" if it serves the social purpose of minimizing human suffering. This view seems to have been first proposed by the Italian Cesare Beccaria (1775).[15] The idea is that the purpose of all social arrangements should be something like "the greatest good of the greatest number," which is the central creed of the movement in moral philosophy known as *utilitarianism.* The term was coined by Jeremy Bentham (1748–1832), "spiritual founder" of University College, London, where his preserved skeleton, dressed in his own clothes, with a wax head, still resides in a glass cabinet. But utilitarianism is probably most associated with the English prodigy, philosopher and polymath John Stuart Mill (1806–1873).[16]

The utilitarian view is that punishment can be justified to the extent that it minimizes general suffering. *Suffering* includes the damage to society done by criminals, the damage to individual criminals done by just punishment—and the cost of errors: failures of the system that lead to punishing innocent people. Errors are especially damaging because, as we saw in earlier chapters, any failure of contingency (punishment of the innocent, failure to punish the guilty) much reduces both the incentive effect of reward and the deterrent effect of punishment. Moreover, if unjust punishment is frequent, the law itself is brought into disrepute and society needs to deal with new set of problems. So everything points to the importance of establishing causality and guilt. Crime must predict punishment, in the sense I described, if it is to be an effective deterrent.

There remains the mighty problem of measuring collective benefit or loss, of comparing one person's pain or joy with another's. This has always been the Achilles heel of utilitarianism, and various solutions, some even involving experiments and data, have been proposed. All I can say here is that there is no consensus, although it is usually possible to get some agreement in particular cases.

In the utilitarian view, the justification for legal punishment is *deterrence.* The optimal level of punishment (for a given crime) is the level that minimizes the sum of two quantities, the cost to the criminal (and innocent defendants convicted in error) of legal punishment and the benefit to society of *future crimes deterred.* The logic is this: As the level of punishment is increased, the level of crime in society decreases, but the suffering of criminals and those wrongly convicted increases. There should therefore be an optimal level of punishment where these two lines cross, at the point where the net social cost is a minimum.

Deterrence is not the only possible justification for punishment. Some legal scholars have argued that deterrence should not count at all, only *retribution* matters: "The punishment should fit the crime." One eminent legal scholar is quite explicit: "Of the possible functions for criminal law, only the achievement of retributive justice is its actual function."[17] This is a venerable position that cannot be ignored. But it also has its pluses and minuses. Achieving consensus on what *is* retributively just is likely to be even more difficult than getting agreement on what minimizes general suffering. "An eye for an eye" used to be considered just, but now (in Europe and the United States, at least) the *lex talionis* would be considered unduly harsh. Sharia law recommends amputation as the punishment for theft; the Common Law of England recommends more moderate punishment. The near-universal agreement that punishment for attempted murder should be less than for successful murder strongly supports the idea that judicial punishment should have some retributive component and not be deterrent only. But, since punishment certainly *does* deter, it seems unwise to formulate criminal justice policy without taking deterrence into account.

Some legal scholars judge the utilitarian view too narrow, but few find it to be completely irrelevant. It is perfectly consistent with Skinner's pragmatic approach to such problems. So why does he object to judicial punishment? One reason is his objection to the concept of personal responsibility, based on his critique of "autonomous man." The other reason is his contention that punishment doesn't work. I discussed some objections to his view of responsibility in an earlier chapter. Let's look again at his critique and then at some data on the effectiveness of punishment.

Responsibility

Skinner objects to "responsibility" for two reasons: First, because responsibility implies the potential for punishment, to which he is universally opposed, supposedly on the grounds that it does not work very well. And second, because he mistakenly assumed that personal responsibility rests on the idea of "autonomous man," which he believed he had refuted. Like Isaiah Berlin (Chapter 10), he thought that determinism and responsibility are incompatible. Let's look first at "autonomous man."

Respon'sible, liable to be called to account or render satisfaction: answerable: capable of discharging duty: able to pay.[18] The old Chambers's English dictionary gives a behavioristic definition of responsibility. A person is responsible if he can respond appropriately to correction. To "respond appropriately" means, of course, to respond in a *predictable way.* The alternative, responding to reward and punishment in an unpredictable way, is not only inappropriate but would make reward and punishment quite pointless.

For Skinner, predictability = determinism = no free will. He also thought that the legitimacy of judicial punishment rested on the idea of free will. But, as this argument shows, it does not. *Au contraire,* judicial punishment makes sense *only* if behavior can be modified in predictable ways. That's why we don't punish crazy people.

Isaiah Berlin's problem is a little different. He proposed a very simple definition of freedom: "I am normally said to be free to the degree to which no human being interferes with my activity."[19] But "interference' is not, of course, a simple concept. It requires judgment; it is, in other words, a subjective matter. I am free if I feel free.[20]

Skinner defines "autonomy" as "absence of causation." There are philosophical problems with this idea, but even if it were true, the legitimacy of just punishment does not depend on it. The truth is precisely the opposite. It is precisely because people *are* sensitive to contingencies—their behavior *is* subject to causal influences—that punishment is used. If criminal behavior is predictably deterred by punishment, the justly punished criminal is less likely to disobey the law again, and serves as an example to other potential lawbreakers. But if behavior were unpredictable and unaffected by contingencies—if it were uncaused, in Skinner's caricature of autonomous man—there would be absolutely no point to punishment (or any other form of behavioral control), because it would have no predictable effect. Thus the idea of personal responsibility cannot be dismissed because behavior is determined. On the contrary, responsibility depends on a degree of determinism.

At least one distinguished behaviorist agrees, and disagrees with Skinner. Here is the comment of his colleague, philosopher W. V. O. Quine:

> I deny not the existence of mental phenomena but the utility for law of the concept of mind in which intentions and free will figure. "The division of acts into some for which a man is regarded as responsible, and others for which he is not, is part of the social apparatus of reward and punishment: responsibility is allocated where rewards and punishments have tended to work as incentives and deterrents." And being social rather than philosophical in purpose, the allocation of responsibility need not follow the division between free and coerced acts. A person who . . . kills in self-defense is excused from criminal liability, but not the killer who would not have killed had he not been raised in a poor home by harsh parents.[21]

It is interesting that Skinner was perfectly aware of the legal view of responsibility, but failed to make the connection to deterrence:

> Was So-and-So aware of the probable consequences of his action, and was the action deliberate? If so, we are justified in punishing him. But what does this mean? It appears to be a question concerning the efficacy of the contingent relations between behavior and punishing consequences.[22]

Just so; but the utilitarian point is not so much to change the behavior of the perpetrator as to deter others like him.

What remains, therefore, is Skinner's criticism that punishment is not so much wrong as ineffective. Is it?

Punishment

"Holding a man responsible" is nothing more than making him aware of the aversive contingencies that enforce punishment for misbehavior. Because human beings, unlike pigeons, can learn about contingencies without actually experiencing them (Skinner calls this *rule-guided* behavior, in contrast to the *contingency-governed* behavior of nonverbal animals), awareness of a punishing contingency will usually result in obedience to it. The aversive stimulus need never be experienced by the law-abiding citizen. Thus, even though punishment has inevitably a cost as well as a benefit, its use in civilized societies will usually be minimal. We cannot, therefore, condemn the idea of personal responsibility because it implies the possibility of punishment.

Punishment is an example of what Skinner terms *aversive control,* and one clear value that emerges from his writings is unequivocal opposition to it. He doesn't argue the case on moral grounds, of course, but on grounds of inefficacy: "Reward and punishment do not differ merely in the direction of the changes they induce [there is in fact continuing debate in the technical literature about whether or not this is true]. . . . Punished behavior is likely to reappear after the punitive contingencies are withdrawn."[23] Later on, he adds that another problem with aversive control is that it gives rise to "counterattack." People will fight attempts at aversive control. In place of punishment, Skinner advocates exclusive use of positive reinforcement because it works better.

Skinner's claim is false. Positive reinforcement is not universally more effective than punishment. Laboratory studies do *not* show that punishment is always less effective than reward. Indeed, under many conditions, punishment is quicker and more effective than reward. Parents of young children can attest—and laboratory experiments confirm—that it is easier and faster to eliminate unwanted behavior through punishment than by the indirect means (such as rewarding a competing behavior) required by positive methods. There are few direct experimental comparisons of punishment versus the positive-reinforcement alternative, for ethical reasons. But when the effectiveness of rewarding a behavior incompatible with the undesired behavior versus punishing that behavior directly are directly compared, punishment wins.[24]

To Skinner's objection that the behavior returns when punishment is withdrawn, there is an obvious response: Rewarded behavior also ceases when the reward is withdrawn. And in fact there are some kinds of aversive control that have effects much *more* persistent than positive reinforcement. Behavior that is maintained by what is called an *avoidance* schedule may persist indefinitely when the aversive stimulus is withdrawn. Behavior reinforced positively usually ceases when the positive reinforcement ceases.

An example of an avoidance schedule is *shock postponement* invented and studied by Skinnerian Murray Sidman. The rat subject receives brief electric shocks every 20 s (for example). But if he presses a lever, the next shock is postponed for 20 s. By pressing the lever more often than every 20 s, the rat can avoid shock completely. Such a schedule is sometimes difficult to learn, but once learned the behavior may persist indefinitely, even if the shock generator is turned off[25]—especially if a few random shocks are delivered occasionally. Aversive control is neither less effective nor less permanent than control by positive reinforcement.

Punishment and aversive contingencies generally do have some negative effects beyond the inevitable pain they deliver. Avoidance procedures can lead to real "superstitions," activities that have no relation to the actual reinforcement contingencies but occur anyway. The main reason is that these procedures provide incomplete corrective feedback. For example, it is quite possible (although admittedly tough to prove) that the myriad prohibitions and pat-downs imposed on airline passengers—what one critic has called "security theater"[26]—reflect the fact that these procedures are in effect responses to a shock-postponement schedule, a procedure with imperfect feedback: "We ask them not to carry 2-in penknives, or small bottles of shampoo, and look, no terrorist attack! It must be working!"

The skewed incentives of TSA agents probably also play a part. After all, if there is an attack, the agent who let the terrorist through will be in deep trouble. But the inconveniences visited on travelers are their problem, not the agent's. Nor does the system take any account of the effect of these humiliating procedures, long continued over many years, on the morale and moxie of the American people. Fearful airline travelers are now well trained in habits of passivity and unquestioning obedience to silly rules and arbitrary constraints. These are probably not healthy habits of mind for a vigorous democracy.[27]

What about Skinner's "counterattack," the bad side effects of punishment? People do indeed try to evade or eliminate aversive contingencies. The criminal seeks to avoid punishment for his crime, oppressed citizens may revolt, the guilty suspect attacks the police officer. Organized rebellions, like the French and Russian Revolutions are usually associated with periods when aversive contingencies are relaxed rather than with their high points, however. But Skinner would probably have argued that without the contingencies, the rebellions need never have occurred.

Again, counterattack is not restricted to aversive contingencies. Positive reinforcement can also produce something like counterattack. Skinner himself discusses one example. Some schedules of positive reinforcement, such as fixed-ratio schedules, are very effective in generating responding at a high rate. As Skinner frequently points out, *piecework* (payment per item produced) is just such a schedule. Yet piecework notoriously generates strong counter-control. Labor unions have universally condemned it, and the practice survives mainly in professions such as medicine, law, and trading in stocks and bonds where the reinforcers (dollars per reinforcer) are inordinately large. Animal studies show similar effects: So long as the reinforcer is large enough, a rat will make up to 5,000 lever presses to get one.[28] Otherwise rats show an increasing reluctance to respond as the ratio of responses to reinforcers is increased.

Skinner also objects to aversive control because of its undesirable side effects. But positive reinforcement also has undesirable side effects. The ambitious student who does charitable work not in order to help poor people but because it will look good on his *vita;* the researcher who fakes his data in order to win a research grant; the financier who cheats widows and orphans to make a killing in the market; not to mention common thieves, cheats, robbers and embezzlers all show "counter-control" of the same sort shown by people subject to aversive contingencies. Flatterers, the objects of their flattery, spoiled children, divas, absolute monarchs, presidents and prima donna media stars—the entire "celebrity culture"—all attest to the ill effects of too much positive reinforcement.

The good Skinnerian may object that the problem with the spoiled child is not excess of positive reinforcement, but a poor *schedule* of reinforcement. The kid was rewarded for the wrong things. But of course the same argument can be offered for the violent man abused as a child: His problem may be not the punishment he received, but the fact that it was excessive and indiscriminate.

In short, any form of behavioral control, positive or negative, can misfire. There is no reason to prefer positive reinforcement to punishment—other than our empathy with the person who is punished. And that may well be mitigated if we believe the policy will reduce the number of victims of crime better than any alternative.

Deterrence

> "There was a man," remarked Captain Eliot, "who was sentenced to death for stealing a horse from a common. He said to the judge that he thought it hard to be hanged for stealing a horse from a common; and the judge answered, 'You are not to be hanged for stealing a horse from a common, but that others may not steal horses from commons.'"
>
> —Patrick O'Brien[29]

The utilitarian view of punishment provides a simple answer to the abuse excuse. Let us concede (although it is impossible to prove in any specific case) that violent crime is often the product of an abusive childhood. The infliction of punishment may still be appropriate because of its deterrent effect. The fact that his past behavior was caused by something or other has no bearing on the criminal's present susceptibility to deterrence, or on the likelihood that others with similar histories will be deterred by observing his punishment. Indeed, if a person's criminal behavior can be traced to absence of appropriate and systematic punishment for bad behavior in the past, then punishment may well be what is needed now.

Even if we concede that a defendant committed the crime because of his past history, we need to know a bit more abut that past history to judge the justice of the punishment. In the case of the Menendez brothers, for example, it's pretty clear that one aspect of their past history—what they had learned of the California legal system—led them to think that they could get away with their crime. But this hardly exonerates them. On the contrary, it suggests a thought-experiment test for culpability. Suppose that a prognosticating angel had whispered in Erik Menendez's ear as he was about to pull the trigger: "If you kill your parents, you will go to jail for life." Would he have fired? Obviously not, since his belief that he would get away with the crime is one reason he committed it. Hence he is fully responsible. On the other hand, if the same angel had said a similar thing to Daniel M'Naghten, he would have killed Drummond anyway because he was obeying the voice of God. Conclusion: not responsible.

Only when punishment is likely to be completely *in*effective as a deterrent does the law quite properly limit its use.[30] If the criminal is insane, or if injury was the result of self-defense or the unintended consequence of actions whose harmful outcome was unforeseeable, no guilt is attached to the perpetrator and no punishment is given—presumably because punishment can play no role in preventing the recurrence of such acts. Traditional legal practice is often surprisingly wise.

This argument is perfectly behavioristic. The utilitarian case for personal responsibility rests entirely on the beneficial *collective* effects of just punishment. It does not rest on philosophical notions of individual autonomy or personal morality, although such notions may play a role in training the young. Skinner was perhaps prevented from taking this line by two things: his deep-rooted and fundamentally prejudicial objection to punishment; and the fact that the arguments I have just made are close to arguments that are relatively commonplace in the literature of jurisprudence. By abandoning his objections to punishment, Skinner would have destroyed the uniqueness of his position—which is something he was always at pains to maintain, most obviously through the adoption of an idiosyncratic vocabulary.

Behavior-Control Problems

Skinner's case for behavioral control is similar to the argument of the rational-choice economist. The economist says: Tell me what people want (usual assumption: money). Tell me the rules by which they can get it (e.g., the financial incentives); and I can predict what they will do. Skinner says: Show me the reinforcement schedules that are operating, and I will predict the behavior. Rational-choice economists and naïve reinforcement theorists usually end the story there. For both, once the contingencies are set, the behavior is perfectly determined. If the hungry pigeon must peck a key ten times to get a bit of food (a fixed-ratio 10 schedule of reinforcement), it will inevitably learn to do so and go on to develop the characteristic stereotyped pattern of behavior. If single women are paid substantial amounts of child support, fewer women will marry, and the rate of illegitimacy will increase.[31]

It is hard to overestimate the pervasiveness of the idea of reinforcement contingency in human social thought. The term and the experimental method are new; the basic idea is not. Carrot-and-stick "technology" is an old story and it has led to practices that are generally very effective. Think, for example, of the "behavioral technology" involved in the workings of the great sailing ships of the eighteenth and early nineteenth centuries so vividly described in Patrick O'Brian's novels. A single "ship of the line" might carry 1,000 men, each a cog in a vast machine to work 100 guns and control dozens of sails in a coordinated way to attack an enemy or ride out a storm. Without skilled sailors with habits of automatic obedience, such ships must soon have perished, as many indeed did. But most did not, weathering storms, reefs and lee shores that all pose extraordinary risks for a cumbersome vessel entirely at the mercy of external forces. The large rewards, often from plunder, and the often severe punishments that maintained this efficiency are well known and often deplored. Yet without them, the tight control necessary to the survival of large sailing ships alone for months on the high seas might well have been impossible.

On a less heroic scale, the behavior of automobile drivers is quite sensitive to the penalties for motoring infractions. Drivers in many European countries seem to pay little attention to speed limits, for example, because penalties for speeding are rarely enforced. But drivers in those U.S. states that stringently enforce speed limits are much more careful, even when the limit is well below what most would judge safe. All governments know the power of tax code to boost some activities (like house ownership in the United States and agriculture in Europe) and inhibit others (like alcohol and tobacco consumption).

Contingencies do not always work as intended, however. The failures are of two kinds: Either the subject is smarter than the experimenter, or the reverse. Examples of the first kind are tax "loopholes." A provision designed to facilitate one kind of activity is turned to unintended uses by ingenious tax avoiders. As the fraction of the national treasure taken in by governments tended to increase over the past century, tax law has become a kind of arms race in which laws are drafted for one set of purposes and then turned by taxpayers to quite others.

The complex and indirect system of regulation of financial markets is notoriously ineffective. Inept and lobbyist-crafted regulation allowed clever financial players to make huge gains and pass losses on to others in a spiral that led to the financial crash of 2008. Similar processes have driven many earlier crises.[32]

But contingencies may also fail because the subject is dumber, or more constrained, than the experimenter thinks he is. Pigeons (and even, alas, many human beings) cannot learn calculus, for example, and no matter how rewarding the schedule, a bird that must get its food only by solving equations will starve. So there are capacity limitations: Pigs cannot fly and dogs cannot speak. But, as we saw in Chapter 6, there are also limitations of a more subtle kind. The phenomenon known as instinctive drift shows that although the contingencies favor one thing—and it is well within the organism's capacities—the organism may nevertheless do another.

Procedures that present painful stimuli (aversive schedules) provide many other examples. For example, if two rats, strangers to each other, are placed together in a cage and intermittently shocked through the floor, they will attack each other and this will prevent them from learning to press a lever to prevent shock delivery. Even isolated rats find it difficult to learn an avoidance response because the shock induces instinctive reactions, such as "freezing," that interfere with lever pressing. Most surprisingly, many animals can actually be trained to produce painful stimuli. After an appropriate training history, cats and monkeys will press a lever that occasionally produces painful electric shock.[33]

Aversive contingencies may fail to achieve their intended objective if they are too severe because of these "misbehavior" effects. As in the rat example, punishment that is excessive produces behavior that competes with the desired behavior and thwarts aim of the punishment regimen. In human beings, punishment that is perceived as unjust also elicits reactions (usually aggressive) other than those intended. Literature provides many vivid examples where the excessive punishment fails to yield the desired behavior. For example, in the seventeenth-century play *Surgeon of Honor* by Spanish writer Calderon de Barca, the clown-servant Coquin is given the ultimatum that he must make the King laugh—or else have all his teeth pulled out. This particular aversive contingency is more likely to leave Coquin in need of a dentist than the King in fits of mirth.

Many of the British penal colonies in Australasia incorporated amazingly sophisticated systems of behavioral control. Some worked satisfactorily, many did not. Norfolk Island, a tiny speck in the Pacific, provides examples of both sorts. Under the regimen of Major Joseph Anderson (in charge from 1834 to 1839), for example, five men might get *1,500* lashes between them before breakfast—for crimes like "singing a song" or "robbing the earth of its seed" (not planting corn properly). "Deranged by cruelty and misery, some men would opt for a lifetime at the bottom of the carceral heap by blinding themselves, thus, they reasoned, they would be left alone."[34] The only convict to leave a record of life on the island at this time wrote of Anderson's even more brutal predecessor James Morisett:

> If you endeavour to take out of [a prisoner] that manly confidence which ought to be cherished in every civilized human being, you then begin the work of demoralization; and it will end in the very Dreggs of debasement & and insensibility to every species of integrity and decency, and eradicate every right feeling in the human breast. You make him regardless of himself, and fearless as to the consequences of doing wrong to others.[35]

Far from producing productive obedience, Morisett's terrifying regime made his prisoners unscrupulous and indifferent to consequences.

Excessive punishment is bad because it is usually ineffective. But what about mild punishment? Because of the almost unanimous condemnation from social scientists, including Skinner and his contemporary, best-selling pediatrician Benjamin Spock,[36] corporal punishment has been almost abolished in American and British schools. It has been replaced with Skinnerian techniques like "time out" or by simply suspending persistent offenders. In the legal system in Britain, young offenders are likely to get not the "birching" (beating) they used to receive[37] but an Anti-Social Behavior Order (ASBO). An ASBO is the legal equivalent of the tired parent who says to an errant child: "If you do that again, I will *really* get mad at you!"

Caning, notoriously, is still legal in Singapore. Uproar ensued in the United States when in 1994 this punishment was inflicted on Michael Fay, an eighteen-year-old American man convicted of theft and vandalism. Conversely, even parental spanking of a child is regarded as abuse in Sweden and many other European countries. Usually the justification offered is scientific. Spanked children grow up to be more aggressive and so on (not that aggression is always a bad thing). But experiments cannot be done and correlational research is never conclusive.

Much of the evidence on corporal punishment is anecdotal, so I will add my own. From the age of 10–18, I went to an English boys' school. It was no private boarding school like Dickens' Dotheboys Hall or George Orwell's St Cyprian's.[38] It was a state day school. But it *was* full of boys, from 10–11 to 18 in age. Caning was permitted, both formally, by the headmaster, and informally—by the art master, who used a T-square to whack the miscreant bent over his desk in front of the class. A roomful of sixteen-year-old boys, in an age before the porn-ready Internet, were thus induced to contemplate esthetically rather than lubriciously slides of the Rokeby Venus and her sisters. But caning happened very rarely. Unlike boarder Orwell, we did not live in fear. On the other hand, the *possibility* of caning made it very clear who was in charge, and discipline was good. But if, as once happened, we got a new teacher who treated us in what would now be regarded as a civilized manner, things deteriorated. I can remember playing cards in the back of the class with my buddies and thinking, "Mr. Hawke-Genn [for that was his name] is pretty interesting; too bad no one [myself included] is paying attention." Whether our lack of attention, even when the material was interesting, was due to this break from the "barbaric" regime we were used to—or just reflected the entropic tendencies of adolescents—I cannot say. My guess is that boys will be boys, unless they know who's boss.

At bottom (so to speak) corporal punishment is a moral issue. Western elites have just come to think that it is wrong. If that is your conviction, it cannot be gainsaid. But the scientific justification for total abolition of corporal punishment is weak to nonexistent. Consider again the case of Michael Fay. The alternative to caning would have been several months in jail, which would have been costly both to Singapore and to Fay. Many prisons simply educate first offenders in how to do crime better. They rarely rehabilitate. On the other hand, the caning is brief and returns the culprit immediately to society. My guess is that Mr. Fay himself would have chosen caning over imprisonment, yet its salutary effect might well be greater.

How about deterrence? Which deters more, pain or incarceration? The answer is far from obvious. So unless society agrees to abhor corporal punishment as something fundamentally immoral, the case for it is quite strong. The fact that support for corporal punishment is now weak may well be because flawed science has been promoted to show that all punishment is not just evil, but ineffective. About the "evil," each must make up his own mind. But ineffective it is not.

How about rehabilitation, which, in addition to deterrence and retribution, is a third function of judicial punishment? Again, Norfolk Island provides an illustration. It was also the site of a much more moderate regime that dispensed positive reinforcement as a way to control and rehabilitate its inhabitants. It resembles in almost every particular the modern behavioral psychologist's *token economy*,[39] still widely used in such mental and remedial institutions as remain after the closures in the United States in the 1970s and 1980s. These ideas were put in place between 1840 and 1844 by one Alexander Maconochie: "Let us offer our prisoners, not favors, but *rights,* on fixed and unalterable conditions."[40] Called the "Mark System," Maconochie's scheme involved sophisticated scheduling of both positive and negative reinforcement. (Negative reinforcement is the removal of an aversive stimulus: here, the convict's time of servitude.)

Good behavior was rewarded with "marks" that went toward a reduction of sentence: 6,000 marks were equivalent to a 7-year sentence, 7,000 to 10 and 10,000 to life—a nonlinear scale corresponding roughly to the disutility of each sentence. ("Time off for good behavior" is the modern, less sophisticated version of Maconochie's "marks.") Marks could also be exchanged for goods; they were "just wages, and will equally stimulate to care, exertion, economy and fidelity."[41]

By all accounts, the Mark System was reasonably successful during its short life, but it was in the end stymied by Britain's need for Norfolk Island to be a place where "[f]elons . . . have forfeited all claim to protection of law," the deterrent *ne plus ultra* for intractable villains. Maconochie's humane system failed of this objective and so was abandoned. Rehabilitation must always be balanced against deterrence. Since deterrence affects many and rehabilitation only a few, the balance tends to favor deterrence. Programs for rehabilitation will usually have a smaller effect on the rate of crime than punishments that simply deter.

Notes

1. Staddon, J. (2012). *The malign hand of the markets* (New York: McGraw-Hill).
2. See http://en.wikipedia.org/wiki/Lyle_and_Erik_Menendez.
3. See, for example, Dershowitz, A. (1994). *The abuse excuse* (Boston: Little, Brown); Horowitz, D. L. (1986). Justification and excuse in the program of the criminal law. *Law and Contemporary Problems, 49*, 109–126; Stocker, M. (1999). Responsibility and the abuse excuse. In E. F. Paul, F. D. Miller, & J. Paul (Eds.), *Responsibility* (Cambridge: Cambridge University Press), pp. 175–200.
4. Livermore, L., & Meehl, P. (1967). The virtues of M'Naghten. *Minnesota Law Review, 51*, 789–856.
5. BFAD, p. 112.
6. To be fair to Aristotle, he also argued that virtue was essential to true happiness.

7. Skinner, B. F. (1961/1955). Freedom and the control of men. In *Cumulative record,* pp. 3–18, p. 6.
8. Cohen, J., & Nagel, T. (2009, March 18). John Rawls: On my religion. *Times Literary Supplement.*
9. There is an excellent account of social justice, its proponents and its critics, on Wikipedia: http://en.wikipedia.org/wiki/Social_justice.
10. Quoted by Hans-Hermann Hoppe: http://mises.org/daily/357.
11. See, for example, Murphy, L., & Nagel, T. (2004). *The myth of ownership: Taxes and justice* (New York: Oxford University Press). There is a review in Staddon, J. (2004). A remarkable book. *Society, 41*(4), 90–92. Retrieved from http://dukespace.lib.duke.edu/dspace/handle/10161/6380.
12. TOJ, pp. 150–151.
13. Sen, A. (2009). *The idea of justice* (Cambridge, MA: Harvard University Press), p. 13. Sen was awarded the Economics Nobel Prize in 1998.
14. Nozick, R. (1974). *Anarchy, state and utopia* (New York: Basic Books); Rothbard, M. N. (1998). *The ethics of liberty* (New York: New York University Press).
15. Beccaria, C. (1992/1775). *An essay on crimes and punishments* (Boston. MA: Branden).
16. See, for example, Shaw, W. H. (1999). *Contemporary ethics: Taking account of utilitarianism* (Malden, MA: Blackwell).
17. Moore, M. (1997). *Placing blame: A general theory of the criminal law* (Oxford: The Clarendon Press), pp. 78–79.
18. *Chambers's Twentieth Century Dictionary* (1901/1950).
19. From Berlin's important essay "Two Concepts of Liberty," which was originally given as a lecture in Oxford, United Kingdom, in 1958.
20. There is an interesting argument about free will that occurred to me as a schoolboy. You can never know if you have free will or not because whether you *feel* free or not, you cannot know whether that feeling itself is free or determined. Ergo, free will is unknowable. You do know whether you *feel* free, though.
21. Quoted in Posner, R. A. (1990). *The problems of jurisprudence* (Cambridge, MA: Harvard University Press), p. 176.
22. Skinner, B. F. (1961/1956). Some issues concerning the control of human behavior. In *Cumulative record,* pp. 32–36, p. 26.
23. BFAD, p. 62.
24. Barrett, R. P., Matson, J. L., Shapiro, E. S., & Ollendick, T. H. (1981). A comparison of punishment and DRO procedures for treating stereotypic behavior of mentally retarded children. *Applied Research in Mental Retardation, 2*(3), 247–256: "Results of the study indicated that for both subjects, all conditions were clearly discriminated and that punishment procedures were more effective for suppressing stereotypies than DRO [differential reinforcement of 'other' behavior]."
25. Laboratory experiments on avoidance schedules are described in chapters by Morse and Kelleher, and Hineline, in Honig, W. K., & Staddon, J. E. R. (Eds.). (1977). *Handbook of operant behavior* (New York: Prentice-Hall).
26. See www.theatlantic.com/magazine/archive/2008/11/the-things-he-carried/307057/.
27. Is it time for the American eagle to be replaced by the American turtle?
28. Collier, G., Hirsch, E., & Kanarek, R. (1977). The operant revisited. In W. K. Honig & J. E. R. Staddon (Eds.), *Handbook of operant behavior* (Englewood Cliffs, NJ: Prentice-Hall), pp. 28–52.
29. O'Brien. P. (1977). *The Mauritius Command* (New York: W. W. Norton), p. 210.
30. Suicide bombing—a lethal compound of fanaticism and high explosives—is an intermediate case. A suicide bomber would not, of course, be deterred by the prognosticating angel. But he is probably not insane. If he is caught in the attempt, justice demands that be punished because we know that he might try again, and

232 Behaviorism and Society

could have behaved otherwise. Psychopaths, who can now be identified (to some extent) by brain activity, physiology and genetics, are another intermediate case. (See, for example, Adrian Raine [2013], *The anatomy of violence: The biological roots of crime* [Pantheon]). Many psychopaths are deterrable. Those who are not still need to be incarcerated to protect the public. The larger question is: What is the proper role of brain physiology in the criminal justice system? Should particular brain signatures be treated as prior criminal records—or as mitigating factors? In fact, brain correlates of criminal behavior are largely irrelevant. What matters is the susceptibility of the criminal to behavioral control. Can his behavior be modified to prevent future law breaking? Unless we can identify brain properties that perfectly predict the effects on behavior of reward, punishment, social factors and so on, the fact that some brain properties are correlated with some personality traits or some past patterns of behavior has no bearing at all on the responsibility of the individual for his actions. We are a long way from understanding brain function at this level.

31. It is irrelevant to the economic argument whether support payments actually reward childbearing or simply remove a disincentive. In the United Kingdom in 2013, for example, children are a huge cost to the middle class, but an exploitable source of income, through uncapped child benefits, for those who have no other income source. Charles Murray has provided a path-breaking analysis of this and related issues in *Losing ground: American social policy: 1905–1980* (New York: Basic Books, 1984).

32. See, for example, *Reckless endangerment: How outsized ambition, greed, and corruption led to economic armageddon* by *New York Times* reporters Gretchen Morgenson and Joshua Rosner (Time Books/Henry Holt & Co., 2011) and Staddon, J. (2012). *The malign hand of the markets* (New York: McGraw-Hill).

33. Byrd, L. D. (1969). Responding in the cat maintained under response-independent electric shock and response-produced electric shock. *Journal of the Experimental Analysis of Behavior, 12*, 1–10.

34. Hughes, R. (1987). *The fatal shore* (London: Collins, Harvill), p. 481.

35. Frayne, L. (1799). *Memoir on Norfolk Island* (pp. 25–26). NSW Colonial Secretary Papers, Vol. 1 (re. NSW 1799–1830). Ms. 681/1, ML, Sydney.

36. Spock's hugely influential book is *Baby and child care* (1946, with revisions up to ninth edition, 2012). Spock never met Skinner but disapproved of him on principle, apparently. See Freedman, D. H. (2012, June). The perfected self. *The Atlantic*, Retrieved from www.theatlantic.com/magazine/archive/2012/06/the-perfected-self/ 308970/.

37. See http://en.wikipedia.org/wiki/Birching.

38. Vividly described in *Such, such were the joys,* published in 1952. The essay is both an indictment of and a partial justification for what would now be regarded as cruel and abusive disciplinary practices. New boy Orwell, aged eight, was repeatedly caned for bed wetting, for example. Nevertheless, he conceded: "So perhaps this barbarous remedy could work, though at a heavy price, I have no doubt." Aversive control, broken by occasional flashes of negative reinforcement (i.e., brief relaxation of omnipresent threat), was the behavior modification of choice at St Cyprian's.

39. See http://en.wikipedia.org/wiki/Token_economy.

40. Hughes (1987), p. 499.

41. Hughes (1987), p. 500.

18 Health Care, I
The Schedule

A new behaviorism can shed light on social issues that may seem at first to be beyond its reach. The last chapter discussed reward and punishment in the context of the justice system. In this one I look at the delivery of medical services. Health care is enormously expensive in the United States and likely to become more so. I will try to disentangle this puzzle from the point of view of reinforcement contingencies—incentives. It turns out that the provision of health care is not a competitive free market with "invisible hand" incentives that drive it toward a better and cheaper product. And it never can be. Attempts to turn it into one have caused costs to achieve escape velocity. Without reform, the United States will continue to devote a ridiculous fraction of its national wealth to treating the sick.

The chapter is a broad survey. I do not deal with the hideous and changing complexities of the health insurance industry, for example. Nor with the metastasizing regulation boosted by recent health legislation. To cover all this in detail would require a library of books and an army of researchers. And the result would be largely incomprehensible, hence of little use as a guide to a better future for health care. I try instead to provide a clarifying perspective.

I refer in this chapter to what I have elsewhere[1] called the *malign hand*. It is the opposite of Adam Smith's *invisible hand*. The two are compared in Box 18.1. The point is that self-interest, even in a market-like setting, is not guaranteed to advance the public good. We'll see why in a moment.

Box 18.1   The Credo of Capitalism

The *Invisible Hand*

When the merchant sells you something "he intends only his own gain, and he is in this, as in many other cases, led by an invisible hand to promote an end which was no part of his intention." *The merchant's self-interest also benefits the customer.*

The *Malign Hand*

To paraphrase Smith: When the shepherd adds another sheep to the common land "he intends only his own gain, but he is in this, as in many other cases, led by a malign hand to promote an end which was no part of his intention." *The shepherd does better by adding a sheep, but the community may not.*

Since 1970, the percentage of U.S. GDP devoted to health care has risen from about 7% to 17% or so in 2009. This fraction of national wealth is much larger than the amounts spent by other developed nations such as Germany (10%) or the United Kingdom (8%). The U.S. divergence from the rest of the developed world in per-GDP and per-capita health spending took place only after about 1980.[2] Why have U.S. health-care costs increased so much? Why have they increased more than costs in our peer nations? The answer seems to be that conventional monetary incentives do not work well in health care. The problems with our health-care system cannot be fixed by the kinds of incentives/reinforcers that work in other kinds of markets.

Health-Care Costs

Health-care systems have changed as medical science has developed. One hundred years ago, medicine was ineffective but cheap. Public health advances until relatively recently were mostly caused by improvements in public hygiene and nutrition. Once you were sick, relatively little could be done about it; and what was done cost relatively little. The "unit" of medical care was either the individual physician or a hospital of modest size that delivered largely custodial care. There was choice. Patients could pick their doctor and, 150 years ago, paid him directly. Many physicians, such as Charles Darwin's father, Robert Waring Darwin (1766–1848), were very successful and became quite rich. Robert Darwin, like many other physicians of the time, adapted his charges to the need, character and ability to pay of his patients. It was the "universal health care" of its day.

Things slowly changed as science advanced after Louis Pasteur (1822–1895) and the discovery of microbes, vaccination, sulfa drugs and finally penicillin and other antibiotics. The first advances were both very effective, like vaccination, and also cheap, so they had relatively little effect on the economics of health care. But since the middle of the twentieth century, after the elimination of much infectious disease in the developed world, expensive chronic conditions came to the fore.

Life expectancy at birth has increased hugely since 1900, from forty or so to older than seventy-seven in the United States and other developed countries now. But most of this change is due to a great reduction in child mortality: In the United States the average life expectancy over the past 100 years has increased by more than 50%. But the age-adjusted expectancy for 60-year-olds has only increased by 10% or so.[3]

The popular impression is that the U.S. population is aging. If true, this might account for the steady increase in health-care costs, because costs increase greatly with age—for example, in 2004, people between sixty-five and eighty-five spent about $15,000 per capita on health care but younger people, between nineteen and sixty-four, spent only $4,500,[4] a ratio of 3.3 to 1; and this ratio had changed little from previous years. But the proportion of the aged in the population has *not* in fact increased in recent decades, and this should not be surprising. If advances in health care have especially benefited infants and young people, then we should expect the proportion of the young in the population to increase and, correspondingly, the proportion of the old to decrease. In actuality the proportion of older people in the population has remained relatively stable—from 1990 to 2000, for example, the proportion of the population sixty or older went from 16.83% to just 16.27%, a negligible decrease.[5] This is changing as the baby boomers age. In many countries, reduced fertility will reduce the proportion of younger people for a while.[6] But it is a fact that across the period when health care took up an increasing proportion of national wealth, the proportion of the old in the population changed little. This means that the huge recent increases in proportion of national wealth devoted to health care cannot be blamed on a matching increase in the proportion of older people in the population. Nevertheless, the old do cost a great deal more than the young, so we should perhaps look there first for the causes of health-care increases.

As people live longer, they became more susceptible to diseases of old age such as arthritis, most cancers, degenerative conditions, dementia, and Parkinson's disease. When these conditions were infrequent (because relatively few people lived long enough to get them), and little but custodial care could be offered to cure them, they had little impact on health-care economics. And in any case, in pre-industrial times, care of the old was usually a family matter. But after World War II, treatments began to be developed that could, if not cure, at least ameliorate and prolong the lives of many cancer sufferers, for example. The real *cure* record is rather mixed, in fact. The incidence of many cancers seems to have *increased* in recent years.[7] To pick a few of the more striking examples, over the period from 1973 to 1999, breast cancer incidence increased 41%, liver cancer 103.7%, female lung 142.8%, prostate 104.9%, malignant melanoma, 155.9%. These were balanced by a smaller number of decreases, but overall, for the more than thirty-five sites listed,[8] female cancers increased by 20.8% and male by 23.9%.

Cure rates have not kept up:

> The number of cancer deaths in the United States has declined for the first time in more than 70 years—the first time since the government starting keeping statistics in 1930—according to an American Cancer Society analysis of government health data.
>
> There were 369 fewer cancer deaths in 2003 (556,902 deaths) than in 2002 (557,271 deaths), the latest years for which statistics are available. Although the decline may seem small compared to the total number of cancer deaths, the American Cancer Society expects the downward trend to continue and is projecting a much larger decrease in 2006.[9]

So that's a decline of just 0.07% in one year. As we just saw, demographics don't seem to be the problem. Older people are more likely to die of cancer than younger people, but the proportion of older people in the population did not change much in the years leading up to 2003. Newer data show that cancer deaths have dropped by 11% in men and 6% in women since 1971, which is hopeful. But much of this improvement is attributable to reductions in smoking rates; relatively little reflects improvements in treatment. The troubling fact is that treatment for cancer has had limited success so far—but has cost much. So in recent decades the proportion of relatively ineffective, expensive and protracted treatments for chronic conditions of older people in the treatment mix has increased.

It is typical of the changes in treatment and diagnosis in recent decades that they tend to be expensive, but add relatively little benefit in "quality-life-years saved."[10] The increased costs have several causes, but evaluating their relative importance is tricky. The most obvious sources are the cost of new diagnostic technology, CT scanners and the like, and the cost of research leading to new medicines, which is reflected in their cost. The relative ineffectiveness of many of the new drugs is something of a puzzle in itself. (I discussed the problems with the methods for drug evaluation in Chapter 9.) But the economics of health care also plays a huge role, as I will show in a moment.

This is some background to all the hand wringing about health-care costs. But despite these problems, until very recently, many health-care providers seem to be doing rather well. New hospital buildings were going up everywhere. Brown University, for example, which suffered quite badly during the financial crash and had to announce staff cuts in 2009,[11] in 2010 broke ground for a new medical center building. Duke University, which suffered less from the crash than Brown, was able to break ground in November 2009 on $700M in new Medical Center construction. In 2010, Cornell University, also faced with a big budget deficit, nevertheless borrowed $285M for a new midtown research building.[12] Stephen Brill, in a long *TIME* magazine article, lists many other things that illustrate the affluence of the health-care industry, from massive new building complexes in Houston and other medical hubs to the substantial, and often partly hidden, remuneration of its executives. The annual compensation of Ronald DePinho, head of Houston's MD Anderson Center, was "$1,845,000. That does not count outside earnings derived from a much publicized waiver he received from the university that, according to the *Houston Chronicle*, allows him to maintain unspecified 'financial ties with his three principal pharmaceutical companies.'"[13] The disproportionate growth of the health-care industry, the increasing fraction of GDP it takes up year by year, and the amount of spare cash sloshing around the system makes health care look a little like a (not so) miniature version of the financial markets. Perhaps the malign hand is at work here also?

Behavioral Economics of Health Care

The economics of health care—the amount and types of incentives for individual doctors and for health-care facilities—are a real mess. There are some paradoxes. The United Kingdom's government-run system, for example, costs about half as much per capita as the United States' allegedly free-enterprise one. It's hard to find other areas where the government is more efficient than a supposedly competitive system, which raises some obvious questions: Does our more expensive health care just mean we are healthier and longer lived than the Brits? How competitive *is* the U.S. system, in fact? Is competition in fact the best way to rein in health-care cost and maintain the level of treatment?

Even though Britain's health care is much cheaper, life expectancy is much the same in the two countries. The United Kingdom is a little ahead, in fact: Life expectancy at birth was 79.4 for the United Kingdom from 2005–2010 but 78.2 for the United States.[14] Here's another comparison: In 2006, per-capita spending for 70%-government-funded health care in Canada was U.S.$3,678 versus $6,714 in the United States, which is 46% government money. Yet Canadian life expectancy is quite a bit greater than in the United States: 80.7 versus 78.6 for a comparable period.[15]

So the U.S. system is much more expensive than health care in comparable countries, but the results—at least as measured by life expectancy—are not better; in fact, they are a bit worse. These are of course very crude comparisons. Life expectancy isn't everything. Indeed, as I discussed in Chapter 11 in connection with life-history strategies, from a long-term common-good point of view, it may not be a good measure at all. And many people die for reasons unrelated to their health—accident, homicide, and so on. Some of these causes are clearly more important in the United States than in the United Kingdom or Canada: We have higher murder and traffic-fatality rates than the United Kingdom, for example. But life expectancy is one of the most reliable measures we have and the fact is that despite paying twice as much, Americans don't live anywhere near twice as long as Canadians or Brits!

Another possibility is that Americans are just naturally sicker than other Westerners, and that's why our health care costs more. But, despite all the negative publicity, the United States is not significantly less healthy than other Western nations with much lower health costs. As a well-known medical commentator points out, "We may be more obese than any other industrialized nation, but we have among the lowest rates of smoking and alcoholism, and we are in the middle of the range for cardiovascular disease and diabetes."[16] We don't pay more for health care because we are sicker.

The opposite hypothesis is that given our bad eating and exercise habits, we *should be* sicker than other Westerners. If we're not, it's just because we get better health care. Hard to disprove that one, but do you believe it?

It is possible that when it comes to ailments that require technically difficult treatments, such as the heart condition that prompted sixty-year-old Newfoundland Premier Danny Williams to head to the United States for surgery in February 2010, the United States may well be a world leader. At the top end, the United States may be best. But for routine health care . . . probably not so good. Bottom line: The United States pays too much for health care.

The effects of new health-care legislation on all this are still uncertain and will in any case take years to play out. But the major problems with the present arrangement are actually pretty obvious. Let's look first at the economics of health-care systems and then at the reinforcement contingencies for individual doctors and patients.

The CON

Health-care systems do not compete much. The evidence is everywhere, but a bit you might not have heard of is the *Certificate of Need.* Check out this example from the State of North Carolina:

> The North Carolina Certificate of Need (CON) law *prohibits health care providers from acquiring, replacing, or adding to their facilities and equipment,* except in specified circumstances, without the prior approval of the Department of Health and Human Services. Prior approval is also required for the initiation of certain medical services. The law restricts unnecessary increases in health care costs and limits unnecessary health services and facilities based on geographic, demographic and economic considerations.
>
> The fundamental premise of the CON law is that increasing health care costs may be controlled by governmental restrictions on the *unnecessary duplication* of medical facilities.[17]

Here's another example, from the State of New York:

> New York's Certificate of Need (CON) process governs the establishment, construction, renovation and major medical equipment acquisitions of health care facilities, such as hospitals, nursing homes, home care agencies, and diagnostic and treatment centers. Through the CON process, the Department seeks to promote the delivery of high-quality health care services and to ensure that facility-based health care services are aligned with community health needs. *The CON process also reins in investments in excess facility capacity and unneeded medical equipment that drive up health care costs for everyone,* without contributing materially to the health of our communities. (italics added)

Many other states have similar laws. What on Earth is going on here? The state government is *preventing* health-care providers from adding freely to their facilities. The states know just what new facilities are "unneeded." No North Carolina hospital—not even a care center for helpless old people—can add a new CT scanner, operating room, or even patient bed, without approval from the North Carolina Department of Health and Human Services.

Just think for a moment what would be the effect if a similar regulatory regime applied to, say, auto service stations. What would happen if the number and facilities of service stations were limited in this way? Would it be cheaper or more expensive to get your car fixed in the future? This not a tough question.

Even a contestant on a celebrity quiz could get it right. The answer is obvious: When you restrict supply, the cost goes up. Yet here we see North Carolina (and thirty-six other states[18]) feeling it necessary to restrict supply in order to keep cost *down*. What on Earth can this mean?

But of course the CON is a cure for the wrong disease. The real problem is that health-care demand is almost completely insensitive to cost. That is why health care is not a "typical" economic product. "Market forces" do not work in the same way for health-care services as they do for other markets.

The collapse of the Soviet Union in 1991 is usually taken as final proof for an argument now firmly associated with the Austrian economists, but perhaps first voiced in the modern era by Adam Smith in 1776: "What is the species of domestick industry which his capital can employ, and of which the produce is likely to be of the greatest value, every individual, it is evident, can, in his local situation, judge much better than any statesman or lawgiver can do for him."[19] In other words: People know best what to do with their own resources. No central planner can gather enough information to predict accurately how much and how many of each of the myriad products of a modern economy will be "needed," and how each should be allocated among consumers.

U.S. health planners seem not to have heard either of Adam Smith or Friedrich Hayek because "identifying need" is exactly what they did by attempting to control the creation of health-care resources. The CON process is just the kind of central planning that destroyed the Soviet Union and the planned economies under its control.

Critics complain that "Obamacare" pushes America toward the dreaded "socialized medicine." What they don't seem to realize is that in many ways we already *have* socialized medicine—since 1964, when New York State passed a law giving the state government power to determine whether there was a need for any new hospital or nursing home before it was approved for construction. The state didn't actually initiate new construction, as it might in Britain or some other European country with government-controlled medicine. But it did control exactly what could be built. Many other states passed CON laws, and the process took off, as part of the federal Health Planning Resources Development Act of 1974.

The history of CONs has some resemblances to the history of mortgage finance I described in the *Malign Hand*: an apparently innocuous and reasonable first step, followed by slow emergence of perverse reinforcement contingencies.

> The basic assumption underlying CON regulation is that excess capacity (in the form of facility overbuilding) directly results in health care price inflation. When a hospital cannot fill its beds, fixed costs must be met through higher charges for the beds that are used. Bigger institutions have bigger costs, so CON supporters say it makes sense to limit facilities to building only enough capacity to meet actual needs.[20]

This argument presumes that the effects of competition, which would normally tend to reduce price as supply is increased, simply do not apply to the health-care industry. A facility that "overbuilds" cannot, apparently, recoup some of the cost in the usual way. A hotel with too many rooms tries to fill more by reducing the price. Apparently hospitals cannot do the same: attract more patients by reducing the price of a bed. Why not? Well, the answer is not that they can't reduce price, it's that they won't because they don't need to—because the system is simply not competitive.

Interestingly, one of the most persuasive arguments against the noncompetitive CON comes from the federal government in a report called *Improving Health Care: A Dose of Competition* (2004). The agencies involved are the Federal Trade Commission and the Department of Justice (anti-trust division). This federal report is critical of practices of *state* agencies, a rare example of the checks and balances envisaged by the Founding Fathers (not quite in the form they designed, and not that the report has had any serious effect!). The report's conclusion about CON programs is admirably clear:

> The Agencies believe that, on balance, CON programs are not successful in containing health care costs, and that they pose serious anticompetitive risks that usually outweigh their purported economic benefits. Market incumbents can too easily use CON procedures to forestall competitors from entering an incumbent's market. . . . Indeed, there is considerable evidence that CON programs can actually increase prices by fostering anticompetitive barriers to entry. [No kidding!]

It's not difficult to see what has happened. When certificates of need were first introduced—at around the same time that Medicare and Medicaid began to grow—expensive new facilities could easily be charged off to these new sources of money. There was a new pool of eligibility and health-care facilities expanded to suck up the business it offered. Medicaid is funded jointly by the states and the federal government, so the states had an immediate interest in limiting cost growth. The feds had rather less interest, for three reasons. First, health-care was a smaller fraction of their total budget; second, unlike many states, the federal government is not subject to a balanced-budget law; and third, the feds are always free to print money.[21] So the states acted first. To stop the bleeding—the new demands on state contributions to Medicaid—states introduced the CON requirement, which was intended to limit the ability of hospitals to exploit these new sources of income.

But of course, the states' actions represent the malign hand: short-term benefit, limiting demand, followed by long-term cost, limiting supply. By seeking relief *now* from the increased cost posed by expansion of health-care facilities, the states limited the relief that would eventually come from their expansion and competition.

On the other side of the table, hospitals and other health-care organizations were presumably unhappy at first about the states blocking their expansion plans. But they very soon must have seen the advantages of the CON system and many other competition-limiting regulations to them, as established health-care institutions: "[F]ew things are more foreseeable than that a trade or profession empowered to regulate itself will produce anticompetitive regulations."[22] Agreeing to regulation by the state can have the same effect. It is pleasant, though surprising, to see that even local journalists, who are not especially savvy about economic matters, are beginning to catch on. "WakeMed, Duke, Rex [three North Carolina hospitals] try to block newcomer" is a recent headline. With admirable directness, the article goes on to say, "The county's established health providers don't want to face a powerful new competitor on their home turf"[23]—reacting to the efforts of outsider Novant to build a new facility in North Carolina's Research Triangle.

The CON process is just like the infamous tobacco master Settlement Agreement (MSA)[24]—not that medical institutions will like being compared to the tobacco companies! But health centers, even many nonprofit ones, are businesses at heart—although some are more dominated by the bottom line than others. And most successful businesses are supremely pragmatic, doing whatever it (legally) takes to prop up the bottom line. So, just like Philip Morris and the other established tobacco companies, health centers all acquiesced in severe controls—because, like the tobacco MSA, the CON regulation and its like erect *barriers to entry,* limiting the ability of new clinics and other competing health-care entities from coming into existence. It is no surprise, therefore, to find that "in researching the scholarly journals [as of 1995], one cannot find a single article that asserts that CON laws succeed in lowering healthcare costs."[25] Very similar federal restrictions in the mammoth 2010 Affordable Health Care act have similarly elicited only faint mewing noises from many large medical organizations. They think they can do better with them than without.

At the same time that state regulations were beginning to slow down competition, the amount of money available through Medicare and Medicaid was ramping up. Medicare and Medicaid as a fraction of GDP increased from zero in 1965 to 4% in 2005. Over the same period, total health-care costs increased from 7% to 14%. So, not all the increase in health-care costs can be directly attributed to Medicare/Medicaid. But then, markets don't work in such a proportional way. If the government starts buying more cars, and the supply of cars remains the same, the prices of all cars, those it buys and those you and I buy, will all go up.

In addition to restraints on competition between medical centers, the incentives for individual physicians are also skewed in several ways.

Paying for Treatment, Not Results

A health system usually charges by what it does, not by what it achieves. Returning to the auto-service comparison, it's as if you took your car to a mechanic to fix that annoying noise and you get it back after a day with a bill for $250—and still the noise. If you complain, the mechanic lists all the ineffective things he did and has charged you for. This kind of thing is uncommon in the auto-service business. Only if a problem requires a particularly expensive diagnostic procedure will the service station charge for it. Usually, it's payment by results. Not so for health care. The patient, or more probably, his or her health-care insurance, is billed for time and procedures, irrespective of results.

Treatment-based profit thrives on uncertainty. The less certain you are about a patient's condition, the more tests you can prescribe. If there is no magic bullet, vaccination or an effective antibiotic—a situation very common for the chronic diseases of old age—the more "let's try this" treatments the curious—or profit-oriented—physician can plausibly offer. Perhaps the fact that older people not only suffer more chronic conditions than younger ones, but also suffer from more conditions that are difficult to diagnose and cure, accounts for part of that huge disparity in health-care costs between young and old.

It's not just "payment for treatment not results." Health-care providers, doctors, nurses and even hospital administrators, do not know and are not really interested in finding out, the costs of the procedures they recommend and implement. News stories with headlines like "How much will surgery cost? Good luck finding out"[26] pop up constantly in the media. "Here's why," says *Consumer Reports:* "The contracted prices that health plans negotiate with providers in their networks have little or nothing to do with the actual quality of services provided and everything to do with the relative bargaining power of the providers."[27] Yes, bargaining power, that's the key. And the bargaining is done not by medical personnel but by a specialized and highly paid cadre of lawyers and accountants quite remote from the providers of health care. More on bargaining power in a moment.

Third-party payment is a well-known problem in health-care economics. The patient initiates the process; the doctor decides on the treatment (and may benefit directly from his decision under some conditions); but a third party—the health-insurance company—usually pays.

Clean separation between who pays—the insurer—and who controls the outcome, is usual in most insurance. In accident or life insurance, for example, the insurable event is completely out of the control of the two parties to the insurance, company and customer. You do not choose to die[28] or to have an accident.

Not so with health insurance. The disease condition may not be under the control of the patient, but it's his decision to go to the doctor, he reports on his symptoms and the doctor decides on the treatment and thus the cost to insurance. Both the probability of an insurable event—am I sick or not?—to some degree; and the cost—what is the test/treatment?—are under the control of people, patient and doctor, who are in a position to benefit from insurance payout. The doctor benefits more or less from each insurance payment, and treatment benefits the insured patient but costs him or her little or nothing.

It is an elementary rule of the insurance industry that the existence of insurance should not affect the risk of the insured event. The extreme example is what writer V. S. Naipaul in his great novel *A House of Mr Biswas* called "insureanburn." Apparently some Indians in Trinidad made a habit of buying cheap houses, insuring them for more than they paid, and then setting them afire and collecting the insurance. This is not a good business model for any insurance industry. It doesn't work for medical insurance either.

The risk to which an insurer is exposed is just the chance of the insured event *times its cost*. But of course the very existence of medical insurance affects the cost of the "event"—treatment—in at least two ways: First, immediately, because the physician controls the treatment, and hence, the cost. But there is a second, delayed effect: The prices of tests and treatments are likely to increase as insurance-driven demand increases, especially if supply is limited (see CON, above).

A third effect is that, paradoxically, insurance companies can often negotiate *cheaper* rates than those paid directly by patients—bargaining power, again. So patients who pay their own bills and therefore have the most incentive to shop around, are in fact discriminated against to the point that they have negligible market influence. The power of monopsony—monopoly buyer—is one of the few cost restraints that seem to work in the health-care business.

No one who has a good health-insurance plan pays much attention to the "bills"—which are often clearly labeled, in fact, *this is not a bill*. (The rest of the bill is probably completely incomprehensible.) It's the malign hand in boldface: the unnecessary cost of any overuse of medical facilities is shared and delayed; the benefit, seeing the doctor and getting the surgery or whatever, is immediate. Eventually each beneficiary will have to pay a little more. But the overusing hypochondriac pays no more than the underusing medical nihilist.

There is no decisive solution to all these problems. But providing more balanced incentives to both doctor and patient can help, as we'll see in a moment.

Credentialing

Two hundred years ago little formal training was required to become a lawyer, a teacher or even a doctor. But, as time passed and medical science advanced and some quack doctors did bad things, government stepped in to protect the public by requiring credentials for the legal practice of medicine. After suitable training, the would-be doctor got a piece of paper certifying to both his character and his technical competence, either as a general practitioner or a specialist of some kind.

Why not let people figure out how good a doctor is on their own, a free-market advocate might ask? Why do you need any credentials at all? Well, when both the good and the harm a doctor could do were both relatively limited, that might have been a reasonable question. But for the past seventy-five years or so, the levels of skill, support and equipment doctors require, and the serious damage—to the patient and his bank account—they can do has risen.

The information-asymmetry problem (below) is much worse now than in centuries past when nobody knew very much. Now some kind of certification is obviously necessary. Whether it is best provided by the state, or by private entities like *Consumer Reports* or Underwriters Laboratories—or simply through the reputations of established medical schools—is another matter.

Credentialing may be necessary, but however it is administered, it inevitably limits the supply of practitioners, increases their costs and causes changes in the supply of physicians to lag behind changes in demand. Credentials in the United States cost more in time and money than in most other countries: "Becoming a doctor in the UK is considerably more streamlined than in the USA," says the BBC.[29] Most U.K. doctors start training at eighteen, right out of high school. After five or six years in medical school, they have their first qualification. In the United States, on the other hand, medicine is a graduate degree, adding four more years to the four necessary to get a bachelor's degree (versus three in the United Kingdom): a total of at least eight years versus five or six in the United Kingdom.

And it's very expensive. There are few scholarships for the MD degree in the United States and most medical graduates end up owing huge amounts. From the AMA website[30] we find the following chilling statistics: Average medical student debt in 2009 is $156,456; 79% of graduates have debt of at least $100,000; 87% of graduating medical students carry outstanding loans. This much indebtedness surely forces young doctors to pay attention to financial issues, even if they would much rather think about their patients.

Again, the situation in Britain is very different. Both undergraduate and graduate education are relatively inexpensive by U.S. standards. Undergraduate tuition was essentially free until a £3,000 ($4,500) undergraduate "top-up" fee[31] was introduced in 2006. Medical school also costs less than in the United States, although United Kingdom costs are rising. In 2009, "a British Medical Association poll of more than 2,000 [medical] students found those now starting their studies face debts at graduation of nearly £40,000"[32] ($60,000)—a lot, but much less than the $150,000 owed by U.S. students.

U.S. doctors may well feel that their training is worth the additional cost (psychologists call this "cognitive dissonance"—look it up!) but, as we've seen, U.S. health statistics don't really bear this out. By allowing more competition among credentialing bodies, or by changing the composition of licensing committees, U.S. costs could certainly be brought down. For example, medical licensing boards now are composed almost entirely of physicians—that is, of individuals who have a financial interest in limiting entry to the profession— the fewer doctors, the higher their fees: supply and demand at work. Of course, licensing of doctors does require the expertise of doctors. But they should not dominate licensing committees. They should be in a minority, with the majority made up of disinterested but scientifically proficient people charged with relaxing barriers to entry as much as possible. Physician members who want to restrict entry will then have to persuade the nonphysician majority that the criteria they propose are scientifically justifiable.

Patients and Doctors

Incentives for individual physicians and their patients are also perverse in almost every way. Most of these problems have been known for quite a while, although new details continue to emerge: Patients and doctors suffer from *information asymmetry*. The physician knows much more than the patient about the possible causes of, and cures for, his condition. But the patient knows much more about his or her symptoms, his history, and irrelevant factors (such a desire to get off work or win a lawsuit) that may affect his presenting story.

But much more important than information differences are motivational differences—termed *misaligned incentives* by economists. I will argue that these problems are an example of the animal "misbehavior" I discussed in Chapters 6 and 7. They are the result of a bad reinforcement schedule.

The physician is supposed to be motivated to make his patient healthy. Probably most are; but the economic incentives can sometimes lead doctors in quite a different direction. Here is a striking example. *New Yorker* contributor, surgeon Atul Gawande, compared health costs in two similar communities in Texas: McAllen and El Paso.[33] They attracted his attention because one of them, McAllen—the Square Dance Capital of the World and location for the iconic western movie "Lonesome Dove"—has much higher health-care costs than the other:

> McAllen . . . is one of the most expensive health-care markets in the country. Only Miami—which has much higher labor and living costs—spends more per person on health care. In 2006, Medicare spent fifteen thousand dollars per enrollee here, almost twice the national average. The income per capita is twelve thousand dollars. In other words, Medicare spends three thousand dollars more per person here than the average person earns. . . .
>
> El Paso County, eight hundred miles up the border, has essentially the same demographics. Both counties have a population of roughly seven hundred thousand, similar public-health statistics, and similar percentages of non-English speakers, illegal immigrants, and the unemployed. Yet in 2006 Medicare expenditures (our best approximation of over-all spending patterns) in El Paso were $7,504 per enrollee—half as much as in McAllen.

The reason that McAllen's costs are so high is not that its people are much less healthy than El Paso's. Nor does McAllen deliver a much better level of health care than El Paso: "Medicare ranks hospitals on twenty-five metrics of care. On all but two of these, McAllen's five largest hospitals performed worse, on average, than El Paso's." So, $7,000 more per capita for health care in McAllen, but slightly worse delivered care than El Paso.

So why are McAllen's health-care costs so high? Some obvious explanations don't work. Malpractice, for example: Is malpractice insurance especially high? Is "defensive medicine"—prescribing unnecessary tests and procedures to ward off malpractice suits—more prevalent in McAllen? Not likely, says Gawande, since Texas capped pain-and-suffering awards at $250,000 a few years ago and lawsuits went down "practically to zero"—and, I can add, why should McAllen suffer more from lawsuit-avoiding defensive medicine than El Paso when both are in the same legal jurisdiction?

The answer is that McAllen's higher costs *are* the result of overprescribing tests and procedures, but the reason has nothing to do with malpractice insurance. And these bad practices were especially common in certain institutions, such as Doctors Hospital at Renaissance, in Edinburg, one of the towns in the McAllen metropolitan area.

What is going on in McAllen reminds me of a similar process in the financial markets. When people understand the product, they tend to make straightforward rational decisions. Comparing two fixed-interest-rate loans, for example, it's easy just to choose the lowest rate. But when people are comparing complex derivatives—when they don't really have a clue what is going on—investors rely on authority or on the behavior of other people: "herding." In other words, when they understand the situation, people are guided in a sensible way by the relevant factors. Doctors seem to behave in the same way. When diagnosis and treatment are clear, doctors all follow the standard pattern. But when they aren't, when doctors don't really understand the problem, then they are much more likely to be driven by "other factors."

So it seems to be in McAllen and many other places where medical costs are especially high. In the high-cost areas, the "other factors" drive doctors to overprescribe. Gawande quotes a study[34] that

> surveyed some eight hundred primary-care physicians from high-cost cities (such as Las Vegas and New York), low-cost cities (such as Sacramento and Boise), and others in between. The researchers asked the physicians specifically how they would handle a variety of patient cases. It turned out that differences in decision-making emerged in only some kinds of cases. *In situations in which the right thing to do was well established—* for example, whether to recommend a mammogram for a fifty-year-old woman (the answer is yes)—physicians in high- and low-cost cities made the same decisions. But, *in cases in which the science was unclear,* some physicians pursued the maximum possible amount of testing and procedures; some pursued the minimum. And which kind of doctor they were depended on where they came from. (my italics)

Now perhaps we can begin to see why the diseases of old age, often hard to diagnose and always hard to really cure, are so expensive. These are just the cases where doctors may be tempted to overtest and overprescribe.

The doctors unconsciously follow well-known behavioral principles. In very many cases, the factors that contribute to the strength of a behavior are more or less additive. When the treatment for a given condition is well established, it has high strength; other factors, like economic incentives are relatively weak. The standard treatment is therefore prescribed. But when there is uncertainty, no other treatment has high strength so that "other factors," which may favor a generous selection of expensive treatments, come to the fore.

Notes

1. Staddon, J. (2012). *The malign hand of the markets* (New York: McGraw-Hill). The example is from the famous *tragedy of the commons,* but the same process can operate in nonagricultural settings.
2. See http://economix.blogs.nytimes.com/2009/07/08/us-health-spending-breaks-from-the-pack/.
3. See http://mappinghistory.uoregon.edu/english/US/US39-01.html has an excellent interactive graph showing age-adjusted life expectancies.
4. Hartman, M., Catlin, A., Lassman, D., Cylus, J., & Heffler, S. (n.d.). *U.S. health spending by age, selected years through 2004: Recent trends indicate that per-person spending for the oldest elderly is growing more slowly than spending for all other age groups.* Retrieved from http://content.healthaffairs.org/cgi/content/abstract/27/1/w1.
5. See www.censusscope.org/us/chart_age.html.
6. Last, J. (2013). *What to expect when no one's expecting* (Encounter Books), http://jonathanlast.com/.
7. This measure is not as straightforward as it seems because diagnostic techniques and criteria changed over this period. But the trend is probably correct.
8. See www.preventcancer.com/losing/nci/appendix_2.pdf.
9. See http://environment.about.com/od/healthenvironment/a/uscancerdeaths.htm.
10. This is a measure used by the British National Health Service. I discuss it in Chapter 19.
11. See http://stac.ri.gov/assets/297/Med_school_4_27_10.pdf .
12. See http://weill.cornell.edu/news/releases/wcmc/wcmc_2010/05_26_10.shtml .
13. Brill, S. (2013, February 20). Bitter pill: Why medical bills are killing us. *TIME* magazine. http://content.time.com/time/magazine/article/0,9171,2136864,00.html, But see also www.forbes.com/sites/chrisconover/2013/03/07/5-myths-in-steven-brills-bitter-pill-part-2/.
14. See http://en.wikipedia.org/wiki/List_of_countries_by_life_expectancy.
15. See http://en.wikipedia.org/wiki/Comparison_of_the_health_care_systems_in_Canada_and_the_United_States. See also www.creditloan.com/blog/healthcare-costs-around-the-world/ for more summary comparative health expenditure data.
16. Gawande, A. (2009, June 1). The cost conundrum: What a Texas town can teach us about health care. *New Yorker.* www.newyorker.com/reporting/2009/06/01/090601fa_fact_gawande.
17. See www.dhhs.state.nc.us/dhsr/coneed/index.html; www.health.state.ny.us/facilities/cons/.
18. Most of the states that don't require CONs have some comparable restrictions on the supply of medical services.
19. *The wealth of nations*, e-version.
20. For a summary of the history of the CON, see www.ncsl.org/IssuesResearch/Health/CONCertificateofNeedStateLaws/tabid/14373/Default.aspx.
21. Staddon (2012).
22. Havighurst, C. H. (2006, June). Contesting anticompetitive actions taken in the name of the state: state action immunity and health care markets. *Journal of Health Politics, Policy and Law, 31*(3), 587–607.
23. See www.newsobserver.com/2010/09/07/668161/wakemed-duke-rex-try-to-block.html.

24. See Derthick, M. (2005). *Up in smoke: Legislation to litigation in tobacco politics,* 2nd ed. (Washington DC: CQ Press); and Staddon, J. (2013). *Unlucky strike: Private health and the science, law and politics of smoking* (Buckingham, UK: University of Buckingham Press).
25. Quoted in Roy Cordato's excellent 2005 critique: www.johnlocke.org/policy_reports/display_story.html?id=62.
26. See www.nbcnews.com/id/50748682/ns/health-health_care/#.UUeGXBysh8E.
27. See www.consumerreports.org/cro/magazine/2012/07/that-ct-scan-costs-how-much/index.htm.
28. Most life insurance policies are voided by suicide.
29. See www.bbc.co.uk/dna/h2g2/A717527.
30. See www.ama-assn.org/ama/pub/about-ama/our-people/member-groups-sections/medical-student-section/advocacy-policy/medical-student-debt.shtml.
31. Recently upped to £9,000.
32. See http://news.bbc.co.uk/2/hi/health/8126233.stm.
33. Gawande (2009).
34. Sirovich, B., Gallagher, P. M., Wennberg, D. E., & Fisher, E. S. (2008). Discretionary decision making by primary care physicians and the cost of U.S. health care. *Health Affairs, 27*(3), 813–823.

19 Health Care, II

The Context

So what are these "other factors" that lead physicians to overprescribe when they are uncertain about a patient's condition? They have to do with the prevailing culture among physicians, what I have called context or *labeling* in the operant learning of animals. In humans, as in animals, the type of reinforcer matters. For example, one of the very best hospitals in the world is the Mayo Clinic in Rochester, Minnesota. It also boasts one of the lowest costs in the country—$8,000 less per capita than McAllen, according to Gawande, and in the bottom 15% for the country. The culture at Mayo is collaborative and patient centered—and doctors are paid a salary. In other words, an individual Mayo doctor gains *nothing* financially from prescribing treatment versus no treatment, or one treatment versus another. His reinforcements are social, from success in curing patients and via collaboration with other doctors, rather than pecuniary.

But most doctors are not paid straight salaries. Most physicians in the United States are paid on what is basically a piecework basis. Behavioral psychologists call this a "ratio schedule," and notoriously it tends to generate a very high level of the rewarded activity, especially if payoffs are large. If doctors are paid according to what they prescribe, they will tend to prescribe a lot. One commentator summarizes the situation this way:

> Compensation plans in the 1990s were very complicated, and included such things as participation in the group and patient satisfaction, which involved very complex formulas. Today, they [models] are moving back to a focus on *productivity, efficiency, and the amount of dollars a physician brings in.*[1]

Let's deconstruct this a bit. By "productivity" is meant not any measurable improvement in patient health, but time spent per dollar billed; "efficiency" refers not to the patients' time and cost, but to the physician's time and facilities cost. The prevailing model for many large medical centers seems to be a salary or net-income guarantee with a potential bonus or incentive add-on. The way the bonus is computed differs from institution to institution—some have a threshold (you get a fraction of your billings once they exceed an amount $X), sometimes it's a straight fraction and so on. Another version is like the "shared tips" policy in many restaurants: The physician gets a base salary plus a fraction of the total billings based on the number of physicians and their hours of work.

The fact that compensation before 1990 or so was more complex and less dollar-incentive-based may provide part of the explanation for the divergence in growth rate for American health care versus health care in other nations. As the possible gains to physicians from overusing treatments and tests increased, so did overall cost.

This process is particularly acute in Gawande's comparison: In El Paso, doctors were doctors. In McAllen, doctors worked just as hard, but they tended to be businessmen rather doctors in their outlook. In El Paso, the label was "patient care"; in McAllen it was "health business." A hospital administrator told Gawande: "In El Paso, if you took a random doctor and looked at his tax returns eighty-five per cent of his income would come from the usual practice of medicine,"[2] but in McAllen the doctor bit would be much less. McAllen doctors owned medical facilities and imaging centers, not to mention strip malls and orange groves. They thought about money a lot and owned facilities whose profits they could enhance by their actions as doctors. Much—perhaps most—of their income came from business, not directly from their work as physicians. The result: overtreatment, overprescription and massively increased medical costs in McAllen.

Selection and Variation

There are parallels to the McAllen–El Paso comparison in the behavioral economics of the animal laboratory. In the selection-variation process that underlies all adaptive behavior, variation, the repertoire of behavior the organism brings to a situation, depends on the type of reinforcer—reward or punishment—that is on offer. If physicians work for money, they behave differently than if they work for something much harder to define: the health of the patient. If a dog is trained using food treats, for example, he will behave differently, and generally less intelligently, than if the reinforcer is social. Here are a couple of examples.

First, a very simple example, just to show that the type of behavior you get depends, at least initially, on the type of reward you use. If a pigeon, for example, is trained like one of Pavlov's dogs, with a brief stimulus, like a light flash, that is immediately followed by reward, the "conditioned" behavior that develops depends on the type of reward. If the pairing is light-food, for example, the pigeon begins to peck in the grasping way that it uses to pick up grain, with open beak. But if the reward is water, the beak is closed, because pigeons suck up water.[3] Chapter 7 showed how the intensity of motivation—"arousal"—and type of reward affects the kind of behavior that you can get.

The conventional food-reward-based method for training dogs is something called "clicker training." First you operate a hand-held clicker a few times and every time you click, immediately give the dog a treat. He soon comes to associate the clicker with the treat. After he's learned this, you begin to reduce the food ratio: operating the clicker without pairing it with food a few times in between treats. This is called "intermittent reinforcement," and if it's done properly, the clicker retains its reward properties even though it signals food only intermittently. Now you can use the clicker by itself as a reward. If you want to animal to sit, for example, you can give it a click for "successive approximations" to sitting until it reliably responds to the "sit" command with a proper sit.

This is the method used by many dog-show trainers to get their often dim-witted charges to behave predictably while they are being probed by show judges and run around the ring by sturdy middle-aged ladies in tweed skirts. And it works very well to train a limited range of activities, so long as the dog is hungry enough. But the necessary behavior disappears when the dog is not hungry or sees that no treat is in the offing.

But trainers of those sheepdog geniuses, Border collies, do not use clicker training. They rely on the social bond between dog, shepherd and sheep. "Sniffer" dogs and dogs to aid the handicapped are trained in the same way. The sheepdog comes from the manufacturer with the herding instinct built in. I will never forget seeing my uncle's young Border collie, which had, as far as we knew, been completely sheep-deprived growing up in London, attempt to herd groups of children on his walks on Hampstead Heath (no leash laws in those days!). And there are many films of young sheepdogs trying to herd on their very first exposure to sheep.[4] But the shepherd must mold this instinct, make it more precise and bring it under his control. The result of this long process is an awesome independence and tenacity in doing the job for which the dog is fitted by nature and for which it has been long trained.

There is a famous example from nearly 200 years ago that still moves me. On February 22, 1818, *Blackwood's Magazine* in Edinburgh published a letter from the "Shepherd Poet" James Hogg (1770–1835), which recounted an amazing feat by his sheepdog Sirrah. He describes how he first got Sirrah:

> [When I bought him, Sirrah] was scarcely then a year old, and knew so little of herding that he had never turned a sheep in his life; but as soon as he discovered it was his duty to do so I can never forget with what anxiety and eagerness he learned his different evolutions. He would try everywhere deliberately till he found out what I wanted him to do, and when once I made him understand a direction he never forgot or mistook it again. Well as I knew him, he often astonished me, for, when hard pressed in accomplishing the task he was put to, he had expedience at the moment that bespoke a great share of reasoning faculty.

No treats, no clicker training, needed for Sirrah! His extraordinary achievement took place during a long night a few years later when 700 lambs, under Hogg's charge but newly separated from their dams, escaped on to the Scottish moor. When they realized at midnight what had happened, Hogg and a helper went out and began to search. They could not see the dog in the dark, but Hogg spoke and whistled to him nonetheless. They looked for the lambs until daybreak. Failing to find them, or the dog, they concluded that they must return to their master and tell him his whole flock of lambs was lost. But then:

> On our way home, however, we discovered a body of lambs at the bottom of a deep ravine . . . and the indefatigable Sirrah standing in front of them, looking all around for some relief, but still standing true to his charge. . . . When we first came in view of them, we concluded that it was one of the divisions of the lambs. . . . But what was our astonishment, when we discovered that not one lamb of the whole flock was wanting! How had he got all the divisions collected in the dark is beyond my comprehension. The charge was left entirely to himself from midnight until the rising of the sun; and if all the shepherds in the Forest had been there to have assisted him, they could not have effected it with greater propriety.

So this lone dog, unsupervised, and treatless, managed to round up 700 straying lambs through the whole night because of his devotion to his work and his great training. Is it too fanciful to compare the money-motivated medics of McAllen to clicker-trained pooches, and real physicians to Sirrah? The traditional training of medical residents, which Gerald Edelman describes below, looks much more like James Hogg and Sirrah than the robotic canines of dogshow beauty contests. Perhaps this kind of training, tough and exhausting as it is, is why many, perhaps most, physicians manage to resist the misaligned financial incentives, the bad reinforcement contingencies, they so often work under.

Conditioning

Physicians in the United States go through particularly rigorous training. The period of residency, right after medical school and before independent practice, is particularly tough. Gerald Edelman, MD, PhD, Nobel prizewinner and scientist-raconteur *nonpareil,* in an interview talks about an episode during his own residency that captures both the good and bad things about the process. He was then at one of the great world hospitals, Massachusetts General,[5] in Boston:

> I was hardly ever, in fact, home. We lived on Beacon Hill which was right across from the Mass General Hospital which was just an amazing place. It had this sense of history; I remember they had this lecture room called the Ether Dome, where ether was first administered successfully, and it conveyed great humanity, with history, [and] with an incredible expertise at medicine.
>
> I remember one episode, though, which sticks in my mind, and that is this business of staying up all the time and praying that you could get to

bed; and I remember that I was loaned out by the Medicine Department to Pediatrics and there was a rather sick kid who had a diarrhea that was causing imbalance of the electrolytes and the kid could actually have died. In those days we didn't have computers, we used slide rules and I figured out what was called in those days Gamble's formula, stuck the intravenous in and the kid seemed to be improving after two hours of watching, and then I remembered that I had to give Grand Rounds to the Massachusetts General Hospital within four hours.

That means putting on a clean white uniform and being prepared to be published in the *New England Journal of Medicine*. So I had a sort of discrepant, well contradictory, choice—should I sleep in a four-foot bed next to this very sick kid, or should I go back to the residents' quarters after training the nurse? So I trained the nurse, went through it twice and said, if the temperature does this do that, if this happens do this, now repeat, and she repeated it all and I staggered back to the residents' quarters, walked up four flights of stairs, hit the place that takes you to the roof, realized that that means I go down one, went down one and flopped into bed.

The rest of it I don't remember. It was recalled to me however by the nursing supervisor who called me up and said what the hell are you doing with my girls? . . . I said what are you talking about? It turned out that the girl called me and, she said—the nurse—the temperature's 102.6. And I said, out of my coma, "put the kid in a brown paper bag and send it to the laboratory."

I went to my Professor, Bauer, and said, you know, this can't go on! He said—yes it can! Get back to work.

Well these days they don't do that. They've relaxed the other way. And it is an interesting thing that in those days it was considered to be essential, an essential part of the job, to really be on it all the time. I guess the worst were the neurosurgeons. And I guess the worst outcome of that was a lot of divorces. But whatever it was, it was an interesting and memorable experience to be in that great institution.

This interview was filmed in 2005 when Edelman was seventy-six; the period he was referring to was the mid-1950s. Edelman thinks that residency may not quite as heroic these days, but Atul Gawande, who was a resident in the late 1990s, reports similar experiences.[6] Residency is still a pretty tough business in the United States or the United Kingdom.

Just how does residency work? It is both a filter and a trainer. Like Sirrah the Border collie, human beings have instincts, ready-made patterns of behavior, independent of experience. Sirrah was bred for herding but "knew so little of herding that he had never turned a sheep in his life; but as soon as he discovered it was his duty to do so I can never forget with what anxiety and eagerness he learned his different evolutions." In other words, once he saw a sheep for the first time, the sheep herding "evolutions" were activated and needed only to be guided and controlled by the shepherd. Dogs have relatively few instincts, but humans, far from lacking instincts, have not few but many: "[N]o other mammal, not even the monkey, shows so large an array," as William James puts it in his wonderful chapter on instinct.[7] And, just like dogs, some of us have one set, and others have another, although, unlike dogs, we have not been specifically bred for ours (it's natural, not artificial selection).

Instincts are one kind of behavioral variation, a part of the emitted, potentially operant, repertoire. They are like trial balloons. At a certain age and in certain circumstances, the pattern emerges and if it is reinforced—if the sheepdog encounters some sheep—it will blossom and develop. If not, it may fade. Medical residency, like many other professional apprenticeships, seems to take advantage of these processes. It selects those individuals for whom medical care, or the skills of surgery, or the structures of biochemistry are naturally enjoyable and reinforces them. At the same time, it rejects those who find these activities difficult or unpleasant. The "boot camp" residency process filters out the physically weak and the weakly motivated.

Residency has important effects on the behavior of doctors during the rest of their professional lives. It makes medicine much more hierarchical than many other professions. The contrast is particularly apparent in a university with a medical school. In the university, typically a department head has responsibility but little power; but for her (increasingly it is a "her" in academe) counterpart in the medical school it is quite different: responsibility *and* power. Department headships in universities tend to rotate among the faculty; in medical departments, department heads hold their positions for much longer, often until retirement. Heads of surgery and medicine are powerful figures in medical schools; there are no comparable figures among academic departments of English or physics or psychology. Residency training may also give medical doctors excessive respect for authority. I have never seen such enthusiastic encomia delivered to my academic colleagues as those commonly offered in always-lavish medical-school celebrations. Nor have I seen such quick recourse to authority figures as a way to settle scientific arguments.

But residency is also an intense period where the young doctor's life is totally dominated by patient care. He is making little money and has no chance to augment his income. He is devoting every waking hour to looking after patients. In other words, residency is the time when young doctors absorb the ethos of the medical profession. Their experience as residents surely offers some protection against the distractions of misaligned financial incentives when they begin independent practice. It certainly works for many doctors, since the misalignment is close to universal, but the costly practices of McAllen are not—yet.

The Drug Industry

Pharmaceutical products—drugs—are a major contributor to health-care costs, even (or perhaps partly because) the production of new drugs has declined exponentially over the past six decades, for reasons that are still a matter of debate.[8] Drug manufacture suffers from a uniquely bad set of incentives. In the auto industry, for example, incentives for individual manufacturers are reasonably well aligned with the common good. It may pay an individual manufacturer to make cars that wear out quickly, so consumers will turn them over quickly and so spend more. But in the auto market, consumers have choice and extensive reliability information, so they soon quit buying dodgy vehicles. Hence manufacturers strive to make their cars reliable. Much the same is true for every other aspect of the car: its safety, comfort, cost, etc. In every case, the manufacturer's interest is pretty well aligned with the consumers'.

Little of this is true of the drugs industry. Parallel to the lifetime of a car is the permanence of cure for a disease. Penicillin, vaccination and the like are pretty permanent in their effects. You give the patient a short course, and he's soon free of the condition. But not much drug or vaccine is needed, so not much profit can be made. Hence, drug companies have little incentive to look for the new penicillin or a new vaccine. What's good for them are drugs for chronic, essentially incurable conditions, drugs that must be taken every day forever—or for as long as the patient is above ground. Box 19.1 shows the ten most profitable drugs, as of 2013.[9] Notice that all are for chronic conditions, ranging from high blood pressure to depression. These drugs mitigate or control the symptoms of the conditions for which they are prescribed. None—*none*—provide a permanent cure in the fashion of a vaccine or an effective antibiotic. If this is what makes money, it makes perfect sense for drug companies to devote most of their research to looking for drugs like these, not vaccines or real cures.

How might this problem be fixed? Well, one way would be to adjust the life of drug patents to reflect the duration over which the drug must be taken. A drug that must be taken for life would have a short patent—maybe five years. This would allow for early competition from generics and a consequent reduction in price after just a few years. But a drug or treatment that is brief and effective, like a vaccine or antibiotic, would have a long patent, to enable the manufacturer to recoup his investment over a longer period. The point is to bring the reward to the company from a new drug into balance with its beneficial effects. The incentive to find real cures, rather than palliatives, would be increased. Perfect balance can never be achieved, but at present benefit to society and profitability are almost opposite. This is a complex issue and obviously needs more analysis, more than seems to have been devoted to it so far. But something could, and should, be done to improve matters.

Government, which should be working on these incentive problems, in the United States, at least, is contributing to them. One of the few counter-forces to a monopoly is *monopsony*—monopoly buyer. Health insurance companies in the United States make use of this power, and often pay less for a given procedure than a private buyer. In a kind of natural experiment, we can compare what individual buyers can achieve through competition with what insurance companies can achieve through oligopolistic purchasing power. The answer

Box 19.1   Best-Selling Drugs

1: **Lipitor** (Pfizer) Consistently ranking No. 1, Lipitor is number one by a wide margin. Its annual sales of $12.9 billion were more than twice those of the next drug on the list. Lipitor treats high cholesterol, a major risk factor for heart disease.

2: **Plavix** (Bristol-Myers Squibb/Sanofi-Aventis) This medication is used to prevent heart attacks and strokes. Although it has risen to the second spot on the list, its sales were a mere $5.9 billion, less than half those of Lipitor. However, Plavix had 2.5 times the annual growth of Lipitor.

3: **Nexium** (AstraZeneca) You probably know this drug as "the purple pill," and its sales numbers certainly merit the royal hue. Nexium, prescribed for heartburn and acid reflux, had sales of $5.7 billion, with an annual growth of 16.7%.

4: **Seretide**/Advair (GlaxoSmithKline) Although it's ranked No. 4, this asthma inhaler is in the No. 1 spot when it comes to annual growth. Sales for Seretide/Advair were just slightly lower than those for Nexium, coming in at $5.6 billion.

5: **Zocor** (Merck) This is another medication used to treat high cholesterol and prevent heart disease. In 2005, Zocor had global sales of $5.3 billion, and its annual growth wasn't shabby either, at 10.7%.

6: **Norvasc** (Pfizer) The second biggest seller for manufacturer Pfizer, Norvasc is used to treat high blood pressure. It had global sales of $5 billion in 2005 and an annual growth rate of 2.5%.

7: **Zyprexa** (Eli Lilly) Used to treat schizophrenia and bipolar disorder, Zyprexa is Eli Lilly's top-selling drug. In 2005, it had global sales of $4.7 billion. However, unlike other drugs on the list, Zyprexa experienced a significant decrease in annual growth—a dismal 26.8%.

8: **Risperdal** (Janssen) This is the world's most commonly prescribed atypical antipsychotic medication. At $4 billion, its sales were lower than Zyprexa's, but it had a much larger annual growth rate at 12.6%.

9: **Prevacid** (Abbott Labs/Takeda Pharmaceutical) A popular drug that treats heartburn, Prevacid had global sales of $4 billion in 2005 and an annual growth rate of 0.9%.

10: **Effexor** (Wyeth) An antidepressant, Effexor had $3.8 billion in sales in 2005 and an annual growth rate of 1.2%.

couldn't be clearer: Competition is ineffectual, but big buyers can negotiate lower prices. Health services are not a simple competitive market.

The largest monopsonist is of course the government. Medicare does exert considerable control over its costs for medical care. In general, Medicare pays less for a given treatment than do commercial insurers, and still less than a private individual. What about drugs? Medicare should pay much less here also, but it doesn't, because the law forbids Medicare to negotiate drug prices. In 2003, the government extended a Medicare drug benefit. But "[a] provision in the law that prohibited government from bargaining for prices on drugs was, in effect, a gift of some $50 billion or more per year to the pharmaceutical companies."[10] So, in a case where government could clearly act to restrain costs, it is forbidden from doing so. This rule was a victory for lobbyists, a failure of legislators and a big loss for the American public.

***

Health-care incentives are a mess. In the few cases where competition makes sense—between health-care institutions—it is blocked by law; and there are few checks to the steady drive by health centers to grow and absorb others so as to achieve monopoly status. Training medical personnel so that the reinforcers that are effective for them are not financial but the health of their patients, has been partially solved through a grueling and often criticized training process: internship and residency. Patient care cannot be a truly competitive market. Patients don't know enough about treatment efficacy and don't for the most part decide on the basis of price. But costs can be controlled via monopsony. Alas, in drug purchasing, a prime area for price-control negotiation by the government as a major purchaser, negotiation is forbidden. In short, the U.S. healthcare system is neither fish nor fowl; it is not competitive where competition might work and it is not controlled where controls might work. It is no wonder the United States pays twice as much for health care as other nations and gets, if anything, rather less.

Notes

1. David Cornett, regional vice president of client services for Cejka Search in St. Louis, Missouri: www.nejmcareercenter.org/article/physician-compensation-models-the-basics-the-pros-and-the-cons/ (my italics).
2. Gawande, A. (2009, June 1). The cost conundrum: What a Texas town can teach us about health care. *New Yorker.* www.newyorker.com/reporting/2009/06/01/090601 fa_fact_gawande.
3. There is a nice video of this effect of reward type at www.youtube.com/watch?v=50EmqiYC9Xw.
4. Check out www.youtube.com/watch?v=B0sO1wdBhMY, for example.
5. See www.webofstories.com/play/gerald.edelman/6.
6. See www.slate.com/id/2666.
7. James, W. (1890). *Principles of psychology*, Chapter 24. James also described the phenomena later studied and labeled by ethologists as *imprinting* and *vacuum activity:* http://psychclassics.yorku.ca/James/Principles/prin24.htm.
8. Scannell, J. W., Blanckley, A., Boldon, H., & Warrington, B. (2012, March). Diagnosing the decline in pharmaceutical R&D efficiency. *Nature Reviews Drug Discovery, 11*, 191–200. This problem is complex, but it is likely that diminishing returns is a major problem: As cures are found for more diseases, the effort required to deal with those that remain necessarily increases.

 9. See http://health.howstuffworks.com/medicine/medication/10-most-profitable-drugs10.htm.
10. Stiglitz, J. E. (2012, June 4). *The price of inequality: How today's divided society endangers our future* (New York: Norton), pp. 48–49, Kindle edition. Stiglitz won the Economics Nobel Prize in 2001. The UK National Health Service bargains vigorously with drug companies, however: see, for example, *Drug Pricing,* Houses of Parliament, Parliamentary Office of Science & Technology, POSTNOTE, 364, October 2010.

20 Reinforcement and "Socialized" Medicine

"Socialized" medicine gets very bad press in the United States. It is accused of inefficiency, excessive bureaucracy and poor results. Yet the relevant numbers show that the British system, for example, has fewer high-paid executives, medium-paid middle managers, and low-paid keyboard tappers than the United States, yet it gets better results by many measures. Surprisingly—since it is after all "socialized" and the United States, nominally, is not—the United Kingdom actually pays a great deal more attention to the reinforcement schedule under which medical people must operate than the United States does. This chapter looks at U.K. "socialized" medicine in a bit more detail.

Established in 1948 as part of a wave of social welfare legislation after World War II,[1] the British National Health Service (NHS) is the world's largest taxpayer-funded, single-payer health service. It delivers more than 87% of the country's health care and spends about 8.4% of the country's gross domestic product, half as much as in the (slightly more affluent) United States. In the United States in 2005, the figure was 15% and the public fraction (Medicare and Medicaid) just 5%.[2] By these measures, the U.K. system is much more socialized than ours. Yet the Brits and other European nations spend *much more* time worrying about health economics and how to align economic incentives with health-care outcomes than we do in the United States. It's hard to get a precise figure, but there are many university centers for health economics in the United Kingdom, and almost none in the United States, a country about six times as populous. A Google search in 2009 for "health care economics U.S." yielded "about 17,900,000 results," a large number, it would seem—until you do the same thing for "health care economics U.K." and get "about 131,000,000 results." In the study of health-care economics, at least, the United States seems to be lagging well behind.

Brits must all register with a general practitioner (GP, called a personal-care provider—PCP—in the United States) whom they are free to choose. GPs are not supposed to refuse any potential patient. With the exception of emergency treatment, patients can gain access to NHS hospital or consultant (specialist) care only if they are referred by their GP. The "gatekeeper" status of GPs in the United Kingdom gives them a higher status than in the United States where they are, consequently, in chronically short supply. The physicians and health-care institutions in the United Kingdom are subject to a plethora of incentives intended to enhance efficiency. One may well quarrel both with how "efficiency" is measured and with the government control that forces the vast majority of U.K. doctors to work for the National Health Service as salaried employees (even though they are officially "independent contractors"). And government, as health "czar," inevitably suffers from the *quis cutodiet . . .* problem, which is only partly mitigated by the democratic process. Nevertheless, as we saw with the Mayo Clinic example, by separating remuneration from prescription, a relatively fixed salary makes it easier for doctors to make judgments based on the needs of the patient unbiased by any personal financial consequence.

Beginning in June 2009, after a huge boost in 2008, NHS doctors get a basic salary, ranging from £33,285 p.a. (about $50,000) for junior doctors (residents) up to a maximum of £176,242 for senior consultants (specialists like neurosurgeons, radiologists or anesthesiologists).[3] On top of their salary, most are offered various incentive payments. The way these are computed has changed over the years. At first, these add-on payments were based on easily measurable factors like workload and cost. More recently, attempts are being made to relate them to something more fundamental but much harder to measure, namely health outcomes, quantified as the Orwellian-sounding "QALYs"— *quality-adjusted life years.* An "intervention"—treatment, drug, surgery, etc.— is evaluated according to the number of QALYs it adds to the patients life:

> The QALY is based on the number of years of life that would be added by the intervention. Each year in perfect health is assigned the value of 1.0 down to a value of 0.0 for death. If the extra years would not be lived in full health, for example if the patient would lose a limb, or be blind or have to use a wheelchair, then the extra life-years are given a value between 0 and 1 to account for this.[4]

I see . . . so if a paraplegic rates a QALY of 0.2 (for example) does a quadriplegic get a 0.1? Just who makes these judgments? Well, there are several methods, all problematic.

The effects on an individual patient of a possible "intervention" are evaluated in terms of "QALYs saved." For example, suppose we are looking at two patients, a thirty-year-old man who needs a heart-valve replacement and a seventy-year-old woman with essentially the same problem. Obviously the expected QALY gain from operating on the man—forty or more years—will be much larger than for the woman—no more than twenty years, probably. If resources are limited, as they almost always are, the choice is clear: The young man gets the surgery sooner than the elderly woman. The QALY method is obviously controversial because it is a way to ration health care. On the other hand, since health-care resources are usually limited, this method does allow them allocated in the way that is that is "optimal," doesn't it?

But should health care be "allocated" by government at all? The QALY combines in equal measure an eminently reasonable, if necessarily imperfect, utilitarian system for rationing health care, with what will seem to many people an almost inhuman insensitivity to individual human beings. The idea that a government agency—the oxymoronic NICE[5]—can decide just how much your suffering is worth relative to mine or John Doe's will also be repellant to many people. Economists have wrestled for years with the problem of *interpersonal utility,* and problem is epistemologically undecidable. Are you suffering more than I am, or do you just whine more? Are a thousand dollars worth more to you than to Lloyd Blankfein (CEO of Goldman Sachs)? Well, of course they are, say some economists, because every good is subject to diminishing marginal utility: The more you have, the less you want a bit more. Since Mr. B is much richer than you, each additional dollar is worth less to him. This is one form of the equity argument for "spreading the wealth" via progressive taxation.

The economist's argument certainly works for individuals: It's true for most people that the more money, or cars or houses, they have, the less interested they are in having more. But the same may not be true from one person to another. What's true for Lloyd and true for John may not be true when Lloyd and John are compared. Maybe Mr. Blankfein is so much richer than you *just because* he really cares about money (he is in the financial industry, after all!). Just suppose that every dollar is especially valuable to him, even more than it is to you. If so, it's really not fair to take a larger fraction of his money than yours. Philosophy suggests that this issue is not decidable. Your value is not comparable to mine.

Many discussions of NHS policy revolve around the idea of equity. But this philosophical digression makes the point that most equity arguments are based not on the unknowable utility of money (or anything else) to each person, but on a belief in the absolute value of equality—of *result.* The ideal society, according to this view, is one where all earn the same. The ideal NHS is one where all treatments yield the same QALYs. But do we all agree that this goal is right? If not, who shall decide?

In a capitalist society, the solution is the market. If you care more about this picture or this treatment than I, then, other things being equal, you will be willing to pay more and the issue is decided in an objective way. But if you are richer than I, then . . . see the previous two paragraphs. In other words, there is no objective solution to the redistribution issue. Ideologies compete and the battle continues.

Capitation and Targets

Currently about 70% of British GPs are paid via a mix combining salary with incentives:

> GPs have traditionally been offered a wide range of direct financial incentives, via a national contract that offers a mix of remuneration methods, including fee-for-service (about 15 percent of GP income), *capitation*

(40 percent), salary (30 percent), and capital and information technology (IT) (15 percent). The fee-for-service element includes incentive payments for reaching coverage targets for services such as vaccination and cervical cancer screening.[6]

You can get an idea of the difficulty of "incentivizing" medical care by looking at what seems at first like a very simple way of introducing market forces into a socialized system: capitation payments to individual doctors. The idea is that in addition to his base salary, a general practitioner (GP) gets a small fee for each person who chooses him as a personal physician (i.e., for everyone on his "list"). (This only works for GPs, not specialists, called "consultants" in the United Kingdom.) Unlike fee-for-service, the capitation payment does not "incent" a doctor to prescribe. What it does is encourage him—whether by bedside manner or effective treatment or some combination—to get patients to sign up with him. So "patient satisfaction" is in effect the criterion for the incentive payment. Looks like a good idea, right? But wait.

The problem with capitation, of course, is that all patients are not equal. A sixty-five-year old woman is likely to require much more care, much more of the doctor's time and many more NHS resources, than an eighteen-year-old boy. What is to prevent doctors shedding older, more costly patients in favor of younger healthier ones?[7] (They are not supposed to, of course, but there are ways.) The NHS has carried out several experiments to try and solve this kind of problem and see which incentive scheme works best.

In an experiment on decentralizing, for example, a number of practices (groups of physicians) were given an annual budget to buy routine supplies for secondary care and drugs (rather than relying on a central supplier). The experiment ran from 1991 to 1998; eventually more than half of NHS patients were involved. It worked pretty well. Practices reduced inpatient procedures by about 5% relative to nonfundholders and patient waiting times were shorter.

Another set of experiments involved explicit targets. For example, each GP was offered a financial incentive of £3,000 per annum, which had to be repaid if targets for thirteen chronic conditions were not met. The conditions were such things as such as hypertension, angina, heart failure, and epilepsy. The quality standard for hypertension (for example) was that at least 85% of patients should have blood pressure below 160/90 unless there is a documented valid reason for exceeding those values. The outcome was assessed via interviews, and the scheme did indeed seem to produce improvement in the management of chronic conditions. The doctors liked the informational feedback; it showed some that they were not doing as well as they thought. But there were also unintended effects. Too many patients were referred up the line to secondary care so that specialists, who were not reimbursed for the extra work, were sometimes overloaded. Disease conditions not covered by the scheme, like mental health, may have received reduced care.

This scheme was modified and a new "contract" launched in 2004. Now a sum equal to about 18% of GP income was to be awarded based on performance measures. "Points" are allocated based on quality indicators in seven areas of practice. About half are for "clinical quality"; other areas are assessed based on organization and patient experience. The clinical indicators cover ten areas, such as coronary heart disease (the most important), hypertension and diabetes. The scheme is modified every few years.

Managing all this, of course, is a growing health bureaucracy that makes the assessments and deals with hundreds of practices. And understanding the scheme is not simple. Here is a description of the capitation formula, from a *98-page* booklet describing how the system works in a way that is "accessible to non-specialists, and satisf[ies] the needs of those requiring a fuller understanding of how the formula works." Read and learn:

> Four elements are used to set PCTs' [primary care trusts—the local units of GP care] actual allocations:
>
> (a) weighted capitation targets—set according to the national weighted capitation formula which calculates PCTs' target shares of available resources based on PCT populations adjusted for
> (b) their age distribution
> (c) additional need over and above that relating to age
> (d) unavoidable geographical variations in the cost of providing services (the market forces factor (MFF))
> (e) recurrent baselines—which represent the actual current allocation which PCTs receive
> (f) distances from targets (DFTs)—which are the differences between (a) and (b) above. If (a) is greater than (b), a PCT is said to be under target. If (a) is smaller than (b), a PCT is said to be over target
> (g) pace of change policy—which determines the level of increase which all PCTs get to deliver on national and local priorities and the level of extra resources to under target PCTs to move them closer to their weighted capitation targets. PCTs do not receive their target allocation immediately but are moved to it over a number of years. The pace of change policy is decided by Ministers for each allocations round.[8]

Is all that perfectly clear? The Hayekian specter of central planning and its built-in problems looms large over the NHS. Obviously if capitation, one of the very simplest incentive schemes, requires this kind of documentation, then the others must be truly horrendous—and they are. The rate of growth of the managerial bureaucracy is beginning to exceed the growth in numbers of doctors and nurses.

So, although the NHS works more or less adequately, the list of problems is beginning to grow. The following account is pretty typical of complaints in the United Kingdom about the NHS in comparison with other systems:

Many respondents compared the British system unfavourably with their experiences abroad in Europe, in the United States and even in China (where there is speedy service, smiling staff and the medicine tastes better, evidently).

. . . [A] lawyer in Spain, said he had lived in several countries but the Spanish system was the best he had encountered. "I have nothing but praise for it. It works without undue delays, you make appointments on the internet or by text message and the doctor has your history on his computer." He added that even after an operation that was free, patients received a letter detailing the cost to underline the expense of healthcare. It is clear there are lessons to learn from abroad. . . .

None of the professionals disagreed that there were systemic flaws in the system. One consultant blamed a lack of resources, arguing that extra money was making a big difference but also bemoaning how much had been wasted on the "scandalous" new GPs' contract, and elsewhere. Some were advocates of choice and competition, while others worried that it might work well in cities but do little in sparsely populated areas. But clearly, health-service staff want more responsibility and more freedom to innovate and improve. They don't fear transparency. They know there are problems, they know some patients are being failed, and they desperately want to provide better care.

Several attacked an over-centralised system, which has seen local decision-making eroded and the evolution of a top-down service dictated by Whitehall. . . . [A] management development and training expert who became involved with the Scarborough and Bridlington NHS Trust, blamed this for many problems she encountered—which were so severe that theatre nurses went to public meetings to discover what was happening at their hospital and the trust has since had three chief executives in three years.[9]

My personal experience with the NHS—during lengthy stays in the United Kingdom, and via elderly and ailing relatives who live there—has actually been rather good. I have always been able to see a neighborhood doctor for minor ailments with much less delay than in the United States. Doctors, or district nurses, still do house calls on occasion. My mother, in her eighties and nineties, was always well and promptly treated and got operations without undue delay; so also my father who eventually died of prostate cancer in his eighties. My once-athletic and vigorous brother-in-law, long ailing with an incurable and often disabling condition, received operations and the attention of London consultants with few of the delays and complications one often reads about. By some criteria, he should not have been treated for some things because his prognosis was so bad. But as far as I know, proper treatment was never delayed or denied. An excellent BBC series, "Keeping Britain Alive," documents the work of the NHS in one day in October 2012.[10] It's well worth a look to get an idea of how this huge operation works on the ground.

There is of course what they call in the United Kingdom a "postcode lottery,"—that is, medical performance in some areas is much better than in others. But my folks and I have lived in several places, only one of which was relatively affluent. All have been medically pretty adequate. Are they representative? I have no reason to doubt it.

As with centrally planning the whole economy, planned "incentivizing" is not a royal road to excellent health care. Incentives—explicit reinforcement contingencies—can work when two conditions are satisfied: the objective/reinforcer can be defined precisely in advance; and the consequences of action are certain. Incentives therefore work well for the garage that fixes your car, the painter that paints your house or the plumber who clears your drains. They can also work for well-specified routine health treatments like vaccinations (everyone should have them) and mammograms (women should get them after age fifty)—things for which a checklist is appropriate.[11] But most health care, especially for the elderly, is not like this: The outcome, improvement in health, cannot be precisely specified in advance for every disease condition in every patient; and the treatments for many conditions may take years to have their often-uncertain effects. In such a complex situation, every incentive scheme can be "gamed"; every scheme will tend to bias patient care in one way or another. What is certain is that every new scheme also adds to a swelling enforcement bureaucracy. It's hard to avoid the conclusion that all these clever and well-intentioned attempts to social-engineer the economy of the British NHS seem just to show what a futile exercise such engineering is likely to be.

The alternative to playing with incentives is to first seek a compensation arrangement that disengages the physician as much as possible from the bad incentives of "fee-for-intervention." This is of course impossible to do in a way that does not conflict to some extent with doctors' freedom to practice as they wish. So the profession will probably have to live with misaligned incentives for a while, perhaps forever.

More important, therefore, is to reemphasize the selection and training of medical personnel. The residency process in the United States is both a filter and a reinforcement schedule. It filters out those with insufficient stamina or dedication to medicine, and it conditions those who continue—to be guided and rewarded by their effect on patients' health rather than by financial or other irrelevant incentives. When they do finally practice, therefore, properly trained doctors may be able to resist the inevitably bad financial incentives of the fee-for-service system.

So, with all these problems, why *is* the British NHS cheaper than the U.S. system? Not because it's more competitive (although in some ways, it is), but simply because it is single-payer. The government puts a lid on total cost and that's that. Monopsony rules.

***

There is simply no way that medical care in the modern era can be treated as a standard commercial product. The health-care market is different from markets for cars or groceries. The doctor knows more than the patient; the patient often doesn't have the luxury of shopping around—demand for health care is inelastic, in the economist's jargon; and it's all usually paid for by someone else, a third party.

But U.S. health care has clearly been made unnecessarily expensive by limiting competition where it might actually work: between health-care centers. The CON laws explicitly limit the expansion of old facilities and the creation of new ones. The malign hand—short-term gain yielding long-term loss—has worked quite effectively to keep health-care costs high and maintain the affluence of existing centers. Credentialing increases cost. Making medical education cheaper would also reduce financial pressures on young doctors and allow them to be less attentive to monetary rewards.

The financial-reinforcement contingencies are also bad to the extent that they reward doctors, directly or indirectly, based on what they prescribe. The best care seems to be associated with places, like the Mayo Clinic, that pay doctors a salary, so they have no direct financial interest in what they prescribe.

The rigorous residency ("junior-doctor" in the United Kingdom) process, so puzzling to outsiders, may be a vital element in health care. The idea is hard to test, but perhaps residency so conditions young doctors that when they are finally exposed to the unfortunate incentives of regular medical practice, most can successfully resist, and retain the focus on the patient that dominated during their residency. Perhaps residencies should come earlier in medical training and last a bit longer, less schooling, more treating—and less expense.

None of these fixes—abolition of the CON and enhanced competition among health centers, freedom to price-bargain with drug companies, less restrictive credentialing, reform of physician incentives, more practice and less formal training—plays a significant role in the massive 2010 Affordable Health Care Act.

Notes

1. The plan was embodied in the enormously popular and influential 1942 report of a committee chaired by Sir William Beveridge: http://en.wikipedia.org/wiki/Beveridge_Report.
2. See http://en.wikipedia.org/wiki/File:U.S._healthcare_GDP.gif.
3. See www.nhscareers.nhs.uk/details/Default.aspx?Id=553.
4. See http://en.wikipedia.org/wiki/Quality-adjusted_life_year.
5. National Institute for Clinical Excellence, now the slightly less threatening National Institute for Health and Care Excellence.
6. Smith, P. C., & York, N. (2004). Quality incentives: The case of U.K. general practitioners: An ambitious U.K. quality improvement initiative offers the potential for enormous gains in the quality of primary health care. *Health Affairs, 23*(3), 112–118 (italics added).
7. Glennerster, H., Matsaganis, M., & Owens, P. (1994). *Implementing GP fundholding: Wild card or winning hand?* (Buckingham: Open University Press).
8. (2008). *Resource allocation: Weighted capitation formula,* 6th ed. (Leeds, United Kingdom: Department of Health).

9. See www.independent.co.uk/opinion/commentators/ian-birrell-the-nhs-is-flawed-heres-the-evidence-1778276.html.

10. See www.bbc.co.uk/blogs/tv/posts/Keeping-Britain-Alive-The-NHS-In-A-Day. The affection Brits have for the NHS is nowhere better illustrated than by Danny Boyle's 2012 Olympic Games Opening Ceremony: www.dailymail.co.uk/news/article-2180227/London-2012-Olympics-Some-Americans-left-baffled-tribute-NHS-Mary-Poppins-Opening-Ceremony.html.

11. Gawande, A. *Annals of medicine: The checklist:* www.newyorker.com/reporting/2007/12/10/071210fa_fact_gawande.

21 Teaching

Few cognitive psychologists have much to say about teaching, probably because laboratory experiments on perception and memory are rather indirectly related to real-life education. The relationship between laboratory psychology and teaching is rather like that between physics and bridge building, as one blogger put it.[1] Physics doesn't tell you how to build a bridge, although it may help to explain why the one you just built doesn't fall down.

Much the same is true of radical behaviorism and teaching. The pigeon in a Skinner box is also pretty remote from a child in an overcrowded classroom. This did not prevent Skinner from writing at length on the topic of teaching.[2] Nevertheless, he was right that we can learn something about how to teach from behaviorism, though not in the very simple way that he proposed.

Skinner's starting point was the procedure called *shaping by successive approximations,* which I mentioned briefly in earlier chapters. This is the method long used by animal trainers to teach animals tricks. Skinner studied and promoted the method as a systematic way to get from the animal's initial repertoire to the trick or task that the trainer wants to teach. The idea is that if the animal doesn't show the behavior you want, reinforce a likely *precursor* of the target behavior and move on from there.

It is hard to improve on Skinner's description of this process:

> A pigeon, reduced to 80% of its *ad lib* weight, is habituated to a small semi-circular amphitheater and is fed there for several days from a food hopper, which the experimenter presents by closing a hand switch. The demonstration consists of establishing a selected response by suitable reinforcement with food. For example, by sighting across the amphitheater at a scale on the opposite wall, it is possible to present the hopper whenever the top of the pigeon's head rises above a given mark. Higher and higher marks are chosen until, within a few minutes, the pigeon is walking about the cage with its head held as high as possible. In another demonstration the bird is conditioned to strike a marble placed on the floor of the amphitheater. This may be done in a few minutes by reinforcing successive steps. Food is presented when the bird is merely moving near the marble, later when it looks down in the direction of the marble, and finally when it pecks it.[3]

In the first of Skinner's examples, the precursor behavior is obvious: Raising the head a little is the obvious precursor to raising it a lot. The second is less obvious: How do you begin to reinforce the bird for pecking a marble when it neither pecks nor looks at it? Skinner offers one solution; doubtless there are other sequences that would be effective. The general point is that there is a natural progression of repertoires that ends up with a given target repertoire. For "easy-to-learn" activities, there are many such progressions; for an activity that is hard to learn, there may be only one or two—or none. If you begin at the wrong place, therefore, the pigeon—or the child—may never learn the target task.

Another influence on Skinner derived, I believe, from his dislike for aversive contingencies, for any kind of punishment. Students, Skinner thought, are "punished" when they make mistakes. Wouldn't it be better, therefore, to "shape" their behavior in such a way that they achieve mastery without having to make any mistakes? One of his own students, Herb Terrace, provided laboratory support for "errorless learning" when he showed in his PhD dissertation that by gradually fading in the negative stimulus, pigeons could learn to respond to a red illumination of the response key (S+, reinforced with food) and not to an alternating green illumination (S–) without ever responding to the green.[4] Given laboratory "proof of concept," the next step for Skinner was to put his mechanical skills to work designing a *teaching machine.* In that pre-PC age, teaching machines were small boxlike mechanical devices that presented a question, allowed the student to answer and advance to see whether he was right or wrong and also to see the next question.[5]

Teaching machines were all the rage for a while. The *Encyclopedia Britannica* hired bright young graduate students from MIT like Daniel Bobrow (later to become an artificial intelligence pioneer) to put together programmed instruction texts that presented difficult material, like math, in bite-sized chunks. But the method was not the revolution in education that Skinner had hoped for. It worked adequately for very well-specified target behaviors, like spelling, simple math or learning a technical vocabulary, but not so well for complex tasks whose endpoint might be defined as much by the learner as the teacher. I discovered this myself when I worked briefly at Harvard with James Holland, an associate of Skinner's, who ran a programmed instruction project.[6] My aim was to see if random questions popping up while a student was reading a text would act as reinforcers and improve learning. The text I chose was an excellent history book by Jacob Bronowski, polymath and later TV presenter,[7] and Bruce Mazlish, an MIT historian, *The Western Intellectual Tradition* (Harper, 1960).

The experiment was a failure. The book was too good, and so were the students. They did much better just reading it and flipping from place to place as their interests dictated. I daresay they came up with their own questions and were just annoyed by mine. The point is that learning at this level has little to do with the shaping of pigeons. In the pigeon case, the response is either already learned, like pecking, or a well-defined motor pattern. The pigeon that knows how to peck must then just be taught when and where to peck. The aim of the reinforcer is to control a familiar response: direct it and strengthen it.

Even in shaping a new response, the endpoint is always well defined, and well within the animal's capacity. But in most education that is worth the name the point is not to strengthen an existing response but to get an idea to occur for the very first time. For that task, programmed instruction is no help at all—and may be even a hindrance. Shaping of course may have some application. But for shaping to work, you need to know the endpoint. Again, for advanced subjects, the kind of thing typically taught in a university, the instructor may not know the endpoint. Students must often discover it for themselves.

There is another way to approach teaching from a behaviorist point of view. Teaching is not about selection—reinforcement—so much as about *variation,* getting the right response, right idea, to occur for the first time. To illustrate, let me begin with an anecdote due to British evolutionist Richard Dawkins. It is a moving account[8] of "Sanderson of Oundle"—Oundle, a British boarding "public"[9] school famous for its output of talent, and Sanderson, its headmaster early in the 20th century:

> Sanderson's hatred of any locked door which might stand between a boy and some worthwhile enthusiasm symbolised his whole attitude to education. A certain boy was so keen on a project he was working on that he used to steal out of the dormitory at 2 am to read in the (unlocked, of course) library. The Headmaster caught him there, and roared his terrible wrath for this breach of discipline (he had a famous temper and one of his maxims was, "Never punish except in anger"). . . . [The] boy himself tells the story.
>
> "The thunderstorm passed. 'And what are you reading, my boy, at this hour?' I told him of the work that had taken possession of me, work for which the daytime was all too full. Yes, yes, he understood that. He looked over the notes I had been taking and they set his mind going. He sat down beside me to read them. They dealt with the development of metallurgical processes, and he began to talk to me of discovery and the values of discovery, the incessant reaching out of men towards knowledge and power, the significance of this desire to know and make and what we in the school were doing in that process. We talked, he talked for nearly an hour in that still nocturnal room. It was one of the greatest, most formative hours in my life. . . . 'Go back to bed, my boy. We must find some time for you in the day for this.'"

Dawkins adds, "That story brings me close to tears. . . ."

This story shows a kind of creativity in teaching and a kind of spontaneous flowering in learning that seems to lie quite outside the rhetoric of "successive approximations" and the teaching of tricks. Sanderson's pupil was not "shaped" to show an interest in metallurgy. Undoubtedly he had felt Sanderson's ire for past errors, as he felt it now for breaking the school rules. And yet, under Sanderson's tutelage, in the environment Sanderson had created, he developed a passionate interest in learning of the kind we should love to see in our own students.

But are these examples fair criticism? Some radical behaviorists will object that I am merely countering science with anecdote. Isn't this just the anthropomorphism of George Romanes[10] and your grandmother warmed over? I don't think so. To explain why, we need to go back to what the science really is.

Skinner made at least two great discoveries in his analysis of operant behavior. One was hardly original at all; yet it is the one for which he has gotten the greatest credit—and which he himself thought the most important, namely the principle of reinforcement. But humanity knew about carrots (although they were usually paired with sticks) for countless generations before Skinner came along.[11] And, as we've seen, even reinforcement learning was experimentally demonstrated, and epitomized in the Law of Effect, by Thorndike, some time before *The Behavior of Organisms*.

So I think that Skinner's second contribution is more important than the reinforcement principle, but, because it is still not fully understood, it has received much less attention. It is the idea that operant behavior is *emitted,* that it is essentially spontaneous, at least on first occurrence. In this book I have discussed at some length the Darwinian metaphor, the idea of selection and *variation.* Variation was Darwin's term for the then-unknown processes that produced variants (variant phenotypes, as we would now call them) from which natural selection would pick the winners. In similar fashion, the processes that govern the emission of operant behavior produce an initial repertoire from which reinforcement can then select.[12] Reinforcement affects variation also, of course, not just as a selector, but also as a contributor to the labeling or framing of the situation. It helps the subject assess just what kind of a situation he is in. Food reinforcement will induce a food-related repertoire, social reinforcement, socially related behavior and so on.

The very best teaching is not really about selection at all, but about variation. Sanderson dispensed rather few obvious reinforcements and not a few punishments. He sought not to eliminate errors but to foster the tenacity and persistence that allows kids to learn from them. He created at Oundle an environment that got his boys thinking about things like metallurgical techniques and, I daresay for Dawkins, the wonders of biological evolution. No treats were dispensed to achieve these ends. Instead a culture was somehow created in which the boys, in their private thoughts and in their discussions and debates with others, were passionately attracted to topics with some intellectual weight. Sanderson manipulated not through the dispensing of rewards, but through labeling or framing. He thus set up a culture that favored what Skinner might have called the emission of creative operants.

How this works is still a matter of art rather than science. "Culture" involves some understanding of those antecedents of behavior we term "thoughts," "attitudes," "expectations." They are not mental fictions, nor does their study require introspection. What is needed is an understanding of how the environment created by a school interacts with the patterns of behavior pupils bring with them, from nature, home and the street, to produce good or bad performance in learning tasks. Attitudes and expectations are just the names we give to the effects of that environment. Understanding how this works is a task that takes us well beyond pigeons in Skinner boxes or sophomores remembering word lists.

The education establishment is aware of what I am calling behavioral variation. They have something of an obsession with "self-esteem," which is a crude way of addressing the "variation" issue. If a pupil has high self-esteem, we might expect him to be more willing to try out alternatives and be creative. But, of course, "self-esteem" may also lead to smugness and self-satisfaction. It is a poor proxy for the kind of behavioral variation induced by the very best teachers.

All we can be sure of is that the causes of effective behavior in challenging situations are complex, involving both nature and nurture in an uncertain mix. But three things seem clear: That there are processes in creative teaching that are understood in an intuitive way by great teachers, like Sanderson of Oundle. That the Darwinian framework for behaviorism shows that processes of variation exist, even though they have been sorely neglected in favor of an almost exclusive focus on reinforcement as selection. And that behaviorists need to take time out from pressing the "reinforcement" lever, and look beyond the selectionist simplicities of radical behaviorism to those engines of variation that motivate pupils and yield truly creative learning.

Notes

1. See www.britannica.com/blogs/2009/04/what-can-cognitive-psychology-do-for-teachers/.
2. Skinner, B. F. (1961). Why we need teaching machines. *Harvard Educational Review, 31,* 377–398.
3. Skinner, B. F. (1959). *Cumulative record* (New York: Appleton-Century-Crofts), p. 48.
4. Terrace, H. S. (1963, January). Discrimination learning with and without "errors." *Journal of the Experimental Anaysis of Behavior, 6*(1), 1–27. Retrieved from www. ncbi.nlm.nih.gov/pmc/articles/PMC1404228/.
5. Skinner illustrates the operation of an early teaching machine in this video: www. youtube.com/watch?v=EXR9Ft8rzhk.
6. Holland and Skinner (1961) put together a programmed text, *The analysis of behavior: A program for self-instruction* (New York: McGraw-Hill) to teach material from Skinner's class at Harvard. Skinner's (1968) thoughts on education were published in his *The technology of teaching* (New York: Appleton-Century-Crofts).
7. Bronowski later wrote and presented the acclaimed BBC-TV series *The Ascent of Man* (1973).
8. *The Guardian,* Saturday, July 6, 2002.
9. British public schools are now private, of course. But they were all founded before the existence of state-supported public education, as ways to educate poor but talented boys (yes, mostly boys!). As the state took over their function, they had to find another one, which turned out, usually, to be as elite private boarding schools. Now many are coed and take day scholars—and are usually called "independent" schools.
10. George Romanes (1848–1894), author of *Animal intelligence* (D. Appleton and Company, 1882/1892) and several other books and papers comparing the cognitive capacities of animals and humans.
11. Although they did not know the details, the concept of reinforcement contingencies and the myriad data on reinforcement schedules discovered by Skinnerians.
12. See Catania, A. C., & Harnad, S. (Eds.). (1988). *The selection of behavior: The operant behaviorism of B. F. Skinner* (New York: Cambridge University Press), for a set of papers on Skinner and the Darwinian metaphor.

Index